T0312058

Playing Fair

Game Theory
and the
Social Contract Volume I

Playing
Fair

Ken Binmore

The MIT Press
Cambridge, Massachusetts
London, England

This book was set in Computer Modern by Ken Binmore.

Library of Congress Cataloging-in-Publication Data

Binmore, K. G., 1940–
Playing fair: game theory and the social contract / Ken Binmore.
v. cm.
Includes bibliographical references and index.
ISBN-13 978-0-262-02363-4 (hc. : alk. paper)   ISBN-13 978-0-262-52943-3 (pb. : alk. paper
1. Game theory. 2. Social contract. 3. Political science-
-Philosophy. I. Title.
HB144.B56   1994   93-29610
519.3—dc20   CIP

Playing Fair

is dedicated
to my daughter

Emily

who knows
no other way
to play.

The Dog.

Pub.d June 18, 1805 by R. Phillips N 6. Bridge Street Black Friers

William Blake's allegorical illlustrations are justly famous. This shows a young
author awaiting a reviewer's verdict on his pet project.

Apology

Mr. Thomas Hobbes writes to me, I wonder not if Dr. Wallis, or any
other, that have studied Mathematicks only to gain Preferment, when
his ignorance is discovered, convert his study to jugling and to the
gaining of a reputation of conjuring, decyphering, and such Arts.

Aubrey's *Brief Lives*

This is a work of political philosophy written by a Grandma Moses of
an author who is neither a political scientist nor a philosopher. I am a
mathematician-turned-economist and can only hope that political scientists and philosophers will be patient with the lack of scholarship in their
disciplines that my background makes inevitable. The excuse for writing
at all is my belief that much insight can be gained into ethical matters
by approaching them systematically from a game-theoretic perspective. If
nothing else, I therefore hope to spread the gospel that game theory is an
indispensable tool for the political philosopher. And for this purpose my
background has its advantages.

Those who have no mathematical training at all will find this a difficult
or even an impenetrable book. This seems unavoidable if what I have to
say is not to be misunderstood. But no fancy mathematical techniques are
required. Nor have I attempted to dot every mathematical i or cross every
mathematical t. The arguments are formal only where it seems absolutely
necessary. What then are the mathematical prerequisites? Here I can do
no better than to quote from the preface to Luce and Raiffa's [158] *Games
and Decisions*:

> ...probably the most important prerequisite is that ill-defined qual-
> ity: mathematical sophistication. We hope that this is not a quantity
> required in large measure, but that it is needed to some degree there
> can be no doubt. The reader must be prepared to accept conditional
> statements, even though he feels the suppositions to be false; he must
> be willing to make concessions to mathematical simplicity; he must be
> patient enough to follow along with the peculiar kind of construction
> that mathematics is; and, above all, he must have sympathy with the

method—a sympathy based upon his knowledge of past successes in various of the empirical sciences.

In so far as apologies are necessary on the mathematical content of the book, they need to be tendered to mathematicians, and particularly to mathematical economists. As a mathematician, I used to write in a very formal style, and it may be that, like many converts, I have allowed the pendulum to swing too far in the other direction. It is certainly correct that the truly formal parts of the discussion are infrequent and that these are patched together with appeals to intuition that some mathematical economists will find irritatingly imprecise. If these appeals to intuition were capable of being defended by obvious[1] formal arguments, such irritation would be unjustified. But this will seldom be the case. It will not even always be "obvious" what the formal setting for a rigorous discussion would be. I agree that the need to reach a wider audience is not an adequate excuse. But I don't think this book would have got written if I had tried to do a better job on the formal side. Nor do I have much sympathy with the view that one should either say something formal or else say nothing at all.

Apologies also need to be made about the scope of the material. The models contain only two representative agents. This is certainly an improvement on those macroeconomic models with only one representative agent, but I am well aware that coalitional issues matter a great deal in this context and that a treatment that confines itself to only two agents does not even allow the difficulties to be expressed. Moreover, most of the concerns of political scientists about the organization of the "ideal state" are simply abstracted away. My belief is that what remains to be studied after the gross simplifications that are made remains worth studying. However, I see that this is not a view which will meet with universal acceptance. But probably acceptance will be readier among the "mathematically sophisticated", and others will not be reading this book anyway.

I also want to apologize for writing *so much*, particularly since I am fully conscious of the fact that I repeat myself a great deal. Two thick volumes of verbiage would be an absurd extravagance if I had chosen to confine my attention to the positive aspects of my theory. However, my experience in trying to put across ideas in this area has taught me that it is not enough to say why what you think is right, you must also say why you think others are wrong. Much of the book is therefore hatchet work in which I try to clear some ground in the jungle of confusion for my own tender plant to grow. On top of this, there is the problem that it is almost impossible to say anything whatever in a moral context without inadvertently using the

---

[1]The mathematician Hardy defined an "obvious result" to be one for which it is easy to think of a proof.

terms and phrases of one of the many prepackaged collections of views that are on offer. One then risks being automatically categorized as belonging to some Ism or other. I try to deal with this problem by saying things that really matter in several different ways and in several different places. Sometimes I invite readers to skip sections if they are satisfied with earlier passages on the same topic, but I suspect that this is a compromise that will satisfy nobody.

Those who already know game theory reasonably well will have more reason than most to skip substantial sections of the text. However, in spite of the advice offered in the *Reading Guide* that follows this *Apology*, such readers will not always find it easy to isolate the purely instructional passages from those in which I have something new to say. Game theorists will also perhaps feel that I devote far too much time to foundational questions in game theory. Apologies are certainly due in respect of the arrangement of the instructional material. In planning how to write the book, I made a deliberate decision to weave the game-theoretic instruction into the fabric of the book, rather than to confront newcomers to the subject with a large and undigestible introduction that would inevitably be very difficult for those unused to thinking in the abstract style of the mathematician. It may be that such a strategy fails to please even the newcomers to game theory, but at least I can claim that my intentions were good on this count.

As for the time spent on foundational issues, I have already apologized for writing so much. However, those brought up on game theory should appreciate that there is a very large constituency of social scientists and philosophers who are highly suspicious of orthodox game theory. They do not see why their own attempts to resolve game-theoretic problems are any less convincing than the abbreviated accounts of the work of game theorists that they read about in popularizing articles. I did not understand this myself until I submitted an article to a distinguished political science journal that was rejected by both referees on the grounds that "the author does not understand that the purpose of studying the Prisoners' Dilemma is to explain why cooperation in the game is rational". This constituency is unwilling even to grant that the conclusions of game theorists follow logically from their assumptions, let alone that game-theoretic assumptions have any relevance to the world of our everyday experience. I know that such hard-liners are unlikely to read this book or to be convinced if they do, but I have made what seems to me a valiant attempt to reach them for which I do not think apologies are really appropriate. However, when explaining why various fallacies are fallacious, it is hard to avoid becoming patronizing, even though this can only be counterproductive in seeking to reach a hostile audience. I know that it will do me little good to apologize for falling into this trap where I have done so, but I can at least register my recognition that it is a bad mistake to have made.

Some readers will also feel in need of an apology because I do not always treat weighty subjects with the seriousness they properly deserve. Nor am I very respectful of the great thinkers of the past. Even the magnificent illustrations from the works of William Blake that head up each chapter are sometimes chosen for the most frivolous of reasons. Let me say in my own defense that an argument does not have to be dry in order to be correct. Nor does a great thinker have to be right about everything in order to be great. And the exuberance of William Blake's art is proof against any attempt to cheapen it. On the other hand, nothing excuses a failed attempt at humor.

I do not know what to say about the originality of the ideas. Ideas that I thought were my own I have often found later to be commonplace in literatures with which I was not familiar. Almost certainly there remain attributions that I ought to be making if I knew the relevant literature better. Let me apologize in advance to those whom I have failed to quote from ignorance. At the same time, not everybody to whom I have sought to attribute ideas has been entirely happy with the attribution. In particular, neither Harsanyi nor Rawls, from whom I have borrowed a great deal, would wish to be associated with the manner in which their ideas have been repackaged. Let me therefore also apologize in advance to those who feel that I have quoted them or others inappropriately.

To women I have to apologize for having abandoned my initial attempt to be neutral in my use of pronouns. I have succeeded in doing so elsewhere, but, in a work of this length, the necessary circumlocutions become increasingly burdensome.

I have also to apologize to those who commenced reading them, for abandoning my planned sequence of papers on the social contract, of which I had written the first four. (See Binmore [30, 34, 23, 35, 36].) It seems that one cannot successfully chop up the subject into small digestible pieces. The attempt generates too many misunderstandings to be worthwhile. All the balls have somehow to be kept in the air at the same time. In looking over what I had written, I see that my juggling talents were often not up to the task. All I can say in mitigation is that juggling is not nearly so easy as it looks.

To those who reviewed my typescript, I have to aplogize for not always taking their advice. However, I do very much want to register my gratitude for the reviews, which were uniformly thoughtful and sometimes came in the form of a line-by-line commentary. I hope that I have succeeded in clarifying at least some of the points that the reviewers found obscure and that the errors they came across have been eliminated without too many new errors being introduced along the way.

Finally, I even have to apologize for the layout of the book, together with such idiosyncracies as punctuating "like this", instead of "like this."

I typeset the book myself using Leslie Lamport's LaTeX, which is an adaptation of Donald Knuth's mathematical typesetting program TeX.

In spite of all these apologies, the truth is that I do not really feel very apologetic. Perhaps all I have done is to select some old wines to be decanted into new bottles. But the new labels are bright and attractive and may perhaps describe the wine better than the old labels. And even if my own attempt to be original is judged a failure, perhaps others will succeed in planting sturdier plants in the space my hatchet has cleared.

Contents

Those who tread every step of the way are often weary at the journey's end.

Reading Guide

> ...the writing of many books is endless and excessive devotion to books is worrying to the body.
>
> Ecclesiastes

In John Bunyan's *Pilgrim's Progress*, Evangelist sternly instructs Christian that only by following the strait and narrow path to the Celestial City will he be relieved of his burden. However, I am more like Bunyan's Worldly Wiseman than his Evangelist. Not only do I share Worldly Wiseman's view that relief for those who carry burdens is to be found not so very far away in the town of Morality at the house of Mr. Civility, I also think that each person must decide for himself whether the virtue that accrues from treading every step of the approved path is really worth the time and effort that it takes.

As the *Apology* explains, the strait and narrow path that will be followed by those who read every word of this book is long and sometimes tortuous. There are occasional long detours through material that many readers will think superfluous. At one time, I even considered subtitling the book *Life, the Universe and Everything*[2] to give due warning of how far afield I sometimes stray. Moreover, I have made a point of repeating the really important ideas again and again as the book proceeds, because I am weary of being misunderstood and see no way to insist that I literally mean what I say other than by straightforward repetition. Nothing is more galling than to propose a tautology that critics reject on the grounds that it is a contradiction proposed by somebody else. Often the recycling of an idea may be unobtrusive because of the change in context, but I cannot guarantee that this will always be the case. In any case, although I hope that everything I have written will be of interest to someone, there will be much that any but the most dedicated and patient reader will wish to skip.

Although there will be few economists, political scientists, or philosophers who actually correspond to the stereotypes attributed to their pro-

---

[2]For those who do not know, this is the title of a best-selling science fiction spoof by Douglas Adams.

xvii

fessions, my names for the three typical readers I plan to consider will be Economist, Politician, and Philosopher. All three have open minds about the contribution that game theory may be able to make to moral and political philosophy, but they differ in their backgrounds and interests.

Economist knows game theory fairly well. He is accustomed to the use of Nash equilibria in economic models and has always felt that the folk theorems of repeated game theory are somehow relevant to how societies hold together. However, he does not have much interest in academic moral philosophy. Still less does he want to get involved in the metaphysical debates that engage the attention of those who work in the foundations of game theory. He is, in brief, one of that happy band of brothers who begin to call for the "bottom line" at economics seminars even before the speaker has mounted the rostrum.

Politician is not in so much of a hurry as Economist. He also knows less game theory. Indeed, part of his reason for reading this book is to straighten out his thoughts on some of the game theory ideas with which the political science literature often plays so fast and loose. I suspect that Politician will remain skeptical about most of what I have to say about the social contract, but I hope that he at least will be persuaded that game theory is such a powerful tool that it is worth learning to use it correctly. If I fail to convince readers on this score, then I shall have failed altogether.

Philosopher knows as much game theory as Economist and is even less hurried than Politician. He has already thought through much of what I have to say for himself. He is therefore not so much interested in the general points that the book has to make, as in the viability of the framework within which I make the points. He will care very much about why one assumption is made rather than another. He will be familiar with alternative theories and wish to know how I think my own theory should be defended from the criticism that will be directed at it by followers of such rival theories. He will probably also be a harsh critic himself. I fear that my attempts to satisfy him will be found wanting. However, on certain topics, I have done my best to keep him happy.

To help these three stereotypes to find their way through the book, each section is labeled with one of the three marginal symbols shown below. The three symbols are meant to represent different levels of conceptual difficulty. The more boxes that are nested, the greater the conceptual depth. Economist, Politician, and Philospher will all will wish to read the first-level material. This is the level at which I describe my theory of the social contract. Economist may perhaps browse at the other levels, but will not usually feel that his time has been well spent in so doing. Politician will wish to take on board the instructional material in game theory developed at the second level. My guess is that he may also be tempted to get embroiled in the foundational material offered at the third level, but I would strongly advise against this at a first reading. In contrast to Politician, Philosopher will only skim the second-level instructional material in order to concentrate on the foundational issues discussed at the third level.

(a) First level   (b) Second level   (c) Third level

Finally, let me insist again that I have not written this book with a view to its being read line by line. If a particular passage is tangential to your interests, please skip forward immediately. Even Economist, Politician and Philosopher would probably be unwise to follow the advice given in this reading guide all the time. Professional game theorists might even consider skipping the whole of the current volume, *Playing Fair*, and beginning with Chapter 1 of the second volume, *Just Playing*.

Abstract of Volume II

The four long chapters of *Playing Fair*—the first volume of *Game Theory and the Social Contract*—will be followed by four more long chapters in a second volume to be called *Just Playing*. The content of this second volume is briefly summarized below.

Chapter 1: Nuances of Negotiation. This chapter contains an account of the modern theory of rational bargaining. Its emphasis is on when, how and why to use the Nash bargaining solution. The chapter contains little political philosophy and will perhaps serve as an introduction to bargaining theory for a variety of applications.

Chapter 2: Evolution in Eden. This chapter reconstructs Rawls à la Harsanyi or Harsanyi à la Rawls, depending on your point of view. If one insists that those in the original position are *committed* to the deal that they reach behind the veil of ignorance, then it is argued that only a utilitarian social contract is viable. However, the weights that a utilitarian rule attaches to each individual's utility are not given by God. Social evolution operating in the medium run will alter the manner in which interpersonal comparisons are made until the utilitarian social welfare function being used by society leads to the same outcome as would be obtained using the Nash bargaining solution. All moral content in the supposedly utilitarian society will thereby be leached away. In the long run, personal preferences also adjust until the Nash bargaining solution yields the same outcome as a Walrasian equilibrium.

Chapter 3: Rationalizing Reciprocity. This chapter is about the mechanics of repeated games. These provide a game theorist's arena for discussion of Hume's contention that moral laws are "merely" rules for coordinating on equilibria in the game of life. Such rules need no policing from outside the system. The rules police themselves by calling for approval to be withdrawn from those who do not reciprocate the favors accorded to them by others. Nor are they necessarily invented by legislative bodies. Those that are most important to us are exclusively the product of social and biological evolution.

Chapter 4: Yearning for Utopia. This final chapter offers my own version of a social contract theory. It differs from those of Harsanyi and Rawls in not calling for citizens of a society to regard themselves as being committed to some hypothetical deal that would supposedly be agreed by persons placed in the original position at some past time. Instead, the original position is proposed as a device to be available at all times for the purpose of coordinating on an *equilibrium* in a repeated "game of life". No coercion is needed to persuade people to honor such a social contract, provided that they are guided by their own enlightened self-interest. It is shown that the use of such a social contract leads to the same outcome as the use of a non-utilitarian social welfare function referred to as a proportional bargaining solution in the literature on cooperative games. The stability of this social welfare function in the presence of evolutionary pressures is then studied along the same lines as in Chapter 2.

Leviathan is the sea monster in this illustration by William Blake. "He is King over all the Children of Pride".

Chapter 1

A Liberal Leviathan

What is Whiggery?
A levelling, rancorous, rational sort of mind
That never looked out of the eye of a saint
Or out of a drunkard's eye.

W. B. Yeats

1.1 Whiggery

Why write a book like this? My own motivation lies in the conviction that there is a viable and respectable defense for at least some of the liberal ideas that have been contemptuously brushed aside in the last decades of the twentieth century.

So thorough is the triumph of conservatism that current newspeak even makes it difficult to use the word *liberal* without inviting unwelcome associations. Bourgeois liberals like myself find ourselves tarred with the same brush that somehow simultaneously suffices to smear both laissez-faire extremists of the far right and bleeding-heart welfarists of the far left. It therefore seems to me that a case exists for reviving the word *whiggery* to describe my kind of bourgeois liberalism.

Whigs like myself are definitely not in favor of conserving everything as it is. We do not like the immoral society in which we live. We are therefore in favor of reforming it. But the fact that we are not hidebound conservatives does not make us socialists. Nor is whiggery some wishy-washy mixture of left-wing and right-wing views. Indeed, a whig finds such a compromise hard to envisage. How can one find some median position between those who fix their attention on the wrong problem, and those who do not see that a problem exists?

1

In illustration of this last point, consider the following passage that appeared in the *Guardian* newspaper of 25 May 1988 during a British general election campaign. Its author, Bryan Gould, was a leading spokesman for the Labour Party. Mrs. Thatcher, whom he quotes verbatim (if somewhat out of context), won the election on behalf of the Conservative Party.

> For Mrs. Thatcher, "There is no such thing as society". There is only an atomised collection of individuals, each relentlessly pursuing his or her self-interest, some succeeding, some failing, but none recognising any common purpose or responsibility.

This quotation epitomizes the errors of both the left and the right. Both are wrong at a fundamental level because their implicit models of man and society are not realistic about "the nature of human nature". Consider Mrs. Thatcher's denial of the existence of society. This we may charitably interpret as a denial, not of the existence of society *per se*, but as a denial of the existence of society as interpreted by her opponents of the left. As Bryan Gould is trying to say, the left shares Hobbes' [117] vision of society as being more than just a collection of individuals or households. It is rather a social organism, or as Hobbes would have it, a Leviathan, constructed from but transcending the human beings that form its constituent parts— just as human beings are constructed from but transcend the organs that make up their bodies. However, unlike Hobbes, leftists see Leviathan as being moved by a "common will" or motivated towards a "common good" to which the strivings and aspirations of its constituent human parts are properly to be subordinated.

Left or Right? I believe that Mrs. Thatcher was right to reject the leftist Leviathan as a model of what society is or could be. A view of human society that sees Leviathan simply as an individual on a giant scale, equipped with aims and preferences like those of an individual but written large, would seem to place man in the wrong phylum. Perhaps our societies would work better if we shared the genetic arrangements of the *hymenoptera* (ants, bees, wasps, etc.), or if the looser genetic ties that link members of human families extended across society as a whole, so that rhetoric about all men being brothers were actually true in more than a metaphorical sense. But this is not the case, and all that can be expected from "reforms" based on such misconceptions about the human condition is that they will fall apart in the long run, leaving behind a sense of disillusionment and a distaste for reformists and for reform in general. Indeed, is not this precisely what we have witnessed in recent years? Even as I wrote this book, the seemingly monolithic Soviet empire at last collapsed under the weight of its own contradictions and old-time conservatives have emerged from the backwoods to rejoice at the fall of socialism.[1]

The truth about society is much more complex than either the left or the right is willing to admit. As that most conservative of Whigs, Edmund Burke [142, p.99], so aptly explains:

> A nation is not an idea only of local extent and individual momentary aggregration, but it is an idea of continuity which extends in time as well in numbers and in space ... it is made by the peculiar circumstances, occasions, tempers, dispositions, and moral, civil, and social habitudes of the people, which disclose themselves only in a long space of time.

However, a conservative avatar like Mrs. Thatcher sees no reason to consider such a sophisticated Leviathan. For those like her, a rejection of the naive Leviathan of the left is a rejection of all Leviathans.

This is the fundamental error of the right. It may be true that to speak of the common will or of the common good is to reify the nonexistent, but there are other nouns to which the adjective "common" can sensibly be attached. In particular, nobody is likely to complain that we are reifying the nonexistent in speaking of common *understandings* or *conventions* in society. A conservative may feel that to concede this is to concede little of importance. No doubt common understandings exist, but surely they are too fragile and ephemeral to be other than peripheral to the way society operates? Along with many others, I think this view is badly mistaken.[2] Far from being peripheral to society, such common understandings constitute the very warp and weft from which society is woven. Leviathan is more than the sum of its parts precisely because of the commonly understood conventions stored in the brains of its citizens *and for no other reason*.

It is hopeless to think of convincing those on the far right of such a proposition. They prefer to wear blinders rather than admit that society is based on such a seemingly precarious foundation. Certain conventional arrangements, particularly those concerned with private morality and the

---

[1]When such reactionaries learn anything from history, they always learn the wrong lesson. What we have witnessed is not the triumph of the free market economy over socialism. Only rarely in the Western democracies does the allocation of goods and services approach the ideal of a perfectly competitive market. We are all welfare states now—and where "free" markets do operate, their institutions are often badly corrupt. Nor did the Soviet empire that fell come close to the socialist ideal. What we learn from its fall is only what George Orwell's [198] *Animal Farm* taught us years ago. Institutions that do not recognize that their officers' incentives are not consistent with the goals of the institution will necessarily be corrupted in the long run. Rather than rejoicing at the fall of socialism, we would do better to look to the motes in our own eyes.

[2]Among modern writers, particular mention should be made of Schelling [229], Lewis [152], Ulmann-Margalit [262], and Sugden [254], but the general contention is that of Hume [128].

preservation and transference of property rights, they recognize; but not as artificial constructs shaped by social evolution or human ingenuity. They dimly perceive such matters as being determined by some absolute standard of "right" and "wrong" and hence as immune to change. Other conventional arrangements that they cannot ignore, they are anxious to sweep away in favor of the market—of whose intrinsic "rightness" as a distributive mechanism they will tolerate no doubts.

But this book is not directed at conservatives from the backwoods. It is a piece of rhetoric aimed at open-minded conservatives. Those of us who live in bourgeois comfort need to be continually reminding ourselves that Nature has not provided us with any warranties for the continuation of our cozy way of life. All that stands between us and anarchy are the ideas that people carry around in their heads. Our property, our freedom, our personal safety are not ours because Nature ordained it so. We are able to hang on to them, insofar as we do, only because of the forbearance of others. Or to say the same thing a little more carefully: given society's currently dominant but precarious system of conventions, we continue in the enjoyment of our creature comforts simply because nobody with the power to do so has a sufficient incentive to deprive us of them. Or, at least, not right now.

Such a bleak view of the way things are is admittedly simplistic. But is it so very far from the truth? If you doubt it, drive downtown to your local ghetto and watch what goes on when a community's common history and experience fill people's heads with a set of conventions and customs that are very different from your own. Or read a newspaper report about those countries in which the old common understandings have broken down and new common understandings have yet to emerge. In any case, it does not seem to me that the conservative thinker to whom this book is addressed can consistently seek to categorize human behavior in terms of enlightened self-interest and simultaneously paint a more rosy picture of how society holds together.

Nobody would claim that the current systems of commonly understood conventions that regulate life in the major societies of the West are ideal. It would be nice, for example, if one could take the dog for a walk in the park without fear of being mugged. Or if one did not have to be apprehensive about AIDS and the drug scene when a teenage child is late coming home. And so on. These are examples of problems that a whig traces to the existence of injustices and inequalities in the structure of society. There is, of course, no shortage of other problems. It would be pleasant if the air we breathe and the food we eat were unpolluted. Or if we were not at risk from war, nuclear or otherwise. Or if our taxes were not squandered so flamboyantly. But it is problems of justice and inequality that will be central to this book.

Reform. What is proposed is very moderate. Indeed, it is so moderate that no conservative need fear becoming tainted in trying on the ideas for size. Marxists, on the other hand, will have nothing but contempt for such bourgeois proposals. For progress to be made, it is necessary for the affluent to understand that their freedom to enjoy what their "property rights" supposedly secure is actually contingent on the willingness of the less affluent to recognize such "rights". It is not ordained that things must be the way they are. The common understandings that govern current behavior are *constructs* and what has been constructed can be *reconstructed*. If the affluent are willing to surrender some of their relative advantages in return for a more secure environment in which to enjoy those which remain, or in order to generate a larger social cake for division, then everybody can gain. To quote Edmund Burke [142, p.96] again:

> Early reformations are amicable arrangements with a friend in power; late reformations ... are made under a state of inflammation. In that state of things the people behold in government nothing that is respectable. They see the abuse, and they will see nothing else ... they abate the nuisance, they pull down the house.

People like Edmund Burke, who propose reform with the primary objective of conserving what they can of the past, have been called reforming conservatives. They are to be contrasted with conservative reformers like myself, who actively wish to reform the society in which they live, but are conservative in the reforms they propose because they see no point in creating a society that is unstable. However, both reforming conservatives and conservative reformers are whigs in that they hope to create institutions that will organize trade-offs between different sections of society, so that the system of common understandings that form the fabric of our society can be continually reformed in directions which everyone involved agrees are better. A conservative who is supicious of reform may argue that social evolution does this for us already. But, as Edmund Burke would have been the first to explain, conservatives did not need to wait to observe city blocks being burned to the ground before deciding that more in the way of black emancipation was required. As the adage has it: an ounce of prevention is worth a pound of cure.

Social Contracts. It will perhaps now begin to be clear what I have in mind in practical terms when speaking of a "social contract". However, this book is not about practical matters. It is an attempt to provide some logical underpinnings for the species of bourgeois liberalism that I am calling whiggery. Such logical underpinnings are to be found in the theory of games. When translated into this language, what I have been saying so far about whiggery goes something like this. We are all players in the game of life, with divergent aims and aspirations that make conflict inevitable. In a healthy society, a balance between these differing aims and aspirations is achieved so that the benefits of cooperation are not entirely lost in internecine strife. Game theorists call such a balance an *equilibrium*. Sustaining such equilibria requires the existence of commonly understood conventions about how behavior is to be coordinated. It is such a system of coordinating conventions that I shall identify with a social contract.

Whigs argue that it is sensible to look at the whole class of social contracts that are feasible for a society, and to consider whether one of these may not be an improvement on our current social contract. Left-wing socialists agree that what we have now could do with being reformed, but do not understand that there is a feasibility constraint. They therefore propose social contracts that are unworkable because they call for behavior that is not in equilibrium. The utopias they envisage are therefore unstable. Right-wing conservatives understand the need for stability only too well, although they often forget that what was stable yesterday need not be stable today. However, in concentrating on the need to sustain our current social contract, they lose sight of the opportunity to select a better equilibrium from the many available.

In saying these things, I am conscious that the risk of being misunderstood is very great, but there is no point in trying to elaborate my position at this stage. What I shall do instead is to reiterate it using the lines of verse from Yeats at the head of the chapter as a text.

Yeats is right that whigs worship rationality. They believe that the way to a better society lies in appealing to the enlightened self-interest of all concerned. Yeats is also right that whigs are levelers, and if this seems rancorous to unreconstructed Tories like Yeats, it is because they do not see what is in the best long-run interests of people like themselves. Yeats also tells us that whigs are not saints. He is right about this also. Not only are whigs not saints, they do not think that most of us have the potential to become saints, as the more naive thinkers of the left would have us suppose. People might be temporarily persuaded to put the "interests of the community" ahead of their own selfish concerns. But a community based on the assumption that its citizens can be relied upon to behave unselfishly much of the time simply will not work. Finally, Yeats is right that whigs see no reason to behave like drunkards lurching from crisis to crisis. Planning and reform need not be dirty words. They do not require the existence of a mythical "common interest". We can plan to institutionalize new "common understandings". Nobody need make great sacrifices in the process once it is understood that it is not in the self-interest of the "strong" that they always let the "weak" go to the wall. We can go from the old to the new *by mutual consent*. We do not need to set up stultifying and inefficient bureaucracies along the way. Nothing prevents our planning to use markets wherever markets are appropriate, but a society that relies *only* on market institutions is a society that is leaving much of its potential unfulfilled. What is being described is a bourgeois conception of a liberal society. One should therefore not expect it to lead to some kind of utopia. Utopias are typically founded on misconceptions about human nature and hence are doomed to fail. Nor does there seem much point in adopting a point of view that evaluates what we have now by comparing it to such ideal but unattainable societies.[3] All that can be achieved by so doing is to distract attention from improvements that actually are feasible.

1.2 DeKanting Rawls □

The previous section may have left the reader with an expectation that matters of practical politics were to be discussed. The fact that philosophers' names are listed in Figure 1.1, rather than the names of men of action, will help to dispel any such false impression. What is to be offered is not a theory of political action. It is at best a prototheory that might perhaps one day be incorporated into the foundations of a theory of political action.

My concern is with the philosophical and moral positions that lie beneath the attitudes adopted by politicians and the factions that they represent. Any genuine meeting of minds on policy issues would seem unlikely unless some consensus is possible on such fundamental questions. To those whose understandable reaction is that it is hopelessly academic to attack the problem at this level, I can do no better than offer the traditional quotation from Keynes [140]:

> ...the ideas of economists and political philosophers, both when they are right and when they are wrong, are more powerful than is commonly understood. Indeed, the world is ruled by little else. Practical men, who believe themselves to be quite exempt from any intellectual influences, are usually the slaves of some defunct economist. Madmen in authority, who hear voices in the air, are distilling their frenzy from some academic scribbler of a few years back.

---

[3]Or, worse still, in allowing our foreign policy to be guided by such an attitude. A reform that was successful in one society need not be successful in another society—i.e. what proved to be feasible here need not be feasible elsewhere. In particular, it is far from obvious that we act in our own best interests if we unthinkingly seek to remodel our neighbors in our own image. Reforms need to be tailored to the system of common understandings that currently operate in a society: not to those which once operated in our own society.

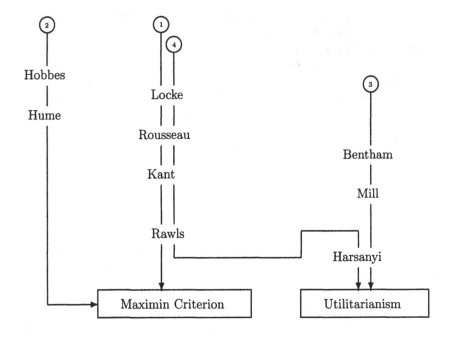

Figure 1.1: Philosophical ancestries

Perhaps academic scribblers like myself take undue comfort from such thoughts. On the other hand, it may be that, if enough of us scribble sufficiently long, the madmen in authority will distil some less simplistic brews than those on which they currently get high.

The keystone name in Figure 1.1 is that of Rawls [209, 208, 214] whose *Theory of Justice* is often described as the outstanding work in political theory of the twentieth century. For those who are not Rawlsian scholars, it should be explained that Rawls [210] began to revise the views expressed in the *Theory of Justice* within a few years of its publication. He thereby anticipated, for example, some of the criticisms implicit in the work of authors like Macintyre [160, 162, 161], Sandel [226], Taylor [260] and Walzer [270], whom Mulhall and Swift [184] group together as members of a loosely defined school of *communitarians*. The so-called new Rawls [211] now offers a theory that is less ambitious in its scope and therefore far less vulnerable to charges of inconsistency or unacknowledged cultural bias.

Doubtless Rawls was right to accept the existence of blemishes in his *Theory of Justice*, but I very much regret his retreat from the visionary philosophical position of his younger self. It should therefore always be understood that it is this younger Rawls whom I have in mind when I refer to his work. Sometimes it follows that I will find it necessary to criticize positions that the later Rawls no longer holds. But here my view is usually that the later Rawls is overly defensive. He will often not like the manner in which I seek to regroup his forces for a counterattack on his critics. Indeed, it will emerge almost immediately that I differ from Rawls very sharply at a very fundamental level. However, I hope he will feel that I have been sufficiently influenced by his earlier self that my attempt to make a contribution can still be counted as being Rawlsian in spirit.

My analysis makes use of Rawls' notion of the *original position* and arrives, after much huffing and puffing, at a conclusion that bears a close family resemblance to his *difference principle*.[4] Moreover, I agree very much with the younger Rawls [214, p.121] when, in speaking of methodological questions, he observes that "We should strive for a kind of moral geometry with all the rigor that this name connotes." Why not then simply commend the reader to Rawls' [214] *Theory of Justice*? In brief, I share the aspirations of the younger Rawls for the future of society, but I find myself unable to acquiesce in his "moral geometry".

My differences with Rawls on some foundational issues run very deep— as deep as the gulf that divides Kant and Hume. To pursue Rawls' mathematical metaphor, it is not so much that I have doubts about the "proofs" of his "theorems", or even that I wish to replace his "axioms" by others that I find more congenial.[5] It is the assumptions built into the language in which the "axioms" are stated that I feel the need to contest. My approach is therefore very definitely *not* an attempt to explicate the younger Rawls. On the contrary, its underlying ethos is incompatible with that avowed by Rawls. In brief, I like the big picture that Rawls paints about the nature of a just society, but I find the arguments with which he defends his position unacceptable.

I am emphasizing that my differences with Rawls lie at a deep conceptual level because it is the *foundations* of moral philosophy about which I care.

---

[4]Figure 1.1 disgracefully bowdlerizes Rawls' conclusions. The difference principle calls for maximizing the welfare of the least well-off and hence the use of the term *maximin criterion* in Figure 1.1. However, this is only one component of Rawls' two principles of justice, and by no means the component to which he attaches most importance. It comes into play in his scheme only after certain basic rights and liberties have been secured. Although I am concentrating on distributive justice in this introductory chapter, Rawls' sense of the appropriate priorities is not abandoned in my theory. As explained in Sections 2.3.6 and 2.3.7, my theory requires rights and liberties to be considered prior to distributive questions for the same reason that one must always consider what is feasible before considering what is optimal.

[5]Although I do have doubts about his "proofs", and my "axioms" are often very different from his.

The architectural details of the buildings to be built on the foundations that I propose are very much less important to me. For this reason, I have not sought to obtain conclusions of any great generality. For example, my illustrative societies nearly always have only two citizens. Nor would I feel too unhappy with a reader who argued that what conclusions I do offer are wrong, provided he were willing to grant that my general approach is sound. In this I am like a geometer who uses working hypotheses about the nature of points and lines but is willing to agree that another geometer who uses different working hypotheses may possibly be offering a closer approximation to the way the physical world actually is. What makes us both geometers is not our *conclusions*, but our common understanding of the geometrical *ethos*. When another geometer speaks to me of "points" and "lines", I know that he means exactly what I would mean if I were to say the same thing. But this is seldom true when one *moral* geometer speaks to another—and it is certainly not true when Rawls speaks to me.

The rest of this chapter is structured by contrasting my theory with that of the younger Rawls. However, its chief purpose is to provide a preliminary "fast-forward" through the theory in an attempt to avert the misinterpretations that arose when I began to try to write the material as a sequence of linked but atomic papers (Binmore [30, 34, 23, 35, 36]). Readers found it difficult to get a feel for what was being built because of the attention directed at each particular brick.

My hope is that those who know something of game theory and its putative applications in moral philosophy will skim the rest of the chapter, perhaps pausing here and there to read more closely when I say things that seem unconventional. Those who know nothing at all about the subject could do worse than skip the remainder of the chapter altogether. Everything that is said in the chapter is repeated at least once more later in the book, usually in a less compressed form. However, I know that many readers prefer to read books page by page from beginning to end. In offering a preliminary overview of the theory, I am conscious that there is a risk of losing such readers by making myself insufficiently clear on matters of detail which are important to them but which can only be dealt with adequately in later chapters.

This last difficulty is particularly pressing since several of the bricks from which the theory is constructed are more than a little controversial. Some readers may even be tempted into classifying me as being simultaneously naive and cynical. My views on human nature and the status of moral codes are especially vulnerable to such misinterpretation. Bernard Williams [273], for example, would doubtless regard me as an amoralist.

Let me therefore emphasize that I do *not* share Nietzsche's [191] view that "There are no moral phenomena ... only moral explanations of phenomena." But I do agree with Nietzsche that conventional explanations of moral phenomena typically reify the nonexistent. Like many others, I believe that the actual rules that govern our moral behavior are simultaneously less grand and more complex than those which moral philosophers have abstracted from the mythology of our culture. Insofar as people are conscious of the *actual* rules, they call them conventions, customs or traditions. Such rules are neither absolute nor immutable. They are shaped largely by evolutionary forces—social and economic, as well as biological. If one wishes to study such rules, it does not help to ask how they serve the "good". One must ask instead *how and why they survive.*

Such a view sees moral phenomena as being *naturally* determined, but the naturalism I advocate has little in common with the following definition offered by Mayo [174, p.39]:

> Naturalist theories offer to rescue ethics from perpetual uncertainty, or even meaninglessness, by offering substitute statements which we know how to verify, and claiming that they are equivalent to the original moral judgments.

According to such a definition, the role for a naturalistic theory is to find naturalistic explanations of what is commonly said about moral phenomena. But I am not primarily interested in explaining explanations. On the contrary, the philosophical method that proceeds by asking what it *really means* to make a moral statement like "All men are created equal" seems to me quite hopeless. One might as well look for progress in physics by asking what we *really mean* when we say, "Nature abhors a vacuum". Our ancestors buried no secrets in the language they constructed. They simply rationalized what they saw about them as well as they were able using whatever concepts they had at hand. The allegories and metaphors they used in rationalizing moral phenomena often pack a powerful emotional punch, but we have no good reason to suppose that these rationalizations are any better as *explanations* of the moral phenomena that provoked them than the ancient rationalizations of physical phenomena.

The naturalism I advocate therefore bypasses much that preoccupies conventional moral philosophers. Am I, for example, guilty of perpetuating the Naturalistic Fallacy?[6] Such an accusation will indeed be correct if one chooses to *define* ethical theory to exclude those *oughts* which can be deduced from an *is*. Such a definition, confining the domain of moral inquiry

---

[6]Unlike the puerile version of G. E. Moore [181], Hume's formulation is simply that nothing entitles the deduction of an *ought* from an *is*. Hume's version is irrefutable. If all the axioms and rules of deduction of a formal system relate only to indicative sentences, it is clearly impossible that an imperative sentence can be a theorem of the system. However, this does not worry a naturalist like myself. My "oughts" are all hypothetical imperatives of the form: You ought to eat your spinach if you want to be healthy. This translates into the indicative statement: Refusing to eat spinach is irrational for someone who prefers to be healthy.

to the study of "categorical imperatives" and the like, would force me into
agreement with Nietzsche that there are *no* moral phenomena. Whatever
this book would then be deemed to be about, it would not be morality.

However, I hope there will be at least some readers willing to join me in
seeing such a barren interpretation of the scope of ethical theory as making
as much sense as restricting entry in the Olympic high jump event to one-
legged athletes. Those who are unwilling to follow me this far, or who are
sure that society would fall apart if "moral absolutes" ceased to be widely
regarded as such, need read no further.

1.2.1   Hobbes and the State of Nature

Rawls traces his philosophical ancestry through Locke, Rousseau, and Kant,
as indicated by the central arrow in Figure 1.1. He therefore seeks to establish ideal principles of justice that are to be used as standards of comparison
in evaluating a society. These standards are seen as being determinable by
abstract contemplation, *independently* of the way society is actually con-
stituted at present and of the historical process by means of which society
achieved its current state. This naturally makes his work unpalatable for
such conservative-minded thinkers as Nozick [194]. However, a whig should
perhaps also be cautious about such an approach.

It is fun to make mock of arch-conservatives by identifying them with
the Panglossian view that here and now we have "the best of all possible
worlds". But it is just as silly to propose that we seek to create an impossible world, or to advocate that current institutions be abandoned because
they do not measure up to the way things would be if such an impossible
world were in operation. Since moral geometry has been mentioned, a quote
from Spinoza [251] may be appropriate. In speaking of his forerunners in
moral philosophy, he remarks:

> ... they conceive of men, not as they are, but as they themselves would
> like them to be [and hence], instead of ethics, they have generally
> written satire ... and never conceived a theory of ... politics, but such
> as might be taken for a chimera, or might have been formed in Utopia,
> or in that golden age of the poets ...

I certainly do not want to accuse Rawls of writing satire (although I have no
qualms at directing such accusations at Rousseau or Kant). The quotation
is offered to add some authority to my contention that any ideal standards
of justice that we choose to advocate should be workable in at least one
possible world. Moreover, it should be a possible world that is attainable
from the world in which we currently live by a process that is itself possible,
and not just in some abstractly conceived best of all possible worlds. Of
course, any discussion that goes beyond the most general of generalities will

not be able to meet this criterion to the letter. Whatever model of reality we choose to adopt will necessarily be stylized and simplified. Otherwise its analysis would be beyond our capabilities. The criterion is therefore not intended to be interpreted *literally*. It is intended to serve as a basis for making judgments about the model. Conservatives will be happier with my model of reality than liberals, since my assumptions are largely those of neoclassical economics. But, since I am promising some whiggish conclusions, perhaps liberals will be prepared to suspend judgment.

The State of Nature. The social contract tradition goes way back beyond Hobbes. Gough [91] is a good reference for its historical development. However, it is in Hobbes' [117] *Leviathan* that the social contract idea is tackled using a methodology that is recognizably modern in spirit. In a nutshell, Hobbes saw concurrence on a social contract as the alternative to existence in a "state of nature". Given the anarchic times in which he lived, it is not surprising that he was not optimistic about the capacity of human beings to get along together amicably without policing and supervision. He therefore conceived of the state of nature as being very unpleasant indeed: "the war of all against all" in which life is "solitary, poor, nasty, brutish and short". As a viable alternative, he saw only the voluntary surrender by all of their rights and liberties into the hands of an absolute sovereign. Neither his gloomy view of human nature nor his favored political system will find many modern takers, but his conceptual framework, within which the social contract is envisaged as a rational alternative to a real or hypothetical state of nature, remains deservedly popular.

The Rawlsian theory dispenses with a state of nature. Or, perhaps one should say that Rawls [214, p.12] sees the device of the *original position* as a substitute for a state of nature as understood by Hobbes. The original position is a hypothetical standpoint used by Rawls to make judgments about how a just society would be organized. Members of society are asked to envisage the social contract to which they would agree *if* their current roles in society were concealed from them behind a *veil of ignorance*. From the point of view of those in such an informational state, the distribution of advantage in the planned society would be determined as though by a lottery. The idea is that a social contract agreed to in such an original position would be "fair", the intuition being that "devil take the hindmost" will not be an attractive principle if you yourself might end up with the lottery ticket that assigns you to the position at the rear. Rawls, of course, would not be satisfied to quote such intuitions in defense of the original position. He recognizes that the device embodies intuitions about fairness that people actually do hold in the real world,[7] but seems more comfortable in arguing, for example,

---

[7] ... the conditions embodied in the description of the original position are ones that

that the original position may be viewed "as a procedural interpretation of
Kant's conception of autonomy and the categorical imperative" [214, p.256].
Wolff [275, 276] has been active in criticizing Rawls for discarding the
notion of a state of nature that Wolff regards as essential if a social contract
argument is to be meaningful. My own approach takes the same line.
However, my state of nature is no philosopher's fiction. Nor is it set in the
far past. Instead the state of nature is identified with the way things are
now—the current *status quo*. Since the current *status quo* includes what
society remembers about its history, the social contract agreed to in the
original position will therefore not be independent of history as in Rawls'
theory.[8] My theory is therefore not vulnerable to the telling criticisms of
authors like Gellner [86, p.249] who attack Rawls and most other social
contract theorists for proceeding as though a society were free to discard
its history and plan its future as though it were newly born.

In identifying the state of nature with the current *status quo*, I differ
sharply from such authors as Gauthier [84] and Nozick [194], who follow
a Lockean [157] line in their attitude to the *status quo*. Such Lockean
alternatives involve postulating a state of nature in which anarchy is held
in check by some *a priori* system of "natural rights" or some "natural
division of goods". My reasons for rejecting such fictions as a basis for
discussion will become apparent as this chapter proceeds. Briefly, I agree
with Hume [128, p.493] that, "Philosophers may, if they please, extend
their reasoning to the suppos'd *state of nature* provided they allow it to
be a mere philosophical fiction which never had and never cou'd have any
reality", but there is then no reason why anybody should attend to what
such philosophers have to say. Even if I accept the manner in which they
derive a social contract from the state of nature they propose, why should I
regard their state of nature as having any relevance to my behavior, moral
or otherwise? The question of what is just is simply transferred to that of
deciding what is or is not "natural" in the state of nature.

I find myself much more in sympathy with Buchanan's [50, 49, 51] social
contract theory than with its Lockean rivals, because Buchanan's theory
dispenses with *ad hoc* ethical assumptions about behavior in the state of
nature. Instead we are offered a much more Hobbesian *status quo*.[9] Never-

---

we do in fact accept. Or if we do not, then perhaps we can be persuaded to do so by
philosophical reflection—Rawls [214, p.21].

   [8]The agreed social contract will also depend on history in other ways as well. In
particular, the manner in which interpersonal comparisons of utility are made is also a
function of history in my theory (Section 1.2.7).

   [9]Buchanan sometimes expresses guarded approval of my own view that the state
of nature should be identified with the current *status quo*. However, this is not what
Buchanan [50] intends when using what he calls the "natural equilibrium" as a state of
nature in his best-known work.

theless, it seems to me that Hume's criticism applies as much to Buchanan as to Gauthier or Nozick. What has Hobbes' brutish struggle of all against all to do with human behavior? We were social animals long before we were recognizably human. Let me emphasize, however, that although I differ from Buchanan on how to model the *status quo*, much of what I have to say on other matters simply echoes his more general views on the social contract, which I learned largely from Sugden [254].

An approach that takes the state of nature to be society's current *status quo* requires abandoning Hobbes' very conservative estimate of what is or is not available as a social contract. Instead of having essentially only one viable social contract available as an alternative to a Hobbesian state of nature, it will be argued that there will normally be a wide class of social contracts among which a choice can be made. The manner in which society is organized at present can then be seen as embodying one of these possible social contracts. The problem for a reformist will then be regarded as that of seeking a *new* social contract to which society can be shifted *by mutual consent.*

When will such consent be forthcoming? Here the underlying assumptions will be those of neoclassical economics. Individuals will be assumed to consent to a reform only if it is in their enlightened self-interest to do so.[10] The question then remains: Of those reforms that do not require those whose consent is needed to surrender any of their rights and privileges without adequate compensation, which is to be chosen? For this purpose some guiding principle is necessary to *coordinate* the aspirations of those involved. It is in *this* role that the device of the original position is required in my analysis. When imagining themselves in the original position behind the veil of ignorance, individuals will not be called upon to suppose that they have forgotten how society is organized at present—i.e. the current state of nature. They will be called upon only to imagine that they and their fellow citizens do not know their current roles in society and to envisage what new social contract from the class of implementable social contracts would be commonly agreed to under such an equalizing assumption. It is this social contract that it is to be recommended as the candidate for reformist activity.

A natural objection is that it is "immoral" to advocate such an approach to reform. Surely, it will be argued, slaveholding societies are obviously "wrong". But slaveholders will never consent to surrender their slaves if they are motivated only by selfish considerations. Slavery will therefore necessarily survive.

---

[10]This is not to argue that altruistic behavior will never be observed. Much of what passes for altruism is readily explicable within a neoclassical framework.

Several points need to be made in reply. To begin with, it is not *obvious* that slavery is "wrong" in some absolute sense. Otherwise Aristotle would not have overlooked the fact. Nor would Cicero have been able to represent his callous proposals for the disposal of slaves who had outlived their usefulness as strictures to be observed for *moral* reasons. Our opposition to slavery is a *cultural* phenomenon. Being a child of my culture, I share its distaste for slavery. I also have a strong distaste for the current social institutions that allow some members of our society to be reduced to sleeping in cardboard boxes on trash heaps. Should this distaste ever become widely enough shared, it will then be said that it is "obviously wrong" that a society should tolerate such misery in its midst. However, those who currently argue that it is "obviously wrong" to ignore the plight of the destitute have yet to win the day. It is true that, in anticipating their success in reforming the current social contract, they are using an exceedingly powerful rhetorical device. Nobody likes to be categorized as "wicked". But it is important that we not be deceived by our own propaganda, even though the propaganda is most effective when delivered from the heart. Our social contract does not frown on certain behavior because it is "wrong"; the behavior is said to be "wrong" because our social contract frowns upon it.

Nor is it true that the consent of the slaveholders will necessarily be required in eliminating slavery. If the slaveholders do not form a sufficiently powerful faction, they may be forced to surrender their slaves against their will—although the freedom lobby will not be able to "justify" their behavior by appealing to my version of the original position. If the slaveholders are rational, they will anticipate that slavery has had its day and cooperate in dismantling the institution. If they fight, they will end up losing altogether. If they cooperate, they will be able to trade their consent for whatever it is worth. In equilibrium, they will therefore consent. It will be said that such forced consent is not genuine consent. But, for me, consenting just means saying yes. After all, is it not *always* true that we agree to something because we perceive the alternative as being worse?

It is not even true that slaveholding will necessarily survive when the slaveholders are too powerful to be coerced. For example, the process of reform I advocate will eliminate slavery once a society advances to a state in which the institution has become economically inefficient.[11] The crumbling

---

[11]I share the cynical view that it is to this phenomenon that we largely owe the historical elimination of slavery. Moral outrage is much easier to sustain when it doesn't hurt you in your pocketbook. This does not mean that I think Wilberforce and other crusaders against slavery are not to be admired for their determination and courage: only that their efforts would not have ended in triumph if the time had not passed when slavery was an unqualified economic success. (It is worth noting that the experts claim that true slavery is a relatively rare phenomenon in human societies. Hopkins [120], for example, argues that it has occurred in a total of only five societies, three of which he locates in the post-Columbian New World.)

of state authoritarianism in the former Soviet Union is a gratifying instance of this phenomenon.

But what if the times are such that slavery is a thriving economic institution? Should we then be prepared to tolerate slavery? My answer is that this is a misconceived question since it takes for granted that we necessarily have a choice. In seeking reform, it is necessary to recognize that what cannot be altered must be endured, and that we do better ameliorating what current ills we can, rather than counterproductively striving to put reforms into immediate effect that will only be viable in the distant future, if ever. Disaster after disaster in the developing world can be traced to the stupidity of those who ignore this obvious principle.

Pragmatism. A second natural objection to the approach advocated here derives from my claim that our ethical intuitions cannot usefully be evaluated according to *a priori* absolute ethical standards. How is the device of the original position to be justified by someone who holds such views? If, as will be argued more extensively later, ethical principles are "no more" than common understandings that have evolved to coordinate the behavior of those acting in their own enlightened self-interest, why should anyone care what would happen if the device of the original position were to be added to the list of available ethical principles? Appeals to principles like the Kantian categorical imperative—act only on the maxim which you can at the same time will to become a universal law—cut no ice given such a view of things.

However, there is perhaps something to be learned from the historical fact that philosophers and others have tried so earnestly to provide a clinching argument in support of some version of the do-as-you-would-be-done-by principle[12] and that their readers have been so ready to embrace their conclusions. I suggest that the reason is not that the arguments given carry all before them; it is simply that the principle captures aspects of their own behavior in interacting with others that they recognize but do not fully understand. That is to say, variants of the principle are *already* firmly entrenched as joint decision-making criteria within the system of commonly understood, albeit unarticulated,[13] conventions that bind society together. Moreover, the appeal that the device of the original position makes to our "intuitions" about "fairness" may be traced to the same source. The device can be seen as a stylized attempt to operationalize the do-as-you-would-be-

---

[12]Hobbes' version is characteristically negative: *Quod tibi fieri non vis, alteri ne feceris*—don't do to others what they don't do to you.

[13]Since ... men have *forgotten* the original purpose of so-called just and fair actions, ... it has gradually come to appear that a just action is an unegoistic one—Nietzsche [192].

done-by class of principles that elucidates how to resolve the kind of issue that arises from considering objections like: Don't do unto others as you would have them do unto you—they may have different tastes from yours. In advocating the use of a device like the original position, I therefore do not see myself as calling on people to do something that is inconsistent with their nature as human beings or outside their experience as social animals. All that is being suggested is that a familiar social tool be recognized as such, and then that it be adapted for use on a wider scale. The proposal is entirely pragmatic. If history had tabled some rival to the device of the original position as a coordinating mechanism, I would have been happy to explore the consequences of using such a rival mechanism—and the conclusions to which the analysis led would have been different.

1.2.2   Sen and the Rational Fool

The point of this section is summarized in the following quote from Pareto [199]: "One is grossly mistaken ... when he accuses a person who studies ... *homo oeconomicus* ... of neglecting, or even scorning, ... *homo ethicus.*" This issue needs to be tackled immediately for the sake of those who will have bridled at the statement in the previous section that our underlying assumptions are to be those of neoclassical economics.

Those for whom *homo economicus* is a not a red rag to the bull are invited to skip this section, and to continue the fast-forward through the theory that resumes in Section 1.2.3. Later sections are written with this possibility in mind. This makes for some repetition, but the repeated topics are of such fundamental importance that the tape would, in any case, need to be rewound and replayed more than once.

No discussion of the organization of human societies is possible without taking a view on what people are like. Any such view is bound to be wrong, because it is impossible to encompass the richness and diversity of human nature in a few sentences of text. Nevertheless, if any serious analysis is to be attempted, one cannot follow the example of authors like Elster [70] who seek to list all the multifarious factors that influence the way collective decisions get made. One needs to commit oneself to a specific view about which of the various influences that act upon us are really crucial in understanding what makes us tick. The issue is therefore not which is the right view, but which of all the various possible wrong views creates the fewest distortions.

As noted already, the assumptions about human nature to be made in this book are those of neoclassical economics. People are assumed to act in their own enlightened self-interest. This is a view that needs defense. Paradoxically, it needs to be defended, not only from those who attack it, but also from those who are most vocal in its defense.

It is necessary to defend against the most vociferous supporters of *homo economicus* because they offer themselves as strawmen for his enemies to attack. Consider, for example, the following claim[14] made by Stigler [253]:

> Let me predict the outcome of the systematic and comprehensive testing of behavior in situations where self-interest and ethical values with wide verbal allegiance are in conflict. Much of the time, most of the time in fact, the self-interest theory ... will win.

Doubtless there is more than a hint of mischief in Stigler's espousal of such an extreme position, but let us take him at his word. His reference to empirical testing presumably means that the self-interest to which he refers is to be *narrowly conceived* in terms of goods and services, otherwise he would be guilty of the unlikely crime of saying something without operational content. Sen [242] condemns the supposed rationality of those who pursue such selfish aims without regard to the well-being of those around them. He calls them "rational fools". In this, he echoes Hobbes [117, p.203]:

> The Foole hath said in his heart, there is no such thing as justice; and sometime also with his tongue; serious alleging, that every man's conservation and contentment, being committed to his own care, there could be no reason why every man might not do what he thought conduced thereunto ...

I agree with Sen that an individual who acts only in his own narrowly conceived self-interest would often be behaving foolishly. I also share his doubts about Stigler's predictions. But I do not agree that one should therefore seek to replace *homo economicus* by some version of *homo ethicus*. Nor would Hobbes. In such statements as "... of the voluntary acts of every man, the object is some Goode to himselfe", Hobbes [117] repeatedly makes almost a tautology of the claim that people pursue what they imagine to be in their own best interests. Elsewhere, Hobbes [117] goes so far as to say that this is a "necessity of Nature". I am unwilling to follow Hobbes anywhere near so far. However, I am sure he is right in arguing that those who really understand what is genuinely in their own best interests will have no cause to act the Foole. Unlike Stigler's *homo economicus*, the variety of the species to be considered here will not artificially restrict his attention to aspects of his life that are easy to weigh or measure. His concern will be with his own self-interest *broadly conceived.*

Social Evolution. Stigler seems to me a windmill at which it is pointless to tilt. Not even in Chicago are such views given credence any more. I sus-

---

[14]Magnificently reminiscent of a passage from Plato's *Timaeus*: "We may venture to suggest that what has been said by us is probable and will be rendered more probable by investigation. Let us affirm this".

pect that this is largely because a paradigm is now available that preserves optimization as the underlying mechanism, but no longer sees economic agents as omniscient mathematical prodigies. The new paradigm regards evolutionary forces, biological, social, and economic, as being responsible for getting things maximized.

Socioeconomic forces are of greatest significance in such stories. As a parallel for the word *gene*, Dawkins [62] coined the word *meme* for use in such a context. A meme is a norm, an idea, a rule of thumb, a code of conduct—something that can be replicated from one head to another by imitation or education, and that determines some aspects of the behavior of the person in whose head it is lodged. If the environment is sufficiently stable, one may reasonably look to evolution to bring about an equilbrium in which "inferior" memes have been eliminated. The surviving memes need not necessarily be symbionts, but none will gain ground at the expense of others.

In this story, people are reduced to ciphers. Their role is simply to carry memes in their heads, rather as we carry around the virus for the common cold in the winter. However, to an observer, it will seem as though an infected agent is acting in his own self-interest, provided that the notion of self-interest is interpreted as being *whatever makes the bearer of a meme a locus for replication of the meme to other heads.*

Often such theories are rejected outright on the grounds that they demean the human spirit. This seems to me like denying that broccoli is good for one's health because candy tastes sweeter. It is true that the theory does not square with the flattering stories that we tell ourselves about the way we are. But these stories are themselves just memes. Even the idea of personal identity, the "I", can be seen as "nothing more" than a meme.[15]

But to take such an extreme view would be to oversell the theory. It is enough for the purposes of this book that it be admitted that mechanisms exist which could lead to behavior on the part of *homo sapiens* which mimics that of *homo economicus*, without requiring that *homo sapiens* necessarily thinks the same thoughts as those attributed to *homo economicus*. At his fireside, *homo sapiens* will tell different stories from *homo economicus*, and neither type of story need correlate very well with the actual reasons that the species came to behave the way it does. For example, it may be that we attribute our choosing an action to the fact that our "consciences" incorporate a moral rule that tells us that it is the right and proper action. But the real question is how and why the practice of building this rule into the moral conditioning of our children survives. The simplest possible answer is that it survives because the children so conditioned are successful in establishing themselves as loci for further replication of the relevant meme.

---

[15]And not one that accords particularly closely with the psychological realities.

Of course, far from being narrowly conceived, self-interest is being *very* broadly conceived in this treatment. This is not at all at variance with modern utility theory, which eschews any attempt to rank the various possible *goals* towards which a person might strive as being more or less rational. To be accorded the status of being rational, an individual need only be *consistent* in seeking to attain whatever his goals may be. Sometimes this position is derided as being tautological, and hence without content. Would that this were so! There would then be nothing for me to defend in using *homo economicus* to model *homo sapiens*. However, even if one has faith in the proposition that evolution will act to eliminate inconsistencies from behavior in the long run, the fact has to be faced that evolution has yet to complete its task. Even with his aims broadly conceived, *homo economicus* is at best a distorted and oversimplified image of *homo sapiens*. Like democracy, his only virtue is that all the alternatives are worse. To quote Sen [242, p.11] against himself:

> In defense of the assumption that actual behaviour is the same as rational behaviour, it could be argued that, while this is likely to lead to mistakes, the alternative of assuming any *particular* type of irrationality is likely to lead to even more mistakes.

Love and Duty? Proponents of *homo ethicus* do not agree that all the alternatives to *homo economicus* are worse. They feel that to model man as *homo economicus* is to neglect aspects of his nature that are crucial to understanding how his societies operate. Elster [72], for example, observes that "love and duty are the cement of society". Communitarian political philosophers are seldom so explicit about what holds societies together, but the arguments they offer against the "liberal conception of the self" would seem to take Elster's view as given.

In responding to such criticism, I shall follow numerous others in speaking of *sympathy* and *commitment*, rather than of love and duty.

Both Hume [128] and Adam Smith [248] regarded sympathy as lying at the root of human moral life. Hume [128, p.576] describes how sympathy arises by saying:

> When I see the *effects* of passion in the voice and gesture of any person, my mind immediately passes from these effects to their causes, and forms such a lively idea of the passion, as is presently converted into the passion itself.

This captures the idea that sympathy involves identifying oneself with another person, or perhaps with a group or cause, so closely that one no longer fully distinguishes between one's own personal goals and those of the entity with which one identifies.

If sympathy provides a carrot, then commitment offers a stick. To be committed to a course of action is to carry it through even though alternatives may become available that lead to better outcomes. However, if *homo ethicus* is to be characterized in terms of a capacity to feel sympathy and to make commitments, then there is no need to see him as a separate species from *homo economicus*. In making this point, it will be helpful to use the following quotation from Hobbes [116] for classification purposes:

> The whole nature of man ... may all be comprehended in these four: strength of body, experience, reason, and passion.

For *homo economicus*, strength of body can be translated as what he can do. It determines the set from which it is feasible for him to choose. Experience translates as his beliefs about his environment. Passion corresponds to his preferences.[16] Reason is what he uses to select an action from his feasible set that generates his most preferred outcome given his beliefs.

Nothing says that *homo economicus* cannot be passionate about the welfare of others. Indeed, it is not unusual for economists to assume precisely this in certain contexts. Nor does anything disbar *homo economicus* from making some types of commitment. What kinds of commitment he can make depend on what commitment *mechanisms* are available to him. Such mechanisms come under the heading of "strength of body". If he doesn't want to scratch his ear when it itches, he can strap his arm to his side. He thereby chooses at one time to shrink his feasible set at a later time. Less crudely, he may tamper, not with his future strength of body, but with his future passions. From Hume [128, p.422], we have that: "Nothing has a greater effect both to increase and diminish our passions, to convert pleasure into pain, and pain into pleasure, than custom and repetition." The aversion therapy treatments to which alcoholics sometimes resort provide an extreme example.

Not only is the *homo economicus* paradigm reconcilable with a human capacity for sympathy and commitment, it is also not hard to see why evolutionary forces might lead to their being part of his repetoire. Frank [75] and Boyd and Richerson [45] are among those who argue this case very persuasively. Much empirical evidence can also be marshaled in favor of the proposition that *homo sapiens* has ethical propensities built into his software or his hardware. He votes. He contributes to charity and to public television stations. He tips in restaurants that he does not anticipate visiting again. In many countries, he donates blood without monetary reward.

---

[16]To be precise, modern utility theory does not say that a rational decision-maker *is* a passionate beast; it says that his consistency in making decisions leads him to behave *as though* he were.

Sometimes, he will risk his life in an attempt to save a total stranger. Sometimes, he will sacrifice his life altogether in the name of some abstract cause or principle. The evidence, both factual and theoretical, for the proposition that *homo sapiens* shares some of the virtues of *homo ethicus* seems overwhelming. However, let me repeat that one does not necessarily need to step outside the *homo economicus* paradigm to accommodate most of this evidence.

It would, of course, be very pleasant, if *homo economicus* not only shared some of the virtues of *homo ethicus* some of the time, but shared all of his virtues all of the time. Moral problems would then evaporate. Or, in game theory terms, after modeling the players as specimens of a virtuous variety of *homo economicus*, the games to be analyzed would be trivial[17] because there would then be few opportunities, if any, for conflict. I fear, however, that conservatives are right when they observe that, although *homo sapiens* may be a mixture of Sen's Dr. Jekyll and Stigler's Mr. Hyde, it is Hyde who has the upper hand in situations relevant to a social contract discussion.

In evaluating those situations in which proponents of Jekyll claim him to be predominant, two questions always need to be asked:

- How costly is the behavior?
- How frequently does the situation arise?

If the behavior costs little, or it is called for only infrequently, then a supporter of the Hyde paradigm as a first approximation to human nature need not be overly troubled. He has a sound explanation for why the behavior survives. One would only expect evolution to eliminate it in the *very* long run.[18]

Nearly all the evidence offered against Hyde falls into this category. Mansbridge [169] regards the problem of why people vote as creating a crisis for the optimizing paradigm among political scientists. But what is the opportunity cost of going out to vote on a rainy evening? You get to see a little less television. You don't need to sympathize very much with your party to make voting seem worthwhile when the alternative is the Johnny Carson Show. Even then, the percentage of those who vote in the United States is worryingly low for those who care about democratic institutions.

Sometimes people behave altruistically even when the behavior is potentially very costly indeed. Often such behavior is unconsidered—but not always. Hunt's [129] descriptions of those Poles who chose to help Jews

---

[17]Provided no informational difficulties arise. Even in games where the players have identical goals (team games), matters can become problematic if the players are prevented from communicating their private information to each other.

[18]In the meantime, as Frank [75] explains, the behavior may well be very useful for people with a limited capacity to adapt their behavior flexibly to new situations.

escape Hitler's death camps are particularly telling. But such behavior is rare; otherwise it would not seem so admirable. Much more common are those whose civilized veneer is paper-thin, like the ordinary housewives who turned to savagery when enlisted as concentration camp guards at Ravensbrück.

It seems to me that there is just one exception to the proposition that Jekyll only appears on a regular basis when his selfless activities are cheap. This is when individuals are members of a close-knit insider-group, as in a family, a tribe, a teenage street gang, or an army platoon under combat conditions. And there are good reasons why one should expect such behavior to evolve under such circumstances, as Boyd and Richerson [45] explain.[19] A social contract for the internal organization of such groups must therefore be expected to have a different character than for large modern societies. In particular, utilitarian arguments make a great deal of sense in the former context.

The error of which liberals must beware is to extrapolate from their experience of the good fellowship and mutual trust that they find in their own particular insider-group to society at large. I do not imagine that thieves really treat each other honorably as the adage claims, but if they began to do so, the rest of society would still need to keep its doors and windows bolted and barred. Nor is it entirely obvious that a large society would necessarily benefit overall even if it were possible to persuade its citizens to treat everyone with the same consideration that they show to their nearest and dearest. As de Mandeville [168] aptly observed as long ago as 1714, many of the public benefits we enjoy would not exist if we were not so ready to indulge certain of our private vices.[20]

Love and duty are *not* the cement of modern societies, although they may be the mortar that holds the bricks of a primitive societies together. Modern society is like a dry-stone wall. Its stones do not need cement. Each stone is held in place by its neighbors, and it, in turn, holds its neighbors in place. The mechanism is *reciprocity*. Seemingly altruistic behavior, based on versions of the I'll-scratch-your-back-if-you'll-scratch-mine principle,[21] require no nobility of spirit. Nor do more general versions like "I won't scratch your back if you won't scratch *his*." Greed and fear will suffice as motivations; greed for the fruits of cooperation, and fear of the consequences of not reciprocating the cooperative overtures of others. Mr. Hyde may not be an attractive individual, but he can cooperate very effectively with others like himself.

---

[19]Using models of cultural transmission. The context in which they write is anthropological. I do not know whether they would agree with the next sentence, but it is clear that the larger the group, the less well their models apply.

[20]For an assessment of de Mandeville's work in this context, see Bianchi [21].

[21]Better expressed as "I won't scratch your back if you won't scratch mine."

The Game of Life. My model of man—my strolling player who struts and frets his hour upon the stage—is unashamedly to be *homo economicus*. In game theory and in economics, a player or an economic agent is characterized by his preferences and his subjective beliefs, or as Hobbes would say, by his passions and experience. This will also be true of our version of *homo economicus*. Jekyll and Hyde may be mixed and matched as one chooses in assigning his preferences. If the admixture of Jekyll is sufficiently large, so that he actively cares about the plight of others, then a game theorist's task in solving the games he plays will be so much the easier. My own view, however, is that those who mix in too much Jekyll are unreasonably optimistic. As for his subjective beliefs, their nature will not be made an issue in this book. It will simply be taken for granted that *homo economicus* has beliefs that accurately reflect the information available to him.

Once they have specified an economic agent's passions and experience, economists usually feel they have said everything that needs to be said for the purposes of predicting his behavior in an economic context. However, in a social contract discussion, the other two items on Hobbes' list of the properties characterizing the nature of man are often controversial. This section therefore continues with a discussion of how it is proposed to model an agent's strength of body and the manner in which he reasons.

Recall that Hobbes' strength of body is to be identified with what an agent physically can or cannot do. In game theory, such matters are treated very formally by specifying the rules of the game that he plays in great detail. However, it is not enough simply to observe that an agent's strength of body is to be built into the rules of the game he plays, it is also important to warn against what should *not* be built into the rules of the game. I make the necessary distinction by speaking of a *game of life* and a *game of morals*. An agent's strength of body is determined by the rules of the game of life. The game of morals has additional rules, but these tell us nothing about what an agent physically can or cannot do. As with chess, it is always open to an agent to break those rules of the game of morals that are not also rules of the game of life. As in chess, however, we usually choose not to do so.

Modern social contract theorists often see their task as that of *inventing* an artificial game for society to play. Some authors, for example, envisage Hobbes as advocating that the game played in his state of nature be replaced by an alternative game in which power is concentrated in the hands of a sovereign. Such an invented game would correspond to my game of morals. However, it is of the greatest importance not to confuse such a game of morals with the game of life. It is impossible to modify the rules of the game of life. Its rules embody the unalterable physical and psychological constraints that delimit the players' freedom of action. That is to say, the rules are to be seen as being natural in the sense that a natural scientist would understand this term, and *not* in the sense usually intended when "natural law" is mentioned in a social contract discussion.[22] The "natural laws" that societies invent to regulate their affairs—the rules of their game of morals—will appear in the treatment adopted here as the rules for *sustaining an equilibrium* within the game of life.

In the case of King Canute, for example, the laws and edicts that he chose to promulgate were part of his strategy in playing the game of life. His subjects obeyed him, insofar as they did, not because it was physically or psychologically impossible for them to disobey, but because disobedience seemed an inferior option to obedience. King Canute himself, of course, was not confused at all about these matters—hence his famous demonstration at the seaside of the difference between a man-made law and a genuine law of nature. In distinguishing between the game of morals and the game of life, I am making precisely the same point.

So much for Hobbes' passion, experience and strength of body. But what of reason? This is where I feel most at risk of being misunderstood. The usual arena for debate on such questions is a "toy game" called the Prisoners' Dilemma. This is discussed at great length in Chapter 3. Sen [242] comments on the orthodox game-theoretic approach as follows:

> A more fruitful approach may lie in permitting the possibility that the person is *more* sophisticated than the theory allows and that he has asked himself what preference he would like the other person to have, and on somewhat Kantian grounds has considered the case for himself having those preferences, or behaving *as if* he had them. This line of reasoning requires him to consider the modifications of the game that would be brought about by acting through commitment.

Gauthier [84] has similar things to say about committing oneself to having a disposition to cooperate in the Prisoners' Dilemma.

---

[22]It should be noted that I use "natural law" more widely than some authors would allow. In particular, I do not necessarily assume that a "natural law" is confined to the rules that supposedly govern human interaction in the state of nature, and which a social contract supplants. Hume, for example, regards the notion of a state of nature as an idle fiction, but nevertheless has "natural laws" to propound. When it appears in quotes, I intend "natural law" to signify any postulated *a priori* constraint on human behavior that *cannot* be explained naturally. In defense of Hume's usage, it should be observed that he insists that his particular "natural laws" are cultural artifacts and justifies his terminology only on the grounds that it is a natural law (in the sense that a natural scientist would understand) that the human species have "natural laws". Aristotle [5, p.303] is presumably saying much the same thing in his *Ethics* when he tells us that: "The virtues are neither innate nor contrary to nature. They come to be because we are fitted by nature to receive them; but we perfect them by training or habit."

Authors who write in this vein are, or so I believe, confusing what has to be analyzed with how the analysis is conducted. When a game comes to be analyzed, intelligibility demands that matters like those raised by Sen should *already* have been incorporated into the structure of the game. If the players have the power to alter their preferences or to commit themselves to behaving in certain ways before the play of the Prisoners' Dilemma, then it is not the Prisoners' Dilemma that they are playing, but some more complicated game. It may well be that what would be rational in the Prisoners' Dilemma would be foolish in this more complicated game. But the Prisoners' Dilemma is not some more complicated game. Nor can it be made into a more complicated game by wishing it so. It is more than wrong to argue this way—it is *incoherent*. Players cannot alter the game they are playing. If it seems like they can, it is because the game has been improperly specified.

Morality and rationality must not be confused. In this book, rationality is simply *consistent* behavior. Sen [242] ironically observes that a person can consistently act contrary to his own preferences. However, the theory of rationality that is orthodox in economics makes such behavior impossible for a rational person. The theory of revealed preference, to which Sen is a prominent contributor, *deduces* a consistent person's preferences from the decisions he makes. And the practical reasons for thinking consistency an important characteristic of a decision-maker cannot be lightly rejected. People who are inconsistent will necessarily sometimes be wrong and hence will be at a disadvantage compared to those who are always right. And evolution will not be kind to memes that inhibit their own replication. If a version of *homo ethicus* who behaves irrationally is to be substituted for *homo economicus* as a player in the game of life, then an explanation needs to be given of how the former contrives to survive.

In *analyzing* a game, the players must not be assumed to be able to make commitments that constrain their future behavior.[23] Any commitment opportunities must be built into the rules of the game. Nor does it make sense to attribute goals to the players other than those specified by the game payoffs. If a player cares about the welfare of others, such concerns should already be reflected in the game's payoff structure. At the analytical level, it is *tautological* that *homo economicus* maximizes all the time. An analyst who argues that he will make a commitment not to do so is simply inventing an enforcement mechanism that exists only in his own mind. Nor does it make sense for the analyst to invent new preferences for *homo economicus* that involve his sympathizing with others. Indeed, an analyst has no business inventing anything at all. His business is to analyze

---

[23]Thus, insofar as Gauthier's [84] notion of constrained maximization has a role, it is not at the analytical level.

the model *as given*. It bears repeating yet again that the *rules of the game*
and the *preferences* assigned to a player may well already incorporate the
power to commit and to sympathize to some degree. However, such considerations need to be taken into account when the model is constructed, not
when it is analyzed. It is true that the analyst and the model-builder will
often be the same person. But intelligibility demands that we never forget
which of these two hats we are wearing.

Empathy and Sympathy.   One last possible source of misunderstanding
concerning *homo economicus* needs to be addressed. Sen [242] advocates
the use of "meta-rankings" in moral discussions. Such a meta-ranking expresses a preference over the various possible preference systems that a
person might possess. Harsanyi [109] is in the same ballpark with what
he calls extended sympathy preferences. I agree with both that moral discussion requires some such notion. In fact, I borrow Harsanyi's account
lock, stock, and barrel. Without such an input, there would be no way to
reconcile a model in which *homo economicus* is the leading actor with the
existence of do-as-you-would-be-done-by principles.

More on this point appears in Section 1.2.4. What needs to be emphasized at this stage is that the sympathy in the phrase *extended sympathy
preferences* is *not* the sympathy of Hume or Adam Smith. The modern
term *empathy* captures much better what is involved, and so I shall use
this instead.[24] *Homo economicus* must be empathetic to some degree. By
this I mean that his experience of other people must be sufficiently rich
that he can put himself in their shoes to see things from their point of
view. Otherwise, he would not be able to predict their behavior, and hence
would be unable to compute an optimal response.

Such empathizing must be sharply distinguished from sympathizing as
understood by Hume and Adam Smith. A loan shark might attend a movie
and succeed in identifying with an old lady that the story-line plunges into
deep distress. But nothing then prevents his wiping the tears from his
eyes on leaving the theater and proceeding to use the insights gained in
watching the movie in gouging the next elderly widow to come his way.
Such empathizing is about as far from being sympathetic as it is possible
to get.

1.2.3   Hume and the Social Contract

This section resumes the fast-forward through the theory promised in Section 1.2.1. No apology is offered for replaying some of the themes of the

---

[24] Although I have tried elsewhere not to deviate from standard terminology even when
the meaning of what is standard is controversial.

previous section when they are vital to the discussion. One can always skip passages that seem repetitious.

It will perhaps be evident by now that Kant and other advocates of an *a priori* approach to moral questions are not to be the objects of unreserved adulation in this book. Its hero, insofar as a book that argues in favor of bourgeois values can properly have a hero, is David Hume.[25] Communitarians like Sandel [227], who find fault with the use that Rawls makes of Kant's metaphysical conception of the self, will therefore need to retarget their criticism if they wish to reject the type of Rawlsian liberalism that I defend.[26]

Hume [127] makes fun of what he calls the *original contract*. In reviewing Gauthier's [84] *Morals by Agreement*, Harsanyi [110], whose approach to utility questions will be borrowed at a later stage, expresses similar reasons for rejecting "contractarianism":

> Moral people keep contracts even if they would not be punished for breaking them, because their moral code tells them that contracts should be kept. But before accepting such a moral code, nobody would have any real reason to keep contracts not enforced by external sanctions. Yet this rules out the possibility, even as a theoretical possibility, that the moral codes of a society should be the result of a social contract. For, even if there had been a social contract to accept this particular moral code, nobody would have any good reason to live up to this contract, because, by assumption, this contract would have *preceded* acceptance of the moral code that alone could have given this contract any binding force. In other words, people cannot rationally feel committed to keep any contract unless they have *already accepted* a moral code requiring them to keep contracts. Therefore, morality cannot depend on a social contract because ... contracts obtain all their binding force from a *prior* commitment to morality.

If Harsanyi were right to argue that one cannot be a contractarian without believing that everyone is somehow committed to honor the terms of the social contract, then I would be forced to join Hume in poking fun at "contractarians". But I am not alone in thinking that Harsanyi's character-

---

[25]I am more than a little mystified that David Hume should be so little valued by modern moral philosophers. For example, in Bernard Williams' [272] recent overview of ethical theory, Hume would be mentioned only in passing if it were not for the fact that Williams is anxious to denounce the follies of G. E. Moore. Adam Smith's moral philosophy gets no mention at all. I suspect that the same would also be true of my antihero, Nietzsche, if he were not so magnificently quotable. In brief, my sources of inspiration are not fashionable!

[26]As Section 3.4.2 makes clear, when it comes to the nature of the self, I am something of a communitarian myself.

ization of contractarianism is too narrow. Both Gauthier [82] and Mackie
[164], for example, offer contractarian readings of Hume. However, when I
follow such authors in finding a place for Hume within the social contract
tradition, it should be emphasized that I do not see myself as thereby defending the brand of social contract theory that Hume and Harsanyi criticise
so effectively. In particular, the term *social contract* will not be understood
in the quasi-legal sense adopted, for example, by Harsanyi or Rawls.

I shall emphatically *not* argue that members of society have an *a priori*
obligation or duty to honor the social contract. On the contrary, it will
be argued that the only viable candidates for a social contract are those
agreements, implicit or explicit, that police *themselves*. Nothing enforces
such a self-policing social contract beyond the enlightened self-interest of
those who regard themselves as a party to it. Such duties and obligations
as are built into the contract are honored, not because members of society
are committed in some way to honor them, but because it is *in the interests*
of each individual citizen with the power to disrupt the contract not to do
so, unless someone else chooses to act against his own best interests by
deviating first. The social contract therefore operates *by consent* and so
does not need to rely on any actual or hypothetical enforcement mechanism.
In game-theoretic terms, it consists simply of an agreement to coordinate
on an *equilibrium*.

A natural reaction is to doubt that anything very sturdy can be erected
on such a flimsy foundation. Surely a solidly built structure like the modern
state must be firmly based on a rock of moral certitude,[27] and only anarchy
can result if everybody just does what takes his fancy? As Gauthier [84,
p.1] expresses it in denying Hume,[28] "Were duty no more than interest,
morals would be superfluous".

I believe such objections to be misconceived. Firstly, there are no rock-
like moral certitudes that exist prior to society. To adopt a metaphor that
sees such moral certitudes as foundation stones is therefore to construct
a castle in the air. Society is more usefully seen as a dynamic organism,
and the moral codes that regulate its internal affairs are the conventional
understandings which ensure that its constituent parts operate smoothly
together when it is in good health. Moreover, the origin of these moral
codes is to be looked for in historical theories of biological, social, and political evolution, and not in the works of abstract thinkers no matter how
intoxicating the wisdom they distill. Nor is it correct to say that anarchy
will necessarily result if everybody "just" does what he wants. A person

---

[27] "We hold these truths to be self-evident ... "

[28] "What theory of morals can ever serve any useful purpose unless it can show ... that
all the duties which it recommends, are also the true interest of each individual?"—Hume
[124, p.280]

would be stupid in seeking to achieve a certain end if he ignored the fact that what other people are doing is relevant to the means for achieving that end. Intelligent people will *coordinate* their efforts to achieve their individual goals without necessarily being compelled or coerced by real or imaginary bogeymen.

Self-policing Agreements. The extent to which simple implicit agreements to coordinate on an equilibrium can generate high levels of cooperation among populations of egoists is not something that is easy to appreciate in the abstract. The following chapters will perhaps make it clear why game theorists believe that the levels of cooperation that can be achieved are very high indeed. If not, then Axelrod [14], Schotter [231], and Sugden [254] are among those who have written accessible books that popularize the relevant ideas. At this stage, some quotations from Hume will have to suffice in conveying the general idea. The first quotation from Hume [128, p.490] is very famous indeed:

> Two men, who pull the oars of a boat, do it by an agreement or convention, tho' they have never given promises to one another. Nor is the rule concerning the stability of possession the less derived from human conventions, that it arises gradually, and acquires force by a slow progression ... In like manner are languages gradually established by human conventions without any promise. In like manner do gold and silver become the common measures of exchange ...

Schelling [229], Lewis [152] and Ulmann-Margalit [262] have been effective in seconding Hume's view with many apt examples. Lewis, in particular, pioneered the insight that the conventions of which Hume is speaking require that certain understandings be *common knowledge*[29] in a population of specimens of *homo economicus* that use the conventions. This insight will provide a backdrop to much of what is said in later chapters. Indeed, any game-theoretic discussion along traditional lines is founded on the explicit or implicit assumption that certain matters, like the rules of the game, are common knowledge. At this stage, I want only to reiterate an earlier point, namely that the use of *homo economicus* as a model for *homo sapiens* does not necessarily involve postulating that the two species *think* alike: only that *homo sapiens* behaves like *homo economicus*. Thus, for example, when Frenchmen communicate with each other in French, they behave *as though* certain matters were common knowledge between them, but we need not assert that they have other than a dim awareness of this fact.

---

[29]Something is common knowledge between us if we both know it, we both know that we both know it, we both know that we both know that we know it, and so on.

The next quotation from Hume [128, p.521] is not so well-known, but it
as insightful as its predecessor. As it stands, the passage might almost have
been written by a modern game theorist seeking to explain the methods
by which cooperative outcomes may be sustained as equilibria in repeated
games.[30]

> ... I learn to do service to another, without bearing him any real kind-
> ness: because I foresee, that he will return my service, in expectation
> of another of the same kind, and in order to maintain the same corre-
> spondence of good offices with me or others. And accordingly, after
> I have serv'd him and he is in possession of the advantage arising
> from my action, he is induc'd to perform his part, as foreseeing the
> consequences of his refusal.

In spite of all the eighteenth-century sweetness and light, one should take
special note of what Hume says about foreseeing the consequences of refusal.
The point is that a failure to carry out your side of the arrangement will
result in your being *punished*. The punishment may consist of no more than
a refusal by the other party to deal with you in future. Or it may be that
the punishment consists of having to endure the disapproval of those whose
respect is necessary if you are to maintain your current status level in the
community.[31] However, nothing excludes more active forms of punishment.
In particular, the punishment might be administered by the judiciary, if the
services in question are the subject of a legal contract.

At first sight, this last observation seems to contradict the requirement
that the conventional arrangements under study be *self-policing*. The appearance of a contradiction arises because one tends to think of the apparatus of the state as somehow existing independently of the game of life that
people play. But the laws that societies make are not part of the rules of
this game. One *cannot* break the rules of the game of life, but one certainly
can break the laws that man invents. Legal rules are nothing more than
particularly well-codified conventions. And policemen, judges and public
executioners do not exist outside society. Those charged with the duty
of enforcing the laws that a society formally enacts are themselves only
players in the game of life. However high-minded a society's officials may

---

[30]Note that he goes beyond simple reciprocity between two individuals. If someone
won't scratch my back, a third party may fail to scratch his.

[31]Rawls often refers to "self-respect", but I wonder to what extent we can genuinely
separate the respect we have for ourselves from the respect we are accorded by others.
Perhaps this is what Rawls [214, p.178] means when he says that "self-respect is re-
ciprocally self-supporting". If I am right in interpreting this as a statement about the
existence of equilibria, then here, as in a number of other places, I am not so much
contradicting Rawls, as extending his thoughts further than he chose to do himself.

believe themselves to be, the fact is that society would cease to work in the long run if the duties assigned to them were not compatible with their own individual incentives. I am talking now about corruption. And here I don't have so much in mind the conscious form of corruption in which officials take straight bribes for services rendered. I have in mind the long-term and seemingly inevitable process by means of which bureaucracies gradually cease to operate in the interests of those they were designed to serve, and instead end up serving the interests of the bureaucrats themselves.

MacMullen's [166] *Corruption and the Decline of Rome* is very persuasive in attributing the long fall of the Roman empire to such corruption of its social contract:

> Rome, like any other state, could accomplish large goals only so long as its power patterns permitted. During the better centuries of its history, enormous amounts of psychic and physical energy, the resolve and muscle of its citizens, could be brought to bear mostly on war but also on the spreading of a pattern of effective ties of obedience throughout the Mediterranean world ... It functioned effectively because a generally accepted code of obligations pervaded both its public and private relations. Between these two, in fact, there was little distinction. Gradually, however, a competing code made converts among leaders and dependents alike and diminished the capacity to transmit and focus energy. Both public and private power came to be treated as a source of profit, in the spirit of slaves, freedmen, supply sergeants, and petty accountants. The results were seriously dysfunctional.

Indeed, if MacMullen is to be believed, whole provinces were detached from the Roman Empire in its later years by bands of barbarians who were laughably small in number compared with the provincial garrisons they opposed. It seems that the latter had responded to their incentives by ceasing to be soldiers except in name. Instead they operated as a protection racket whose function was to extort money from local businessmen.

Things are no different in our own time. To put it crudely, the pigs nearer the trough get more of the swill. Cooks are as fat as they always were, and butlers are no less rosy-cheeked. Politicians continue to neglect the welfare of those they represent to chase after the prospect of high office. Bankers and lawyers extract vastly more than the value they add to the funds entrusted to their care.[32] University adminstrators spend the money donated for the advancement of scholarship on yachts and fancy receptions. And so on.

---

[32]In the Roman republic, it was considered disgraceful to take money for acting in a legal capacity!

Money sticks to the hands through which it passes. The guilty parties, of course, react with outrage when it is suggested that they have sticky fingers. And it is true that they mostly made no conscious decision to dip their pinkies in the gluepot. They are simply following the customary practices of their professions—now so sanctified by time and tradition that even the victims will often agree that it is only right and proper that they be led to the slaughter.

Such unconscious and unintended corruption of our institutions is perhaps the major problem that faces a modern society. I believe, for example, that the recent fall of the Soviet empire is an awful warning that we neglect at our peril. It is never enough that a society set up guardians. The question must always be: *quis custodiet ipsos custodes?* And the answer is that we must guard each other. That is to say, in a healthy society, *everybody's* behavior must be in equilibrium, including that of our policemen, both official and unofficial.[33] To rely on policemen for the enforcement of social contracts is therefore to take too small a view. Policemen may enforce some aspects of a society's activities, but the *system as a whole* must necessarily be self-policing.

This talk of guardians guarding each other may well bring to mind authoritarian police states with parallel secret agencies spying on each other's activities. And well it might, since nothing says that stable societies operating in equilibrium have to be the resemble the bourgeois idylls envisaged by Hume. Even tyrannies need to be in equilibrium if they are to survive. As Hobbes [115, p.16] puts it: "The power of the mighty hath no foundation but in the opinion and belief of the people."[34] In modeling societies in terms of the equilibria of a repeated game, one is therefore making no

---

[33]We are all unofficial policemen to some extent in that we accord our neighbors high or low status as though it were a reward or punishment for how they behave. (We are particularly meticulous in assigning low status to those whom we perceive as awarding status improperly to others.) Such unofficial rewards and punishments are much more important in regulating our society than most people are willing to admit. Even those who affect to despise conventional values care desperately for the good opinion of those who belong to the same clique as themselves.

[34]Adam obeys the sovereign because he believes that the sovereign will otherwise order Eve to punish him. Eve would obey the order to punish Adam because she believes that otherwise the sovereign would instruct Ichabod to punish her. Ichabod would obey the order to punish Eve because he believes that otherwise the sovereign would instruct Adam to punish him. Hobbes' clarity on such political realities is obscured only by his insistence that, without a sovereign to coordinate things, an equilibrium would necessarily fall apart. This is an understandable error, given the times in which he lived. On the other hand, Kant [137, p.417] seems to have no grasp of the notion of an equilibrium at all: "...the head of the state alone has the authority to coerce without being himself open to coercion ... if he could also be coerced ... the sequence of authority would go upward into the infinite." He should perhaps have read Hume [126, p.32] more closely.

assumptions about the intrinsic merits of open societies. Nor is any *a priori* role being assigned to the notion of a free market.

Social Consensus? This section has identified a social contract with an implicit self-policing agreement between members of society to coordinate on a particular equilibrium in the game of life. Some apology is appropriate for those who find this terminology misleading. It is incongruous, for example, that the common understanding in France that conversations be conducted in French should be called a "contract". Words other than contract—such as compact, covenant, concordat, custom, or convention— might better convey the intention that nobody is to be imagined to have signed a binding document or to be subject to pre-existing moral commitments. Perhaps the best alternative term would be "social consensus". This does not even carry the connotation that those party to it are necessarily aware of the fact. However, it seems to me that, with all its dusty encumbrances, "social contract" is still the only term that signals the name of the game adequately and that, as Gough [91, p.7] confirms, I am not altogether guilty of stepping outside the historical tradition in retaining its use while simultaneously rejecting a quasi-legal interpretation. Or, if I am guilty, then the guilt is shared with such impeccable authorities as Spinoza[35] and Spencer.

1.2.4 Schelling and Commitment

Rawls has a more traditional attitude to the status of the social contract than that outlined above, and it is important to notice that his view is not consistent with mine. This fact could easily be obscured, since Rawls [214, p.176] recognizes that the enforcement problem exists and seeks to deal with it by arguing that the hypothetical agreement reached in the original position would exclude prospective social contracts that impose "strains of commitment" on its citizens that are beyond their powers to sustain.

For a game theorist, a commitment is a *binding* promise. Since Schelling [229], it has been understood how difficult it is, in real life, to make *genuine* commitments. Ellsberg's [69] kidnapping paradigm is often quoted in this context. The victim would dearly love to make a commitment not to reveal the kidnapper's identity if released. The kidnapper, not wishing to murder his victim and having already received the ransom, would dearly love to be able to believe that a commitment had been made. But once the victim has been released, nothing binds him to keep his promise. To make an

---

[35]Everyone has by nature a right to act deceitfully, and to break his compacts, unless he be restrained by the hope of some greater good, or the fear of some greater evil— Spinoza [252, p.204].

attempted commitment stick in such circumstances, an *enforcement mechanism* of some kind is necessary.

In consequence of such examples, most game theorists nowadays treat commitment very gingerly. Each commitment opportunity, insofar as these exist, is modeled as a formal move within the game itself, as explained in Section 2.5.1. The formal game is then analyzed without further commitment assumptions of any kind being incorporated into the analysis. This means that attention is restricted to *equilibria*. These have the virtue of being self-policing. Nobody needs to worry about the enforcement of commitments when a suitably defined equilibrium is in use because nobody has an incentive to deviate from the play prescribed. Section 1.2.2 explains why I think that alternative views are not so much wrong as incoherent.[36]

An approach that advocates confining attention to such self-policing social contracts can be seen as taking Rawls' position on the "strains of commitment" to its logical extreme. But Rawls is not willing to go this far. The following story, based on his [214, p.167] slaveholder's argument, will serve to indicate, not only that Rawls would not approve of the approach advocated here, but that this would also be true of that large majority of social contract theorists who base their ideas on various conceptions of *a priori* "natural laws".

The Slaveholder's Argument. In preparing his case against utilitarianism, Rawls [214, p.167] considers a slave who complains about his condition of servitude. The slaveholder justifies his position to the slave with the following version of a social contract argument. "If you had been asked to agree to a structure for society without knowing who you would be in that society, then you would have agreed to a slaveholding society because the prospective benefits of being a slaveholder would have outweighed in your mind the prospective costs of being a slave. Finding yourself a slave, you therefore have no just case for complaint." Rawls, of course, denies that a slaveholding society would be agreed to in the original position. But he takes pains to argue that the slaveholder's argument would be correct if it were true that a slaveholding society would have been agreed to in the original position,[37] and explicitly rejects the slave's objection that he sees no grounds for honoring a *hypothetical* contract to which he never actually assented and which postulates a lottery for the random distribution of advantage that never *actually* took place.

---

[36]The opposing view is perhaps best articulated by McClennen [175], insofar as this is possible.

[37]It is as though, in Ellsberg's kidnapping paradigm, we were to argue that the kidnapper will not actually release the victim, but, *if he were to do so*, then the victim would be obliged to honor his promise to conceal the kidnapper's identity.

One may distinguish at least two lines of argument with which the the slaveholder could reply to the slave's objections. In his major line of defense, the slaveholder continues by saying: "I agree that you never actually signed a contract. But this is not the issue. We can compute the terms of the contract that you surely would have wished to have signed if the circumstances of the original position had arisen. Either you must admit that you have a commitment to honor this contract or you have to deny that the device of the original position is appropriate in determining what is or is not fair. As for the lottery, it is not hypothetical. Nature runs the lottery when she chooses who will be born into what station in life." The slave might reasonably observe that it would not have been Nature's lottery that he had in mind in the original position, but some other lottery. Indeed, he would be only too pleased to settle the issue of who should be the slave by tossing a coin right now. But the slaveholder's response is remorseless: "You are not entitled to what I see as a second toss of the coin because, in the original position, you would have made a commitment to abide by the toss of the first coin—that is, to accept whatever role Nature asssigned to you".

I hope it will not be thought that I feel that this is an argument to be taken too seriously, or that Rawls would wish to endorse it. It is offered by way of a *reductio ad absurdem* to indicate what a heavy load a quasi-legal interpretation of the social contract has to bear. In particular, the argument takes for granted that, because one would have *wished* to have made a commitment and perhaps therefore have uttered appropiate words or signed a piece of paper, *therefore* a commitment would have been made.[38] But without a mechanism for making commitments stick, such gestures would be empty. For a person to have *claimed*, whether hypothetically or actually, that he is committed to a course of action is not the same as that person *being* committed to the course of action. As Hume[39] [128, p.306] observes

> ...we are not surely bound to keep our word because we have given our word to keep it.

The slave should point out that, although he and the slaveholder might have *wished* to be able to make commitments in the original position, no magic wand could have been at hand to make such wishes come true.

---

[38]In denying this, I am agreeing with Hare's [103] grounds for rejecting Searle's [234] attempted refutation of the Naturalistic Fallacy. It seems to me no more than a facile evasion to say that the act of making a promise is the reason for keeping it. A reason tells you *why* something is true.

[39]His comment is to be contrasted, for example, with Rousseau's [221, p.257], "...the first of all laws is to respect the laws."

Natural Law? This mention of magic wands raises the question of "natural law". Many proponents of social contract theories would argue that the preceding discussion of commitments and obligation misses the point of a contractarian approach. They believe that ethical considerations can be relied upon to secure the honoring of agreements. In speaking of the "strains of commitment", for example, Rawls [214, p.178] remarks that "self-respect" may be counted upon to take up the strain.[40] But do questions of personal integrity take precedence over questions of social justice? Is it not precisely to elucidate such questions that the device of the original position is posited? What point is there in proposing it as an instrument of reform if there is no *a priori* agreement over what ethical groundrules apply in the original position? Surely *all* ethical considerations should be "factored out" and built into the structure over which those in the original position negotiate.

This is to take a very severe line. No *a priori* moral codes or "natural laws" are to be seen as *binding* those in the original position. As in Sugden [254], a "natural law" will be identified with an ethical convention and the former term not used at all except in relating my position to that of others. *All* such ethical conventions are to be seen as *artificial* and hence needing to be *constructed* in the original position, or reconstructed anew if they are already embodied in the old social contract that maintains the current state of nature. As Hume [128, p.484] puts it: "Tho' the rules of justice be *artificiall*, they are not *arbitrary*. Nor is it improper to call them *Laws of Nature.*"

This attitude to the hypothetical deliberations in the original position leaves the slaveholder in his dialogue with the slave without a magic wand to wave at the end of the story. *Nothing* obliges adherence to the social contract beyond the enlightened self-interest of those who consent to it. In particular, to quote Hume [128, p.516] yet again:

> ... a promise wou'd not be intelligible, before human conventions had establish'd it ... even if it were intelligible, it wou'd not be attended with any obligation.

The assumptions made about the status of promises and commitment in the original position are clearly crucial to the conclusions one reaches. However, I have another reason for stressing the severe line that I think is appropriate.

Having agreed to work with one fiction, that of the original position, there is a temptation to invent further fictions if the analysis does not seem to be taking us where we want to go. But to fall prey to this temptation

---

[40]He says that: "Self-respect is, not so much part of any rational plan of life, as the sense that one's plan is worth carrying out".

is to make nonsense of the idea behind the original position. As when a reformed alcoholic is offered his second drink, it is certainly often very hard to stick to the straight and narrow path of righteousness, especially when this calls upon us to chop the logic very fine as in the slaveholder's argument. Nevertheless, it seems to me vital, in modeling the circumstances of those in the original position, to *minimize* the fictions that are to be hypothesized. In brief, I believe the right approach is to get the basic fiction straight, and then to follow the analysis wherever it goes on the grounds that realpolitik is appropriate even in Cloud-Cuckoo-Land.

Before returning to the slaveholder's story in order to motivate a discussion of precisely *when* appeals to the original position are to be permitted, it may help to summarize progress so far. Up to now in this section, attention has centered on why a hypothetical deal envisaged as being agreed behind an imaginary veil of ignorance at some indefinite time in the past should be regarded as a binding commitment for everyday folk here and now. My response is that this is a when-did-you-stop-beating-your-wife question. The hypothetical deal reached in the original position should *not* be regarded as binding, for the reasons that Hume expresses so eloquently. There is nothing about the circumstances under which people are hypothesized as bargaining in the original position that can justify the assumption that they are bound, either morally or in practice, to abide by the terms of a hypothetical deal reached in the original position. Thus, in my theory, compliance is assumed only when compliance is in the best interests of those concerned.

The Game of Morals. Cutting the Gordian knot in this way solves some theoretical problems, but creates others. The problem to be considered next concerns the *timing* of appeals to the original position. In my theory, it is clear that one can no longer envisage appeals to the original position taking place in some mythical bygone age or in some timeless limbo. Since nothing binds anyone to anything, everybody must always be free to call upon the original position at any time for a reassessment of what is just. In particular, such appeals must be possible right now—upon this very bank and shoal of time. It may be that the current state of nature itself represents a social contract achieved through the use of the original position in the past. But, since nobody is committed to hypothetical agreements reached in the past, nothing prevents the original position being used anew to coordinate the behavior necessary to bring about a further reform. The implications create technical problems,[41] but it is clearly conceptually attractive to be working with a notion of social justice that allows appeals against past judgments

---

[41]Since it will be necessary for those in the original position to predict what will be agreed in possible future original positions, game theorists refer to such problems under

at any time. I recognize that it becomes somewhat anomalous to refer to
a device that may be in continual use as the original position. However,
as with "social contract", it seems the lesser of two evils to stick with the
established terminology.

Although the commitment ladder has been kicked out from beneath our
ingenious slaveholder, he is not left entirely without resource. He can fall
back on a second, albeit minor line of defense. He can argue that there
is no point in the slave demanding a return to the original position for a
reassessment of his current condition, because the judgment that would be
made in any original position convened in the future will be exactly what
the slaveholder claims it would have been in the past; namely, that the
slave will be confirmed in his servitude. In this defense, the slaveholder
abandons his contention that the slave has no right to a second toss of the
hypothetical coin that supposedly determines who will be the slave. Instead
he simply insists that the only right and proper model of the hypothetical
coin toss is that provided by Nature when she decided who would be the
rich man in the castle and who would be the poor man at the gate.

I have heard this line of argument defended vehemently on more than
one occasion, but cannot understand why it should be thought that the slave
might for one moment accord it any credence whatsoever.[42] Why should
any particular lottery, whether run by Nature or not, enjoy some special
status? One can see that such a view would appeal to those who already
know that they have won the lottery, but those who are preordained to lose
will quite correctly regard the argument as nothing more than a ludicrously
inept confidence trick.

In any case, the fiction that people could be persuaded to accept Nature's lottery as somehow fairer or more legitimate than other possible
lotteries that might be used has no place in my theory. Since a lot hangs
on this point, it may be helpful to expand on the details of how I model
the situation. As emphasized repeatedly, a social contract is envisaged as
coordinating behavior on an equilibrium in the game of life. Such coordination is facilitated with the aid of a fictional game that will be called the

---

the general heading of "renegotiation-proofness". Those who know something about
this subject will be relieved to learn that I do not need to borrow anything elaborate or
controversial from this literature.

[42]Such defenders of Rawls go so far astray that they seem to me to fall into an error that
properly belongs to utilitarians. The error is that one can decide whether an outcome is
fair merely by looking at properties of the outcome that do not include how the outcome
was achieved. Suppose, for example, that only one heart is available for transplantation,
but there are two people who need it to survive. Is it fair to toss a coin to decide who
gets it, or should we instead rely on the hypothetical coin toss employed by Nature when
she decided which of the two patients would have the higher social status? Diamond [66]
points out that taking the former position creates a difficulty for some utilitarians, since
in both cases the outcome is that someone dies and someone lives.

game of morals. The game of morals provides what Rawls [214, p.584] calls an "Archimedean point for judging the basic structure of society".[43] The game of morals that I shall study is a twin for the game of life except that it offers the players extra moves that are not available in the real world. To be precise, each player has the opportunity to appeal at any time to the device of the original position. The actual game of morals played by *homo sapiens* is, of course, much more complicated. But I believe that the simplified game of morals that I shall study captures enough of what is going on when we talk about "fairness" to make it worthy of our attention.

Although the rules of the game of morals are not binding like the rules of the game of life, it is nevertheless important not to be half-hearted in analyzing how the game of morals *would* be played *if* its rules were binding. One has to pretend that its players have no doubts that the opportunities offered by the rules of game of morals are genuinely available. In particular, they really do believe that they really can invoke the original position and disappear behind the veil of ignorance, where a lottery really will reshuffle each citizen's place in society so that, for example, a slave really does regard it as possible that he might end up as a slaveholder. And when the original position is invoked, they really do negotiate about what equilibrium in the game of morals should be selected in ignorance of what their role in that equilibrium will be. Such a scenario for the game of morals is, of course, incompatible with the idea that each player will always find himself occupying the same role when returning from behind the veil of ignorance as he occupied before. In fact, the assumption will be that the players in the game of morals believe that the lotteries used at successive appeals to the original position are *independent* of each other.

I saying all this, I am calling for nothing more than the same discipline that a novelist applies when writing a book. He sets his scene and peoples it with characters. But he then works exceedingly hard to invent a story-line that is consistent with these fictions. Our task is similar. When analyzing what players *would* do *if* they were bound by the rules of our game of morals, we must never allow our own consciousness that the rules are a fiction to be shared by our fictional players.

Playing Fair. Once the game of morals has been introduced to serve as an Archimedean point, it is possible to define a "fair social contract" in the game of life. A fair social contract is simply an equilibrium in the game of life that calls for the use of strategies which, if used in the game of morals, would leave no player in the game of morals with an incentive to appeal to the device of the original position.

---

[43]Recall that Archimedes undertook to move the world if given the appropriate tools—and a place *outside the world* on which to stand.

A fair social contract will therefore be an equilibrium in the game of morals, but what must never be forgotten is that it must also be an equilibrium in the *game of life*—otherwise it will not be viable. Indeed, the game of morals is nothing more than a coordination device for selecting one of the equilibria in the game of life. People *can* cheat in the game of morals, just as they *can* cheat when playing Chess. But they have no incentive to do so, because playing the game of morals *as though* its rules were binding leads to an equilibrium in the game of life. No player can therefore gain by deviating unless some other player acts against his own self-interest by deviating first.

I believe that the notion of a game of life and a game of morals being played simultaneously has substantial descriptive validity for the way *homo sapiens* runs his societies.[44] It is the rules of the game of life that determine whether a particular set of behavior patterns can survive. To be viable, a social contract must therefore be an equilibrium in the game of life. But there are many such equilibria. In choosing an equilibrium, we often tell ourselves that we are playing the game of morals and hence choose "fair" equilibria in the game of life. In doing so, the danger we always face is that of failing to understand the relationship that holds between the game of morals and the game of life. When playing the game of morals, it is easy to forget that it is not the game of life. This does little harm as long as we keep playing a game of morals that has evolved to be compatible with the game of life. But the rules of the game of morals that grew up with our species are merely fictions embodied in our culture. People can and do persuade themselves and others to seek to play by different rules that are not adapted to the game of life. For example, they may invent rules for the game of morals that allow commitments to be made. We then find ourselves saddled with ideals and aspirations that would make sense, as Spinoza [251] puts it, only in "some golden age of the poets". As a consequence, humbler goals that are compatible with human nature and the world in which we live are left unrealized.

Justice as a Natural Duty?   This section has focused on the manner in which our differing attitudes to commitment in the original position has on the Archimedean points that we adopt. In particular, the fact that appeals can be made to the original position at any time in my game of morals is highly significant. This concern with timing is not original. A number of authors, notably Dasgupta [58], Hare [104], Calvo [53], Howe and Roemer [123], and Rodriguez [220], have commented on the difficulties that

---

[44]Although I am certainly not claiming that the simplistic models I offer do more than reflect some small part of what matters in the real world.

timing problems create when one seeks to apply Rawls' theory to practical problems. Hare, for example, claims to be baffled by Rawls' use of tenses. My impression is that part of the problem lies in the fact that the younger Rawls [214] does not confine himself to wearing just one hat on this issue. Indeed, the later Rawls [211, p.xvi] agrees that the views he offers on stability in Part III of his *Theory of Justice* are inconsistent with his overall position. However, I shall always understand Rawls [214, p.115] to be sporting the hat he was wearing when he wrote:

> ...a fundamental natural duty is the duty of justice. This duty requires us to support and to comply with just institutions that exist and apply to us. It also constrains us to further just arrangements not yet established, at least when this can be done without too much cost to ourselves.

Nor do I think we can attach very much importance to his proviso about the costs that his reforms will sometimes impose on certain individuals. The later Rawls [211, p.17] is explicit that his reservations about the strains of commitment do not apply when past injustices are to be to rectified. In spite of his ambiguity on stability questions, I therefore think it necessary to classify Rawls, along with Harsanyi, as someone who regards some level of commitment to the terms of the social contract as essential for a workable theory.

I hope this section makes it clear why I think that such an attitude to commitment begs too many questions to be viable. I agree with Harsanyi and Rawls that people often do behave "justly". But we do not need to believe the folkwisdom that is commonly taken as explaining *why* people are often just. I, for one, think it highly unlikely that we come into the world hard-wired with a natural inclination to "do our duty".[45] To paraphrase Hume, it cannot be that we do our duty just because it is our duty to do it. If we are ever to understand what is really going on when we speak of "doing our duty", we need to look beyond our culture's folklore for an explanation. And, in doing so, we shall presumably also discover how it is that the standard folk explanations succeed in surviving.

1.2.5 Rawls and Utility

After owning up to so many heretical views, it is refreshing to have the opportunity to point a finger elsewhere on another matter. Rawls [214] is not orthodox in his decision theory when predicting the conclusions that those in the original position will reach. He dispenses with utility theory

---

[45]Unless one wants to count as "duties" such biological imperatives as reproducing our kind and caring for our young.

in favor of his notion of primary goods. This allows him to evade the difficulties of interpersonal comparison that plague a utility theory approach. He is also unorthodox in his treatment of the uncertainty faced by those in the original position. Instead of describing the hypothetical lottery that determines who will occupy what role in society in terms of subjective probabilities and then making calculations in terms of appropriate expectations, he recalls the well-known difficulties with Laplace's *principle of insufficient reason* and then adopts the maximin criterion as the appropriate "rational" decision principle for those in the original position to use. Since his intention is to defend the lexicographic[46] character of his principles of justice, it clearly weakens the force of his argument, particularly against utilitarian objections, that a controversial lexicographic principle like the maximin criterion has been built into the foundations of his theory. Indeed, his "difference principle" is little more than a direct application of the maximin criterion.

The Garden of Eden. For those unfamiliar with the type of issue raised in the previous paragraph, some explanation will be helpful. More detailed discussion will be provided later as it becomes necessary. As will nearly always be the case in this book, the exposition will be simplified by confining attention to a society with only two members. These will be referred to as Adam and Eve, and one may fancifully think of their problem as that of determining a suitable marriage contract in the Garden of Eden. The set of possible marriage contracts is identified in Figure 1.2(a) with a set X of payoff pairs $x = (x_A, x_E)$. How these payoffs[47] are measured will matter a great deal in the sequel, but all that is important at the moment is that Adam cares only about maximizing x_A and Eve cares only about maximizing x_E.

Identifying the set of all social contracts with a simple set X involves operating at a high level of abstraction. A marriage contract between Adam

---

[46]This is an economist's term indicating that priorities are to be assigned among objects possessing a number of distinct characteristics on an alphabetical principle. The objects are first ranked with respect to characteristic A, and only when they cannot be distinguished on this basis is characteristic B considered. And so on.

[47]The use of the word "payoff" is not meant to imply that the different contracts are being evaluated naively in terms of sums of money. Section 2.2.4 explains the much more sophisticated interpretation derived from modern utility theory that a game theorist intends when he uses this term. In particular, nothing is being taken for granted about ends justifying means. Nor is it implied that Adam and Eve have simplistic views on how the good life should be lived. To adopt Bentham's [17] famous comparison, poetry is not to be neglected because it is hard to measure the joys it brings as compared with the game of push-pin. But nor is push-pin to be neglected in favor of poetry because bourgeois folk think the latter more uplifting. Even the relevance of such elitist attitudes is not to be neglected. If Adam thinks the world would be a better place if Eve were to abandon push-pin for poetry, then this will be reflected in his payoffs.

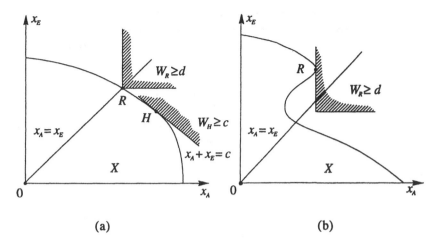

(a)   (b)

Figure 1.2: The Garden of Eden

and Eve actually consists of a set of commonly understood rules for maintaining a long-term relationship. Such a set of rules is seen by a game theorist as determining the strategies that each should use in sustaining an equilibrium in the repeated game that they will play day by day during their marriage. Each such equilibrium determines a pair of payoffs $x = (x_A, x_E)$. The set of all such equilibria therefore determines a set X of outcomes. In idealizing marriage contracts simply in terms of the set X, it follows that nearly everything that a marriage counselor would care about has been packed away in a black box. Or to put the same thought more generally, in looking only at the set X, we are abstracting away the practical details of the moral rules that a society uses in *sustaining* an equilibrium in order to focus on the question of how an equilibrium should be *selected* from those available.

Asymmetries in the set X represent the "inequalities of birth and natural endowment" that Rawls [214, p.100] believes require redress of some kind.[48] Notice that Rawls focuses on inequalities that *cannot* be directly eliminated so that any redress must be through some form of indirect compensation. His emphasis on such inequalities is of some importance since inequalities that can be directly eliminated will not be reflected in the shape of

---

[48]The particular asymmetries built into the set X shown in Figure 1.2(a) are not meant to provoke any debate about the relative capabilities of men and women. After all, X has to be drawn somehow. However, if one chooses, its shape can be taken to be consistent with the view that the biological differences between men and women put women at a disadvantage in the exercise of power without their enjoying adequate compensating advantages—in spite of the testimony of Tiresias to the contrary.

the set X. (They will figure only in the location of the state of nature represented by the current *status quo*.) Some examples may help to explain why.

Consider how things would be under the somewhat bizarre hypothesis that a person's sex was something that could be changed at will like a suit of clothes. If it were also true that Adam and Eve were identical apart from their sex, then the set X would be *symmetric*. It would be symmetric because, for each equilibrium in which Adam acts as the husband and Eve as the wife, there would be an equivalent equilibrium in which Adam acts as the wife and Eve as the husband. One may even imagine equilibria in which Adam and Eve alternate the roles of husband and wife according to some predetermined schedule in which each gets equal time in both roles. When such possibilities are available, the fairness problem is trivialized—and hence the need to emphasize the case when we are powerless to eliminate what makes people unequal.

Ineradicable inequities may arise not only as a consequence of physical constraints, as in the case of Adam and Eve, but also through the action of socioeconomic or political constraints. For example, in the slaveholder's story of Section 1.2.4, an attempt was made to persuade the slave that he should consent to continue to serve his master because it would be immoral for him to seek to be free. However, a slaveholder does not really need the slave's consent to hold him in bondage. He is able to remain the master because he has access to instruments of compulsion that are unavailable to the slave. To propose a "social contract" that calls on him to relinquish his power over the slave without some *quid pro quo* would therefore be to ask for the moon.[49] Recall that only *equilibria* are available as social contracts. However, although the slave may remain a slave, it does not follow that social contract theory is necessarily irrelevant to his situation. Even slaves and their masters must find some way of getting along together. Each such *modus vivendi* will constitute an equilibrium in a repeated game in which the two players are very unequal in their power to punish the other. The resulting set X will therefore be very asymmetric. But we can still seek to select as fair an outcome as we can from the possibilities that are open to us.[50]

---

[49]This does mean that I think we should tolerate slavery in the real world. Although the slave is unable to free himself, it does not follow that *others* cannot force the slaveholder to free him. However, in the slaveholder story one must think of the slave and his master as constituting the whole of society.

[50]I am saying all this quite baldly even though I know that I will be thought wicked by some readers. It will be said to be a travesty to speak of fairness in such a context. But consider a shepherd who treats his dogs badly. Would it not be worthwhile to urge upon him that it is not in his own best interests to abuse his dogs? One can reply that people are not dogs. But slaveholders do not see things this way. Like Aristotle, they have no difficulty in reconciling their morality with holding slaves. They simply categorize their slaves as being "naturally inferior". John Locke seems to have felt much the same

Having discussed the status of the set X, we can now study some criteria for making a selection from X. In Figure 1.2(a), the letters R (for Rawls) and H (for Harsanyi) represent two possible marriage contracts. The former is the point in X at which the "social welfare function" W_R defined by

$$W_R(x) = \min\{x_A, x_E\}$$

is maximized. The latter is the point in X at which the social welfare function W_H defined by

$$W_H(x) = x_A + x_E$$

is maximized. It will be clear why R is said to be selected by the maximin criterion and why H will be referred to as the utilitarian point. Notice that the maximin criterion is lexicographic in that the welfare of the least well-off takes precedence over the welfare of everybody else. Notice also that, when X has the shape illustrated in Figure 1.2(a), the maximin point R is simply the point x on the frontier of X at which $x_A = x_E$. The maximin criterion therefore generates egalitarian outcomes. It does not always literally *equate* Adam and Eve's payoffs, as Figure 1.2(b) demonstrates. This possibility is often emphasized in discussions of Rawls' theory, but it is a possibility that will not arise in my approach since the Folk Theorem of repeated game theory implies that the set X must be convex (and there does not seem much interest in contemplating cases in which X fails to be strictly comprehensive).[51]

So far, this section has proceeded as though a major problem were absent. This is the problem of how different people's payoffs are to be compared. In particular, both in the calculation of the maximin point R and in the calculation of the utilitarian point H, it was taken for granted that the units in which Adam's payoff is measured can be compared directly with those in which Eve's payoff is measured. Indeed, the implicit assumption was that each of Adam's units can be traded off one-to-one against each of Eve's units. Suppose, however, that Eve were paid off in apples and Adam

---

about the lower orders of his time. Far from championing their "natural rights", he argued that even children of the unemployed "above the age of three" should be set to work in "houses of correction" lest they become a burden to the state (Macpherson [167]). Similarly, modern conservatives refuse to recognize that many of those who have been rendered destitute by ill-considered economic policies are just unlucky. Instead, the unfortunate are said to be lazy or inadequate, and hence "naturally inferior". This is one of the reasons that the misuse of the word "natural" in a moral context is so dangerous.

[51] A set X is convex if, whenever it contains two points, it contains the line segment that joins them. It is strictly convex if its boundary contains no straight-line segments. A set X is comprehensive if, whenever it contains a point, it also contains all points with smaller coordinates. For practical purposes, X is comprehensive if Adam and Eve may throw things away. A set is strictly comprehensive if its boundary contains no horizontal or vertical straight-line segments.

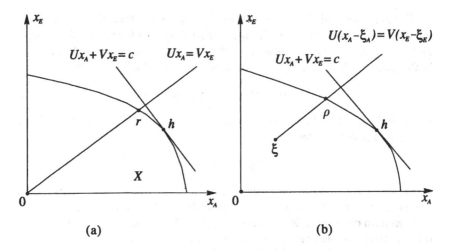

(a)   (b)

Figure 1.3: Weighting the utility scales

in fig leaves, and that they were both in agreement that V fig leaves are
equivalent to U apples—i.e. that one fig leaf is worth U/V apples. Then
it would no longer be appropriate to use the social welfare functions listed
above. One needs instead to redefine the social welfare functions W_R and
W_H to be W_r and W_h, where

$$W_r(x) = \min\{Ux_A, Vx_E\}$$
$$W_h(x) = Ux_A + Vx_E \ .$$

That is to say, the redefined social welfare functions need to *weight* each
person's payoff to take account of how much it is worth relative to the payoff
of the other person. Figure 1.3(a) shows the *weighted* maximin point r and
the *weighted* utilitarian point h that result from the use of the redefined
social welfare functions.

How units are compared on each person's payoff scale clearly matters
a great deal. The location of the *zero point* on each person's scale is also
clearly relevant in the case of the maximin point. Suppose, for example,
that Adam had ξ_A fig leaves to begin with and Eve had ξ_E apples. If one
follows the line advocated in Section 1.2.1 by treating the point $\xi = (\xi_A, \xi_E)$
as the current state of nature, and considers only fair ways to *improve* on
this, then the social welfare function W_R has to be modified yet again to
the function W_ρ defined by

$$W_\rho(x) = \min\left\{U(x_A - \xi_A), V(x_E - \xi_E)\right\} \ .$$

Figure 1.3(b) shows the now much modified maximin point labeled as ρ.[52] The location of the zero points on Adam and Eve's scales do not, of course, affect the location of the utilitarian point which is therefore still labeled as h.

It is now possible to contrast the conclusion to which my analysis leads with that of Rawls. Refer first to Figure 1.1. The central arrow (numbered 1) traces Rawls' route to the maximin criterion. The left-hand arrow (numbered 2) traces my route via Hobbes and Hume to a similar but not identical conclusion. As stated at the beginning of this section, my conclusion bears only a close family resemblance to that of Rawls. To oversimplify disgracefully, I defend the point ρ in Figure 1.3(b) rather than the point R in Figure 1.2(a). However, what needs to be emphasized immediately is that the outcome to be defended is definitely *not* utilitarian.

Primary Goods? The above discussion would be all very well if Adam and Eve really were paid off in fig leaves and apples that could be exchanged in some exogenous market at a fixed rate. But the payoffs they receive from jointly implementing a social contract obviously cannot be so neatly categorized. Rawls[53] [212] seeks to deal with this problem in applying the maximin criterion by measuring the payoffs with an index that assigns appropriate weights to what he calls "primary goods". Those relevant to the immediate issue[54] are "the powers and prerogatives of office", "the social basis of self-respect", and "income and wealth".

Hypothesizing the existence of such an index finesses the problem of interpersonal comparison. But, to pursue the bridge metaphor, it seems to me that this is a situation in which the King must be played directly from hand, and if this means that the trick is then taken by an opponent's Ace, then one must live with the fact that the contract cannot be made. It is not even true that if one were to confine attention to the most mundane of the primary goods, namely income and wealth, that the problem would go away. On this subject, Rawls [212] remarks: "Income and wealth, understood broadly as they must be, are all purpose means (having an exchange value) for achieving directly or indirectly a wide range of ends, whatever they happen to be." It is true that there actually are markets for most economic commodities and hence these can be said to have an exchange

---

[52]In the language of cooperative bargaining theory, ρ is referred to as a *proportional bargaining solution* for the bargaining problem (X, ξ).

[53]Recall that it is the young Rawls who is under discussion. On this subject, as on others, his views have evolved since the publication of *A Theory of Justice* in 1972.

[54]Rawls [214, p.92] also regards a person's "rights and liberties" as a primary good— but not a primary good to be weighed and measured against the others in an index of primary goods. In his theory, no amount of compensation in other primary goods can ever outweigh an inequity in the assignment of rights and liberties.

value. But it is necessary to protest at the implicit assumption that the existence of such markets can be taken for granted in the circumstances of the original position so that the exchange value of economic commodities can be treated as being determined *exogenously*. I believe that the use of the market mechanism for decentralizing production and distribution decisions would inevitably be a major part of any rational social contract of the type being advocated in this book, but to proceed on the assumption that such institutions as markets have an *a priori* legitimacy would seem to destroy the point of a social contract argument. Nor do I believe that the price at which economic commodities are exchanged in markets is independent of the social and political environment within which markets operate.

Rawls [212] responds to the criticism of economic theorists as follows:

> To an economist concerned with social justice and public policy an index of primary goods may seem merely an *ad hoc* patchwork not amenable to theory ... the economist's reaction is partly right: an index of primary goods does not belong to a theory in the economist's sense. It belongs instead to a conception of justice which falls under the liberal alternative to the tradition of the one rational good. Thus the problem is not how to specify an accurate measure of some psychological or other attribute available only to science. Rather, it is a moral and practical problem.

Before replying, two *caveats* are necessary. Firstly, one does not need to subscribe to a theory of the "one rational good" to disagree with Rawls on this issue. In particular, the theory advocated in this book denies the "one rational good", but not in a manner likely to cause distress to economic theorists. Second, the theory of utility that is orthodox among neoclassical economists is not regarded by them as being an attempt to measure scientifically some psychological attribute. Indeed, they respond with horror at the notion that their utility functions somehow measure the excess of pleasure over pain that an individual is experiencing within the privacy of his own skull.[55] The modern theory therefore *disowns* its Benthamite origins and cannot be properly understood if these trappings of its childhood are not entirely discarded. In the orthodox theory, it is regarded as a *fallacy* to argue that a rational individual chooses act A over act B *because* the utility of A exceeds that of B. On the contrary, the utility of A is said to exceed the utility of B *because* the individual never chooses B when A is available. The theory is therefore entirely *descriptive*. In its full glory, not even preferences are attributed to individuals, let alone utility functions. These

---

[55]I do not share the view often expressed that such an interpretation of a utility function is *intrinsically* absurd. But, fortunately, the orthodox interpretation is all that is needed to defend my theory.

are also supposedly deduced from individual choice behavior.[56] A rational
individual is only said to behave *as though* he were satisfying preferences or
maximizing a utility function and nothing is claimed at all about the internal mental processes that may have led him to do so. A utility function, in
the modern sense, is nothing more than a mathematically tractable means
of expressing the fact that an individual's choice behavior is *consistent*.

Moreover, far from subsuming the interpersonal comparisons necessary
to make sense of the notion of "one rational good", the orthodox theory
offers *no basis at all* for such an idea.[57] Nor does the modern theory of
utility necessarily attribute *selfish* preferences to a rational decision-maker.
His preferences can be as saintly as one chooses to imagine, provided that
he is consistent in his saintliness. It is true that economists seldom attribute
saintly inclinations to *homo economicus*, but one cannot *deduce* selfishness
from assumptions that are concerned only with consistency.

However, my difficulty with Rawls' index of primary goods goes deeper.
When he asserts that the construction of such an index is a *moral* problem,
I am at a loss, since it seems to me that *all* moral problems should be
settled in the original position. But how is this to be done if the input
offered to those in the original position is conceived to be a function of
their deliberation? I have a similar problem with Rawls' [214, p.178] notion
of "self-respect" which he offers both as one of the reasons why the social
contract will be observed and as a component in a primary good that is to
be allotted in the original position. The earlier difficulty about the exchange
value of economic commodities is, of course, also of the same character. I
see that Rawls' [214, p.48] notion of a "reflective equilibrium" is intended
to provide a way of bootstrapping through such difficulties. But I have
no idea what the structure is within which the appropriate weighing and
balancing is to take place.

Bayesian Decision Theory. Two problems with Rawls' avoidance of
conventional utility theory have been mentioned. The first is his use of
the maximin criterion as a principle for individual decision-making under
uncertainty. The second is his idea of an index of primary goods to take
care, among other things, of interpersonal comparison problems. On both

---

[56]Of course, rationality assumptions about choice behavior have to be made in order
for such a deduction to be possible. But economists see these *revealed preference* assumptions as being open to scientific investigation (and are even able to claim that pigeons
satisfy the "weak axiom of revealed preference" under certain laboratory conditions). To
this extent, Rawls' characterization of the economists' approach is correct.

[57]It is true that welfare economists often write as though matters were otherwise, but
when it gets down to brass tacks, they usually turn out, like Rawls, to be advocating the
maximization of some commodity index to be defended by appeals to moral intuitions
and practical considerations.

issues, my approach is based on that of Harsanyi [109], whose utility theory
is entirely orthodox.

Harsanyi's [105] criticism of the use of the maximin criterion and Rawls'
[213] reply will not be discussed in detail. In brief, Harsanyi independently
developed an argument based on his own version of the original position.[58]
His argument, however, leads to a utilitarian conclusion, as indicated by
the arrow numbered 3 in Figure 1.1. Harsanyi begins by arguing that the
appropriate theory for those having to make decisions in the face of uncertainty, as in the original position, is that of Savage [228]. Savage built
on the previous work of Von Neumann and Morgenstern [269], whose contribution is recognized by referring to the utility functions of the theory
as Von Neumann and Morgenstern utility functions. The theory itself is
called Bayesian decision theory.[59] The appropriate ideas will be discussed
later in Section 4.5. All that need be said for now is that the theory deduces from certain postulated axioms of rational choice behavior that a
rational decision-maker will behave *as though* he had attached subjective
probabilities to the events about which he is uncertain and were seeking
to maximize the *expectation*[60] of a Von Neumann and Morgenstern utility
function relative to these subjective probabilities. Harsanyi [109] therefore
takes the payoffs available in the original position to be Von Neumann and
Morgenstern utilities. Just as it is not too surprising that Rawls should
derive a maximin social welfare function by attributing the use of the maximin criterion to the individual decision-makers in the original position,
so it is not too surprising that Harsanyi should derive a utilitarian social
welfare function from the attribution of Bayesian decision theory, in which
individuals make decisions by maximizing weighted averages, to those in
the original position.

Reconstructing Rawls à la Harsanyi.   At the root of my own approach
is a *synthesis* of the theories of Rawls and Harsanyi. Harsanyi's use of utility
theory is borrowed and embedded in a rational contracting framework as
envisaged by Rawls. One may say that I reconstruct Rawls à la Harsanyi
or that I reconstruct Harsanyi à la Rawls.[61] If one is willing to assume
that people are, or ought to be, committed to the deal hypothesized to
have been reached in the original position, then the conclusion reached in
this reconstruction coincides with that of Harsanyi. One might express

---

[58]He traces the idea back as far as Vickrey [267]. (Hare [102] traces his version to C.
I. Lewis [150].)

[59]Presumably because, when the theory is being applied, Bayes' rule for manipulating
conditional probabilities gets used a lot.

[60]The expectation of a random variable can be thought of as its long-run average.

[61]Although, understandably, neither author is enthusiastic about being reconstructed
at all. Harsanyi, in particular, believes that a contractarian approach is indefensible.

this by saying that an orthodox approach to utility theory would have led Rawls[62] to a utilitarian conclusion as indicated by the arrow numbered 4 in Figure 1.1. However, this reconstruction does not represent my own position. Recall that my own approach admits no commitment at all to the hypothetical deals reached in the original position. It is this twist on the story that allows me to pull a maximin rabbit out of a hat into which only Bayesian decision theory is placed.

Notice that the appearance of this maximin rabbit implies that the use of utility theory does *not* inevitably lead to a utilitarian conclusion. Moral philosophers who, like myself, reject utilitarianism need therefore not feel it necessary to reject utility theory as well. It is true that *naive* mathematical arguments, such as my reconstruction of Rawls à la Harsanyi, do usually lead to utilitarian conclusions. But to blame utility theory would be like accusing the carpenter's tools for producing a legless table. The mathematical model used in my reconstruction of Rawls à la Harsanyi is naive because, as with the carpenter's table, something was omitted at the design stage. In particular, since the model is static, it cannot take account of the fact that the social contract should be upheld in the face of appeals *at any time* to the variety of social justice dispensed in the original position. To simplify a good deal, the point R in Figure 1.2(a)[63] is attractive, in the context of the slaveholder's argument, because it is invulnerable to demands by whoever may see themselves as the slave that the hypothetical coin should be tossed again; *not* because there is something wrong with Bayesian decision theory.

Interpersonal Comparisons. So far it has been noted that Harsanyi deals with the problem of decision-making under uncertainty by identifying the payoffs with Von Neumann and Morgenstern utilities. But nothing has been said about how such utilities are to be compared between persons. Because Von Neumann and Morgenstern utility functions are cardinal[64] they

---

[62]Although it must be borne in mind that Rawls has reservations concerning the "strains of commitment".

[63]One can also argue in favor of the point R in Figure 1.2(b) on similar grounds, as in Binmore [31], but this requires a little more legerdemain.

[64]A utility function $\phi : X \to I\!\!R$ is said to be ordinal if the *only* information incorporated in ϕ that is relevant to the decision-maker's behavior is the manner in which ϕ *orders* the objects in X. Thus, from the fact that $\phi(A) = 100$ and $\phi(B) = 2$, one is entitled to deduce *only* that the decision-maker acts as though he prefers A to B. The information that $\phi(A)$ is very much larger than $\phi(B)$ does not entail any conclusion about the intensity of his imputed preference for A over B. Another way of saying this is that, if $f : I\!\!R \to I\!\!R$ is strictly increasing and $f \circ \phi : X \to I\!\!R$ is defined by $(f \circ \phi)(x) = f(\phi(x))$, then $f \circ \phi$ is no more and no less informative as to the information it conveys about the decision-maker's choice behavior than ϕ. For a cardinal utility function, the last sentence is valid only if the function $f : I\!\!R \to I\!\!R$ takes the form $f(x) = mx + c$, where m and c are real numbers with $m > 0$. Since $(f \circ \phi)(x)$ is then equal to $m\phi(x) + c$, passing from

can be used to assign a *utility scale* to each individual. Von Neumann and Morgenstern [269] draw attention to the analogy with temperature scales. In each case, one is free to choose a zero point and a unit of measurement for the scale in an arbitrary way, but after these choices have been made, no further room exists for maneuver. One unit on such a utility scale will be called a *util*, just as one unit on a temperature scale is called a *degree*. However, nothing in the Savage theory entitles us to regard a util on Adam's scale as equivalent to a util on Eve's scale. To proceed on such an assumption would be like claiming that two rooms were equally comfortable because a centigrade thermometer in one room reads the same as a Fahrenheit thermometer in the other. To my mind, one of the advantages of a formal approach like that of Savage is that it does not allow one to slip unnoticed into making such errors. If we want to be able to trade off Adam's utils against Eve's utils as, of course, centigrade degrees can actually be traded off against Fahrenheit degrees, then something that links Adam's decision behavior with Eve's needs to be adjoined to the Savage theory. Indeed, if ethical discussion is to be possible at all within such framework, I follow Hammond [95] and Harsanyi [106] in holding that such an addition to the theory is unavoidable.[65]

Further progress depends on returning to the subject of human sympathy raised earlier in Section 1.2.2. This may not seem very relevant at first sight to the issue of the interpersonal comparison of utilities, but the connection will soon be apparent.

1.2.6   Adam Smith and Human Sympathy

Hume [128, p.316] observes that: "No quality of human nature is more remarkable ... than that property we have to *sympathise* with others, and to receive by communication their inclinations and sentiments." It is customary to explain that the word *sympathy* in such statements did not have the same sentimental connotation for Hume and his contemporaries as it has

---

the old cardinal utility function ϕ to the new cardinal utility function $f \circ \phi$ amounts to nothing more than a recalibration of the old utility scale. The old zero point is located at c on the new scale and the old unit of measurement is equivalent to m units on the new scale.

[65]Some economists maintain otherwise. Olson [197], for example, keeps alive a tradition stemming from Lerner [148] in which it is disingenuously claimed that a welfare economist need make no interpersonal comparisons when dividing a dollar between two people about whom he knows nothing beyond the fact that they are averse to taking risks. He should simply split the dollar equally. But, as Friedman [76] points out, Lerner deduces this fact from the assumption that the welfare economist's underlying aim is to maximize a utilitarian welfare function. Sen [243] shows that it need only be assumed that the welfare function is concave, but the use of any welfare function in such a context involves an interpersonal comparison of utilities.

for us. I suspect, however, that the word was as fraught with ambiguity then as it is now. Adam Smith [248, p.10], for example, offers the following apology for its use:

> Pity and compassion are words appropriated to signify our fellow feeling with the sorrow of others. Sympathy, though its meaning was perhaps originally the same, may now, however, without much impropriety, be made use of to denote our fellow feeling with any passion whatever.

The tension between the colloquial and technical uses of the word *sympathy* is compounded by the fact that my theory requires distinguishing between several gradations of meaning in the technical usage. A further quote from Adam Smith [248, p.11] will help to clarify the distinctions that need to be made.

> Though our brother is upon the rack, as long as we ourselves are at our ease, our senses will never inform us of what he suffers ... By the imagination we place ourselves in his situation, we conceive ourselves enduring all the same torments, we enter as it were into his body, and become in some measure the same person with him, and thence form some idea of his sensations, and even feel something which, though weaker in degree, is not altogether unlike them.

My own view is that Hume and Adam Smith were right in identifying the general notion of sympathy as lying at the root of human morality. However, I shall be proposing a more subtle mechanism for the manner in which sympathetic identification influences human behavior.[66] In particular, as in Section 1.2.2, I argue that the type of sympathetic identification that matters in large modern societies is not the crude variety in which one individual so successfully imagines himself into the shoes of another that he no longer fully distinguishes his interests from the person with whom he identifies—so that, in Adam Smith's metaphor, he feels his brother's pain upon the rack in some measure as though it were his own.

Such a crude understanding of how sympathetic identification works is easily incorporated into the *homo economicus* paradigm by assigning him altruistic personal preferences so that he cares for the welfare of others in much the same kind of way as he cares for his own. One can trivialize the problems that social contract theories are designed to solve by going too far down this road. However, as argued in Section 1.2.2, we are not sufficiently antlike for such a modeling approach to make much sense. Thus, although I

---

[66] And it should be noted that Adam Smith proposed a very much more subtle mechanism than the caricature of his ideas presented by most economists who comment on his moral writings.

do not wish to deny that we have some altruistic elements built into our personal preferences, I do not agree with those who argue as though the moral problems that can be solved by appealing to such altruistic preferences are the important problems for a large modern society—and nor would Hume or Adam Smith. Both took pains to emphasize that what people feel for others via the crude type of sympathetic identification under discussion does not have the same status as what people feel for themselves. After all, in the eighteenth century, public hangings were widely regarded as occasions for mirth and merriment at the misfortune of another. For such reasons, both Hume and Adam Smith classified sympathetic elements in a person's personal preferences as being weak forces that required to be buttressed by *social pressures* of one kind or another in order to sustain a moral code.

Insofar as I differ from Hume and Adam Smith on this point, it is in believing that the mechanisms through which social pressures are brought to bear cannot themselves operate without some sympathetic identification between those who are pressured and those responsible for the pressuring. Moreover, it seems to me that, after the role of sympathetic identification in selecting and sustaining a system of social sticks and carrots has been appreciated, it becomes apparent that one does not need to lean heavily on the notion of altruistic personal preferences to explain how our moral arrangements survive. Indeed, most of our moral arrangements then become explicable without any reference to altruistic personal preferences at all.

Empathy. What is the role of sympathetic identification in maintaining the system of checks and balances by which we order our social life? The first thing to do in seeking to answer this question is to abandon the word *sympathy*. This word will then be left free for use in those situations where it is necessary to explain why some people have altruistic personal preferences. Instead the modern word *empathy* will be used. I intend empathy to refer to the process through which we imagine ourselves into the shoes of others to see things from their point of view, but without the final step envisaged by Hume and Adam Smith. That is to say, the process stops short of the point where we supposedly cease to separate our interests from those with whom we identify. Thus, when Adam empathizes with Eve, the understanding is to be that he puts himself in her position so that he can reason things out from her point of view, but without this having any impact on his personal preferences.[67]

In spite of the authority of Adam Smith [248], conservative thinkers may be uncomfortable with a natural capacity for empathy being attributed to

---

[67] This does not preclude his personal preferences having been shaped by *sympathetic* identification, but we shall proceed on the assumption that any such remodeling of personal preferences has been completed before our story begins.

homo economicus. Why does he need to be imagining what goes on inside other people's heads? Are not such psychological issues irrelevant to his proper concerns? In traditional economic models, this is certainly often the case. When individual agents are treated as negligible as in models of perfect competition, or there is only one active agent as in models of monopoly, the problems of how equilibrium is achieved can be successfully evaded. A variety of *homo economicus* that had evolved in such environments would have had no need to invest in a capacity for empathy. However, such a variety of the species would soon be extinct when exposed to oligopolistic environments, as a consequence of its inability to carry through the if-I think-that-you-think-that-I-think chains of reasoning necessary to achieve equilibrium quickly when the number of relevant agents is small.

It is probably uncontroversial that *homo economicus* needs some apparatus to handle such tâtonnements[68] and therefore must be in possession of some apparatus for estimating the *inclinations* of others. The question a conservative will ask is whether following Adam Smith so far necessarily entails accepting a notion of empathy that comes with *sentimental* strings attached. I argue that the notion should indeed be conceived of as coming with strings attached, but that the mental phenomena it is so easy to dismiss as being "merely sentimental" actually exist inside the heads of specimens of *homo sapiens* for sound reasons that no hardheaded businessman should despise. In particular, this view can be defended without going outside the traditional optimizing paradigm of neoclassical economics.

Homo economicus would perhaps have no need to join *homo sapiens* in his capacity for sentimentality if one could always count on equilibria being *unique*. But multiple equilibria have to be confronted, and societies of *homo economicus* therefore require coordinating conventions that incorporate common understandings about which of the available equilibria should be selected. It seems undeniable that *homo sapiens* does settle many coordinating problems by invoking "fairness criteria". I have been involved in some bargaining experiments (e.g., [39]) which suggest that such fairness criteria are more malleable and context-dependent than is often taken for granted, but the fact that subjects tend to describe their behavior in terms of "fairness" is a straightforward empirical fact. But this is an observation about *homo sapiens*. How might fair coordinating conventions, for which the device of the original position may serve as a stylized representative, arise in societies of *homo economicus*? Notice that a fair coordinating convention does not call upon agents to "play fair" when it is not in their

---

[68]From tâtonner, "to grope, to fumble, to feel one's way". Economists use the term to indicate the mental process by means of which agents supposedly evade a costly trial-and-error learning session in real time by predicting what everybody's behavior would be after such a process had settled into an equilibrium so that they can implement the equilibrium strategies *immediately*.

interests to do so. Coordinating conventions select *equilibria*, and so it will be *optimal* for an agent to play fair provided that the other agents do so also.

It is easy to see that primitive societies have a need for insurance institutions. If it is equally likely that you or I will be the lucky hunter tomorrow, then we have an incentive to agree on sharing tomorrow's carcass. But why should the lucky hunter honor the deal tomorrow? Would not such behavior be out of equilibrium? The answer is that, even with unrelated protagonists, a viable insurance arrangement can be predicated on the existence of an ongoing relationship between those involved from which neither has any incentive to deviate. The obvious analogy is with the indefinitely repeated Prisoners' Dilemma.[69] Of course, when the protagonists are *kinfolk*, one does not need to work so hard in justifying cooperative institutions since those involved will be directly interested in the welfare of their fellows for biological reasons. In the language used earlier, their genes may well program a concern for their relatives into their personal preferences. It is therefore among primitive kin groupings that one should perhaps look for the *origins* of fairness conventions. But one is not entitled to defend the *survival* of such conventions in society as a whole on the same grounds that one may defend them within the family.

These remarks on the possible evolutionary origin of fairness conventions, which will need to be defended less airily later, are offered as a preamble to the subject of *empathetic preferences*. Without such preferences, those in the original position would have no basis on which to reach any conclusions, provided we are to take account of the fact that different people have different tastes. This is sometimes not easy to do.

For example, one often reads that Socrates was married to a shrew. But look at things from Xanthippe's point of view. How would you like to have been married to Socrates if you were shorn of your taste for philosophical discussion? My guess is that we would all feel much like Xanthippe about his drinking habits and his failure to support the household adequately.[70]

---

[69]The Prisoners' Dilemma is a simple game in which rational cooperation in the one-shot version is impossible, but in which cooperation can be sustained as an equilibrium in the repeated version. See Chapter 2.

[70]Robert Burton's [52] magnificently self-indulgent *Anatomy of Melancholy* of 1651 has much to say about Socrates' shortcomings: "Theodoret in his tract manifestly evinces as much of Socrates, whom though that Oracle of Apollo confirmed him to be the wisest man then living, and saved him from the plague, whom 2,000 years have admired, of whom some will speak evil as soon as Christ, yet in reality he was an illiterate idiot, as Aristophanes calls him, a mocker and ambitious, as his Master Aristotle terms him, an Attic buffoon, as Zeno, an enemy of all arts & sciences, as Athenæus, to Philosophers and Travellers, an opinionative ass, a caviller, a kind of Pedant; for his manners, as Theod. Cyrensis describes him, a Sodomite, an Atheist (so convict by Anytus) hot tempered, and a drunkard, and prater &c., a pot companion, by Plato's own confession, a sturdy

The point here is that it would be wrong for Adam to imagine how it would be if he exchanged roles with Eve but retained his own personal preferences. He must imagine instead how it would be to be Eve with *her* personal preferences.

The idea of empathetic preferences is not new. Formal treatments of the idea are given, for example, by Arrow [8, 6], Suppes [259] and Sen [239]. Usually such preferences are said to be *extended sympathy preferences*, but I think the risks involved in relabeling the idea are less than those involved in persisting with an attempt to use the word *sympathy* in a sense that differs both from that in ordinary use and from the technical usage of Hume and Adam Smith. Harsanyi [109] adapted the concept of empathetic preferences to deal with the problem of interpersonal comparison in his version of the original position. Rawls [212] is only willing to follow the theory far enough to come up with *ordinal* interpersonal comparisons rather than the *cardinal* comparisons that I follow Harsanyi in believing to be necessary for an adequate treatment.

If an individual says that he would rather be one person under one set of circumstances rather than another person under a second set of circumstances, then he is expressing an empathetic preference. For example, he might remark that he would rather be Eve eating an apple than Adam wearing a fig leaf. Such *empathetic* preferences are to be distinguished from an individual's *personal* preferences. I might very well prefer to wear a fig leaf rather than eat an apple if forced to make the choice. But, if I am aware that apples taste very sweet to Eve and that Adam sees no point in covering his nakedness, then there is nothing strange in my feeling that Eve's situation is preferable to Adam's.

If individual i's empathetic preferences allow him to compare all objects in the set $X \times \{A, E\}$,[71] then it is possible to show, with appropriate auxiliary assumptions, that his preferences must incorporate an intrapersonal comparison of Adam and Eve's utils on the Von Neumann and Morgenstern utility scales derived from their personal preferences. That is to say, numbers U_i and V_i can be found such that he would always be willing to trade V_i of Adam's utils for U_i of Eve's. (Here, of course, only the ratio U_i/V_i really matters.) This comparison is *intra*personal rather than *inter*personal because it takes place inside individual i's head and there is no *a priori* reason why his comparison of Adam and Eve's utils should be shared with that of a second individual j. In order for an interpersonal comparison of utilities to be established, something new has to be added from which

---

drinker, and that of all others he was most sottish, a very mad-man in his actions and opinions."

[71]This is the set of all objects of the form (x, y), where x is any member of the set X and y is either A for Adam or E for Eve.

it is possible to deduce that $U_i/V_i = U_j/V_j$, so that the rates at which individuals i and j are willing to trade Adam and Eve's utils are the *same*. Of course, empathetic preferences are concerned with counterfactual hypotheses. I cannot *actually* be another person. Is it therefore not far-fetched to attribute such preferences to *homo economicus*? A stodgy answer is that the rules of the game played by neoclassical economists permit one to attribute *any* set of consistent preferences to *homo economicus*, but this would seem to beg the issues that matter. The fact is that *homo economicus* does not need empathetic preferences *per se*. But he does need *something* to act as input to whatever device or devices are used when he coordinates with his fellows on an equilibrium. When the device of the original position will serve as a stylized representative for the conventions used for this purpose, then the necessary input consists of empathetic preferences. Other conventional devices may use other inputs.

The question is therefore one of how "natural" it is to impute the use of fairness conventions to *homo economicus* along with the necessary paraphernalia associated with empathetic preferences. An evolutionary route to fairness conventions, requiring only one small step at a time,[72] that begins with insurance institutions arising within family groupings has been proposed already. What is to be suggested now is that the path for *homo economicus* to empathetic preferences also only requires small steps. It has been argued that he does need the capacity to put himself into the shoes of another simply in order to be able to calculate what the available equilibria are. He also needs to be able to put himself in his *own* future shoes to examine what his *own* preferences would be under various hypothetical circumstances in order to make future planning viable for him. All that then needs to be said is that the step to his envisaging one of these hypothetical circumstances to be the counterfactual event that he is someone else requires postulating very little additional apparatus.

Presumably, one would not wish to attribute such an invented evolutionary history to *homo economicus* unless such speculations seemed plausible about the actual evolutionary history of *homo sapiens*. On this I have little to say beyond the fact that I personally do have empathetic preferences, albeit incomplete and of doubtful consistency, and that it seems to me that I use them whenever it occurs to me to question whether another human being is getting away with more than it is reasonable for me to tolerate.

---

[72] As Carl Linnaeus expressed it: *Natura non facit saltus*. Dawkins [61] puts the modern case for predicating the plausibility of an evolutionary story on the existence of a route from the postulated source to the observed end that requires no big leaps. Sometimes I am told that the evidence in favor of theories of "punctuated equilibria" refutes this view. However, even though important evolutionary changes may have occurred relatively quickly compared with geological time in isolated pockets, nevertheless, within each such pocket, small changes must surely have come one at a time.

Moreover, my observation of the behavior of others and the explanations they offer of this behavior suggests that they also think in a like manner. Perhaps the fact that we have such empathetic preferences and use them in this way is an accident of our evolutionary history to which no significance should be attached, but this is not an explanation that I find at all plausible.

1.2.7 Harsanyi and Ideal Observers

The preceding discussion of empathetic preferences is lengthy. The reason for saying so much at this stage is that I am anxious to distinguish my naturalistic position on the interpersonal comparison problem from the Kantian perspective of Harsanyi. He is responsible for introducing a principle into game theory that Aumann [11] refers to as the "Harsanyi doctrine". Harsanyi [109, p.58] expresses the version of the principle that is relevant here as follows:

> ...if Peter had Paul's biological makeup, had Paul's life history behind him, and were currently subject to Paul's environmental influences, then he would presumably have the *same* personal preferences as Paul.

At one level, this is a tautological assertion. If one could indeed abstract away everything that makes Peter and Paul different, then in respect of what remains, Peter and Paul would necessarily be the same. In the context of the original position, it is very tempting to appeal to this apparent tautology. Is not the purpose of the veil of ignorance precisely to remove everything that makes people different so that discussion can proceed on a basis of perfect equality? If so, then we can count on the empathetic preferences held by those in the original position to be the same. Thus $U_i/V_i = U_j/V_j = U/V$ and so the problem of the interpersonal comparison of utilities has been solved: everybody will be agreed that V of Adam's utils are to be traded for U of Eve's.

But a pause for thought is necessary. If Peter and Paul actually do have different empathetic preferences and all that makes them different is abstracted away, then they will be left with *no* empathetic preferences at all. Since they need empathetic preferences to operate in the original position, they will presumably have to *reconstruct* what their empathetic preferences *would have been* if each had no knowledge of his personal history and biological peculiarities. Is such an act of imagination possible? Harsanyi [109, p.60] argues as follows:

> ...a rational individual will try to base his social-welfare function on the "true" conversion ratios between the various individuals' utility units (i.e. on the conversion ratios that would presumably be used by

observers who had full information about these individuals' personal characteristics and about the general psychological laws governing human behavior.). But if he does not have enough information to ascertain these "true" conversion ratios, then he will use his best *estimates* of the latter.

I do not believe it is meaningful to speak of a "true" conversion ratio that can be discovered by adopting the point of view of an ideal observer, any more than I believe that there is a "true" geometry in the sense envisaged by Kant. Ideal observers, even if archangels as in Hare [102], have their limitations. Nowadays, for example, everybody would agree that it would be silly to expect a mathematician, however idealized, to single out the one "true" parallel postulate by pure reasoning. If bricks cannot be made without straw, then even an ideal brickmaker cannot make any bricks if he is offered no straw. Similarly, an ideal observer asked for the "true" conversion ratio for interpersonal comparisons needs some *input* about the society he is to consider.[73] Harsanyi seems to have in mind that the ideal observer is to calculate the empathetic preferences that everybody would have in some hypothetical "primeval state of nature" from which all the influences that make us different are to be conceived as excluded. But I have no idea how such a calculation would proceed. One might argue that the ideal observer's remit does not exclude his being supplied, for example, with a listing of the empathetic preferences that everybody currently actually has. He could then perhaps use social choice theory (although he would need to be careful about Arrow's impossibility theorem) to come up with some aggregated empathetic preference for society as a whole. But which method of aggregation should he use? This seems to raise precisely the issue that the introduction of an ideal observer is intended to evade.

Although I do not feel that an appeal to the Harsanyi doctrine resolves any difficulties in the current context, I do believe that Harsanyi [109, p.60] is broadly correct in making the following factual observation: "In actuality, interpersonal utility comparisons between persons of similar cultural background, social status, and personality are likely to show a high degree of interobserver validity." To make progress on the question of interpersonal comparison, it seems to me we have to ask *why* this should be so. That is to say, we need to dispense with a Kantian-style approach and ask *naturalistic* questions instead.

Rather than follow Harsanyi in supposing that those entering the original position reconstruct their empathetic preferences *de novo* by somehow

---

[73]One might object that *we* would need such input, but who is to say what an ideal observer may or may not be able to do? But remember that the ideal observer has no real existence. He is only a hypothetical entity whose thinking we have to be able to duplicate if he is to be a useful adjunct to the device of the original position.

managing to identify themselves with the point of view of the same ideal observer, I simply suppose that individuals imagine themselves in the original position with the empathetic preferences they actually do have in real life.[74] As Harsanyi observes, there are grounds for supposing that specimens of *homo sapiens* drawn from sufficiently close cultural backgrounds will actually have similar empathetic preferences. What is needed to proceed is some reason why specimens of *homo economicus* drawn from the same society should actually have precisely the *same* empathetic preferences.[75]

Empathy Equilibrium. In orthodox neoclassical economics, an agent's preferences are sacrosanct. The understanding is that an economist has no business questioning the origin of the preferences of the agents he studies. These are simply given as part of the specification of the problem that an economist has to solve. Such an attitude certainly makes a great deal of sense in many strictly economic settings. But, once the arena is widened to include social and political phenomena, it ceases to be sensible to exclude the possibililty that some kinds of preferences may be malleable.[76]

The mechanism envisaged as molding preferences is our old friend evolution. No doubt *biological* evolution has long since weeded out those who have a natural preference for foods that make people ill. Our preferences for clean and healthy foods therefore seem likely to be fairly resistant to change.· On the other hand, the historical evidence suggests that people's preferences among life-styles are very much a construct of *social* evolution, and hence highly vulnerable to modifying influences. Indeed, we seem to have a built-in urge to imitate the behavior of those around us, and the capacity to learn to like what we are accustomed to do. I agree with Frank [75] that strong-minded people can sometimes deliberately exploit this capacity for automating customary behavior patterns to their advantage. However, I do not see such deliberate self-manipulation as having more than a minor role. Nearly all the time, drifts in our preferences are involuntary. It is perhaps not very flattering to our egos to admit that one of our major governing principles is "monkey see—monkey do", but that is the essence of what is being suggested here.

---

[74]The veil of ignorance necessitates that they act as though they have forgotten their own *personal* preferences. They will also need to forget who in real life holds what empathetic preferences.

[75]I am very conscious of the fact that the empathetic preferences that hold sway in a society are largely a *cultural* phenomenon. This is one of the reasons I am reluctant to attempt a multiperson analysis. Each of the interlocking subsocieties from which a real-life society is constructed has its own culture and presumably its own internal empathetic pattern.

[76]Even in strictly economic settings, there are many situations in which consumer behavior would seem best modeled in terms of preferences that are determined by passing fads and fashions.

It would, of course, make nonsense of the use of *homo economicus* as our model of man if his preferences were supposed to be entirely protean. Nor would it be at all realistic to make such an assumption of *homo sapiens*. It is therefore necessary to postulate something about *how fast* preferences may alter. In order to structure the highly stylized assumptions that will be made, it will be helpful to borrow some terminology from the economic theory of the firm. When discussing how a firm can alter its production costs, economists distinguish three time spans: the short run, the medium run and the long run. In the short run, firms cannot alter costs at all. In the medium run, they can alter "variable costs" but not "fixed costs". In the long run, they can alter all costs. We adapt this terminology by replacing costs by preferences. "Fixed preferences" will be identified with an individual's *personal* preferences. The stability attributed to our preferences for fresh food is therefore taken as typical of our personal preferences in general. "Variable preferences" are identified with an individual's *empathetic* preferences. The malleability of our preferences for life-styles is therefore taken as a model for empathetic preferences in general.

Economists are very wisely silent on precisely when one type of time span ends and another begins, and I plan to follow their example. However, the short run should certainly be conceived as being too short for social evolution to operate, although the type of economic evolution that equates supply and demand in markets will be able to operate freely. Similarly, the medium run is too short for biological evolution to be significant.[77]

We can now return to the question of the interpersonal comparison of utility. No attempt will be made to compare anything but the utils derived from people's *personal* preferences. Nearly all decisions are short-run phenomena. Both personal and empathetic preferences are therefore fixed during the decision process. Sometimes, as in the transactions on which economists focus, empathetic preferences are not used at all in making a decision. Such decisions do not call for any interpersonal comparison of utilities, and therefore have no moral content.[78] However, I believe it to be a mistake to argue that most everyday decisions are amoral in this sense.[79] People may not be conscious of the fact that they are comparing utils when deciding what to do, but neither are they conscious of solving differential

---

[77]However, this should not be taken to imply that I believe that economic factors are not significant in determining our empathetic preferences; still less that social factors are not important in determining many of our personal preferences.

[78]Perhaps this is part of what Gauthier [84, p.13] means when he describes the market as a "morally free zone". However, the decision to use the market rather than some other distributive mechanism is very definitely a decision that requires moral input.

[79]Although it has to be remembered that I am referring here to the morality of the real world and not to the various invented moral systems that Spinoza so aptly categorizes as being appropriate only to some "golden age of the poets".

equations while riding a bicycle. As for the big decisions that we think it appropriate to entrust to politicians, these are almost exclusively moral in character.

To understand how we compare utils, it seems to me necessary to follow Hegel in emphasizing the importance of history to the nature of our societies. Such an attitude is arguably not so distant from that of philosophers like Harsanyi and Hare who continue to nurture Adam Smith's ideal observer tradition. In a sense, an ideal observer is little more than a personified summary of a set of general cultural attitudes that we perhaps unconsciously assume we do not need to defend because these are shared by all of those for whom we are writing. But, if we share a set of cultural attitudes, it is because we share a common cultural history. So why not try to build the notion of a common cultural history directly into the analysis? This requires looking beyond the short-run present into the medium-run past. I say the *medium-run* past because this is the period during which our empathetic preferences were forged, and it is these which are envisaged as determining how we make interpersonal comparisons of utility. A legitimate criticism will be that my invented medium-run past is no less fanciful than the ideal observers used by others. However, it does have one major and overwhelming advantage. It opens up an area for analysis that the ideal observer approach treats as a black box. Perhaps there are more satisfactory ways of prizing this black box open, but I have no doubts at all that it is a black box that we cannot afford to leave closed if we are genuinely seeking insight into moral questions.

In the medium run, individual empathetic preferences are shaped by the forces of social evolution, which I see operating primarily through imitation and education. The evolutionary process will cease to operate when an equilibrium is achieved. Such an equilibrium will be called an *empathy equilibrium*. This may be a troublesome idea for economists and game theoreticians who are accustomed to thinking of equilibria as profiles of *strategies*, in which each agent's choice of strategy is made optimally given the choices of the others. But an empathy equilibrium is a profile of empathetic *preferences* that is achieved as the endproduct of an evolutionary process rather than as a consequence of conscious calculation by the agents. To be precise, an empathy equilibrium is a profile of empathetic preferences with the property that each player will always answer no to the following question:

Suppose that I could deceive everybody into believing that my empathetic preferences are whatever I find it expedient to claim them to be. Would such an act of deceit seem worthwhile to me *in the original position* relative to the empathetic preferences *I actually hold*?

The idea of an empathy equilibrium is expressed in the language of game theory because this makes it possible to call upon game-theoretic techniques when the concept is applied. However, there is always a risk of a misunderstanding when such teleological language is used to describe the stable points of an evolutionary dynamic process. In the case of an empathy equilibrium, the chief danger is that it might be thought that something of substance was being introduced into the discussion. However, I want to argue that the notion of an empathy equilibrium is essentially tautological if one is willing to accept that empathetic preferences are a cultural phenomonen transmitted from one mind to another by education or imitation.

What people actually learn from watching each other play the game of morals are not empathetic preferences as such, but *behavior patterns.*[80] These behavior patterns are the memes referred to in Section 1.2.2. An observer may use the notion of an empathetic preference in describing such memes, but it is the memes themselves that are basic. To have a chance of surviving, a meme must be able to replicate itself from one head to another. To succeed in surviving, it must do so at least as fast as any competing meme. I have nothing to say about the manner in which the type of memes with which we are concerned manage this trick—although the question is one of very great interest. My only concern here is with book-keeping questions. Since our agents are specimens of *homo economicus*, only memes that represent *consistent* patterns of choice behavior can lodge in their heads. As explained in Section 1.2.5, modern utility theory *deduces* an agent's preferences from such behavior, and then describes the agent's behavior by saying that he makes choices *as though* optimizing relative to the set of preferences constructed in this way. This view of things makes it impossible that the surviving memes for playing the game of morals should fail to satisfy the criterion for an empathy equilibrium.[81] The reason is essentially that, if someone were able to answer yes to the question posed in the definition of an empathy equilibrium, it would mean that his behavior patterns were not optimal given the preferences attributed to him.

More on the idea of an empathy equilibrium appears in Section 1.3 and in later chapters. In particular, it will be shown that, in an empathy equilibrium, everybody's empathetic preferences are the same, so that $U_i/V_i = U_j/V_j = U/V$. An interpersonal comparison of personal utils is thereby established. We therefore obtain a stylized naturalistic explanation

---

[80]When moral pundits suggest that you should pay attention to what they *say* and not what they *do*, all that they teach is what you should *say* if you want to be a moral pundit.

[81]Provided that everybody's behavior in the game of morals is an open book. I understand that informational questions may be highly significant, not only here but in a number of other places also, but this is an issue that my approach ducks altogether.

of the *origin* of the commonly held weights U and V that an ideal observer approach requires be summoned up from nowhere.

Only after the ratio U/V has been fixed, does it becomes meaningful to use a notion like the proportional bargaining solution to determine a new social contract along the lines my theory recommends. The use of a proportional bargaining solution in locating the new social contract ρ is illustrated in Figure 1.3(b). Recall that ξ represents the state of nature— the current *status quo*. The outcome ρ is obtained from ξ by moving along a straight line until the frontier of the set X of feasible social contracts is reached. The ratio U/V determines the slope of this straight line. Notice that history matters in determining ρ not only through the location of ξ, but also through the determination of U/V.

This completes the discussion to be offered at this stage of what I see as the vital problem of how personal utils get compared. I want to emphasize that I do not see myself as defending any specific set of assumptions about the way the world is on this topic. When assumptions are categorized as being "stylized", this will be a major understatement. All that it seems possible to do without hard evidence is to make plausible guesses about the evolutionary origins of our societies. Any auxiliary models used along the way will necessarily have a Cloud-Cuckoo-Land flavor because of the heroic simplifications that one needs to analyze them. The conclusions drawn from such models can therefore, at best, be compared to the few fossilized dinosaur bones from which experts are able to reconstruct the whole skeleton by speculating intelligently. I can therefore claim no more for my approach than that it signposts a possible path through the thickets of confusion that surround the problem of interpersonal comparison. It would be idle to hope for more than that the signpost points in the right general direction. On the other hand, although I do not want to make any but the most tentative claims for the conclusions of the analysis, I do not feel at all apologetic about my methodology. In particular, it bears repeating that, although progress may require the study of fanciful models, there is no excuse for multiplying the fancies to be considered unnecessarily; nor for using anything other than common or garden logic when the models are analyzed.

1.2.8 Pareto and Mutual Consent

The problems that confront a large modern society are immeasurably more complex than those faced by Adam and Eve when contemplating possible marriage contracts in the Garden of Eden. This section therefore backtracks a little in order to review the new difficulties that arise in the multiperson case. Some readers may prefer to skip forward to Section 1.2.9 so as not to lose the thread of the main argument.

Omitting the material on Pareto-efficiency in the early part of the section will do no great harm. However, I do urge a return to the later part of the section, which insists that the prospects of the powerless be assessed realistically. My liberal heart finds it repugnant that reforms should need to be tailored to the underlying power structure, but my head tells me that bleeding hearts are seldom the authors of workable reforms. Whatever words of wisdom we write on tablets of stone brought down from the mountain, people will still worship their golden calves. We need to cut our reforms to fit human nature rather than pretending that the reverse is possible.

But how are we to analyze the realities of power? On this subject, it is important to recognize that my theory contains a gaping hole where it should contain an account of how and why coalitions form. If game theorists were better at their trade, they would be able to offer a definitive solution to the problem of coalition-formation. But it seems that we shall have to wait a long time for some unequivocal progress in this direction. In the interim, game theorists evade the question by packing the difficulties away into various black boxes invented for the purpose. My particular black box is explained at the end of the section. I appreciate that the danger in adopting such a strategem is that the problems abstracted away may get overlooked altogether. But I am too undisciplined to await further advances in game theory before trying to write about the social contract.

Equity and Efficiency. A much quoted example from Nozick's [194, p.161] *Anarchy, State and Utopia* features a basketball star called Wilt Chamberlain. A leveling government is assumed to redistribute wealth between Wilt and his fans until all have the same bank balance. Wilt then sells tickets for an exhibition of his skills below the price that each fan would actually be willing to pay. He thereby becomes rich, and so the distribution of wealth ceases to be egalitarian. But everybody is better off than before.

The Wilt Chamberlain story appeals to a notion of efficiency introduced by the Italian sociologist Pareto [199]. A reform that improves the lot of at least one person in a society without harming anyone else is said to be a *Pareto-improvement* on the current arrangements. A social situation that admits no feasible Pareto-improvement is said to be *Pareto-efficient*.[82]

A paternalist thinks he knows what is good for others better than they know themselves. Sometimes he will doubtless be right. After all, bread and circuses are a notoriously unhealthy diet for a society. But whigs

---

[82]These are strong definitions. A weak Pareto-improvement is one that makes everyone *strictly* better off. A weakly Pareto-efficient state admits no feasible weak Pareto-improvements. Such a use of the words weak and strong seems less confusing after noting that it is harder to be strongly Pareto-efficient than weakly Pareto-efficient.

like myself think that the cure offered by authoritarians is worse than the disease. We therefore advocate reform whenever the current *status quo* is Pareto-inefficient. Nozick shares the same dissatisfaction with Pareto-inefficient outcomes. Most economists, whether conservative or liberal, feel the same.

Under normal circumstances, a Pareto-inefficient state has many feasible Pareto-improvements. For example, both p and h are feasible Pareto-improvements on ξ in Figure 1.3(b). Economists begin to differ when the question turns to which of all the available Pareto-improvements should be selected. One cannot hope for unanimity in resolving such a problem because no point on the Pareto-frontier of any set X can be a Pareto-improvement on any other.[83]

This book advocates extending the use of the fairness norms that have evolved to solve such selection problems in some situations to a wider class of problems. Conservative thinkers are suspicious of such whiggish proposals and so invent Wilt Chamberlain stories that are intended to spotlight what they perceive as an irreconcilable tension between equity and efficiency.

I agree that there is good reason to be suspicious of the crazier redistribution schemes of the left. An unfair share of a large cake may well be bigger than a fair share of a small cake. But whigs do not propose redistribution schemes that are vulnerable to such criticism. For example, in the Wilt Chamberlain story, a whig who wanted to level wealth would wait until *after* Wilt had given his basketball exhibition. He would then tax the proceeds and redistribute the money among the poor. Wilt would then still end up wealthier than his fans, because too heavy a tax on his prospective earnings would leave him with no inducement to perform at all. Nevertheless, a step would have been taken towards equity without any sacrifice of efficiency.

I think that Nozick [194] often misunderstands Rawls [214] on such matters, and that my position is vulnerable to related misapprehensions. Let me therefore emphasize again that the first step of my approach is to admit only *equilibrium* outcomes as points in the set X of feasible social contracts shown in Figure 1.3(b). Continual interference by outsiders is unnecessary to sustain a social contract x in the set X. The definition of x already internalizes all necessary planning and controls. This includes the provision of adequate incentives for those with special roles to play, together with all administrative costs.

---

[83] A point of X belongs to its Pareto-frontier if and only if all its Pareto-improvements lie outside X. Thus, neither of the points p and h on the Pareto-frontier of X in Figure 1.3(b) can be a Pareto-improvement on the other. If p were a Pareto-improvement on h, then h would fail to meet the defining property of a point on the Pareto-frontier of X. It follows that, when only two players are involved, they necessarily have diametrically opposed preferences over any two points on the Pareto-frontier of X.

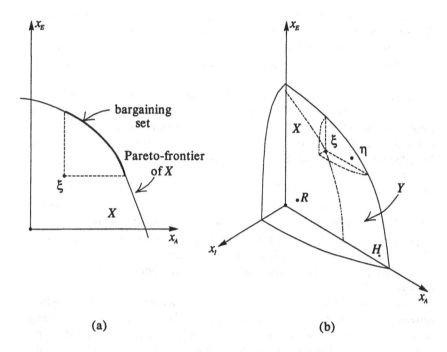

(a)   (b)

Figure 1.4: Bargaining sets

The next step is to identify what Von Neumann and Morgenstern [269] call the *bargaining set*. As illustrated in Figure 1.4(a), this is the set of all Pareto-efficient points of X that are Pareto-improvements on the *status quo* ξ. Coase [56] is the latest of a long line of economists running back at least as far as Edgeworth [68] who argue that a group of rational agents will necessarily move from ξ to some point in the bargaining set, provided that the bargaining costs are negligible. Whigs take this conclusion for granted. But to which point in the bargaining set should society move? The final step is to settle this question using the device of the original position as outlined in Section 1.2.9.

Conflicts between equity and efficiency do not arise if this procedure is followed. Socialist thinkers may complain that the approach makes the set X of feasible social contracts too small and hence excludes options that they would like to see included. But the traditional conservative arguments that seek to characterize the market as the only viable distributive mechanism are allowed no point of purchase.

Planning. An aside is now necessary for those conservatives who find
words like planning and control incongrous in a discussion centered around
the idea of Pareto-efficiency. The First Welfare Theorem guarantees that
the operation of the free market will lead to a Pareto-optimal outcome. So
why interfere and risk ending up with a socially suboptimal result?[84]

It is certainly true that the economists' notion of a competitive equilibrium in a free market can be seen as a game-theoretic equilibrium of a
"market game". But the rules of market games ride on the back of social
and legal institutions whose survival depends on how the individuals in a
society are accustomed to play a much wider game—the game I have been
calling the *game of life*. Even when free market institutions are in place,
it is far from clear that the things which are commonly abstracted away
when a market game is formulated are genuinely irrelevant. For example,
the reasons that Germany and Japan have been so successful in recent years
are not just economic. If one is to explain why they have been better at
creating worldly wealth than their competitors, the obvious explanation is
that they traditionally operate a much tighter social contract.[85]

In reading this book, conservative economists need to keep in mind that
the game of life is played in a much larger arena than a market game. Some
of the fundamental conclusions of neoclassical economics are therefore no
longer valid. In particular, there is no First Welfare Theorem in the game
of life. Equilibria need not be Pareto-efficient. On the contrary, equilibria
with pleasant welfare properties will be the exception rather than the rule in
a socio-political context. A hostile knee-jerk reaction to the idea of planning
is therefore entirely inappropriate. Nobody with any sense denies that the
market is infinitely better at allocating resources than inept, corrupt or
badly informed bureaucrats. But nor is it true that the complexity of the
problems to be faced necessarily makes effective planning impossible, as
claimed by the more extreme followers of Hayek [112, 114]. After all, one
plan that will often work out well is to introduce the market mechanism
into areas where it has not been used effectively before.

Nor should it be thought that my position can be subsumed into the
view that governments merely exist to provide public goods and to internalize externalities, as right-wing economists sometimes naively maintain.
In fact, attempts to describe a social contract in such terms seem danger-

---

[84]The First Welfare Theorem says that the equilibria of perfectly competitive markets
are necessarily Pareto-efficient. Notice that Pareto-optimal is commonly used as a syn-
onym for Pareto-efficient. This makes it easier for the unscrupulous to say that a state
is "socially optimal" when they have only shown that it is Pareto-efficient.

[85]I believe, for example, that it is significant that people will take you to task in Bonn
for crossing the street against a DON'T WALK sign, whereas anyone who sought to do so
in New York would be dismissed as crazy.

ously misleading to me. I agree that part of the role that a government can usefully play is to extend the range of available goods and to assist in creating new markets, but to see a government only in such terms is to wear blinders. Aside from other considerations, it seems obvious that the existence of a well-developed social contract is a *precondition* for the emergence of a market—let alone a government. Even the notion of a private good would not be meaningful in the absence of some of the common understandings that right-wing thinkers insist should be envisaged as abstract public goods.

Just Saying Yes. Suppose that, of all feasible Pareto-improvements on the *status quo* ξ, only η has not been eliminated for some reason or another. Then it is reasonable to say that a move from ξ to η takes place *by mutual consent*. If asked in private whether he wishes to move from ξ to η, no individual citizen will have reason to demur.

Such consent means no more for me than just saying yes. By contrast, social contract theorists who follow Locke [157, p.392] argue that the tacit consent of the citizens in a society somehow "justifies" its current form of government and therefore "obliges" a citizen to obey its laws.[86] Such contractarians read a great deal more into the word "consent" than I intend. However, the following little story will clarify my position.

Eve enslaves Adam and demands that wood be hewn and water drawn. When Adam agrees to cooperate, he consents to act as a slave. But I think it absurd to say that his consent somehow justifies his loss of freedom. As I see it, Adam and Eve are playing a game of sorts. The rules of this game reflect the realities of power. He is manacled and she has a whip. When he labors on her behalf and she responds by treating him less harshly, they are agreeing to coordinate on one of the equilibria of the game. But nothing is gained by saying that their mutual consent *justifies* the agreed equilibrium. Still less does their mutual consent somehow *justify* the underlying power structure.

More generally, I see no point in pretending that we are transcending our cultural prejudices when we pluck a fairness norm from one social environment and use it to judge another. I therefore deny any claim that the device of the original position deserves a high rank on some absolute scale of justice. My interest lies simply in engineering Pareto-improvements by whatever means come to hand. If social evolution had not put the device of the original position in our hands, I would be offering some other theory based on some other coordinating device.

---

[86]Traveling freely on the highway is one way in which Locke argues that a citizen may tacitly register his consent!

Who is my Neighbor? Pareto-improvements require mutual consent. But whose affirmatives are to be counted in the calculus of consent? As Sen [239, p.141] observes in commenting on Rawls:[87] "A half-jocular, half-serious objection to the criterion of fairness of Rawls and others runs like this: Why confine placing oneself in the positions of other human beings only, why not other animals also?" My answer is simple. There is no point in seeking to use the device of the original position to coordinate on an equilibrium with an animal, because an animal is not capable of using such a device. The same is true of the senile, the desperately ill, the feeble-minded and babes in arms.

A narrow definition of a citizen is therefore necessary if the device of the original position is to be used for making reforms. Individuals who lack the knowledge, intelligence or powers of imagination to coordinate successfully with others in society using the device will need to be excluded. But it does not follow that it is "legitimate" that such non-citizens be plundered, exploited, neglected or ignored. In many cases, there will be a bond of sympathetic affection between citizens and non-citizens—as, for example, between a mother and her children or a boy and his dog. However, human nature being what it is, uncuddly animals or schizophrenics are unlikely to be the beneficiaries of such affection.

But other mechanisms that do not require sympathetic identification may also be available. The fact that the original position is not usable does not imply that no *modus vivendi* at all is possible. Other conventions may operate between citizens and various classes of non-citizen—as with the convention that operates between shepherds and sheepdogs. Adam may positively detest children, but still see the necessity that provision be made for their nurture and education, lest the economy fall into disarray when the time comes to pay his pension. Similarly, Eve may not sympathize with those who are currently old or sick, but it will still be expedient for her to endorse an equilibrium in which the old and sick are treated humanely, because she will one day be old or sick herself.

A simple model may help to explain this last point. Consider a society in which old people are all unproductive cripples. To scrape more than the meanest existence, they therefore depend on the charity of the young. But the young have hearts of flint. The plight of the old has no place at all in their personal utility functions. Does it therefore follow that everyone is doomed to live a miserable old age? To see why not, consider the even simpler model described next.

In this society, only one mother and one daughter are alive at any time. At the begining of each period, the daughter of the previous period becomes

---

[87]It is interesting how much less absurd his suggestion now seems after the events of the last twenty years.

old after having given birth to a daughter of her own. While young, she produced 200 loaves of bread. If it were possible, she would eat half the loaves in her youth and store the remaining 100 loaves to eat in her unproductive old age. But bread cannot be stored in this society for reasons that will not be explained. One possible equilibrium requires each daughter to eat all her 200 loaves in her youth. Each mother will then live in misery. A second equilibrium results in each daughter eating half her loaves and giving the rest to her mother. This outcome is a Pareto-efficient, Pareto-improvement on the first equilibrium. But does it represent a *feasible* reform? Can it really be *in equilibrium* for an entirely selfish daughter to give away half her loaves?

As always in an equilibrium discussion, the answer depends on what would happen if a player were not to follow the strategy the equilibrium specifies. Call someone who plays the equilibrium strategy a conformist. Now consider a strategy that requires a conformist daughter to give half her loaves to her mother if *and only if* her mother was a conformist in her youth.[88] A daughter now has a very good reason to support her mother. If she follows her selfish inclinations, then she will not be supported by her own daughter in her own old age.

This primitive *overlapping generations* model shows that the old and sick will not necessarily be neglected, even if nobody cares directly for their welfare at all. But it also has other lessons to teach. A mother in the model is totally powerless. She may perhaps retain her faculties and hence be able to use the device of the original position. But it is pointless for her to seek to coordinate her behavior with others in a game for which she is not a player. To be included as a citizen for the purposes of the original position, a person must have something to trade for his consent. What he has to trade may be very small—as when an enslaved Adam consents to coordinate on an equilibrium with his mistress Eve. But if he is unable to influence the course of events at all, then his voice will count for nothing when an appeal is made to the variety of justice dispensed behind the veil of ignorance.

This issue is raised in the context of an overlapping generations model to clarify my position on the role of future generations. Nobody could be more powerless than someone who does not yet exist. The logic of my approach therefore demands that those who have yet to be born be excluded from citizenship. Their putative consent is irrelevant to fairness decisions made in the present. On this issue, I therefore differ, not only from Rawls [214,

---

[88]The circularity in this definition is only apparent. Notice how the question of who guards the guardians is answered. Someone who who fails to punish a nonconformist is herself branded as a nonconformist.

p.284], but from a long line of distinguished economists, including Arrow [7], Solow [250] and Dasgupta [59].[89]

Rawls [214, p.288] sees a just savings principle emerging from an appeal to an original position in which nobody knows to which generation he belongs. As he comments, only those in the first generation then fail to benefit: they begin the process but do not share in the fruits of their provision. However, an appeal to the device of the original position can be made at any time in my theory. Every generation is therefore a new "first" generation with no commitment to hypothetical deals supposedly made in the past.[90]

Although the putative consent of those who might exist in the future is irrelevant to how coordination is managed in the present, it does not follow that those alive today will make no provision for future generations. For example, in the tale of the selfish daughters, there is only one citizen alive in each period. She therefore makes a social contract with herself for that period. But she would be stupid to neglect what will happen tomorrow in deciding what to do today. When generations overlap, her welfare tomorrow will necessarily depend on the social contract that she predicts will be agreed by those who will then be citizens. She therefore has a strong interest in establishing a *status quo* for their discussion that will lead them to a deal which she regards as advantageous to herself. Her interest will be even stronger if she actually sympathizes with her progeny. It is true that such a mechanism will usually result in less being set aside for the future than a Rawlsian savings principle would recommend. But a second-best species like *homo economicus* must learn to be content with second-best societies. Even the Liberty Bell is cracked.

Coalitions Those rendered powerless by their distance from us in time are to be denied citizenship in our new Jerusalem. But what of those who are distant in social or geographic space?

For example, a foreigner from an alien culture may be accustomed to using the device of the original position. However, different standards for making interpersonal comparisons of utility will doubtless have evolved in his society. An attempt to coordinate with him using the device of the original position is therefore unlikely to be successful. In real life, we coordinate with foreigners in distant lands via our governments. For example, the French and Germans each coordinate on different social contracts in their own national games of life. But France and Germany themselves can

---

[89] The last named work contains an extensive bibliography.

[90] The revised view on this subject offered by the later Rawls [211, p.274] seems only cosmetic to me. His new "present time of entry interpretation of the original position" is largely negated by the imposition of a Kantian proviso that those in the original position should choose as they would wish all previous generations had chosen.

also be seen as players in an international game of life in which yet another social contract operates.

The phenomenon of coalitions acting somewhat in the manner of individual players is not restricted to the international scene. One cannot evade coalitional questions even if attention is confined to the internal affairs of the most stable and insular of nation states. Indeed, it seems to me that the character of a modern democracy is largely defined by the manner in which its coalitional patterns shift in response to stresses and strains.

Modern societies consist of a complex system of interlocking organizational hierarchies that coordinate behavior at many different levels. An attempt to describe the current *status quo* that takes no account of this reality would clearly be futile, as would any similar attempt to describe the potential social contracts to which the society might aspire. Not only do the subsocieties into which society as a whole is split exist, they are essential to its efficient operation.

The existence of subsocieties necessarily requires that distinctions be made between insiders and outsiders. This is not to argue that the irrational dehumanizing criteria currently used to blackball various classes of unfortunates are inevitable or "legitimate". It is simply to accept, as a matter of practical necessity, that we cannot be insiders in everything. Nor need outsiders be seen as opponents. Indeed, two individuals may well be fellow insiders in one subsociety while simultaneously belonging·to rival organizations on orthogonal issues.

One can imagine the device of the original position being used to resolve coordination problems between several such subsocieties with fully briefed delegates serving as representatives of each subsociety. The brief of each such delegate would in turn be decided by a similar use of the original position in resolving coordination problems within each separate subsociety—which will itself typically be split into factions and splinter groups. However, it is inevitable that different standards of interpersonal comparison would arise at different levels and in different contexts. In consequence, a person might well regard one deal as fair when interacting with a fellow insider and something quite different as fair when interacting with an outsider. However, such complexities are beyond my grasp. The immediate moral is simply that it is not enough to ask: Who is a citizen? Once the role of coalitions have been appreciated, one needs to ask the much more difficult question: Who is a citizen *in what*?

For a particularly simple example of how coalitions can matter, consider the diagram of Figure 1.4(b). At first Adam and Eve were alone in the Garden of Eden operating the social contract ξ. When Ichabod happens by, Adam and Eve see the opportunity to use their combined might to enslave him. After Ichabod has been manacled, the set of available social contracts will be Y. If the device of the original position is employed after this sequence of events, the result will be a a social contract η on the Pareto-frontier of Y.

In Figure 1.4(b), the point η is remote from both of the points R and H named after Rawls and Harsanyi in Section 1.2.5. However, there is a deeper lesson. The reason that η is admitted as a member of the set Y is that it supposedly represents a *self-policing* deal—an equilibrium. But what prevents Eve from unshackling Ichabod with a view to creating a new alliance whose aim is to overpower and enslave Adam? What then would prevent Ichabod later unshackling Adam with a view to enslaving Eve?

Such questions about the reasons why some coalitions are favored over others constitute the coalition-formation problem that my treatment abstracts away. In telling the story that accompanies Figure 1.4(b), I took for granted that the original coalition of Adam and Eve would survive the appearance of Ichabod. The shape of the set Y drawn in Figure 1.4(b) assumes that it is commonly understood that neither Adam nor Eve will be tempted to destabilize the potential social contracts in the set Y by forming a coalition with Ichabod.[91]

In a multiperson problem, the points in Y that I shall blithely continue to describe as equilibria are therefore really black boxes that incorporate an unspecified theory of coalition-formation. In the two-person case, Adam and Eve have nobody but each other with whom to hatch plots. Attention can therefore be confined to equilibria that are stable to any deviation by an individual acting alone. Game theorists think they understand such *Nash equilibria* fairly well. But the problems that arise when an equilibrium must be stable in the face of deviations by *groups* of individuals acting in concert is much more problematic. Von Neumann and Morgenstern [269] proposed the first of many theories intended to deal with the question, but none of these theories manage to tackle all the difficulties simultaneously.

The simplest of the approaches that have been suggested discards all social systems that fail to be stable in the face of potential deviations by *any* coalition. The set of potential social contracts that remain would then lie in the *core* of the game.[92] This is an attractive thought for conservative economists. It has been known since the time of Edgeworth [68] that the core outcomes of a market game with very large numbers of players require distributing goods and services in approximately the same way as they would be distributed by the operation of a free market economy.

However, the core of the game of life will typically be empty. That is to say, no social contracts whatever will be stable against potential deviations

---

[91]Both Adam and Eve may see short-term advantages in such a destabilization. After all, Ichabod will readily agree to accept junior status when the alternative is to remain in bondage. But will he continue to be satisfied with junior status once he is free?

[92]Howe and Roemer [123] are among those who have applied the core concept to social contract problems.

by all coalitions. Even if such a social contract could be found, I see no reason why it should monopolize our attention. Most coalitions that might conceivably form can be ruled out from the outset because it will be obvious to their potential members that the prospective gains will be ephemeral at best. The feasible social contracts need to be stable only in the face of deviations by coalitions whose formation is thought to be credible. But game theory is not yet able to say anything sufficiently general about why one potential coalition should be seen as a credible possibility while talk of another is dismissed as mere bombast.

Launching Dinghys?   A sympathetic critic might argue that my theory can be seen as representing the very last stage of the coalition process in which the *grand coalition* of everybody is formed after an appeal to the original position has been made by all relevant interest groups. For example, one might see Adam as a representative man and Eve as a representative woman whose joint task is to find a just settlement of intersex questions. However, even such modest attempts to generalize my two-person examples should be treated with caution, lest one fall into the error of the Marxists by treating abstractly conceived coalitions like Capital and Labor as though they had the single-minded and enduring aims of individual people. The point here is the same as that made in Section 1.2.7 about ideal observers. The preferences revealed by the collective decisions of a group cannot be expected to be as coherent as those made by a rational individual. A delegate representing a group will therefore differ in important ways from a player representing only himself. Indeed, the fact that coalitions will often not behave like monolithic blocs is part of what makes the coalition-formation problem so difficult.

A less sympathetic critic may feel that my inability to cope adequately with the problem of coalition-formation makes my attempts to theorize about social contract questions like putting to sea in a half-built boat. But the problem is not that my boat is unseaworthy. It is rather that a two-person example is a mere dinghy when what we need are ocean liners. However, I see no point in breaking bottles of champagne over the bows of a Republic built in the grand Platonic style unless one can first get some smaller ships to float.

1.2.9   Gauthier and Rational Contracting

The time has now come to return to the problems facing Adam and Eve over their marriage contract in the Garden of Eden. Recall that the set X of Figure 1.3(b) represents all possible equilibrium outcomes in their game of life. This set therefore contains all feasible social contracts. Section 1.2.8 argues that they will choose some point in the bargaining set of Figure

1.4(a). However, Adam and Eve will necessarily have opposing preferences over any two points in the bargaining set. Compromise will therefore be needed if they are to reach an agreement on which point in the bargaining set to select.

We commonly reach such compromises in small groups by negotiating until a consensus emerges. But such face-to-face bargaining is not possible in a large modern society. If Adam and Eve are to serve as an example that is relevant to social contract issues, we must therefore find a way for them to reach a *tacit* consensus. The device of the original position fulfils this function in my theory. However, its use does not free us from the need to consider how rational people bargain. On the contrary, when employing the device of the original position, Adam and Eve need to be so adept at bargaining that they are able to predict what agreement they would reach if they were to bargain behind a veil of ignorance.

What will their prediction be? As with utility theory, the bargaining theory that will be employed in answering this question is entirely ortho-dox among economists and game theoreticians. However, an orthodoxy is largely defined by the heresies it denies. And it matters a great deal that heretical bargaining theories be very firmly denied, since the temptation to import fictions about the nature of rational bargaining into the analy-sis of decision-making process in the original position is very strong. But, as stressed several times already, our aim should always be to *minimize* on such fictions. It is particularly important that no ethical conventions are assimilated into the bargaining analysis. Bargaining in the original position is seen as *determining* such ethical conventions in my treatment. The manner in which the bargaining problem is resolved must therefore be independent of moral considerations.

Some authors see no reason why anything sophisticated on bargaining need be borrowed from game theory at all. For example, Harsanyi [109] knows all about orthodox bargaining theory. But, as he observes, behind his version of the veil of ignorance, everybody is the same and hence their interests are identical. They can therefore relinquish their choice to a rep-resentative or an ideal observer without fear of losing out by doing so.[93] Hare [104] remarks that Rawls' rational contracting story can easily be re-cast in an ideal observer mold. The difference between Harsanyi's ideal observer and Rawls' would then simply be that one maximizes expecta-tions and the other uses the maximin criterion. Elsewhere, Hare [101, p.25] observes that, in the context of an original position in which it is given *a priori* that everybody is the same, it does not really matter very much whether one adopts a rational contracting story, an ideal observer story or

---

[93]Recall that ideal observers were anathema in the context of Section 1.2.7, but here the idea is harmless.

Hare's own "universal prescriptivist" tale.[94] This is my view also.

Why then make a fuss about getting the bargaining story right? It is true that, once an empathy equilibrium has been achieved, everybody in the original position will have the same properties, but this fact is not given *a priori*. As always in an equilibrium story, what happens in equilibrium is determined by what would happen if there were a deviation. Such a deviation would create an asymmetry in the original position that could only be resolved using an ideal observer approach by awkward expediencies of doubtful validity. However, a bargaining approach takes such problems in its stride.

Gauthier's [84] *Morals by Agreement* also attaches similar importance to the bargaining question. Indeed, his general attitudes and aims are close to mine across the board. It is therefore important to make it clear that we differ very markedly on how these attitudes and aims are to be implemented. The most important of our differences lies in our approach to the question of commitment. He believes it can be shown that rational agents will voluntarily observe constraints on the extent to which they maximize. I believe all such arguments to be fallacious. However, the immediate issue is the incompatibility of our views on how bargaining should be modeled. This question is of much greater importance for Gauthier than it is for me since he dispenses with anything resembling the original position. His protagonists imagine themselves bargaining face-to-face with no veil of ignorance. The circumstances in which they bargain and the method by means of which the bargaining problem is resolved therefore have to carry a much greater burden than they do for Rawls.

Which Bargaining Solution? Gauthier's [84, p.146] *Morals by Agreement* is dismissive of "infighting among bargaining theorists", rather as Rawls is dismissive of the arguments of Bayesian decision theorists. And, just as Rawls proposes his own idiosyncratic resolution of the difficulties that Bayesian decision theory addresses, so Gauthier proposes his own idiosyncratic resolution of the bargaining problem. Even the sound of Gauthier's "principle of minimax relative concession" is evocative of the maximin criterion of Rawls. The mainstream game-theoretic position on the bargaining problem will not be defended at this stage. Instead, something will be said about what the mainstream position is, the use that will be made of it, and why I do not believe that the type of argument that Gauthier offers in defense of his notion is adequate.

The bargaining concept that will be represented in Chapter 1 of Volume

---

[94]Hare [102] has his own version of an original position and his own ideal observer approach.

II as the appropriate orthodoxy is called the *Nash bargaining solution.*[95] A Nash bargaining *problem* is a pair (X, ξ) as illustrated in Figure 1.4(a). The point $\xi = (\xi_A, \xi_E)$ and the points $x = (x_A, x_E)$ in the set X are pairs of Von Neumann and Morgenstern utilities that represent the possible outcomes of the bargaining between Adam and Eve.[96] In particular, a point $x = (x_A, x_E)$ is to be interpreted as an idealization of a possible deal available to Adam and Eve. The set X therefore represents the set of all feasible deals. The point ξ is called the *status quo* for the bargaining problem. Nash [190] interpreted this as the outcome that will result if the bargainers are unable to agree. This is an interpretation that needs certain amount of qualification, but it will suffice for now. I take it to be uncontroversial that a rational agreement between Adam and Eve will result in the selection of some point in the bargaining set determined by the bargaining problem (X, ξ). But which point?

The Nash bargaining solution for the problem (X, ξ) can be defined in terms of the social welfare function

$$W_N(x) = (x_A - \xi_A)(x_E - \xi_E).$$

It is the point ν in X at which $W_N(x)$ is maximized. Figure 1.5(a) illustrates the definition. Figure 1.5(b) illustrates the Kalai-Smorodinsky [132] bargaining solution to which Gauthier's [84] argument leads in the two-person case. This is the point κ at which the social welfare function

$$W_{KS}(x) = \min\left\{\frac{x_A - \xi_A}{\eta_A - \xi_A}, \frac{x_E - \xi_E}{\eta_E - \xi_E}\right\}$$

is maximized.

In a recent paper, Gauthier [85, p.178] expresses reservations about his defense of the Kalai-Smorodinsky solution as compared with the orthodox defense of the Nash bargaining solution. But he does not feel it necessary to abandon the former in favor of the latter since, as he remarks, the two solution concepts coincide when the bargaining problem (X, ξ) is symmetric. I do not agree with Gauthier [85, p.178] that one can sensibly restrict attention to symmetric bargaining problems in his approach to social contract

---

[95]It is easy to confuse this with the idea of Nash equilibrium, especially as the latter will be mentioned a great deal—often in the same sentence as the Nash bargaining solution. But their meanings are not even distantly related. For the moment, it will be enough to observe that the former is a statement about *strategies* while the latter is concerned only with *payoffs*.

[96]In describing the Nash bargaining solution, it is being taken for granted here that Adam and Eve bargain face-to-face in full knowledge of their identities. In applying the idea to the bargaining that goes on in the original position, it will be necessary to complicate the situation by taking account of their uncertainties behind the veil of ignorance.

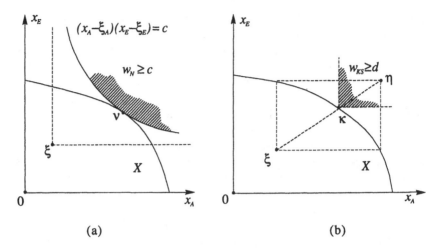

Figure 1.5: Two bargaining solutions

questions.[97] On the other hand, I do not believe that it would be a very significant modification of Gauthier's social contract theory if he were to employ the Nash bargaining solution everywhere that he currently employs the Kalai-Smorodinsky solution. The two solutions are seldom very far apart even in asymmetric bargaining problems. However, except in the current paragraph, I do not plan to discuss Gauthier's second thoughts about the arguments of his *Morals by Agreement*. As with Rawls' *Theory of Justice*, Gauthier's book has been so widely read that I think clarity is better served by criticizing what he used to believe rather than what he believes now.

Neither the Nash bargaining solution nor the Kalai-Smorodinsky solution depend on Adam's utils being comparable with Eve's. For example, in the definition of W_N one may replace x_A and ξ_A by $U x_A$ and $U \xi_A$ respectively, and x_E and ξ_E by $V x_E$ and $V \xi_E$, without altering the location of ν. This signals the fact that, in contrast to the proportional bargaining solution or the weighted utilitarian solution introduced in Section 1.2.5, neither the Nash bargaining solution nor the Kalai-Smorodinsky solution has a viable defense as an *ethical* concept. This is a point on which it is necessary to insist in the case of the Nash bargaining solution, since Raiffa [206] muddied the waters at an early stage by comparing a number of ideas, of which Nash's was one, as candidates for a "fair" arbitration scheme. Since then, the idea that the Nash bargaining solution is properly to be interpreted in this manner has taken on a life of its own and the Nash bargaining solu-

---

[97]If one could restrict the discussion to symmetric situations, it seems to me that one would not need to appeal to game-theoretic ideas on bargaining at all.

tion is routinely rejected on the grounds that it has no merit as an ethical concept. It is, however, *agreed* that the Nash bargaining solution has no merit as an ethical concept. If it had merit as an ethical concept it would be improper to propose it for use in the original position, since this would be to preempt the role of the original position in *determining* what is to be regarded as ethical. When the Nash bargaining solution is used, it is to predict what the result would be, under certain ideal circumstances, if specimens of *homo economicus* were to bargain optimally. The issue is therefore never whether or not one *likes* the result. As with $2 + 2 = 4$, the only issue is whether the result is accurate.

Gauthier defends his approach to the bargaining problem from an identical standpoint and hence similarly claims no ethical merits for the Kalai-Smorodinsky solution. It is instructive to consider his argument. Gauthier [84, p.133] envisages rational bargaining as a two-stage process in which each bargainer i makes a claim y_i followed by a concession to his final payoff of x_i. The rational claims, so Gauthier asserts, are those which maximize y_A and y_E, subject to the requirement that (ξ_A, y_E) and (y_A, ξ_E) correspond to feasible agreements. The bargainers then make concessions according to an unspecified process. This leads to agreement on a utility pair (x_A, x_E). Gauthier defines the "relative magnitude of a player's concession" as $c_i = (y_i - x_i)/(y_i - \xi_i)$. He emphasizes the scale-invariance of this quantity. He next insists that the concessions made by rational bargainers will be chosen so that the larger of c_A and c_E is minimized. This is the "principle of minimax relative concession".

Gauthier's [84, p.143] defense of this last requirement is very brief. He asserts that the condition:

> ... expresses the equal rationality of the bargainers. Since each person, as a utility-maximizer, seeks to minimize his concession, then no one can expect any other rational person to be willing to make a concession if he would not be willing to make a similar concession.

In this quote, the word "concession" is used in two different senses. At its first appearance, no more than Gauthier's algebraic definition seems to be intended. It is, of course, tautologous that a maximizer of x_i is a minimizer of c_i. At its later appearances, "concession" has acquired a more complex meaning that needs more careful examination.

It is certainly attractive to entertain the proposition that no rational person would expect another rational person to take an action that he himself would not take under *identical* circumstances. Having granted this, it is tempting to extend the proposition by requiring that no rational person would expect another rational person to take an action that he himself would not take under *equivalent* circumstances. The question then arises: When are the circumstances under which rational players operate equivalent? Gauthier's answer seems to be: when the sets of concessions from which they choose are the same, other structure being irrelevant. It may be that such a proposition could be defended if the definition of "concession" were tailored to the situation. But Gauthier offers no defense at all for the use of his simple algebraic definition of c_i in this context. It is, for example, unclear why *rational* bargainers should regard the rhetoric involved in making an initial claim as being relevant to any negotiations that follow. It is not even clear that it is meaningful to attempt to discuss such matters without specific reference being made to the bargaining *strategies* available to the players.

This is the nub of the matter. My own view is that no discussion of rational bargaining behavior makes any sense unless one is clear about what the bargainers can or cannot *do* during their negotiations. Once this issue has been clarified, the various ploys available to the bargainers can be modeled as moves in a formal game. If the use of equilibrium strategies in this game leads to a particular solution concept, then one has a defense for that solution concept in respect of those bargaining situations which the formal game models adequately.[98] It is this line of attack, known as the *Nash program*, that will later be used in arguing in favor of the Nash bargaining solution.

The Status Quo. Since Gauthier attributes no ethical virtues' to the Kalai-Smorodinsky solution and his protagonists do not pass behind a veil of ignorance in order to bargain, it follows that any ethical content in his bargaining story, including any interpersonal comparisons of utility, must be concentrated in his choice of the *status quo*. Here he falls back on reinterpreting Locke along lines proposed by Nozick [194]. It will be clear by now why I am unwilling to follow Nozick in making appeals to the Lockean notion of *a priori* "natural rights". I hope I am right in saying that Gauthier shares this view and hence bases his use of the "Lockean proviso" on conventional understandings that are somehow already established when the bargaining begins. If so, then Gauthier is taking for granted that some kind of primitive social contract is already in place to act as a springboard for his bargainers. But why should we accept his account of the nature of this pre-existing social contract? Should not the pre-existing social contract itself be the result of a pre-existing bargain derived from a yet more primitive *status quo*?

---

[98]Gauthier [84, p.129] asks, "Whether there are principles of rational bargaining with the same context-free universality of application as the principle of expected utility maximization?" My answer is no. The Nash program calls for a context to be established and then asks that the appropriate principles *for that context* be *deduced* from the principle of expected utility maximization.

My own treatment simply identifies the state of nature with the current state of affairs in society. Thus the *status quo* in Nash's bargaining problem is simply the utility pair that the bargainers associate with the current *status quo* in society. The deals available to the bargainers are identified with the utility pairs that the bargainers attach to the feasible social contracts, where the term feasible indicates that only agreements on equilibria in the game of life are deemed to be possible. If the bargainers were to confront each other face-to-face, with no veil of ignorance, then the outcome of their negotiation would simply be taken to be the Nash bargaining solution ν for the bargaining problem (X, ξ). However, they have to imagine what the result of bargaining *in the original position* would have been. Behind the veil of ignorance, they do not know their *personal* preferences, and evaluate the possible outcomes of the negotiation in terms of their *empathetic* preferences. The Nash bargaining solution therefore has to be applied, not to the bargaining problem (X, ξ), but to a new problem (T, τ) in which the utilities are calculated from the bargainers' empathetic preferences rather than from their personal preferences. However, the social contract selected by applying the Nash bargaining solution to the pair (T, τ) certainly will assign personal utilities to the bargainers. It will be argued that the selected social contract, when evaluated in terms of *personal* utilities, corresponds to the pair ρ in Figure 1.3(b). Thus the final outcome is what is called a proportional bargaining solution in cooperative game theory. As explained in Section 1.2.5, this can be seen as a modified version of the Rawlsian maximin criterion.

In my treatment, neither the placing of the *status quo*, nor the use of the Nash bargaining solution, nor the mechanism for sustaining the hypothetical bargain (namely enlightened self-interest) depend on any ethical preassumptions. The ethical content of the theory lies *only* in its use of the device of the original position and its account of how interpersonal utility comparisons are built into an individual's empathetic preferences.

Interpretation Matters! One final methodological point needs to be made. If one concentrates on the naive mathematical manner in which the various outcomes advocated by Rawls, Gauthier, and myself are presented in this chapter, one might mistakenly conclude that we are separated only by mathematical quibbling about where to locate the origin of the payoff axes and how to determine the units in which the payoffs are measured. However, this book presents mathematical arguments in a naive style because they are never genuinely important. What matters are always *interpretative* questions.

For example, Gauthier's outcome κ (Figure 1.5) and my proposal ρ (Figure 1.3) can be made identical by choosing U and V suitably in the definition of ρ. Moulin [183] accordingly uses the adjective "Rawlsian" in referring to the Kalai-Smorodinsky solution. However, it seems to me very important that we do not mislead ourselves by proceeding as though two lines of thought that lead to similar pieces of mathematics are necessarily related. *None* of the entities involved in the definition of κ have the same interpretation as those which appear in the definition of ρ. In particular, the interpretation of the point ξ in the two cases is wildly different. The advantage of introducing mathematics into this area is that it allows the intricacies of certain arguments to be handed over to an autopilot so that attention can be focused elsewhere. But, if its use diverts attention from the questions that really matter, then it will have failed in its purpose.

1.3   Behemoth and the Market

This section summarizes how the social contract ideas outlined in this chapter would work in the highly stylized situation faced by Adam and Eve in Section 1.2.5. As in the Garden of Eden, they will be able to sustain their moral integrity only in the short run. In the medium run, corruption is seen as inevitable. In the long run, the values of the marketplace will reign supreme. Hobbes' *Behemoth* is therefore perhaps as relevant to the predicament faced by Adam and Eve as his *Leviathan*.

The Short Run.   In the short run, Adam's and Eve's preferences, both personal and empathetic, are fixed. Their personal preferences may be very different, but interest centers on the case when their empathetic preferences are the same at the time the device of the original position is to be used. In the latter case, they will agree that V of Adam's utils are equivalent to U of Eve's.

An unresolved moral problem is identified with that of choosing a point x in a given set X as explained in Section 1.2.5. It may be, for example, that the points in X represent different ways of exploiting some new technological advance.

Adam and Eve solve such a moral problem by playing the game of morals. The result is that they implement the deal that they would negotiate if they were to bargain about the matter in ignorance of their current and future roles in society, taking into account that any deal they reach needs to be proof against later appeals to the same mechanism. Behind the veil of ignorance, they do not know their personal preferences. They therefore bargain in terms of their empathetic preferences. When the Nash bargaining solution is used to solve the bargaining problem they face behind the veil of ignorance, the solution is therefore expressed in terms of their empathetic preferences. However, the deal that it specifies can also be expressed in terms of Adam's and Eve's personal preferences. When this is done, the result is the proportional bargaining solution illustrated in Figure 1.3(b). This depends on only three things: the set X of feasible social contracts, the social contract ξ that represents the current *status quo*, and the ratio U/V. As explained in Section 1.2.5, such a proportional bargaining solution can be seen as implementing a modified version of Rawls' maximin criterion.

The Medium Run. In the medium run, personal preferences are fixed, but empathetic preferences may vary as a consequence of social evolution. Empathetic preferences are used only for determining how much everyone gets when the device of the original position is used, and so it is only the outcome of morally determined decisions that will contribute to the direction in which empathetic preferences tend to drift.

Since social evolution is a cultural phenomenon, let us provide Adam and Eve with a cultural history so that their behavior patterns in playing the game of morals are conditioned on the experience of many previous engaged couples seeking to negotiate marriage contracts under similar circumstances.[99] Section 1.2.7 argues that, in the medium run, one must anticipate that behavior patterns will change until an empathy equilibrium is achieved. In such an empathy equilibrium, everybody has the same empathetic preferences, and so one has a reason for the assumption that Adam and Eve agree on how their utils should be compared.

However, there is a fly in the ointment. To appreciate its nature, imagine what would happen if Adam and Eve were able to step outside their culture and so separate themselves from the game of morals. They could then negotiate their social contract directly without the need to imagine themselves playing any game except the game of life. If what is said in Section 1.2.9 on rational bargaining is to be believed, they would then agree on the Nash bargaining solution ν for the bargaining problem (X, ξ), as illustrated in Figure 1.5(a). Such a social contract would have no moral content at all[100] for the reasons given in Section 1.2.9. Now return Adam and Eve to their culture *after* social evolution has had time to adapt their empathetic preferences to the problem (X, ξ). One is guaranteed that they then have the same empathetic preferences—but when these empathetic preferences are inserted into the game of morals, the resulting social contract is nothing other than the Nash bargaining solution ν that we just agreed is devoid

---

[99] A purer story would insist that Adam and Eve are the whole of society. In this case, their current behavior would be conditioned only on the circumstances of their past interactions.

[100] Its terms would be dictated solely by the relative bargaining power of the two parties to the agreement. The use of the *symmetric* form of the Nash bargaining solution implicitly assumes that these bargaining powers are equal.

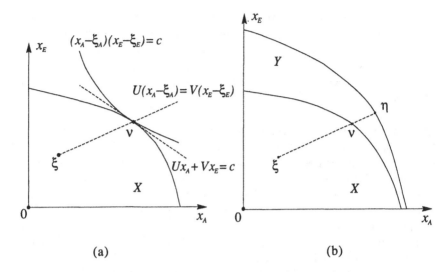

Figure 1.6: Time corrupts all

of moral content. The operation of social evolution in the medium run therefore leaches out all the moral content built into the game of morals. However, it must be borne in mind that this is not how it will seem to Adam and Eve. They will still be playing the game of morals with the empathetic preferences they have inherited from their culture—and they would doubtless wax indignant at any suggestion that their procedures are unfair or amoral.

Figure 1.6(a) illustrates the social contract that will be achieved after social evolution has operated in the medium run. The weights U and V are those derived from the resulting empathetic preferences. As just explained, with these values of U and V, the proportional bargaining solution ρ coincides with the Nash bargaining solution ν. Not only this, it turns out that the weighted utilitarian solution h of Figure 1.3 also coincides with ρ.[101] If what I am saying has some relevance for the societies of *homo sapiens*, it is therefore perhaps not so very surprising that authors like Rawls, Stigler, and Harsanyi should extract such different intuitions from the same data. In the medium run, their reasoning will all lead to the same outcome. However, only Stigler is likely to draw any comfort from this fact!

---

[101] This is no accident. Behind the veil of ignorance, each agent seeks to maximize the weighted utilitarian objective function W_h of Section 1.2.5. (However, the final outcome is not utilitarian because, in the absence of enforcement mechanisms, constraints on what can be agreed must be imposed.)

Back to the Short Run. It would be a mistake to take too gloomy a view of the result just described. The reason is that most decisions are taken in the short run *before* social evolution has a chance to erode the moral content of the game of morals. Consider, for example, Figure 1.6(b). In this diagram, assume that U and V are adapted to the problem (X, ξ). The ratio U/V is therefore determined by first locating the Nash bargaining solution ν for (X, ξ) and then computing the slope of the line that joins ξ and ν. But now suppose that new technological opportunities arise. In Figure 1.6, these are represented by the set Y. The alternative to exploiting the new opportunities this set represents is to persist with the current social contract ν. We therefore have to deal with the problem (Y, ν). If Adam and Eve solve this problem by playing the game of morals, they will use their *current* empathetic preferences. That is to say, they will not use weights that are adapted to the problem (Y, ν) because the weights adapt to new circumstances only in the medium run. Instead they will use the weights U and V that are adapted to the problem (X, ξ). The result will then be the social contract η illustrated in Figure 1.6(b). This is the proportional bargaining solution with weights U and V for the problem (Y, ν).

The Long Run. Lord Acton said that power corrupts. This is certainly true of people, but it is *time* that corrupts societies—and, given long enough, it corrupts them absolutely. It does so by creating a society whose forum for moral debate is the marketplace. To see why I say this, it is necessary to consider what happens to the game of morals in the long run.

In the long run, personal preferences are vulnerable to evolutionary pressures, just as empathetic preferences are vulnerable in the medium run. After evolution has operated in the medium run, the social contract will be the Nash bargaining solution ν shown in Figure 1.6(a). What will happen to this as personal preferences are shaped by evolution in the long run?

To answer such a question, one has to abandon utility space as a setting for the discussion, and to work in terms of physically measurable commodities instead. In a market, each such commodity receives a price that determines the rates at which goods and services may be traded among the agents. A *Walrasian equilibrium* is said to occur when the prices are such that demand for each commodity does not exceed its supply. There is no reason at all why a Walrasian equilibrium should specify a distribution of goods and services that resembles the distribution that would follow from the use of the Nash bargaining solution. Examples can be given where the Nash bargaining solution would assign Adam and Eve an equal amount of each commodity but in which Adam gets nearly everything at a Walrasian equilibrium.

However, the operation of evolution over the long run can be used to establish a connection between the Nash bargaining solution and a Walrasian equilibrium. The mechanism closely resembles that used to establish a connection between the proportional bargaining solution and the Nash bargaining solution in the medium run. We ask that, in the long run, Adam's and Eve's personal preferences should be such that neither would wish to misrepresent their personal preferences, given that the Nash bargaining solution is to be used in deciding who gets what. This assumption forces the outcome that results from using the Nash bargaining solution to coincide with a Walrasian equilibrium.

This story makes the market the final step in a process that first leaches out the moral content of a culture and then erodes the autonomy of its citizens in choosing their own goals. However, I am very definitely *not* arguing that the story justifies condemning the market mechanism. The story simply confirms that there is nothing to be said in favor of the market mechanism on *moral* grounds. As Gauthier [84] puts it, the market is a morally free zone. On the other hand, there is very much to be said in favor of the market in terms of economic efficiency. In particular, it is very much less vulnerable to manipulation by venal officials than other distributive mechanisms—and the story I have been telling provides a partial explanation of why this should be so. One might say that the market is difficult to corrupt because its institutions have adapted to corruption already.

1.4   Elephants and Donkeys

A lot has been packed into this chapter, since it was necessary to distinguish my theory at an early stage from established theories with which it might otherwise be confused. In the rush, sight may have been lost of its relevance to the philosophical and moral positions that underlie the positions people take up on matters of practical politics. Some brief concluding comments may therefore be helpful.

Recall the blind Persian sages who were unable to agree about the nature of an elephant. One felt the trunk and argued that an elephant is a snake. The other felt the elephant's side and argued that an elephant is a wall. Something like this is going on when those of the political left dispute with those of the right. The right emphasizes the role of the individual and, losing sight of the fact that we are social animals, looks to the preservation of our individual rights and liberties, regarding social matters as being best left to Adam Smith's invisible hand. The left grasps the fact that we are social animals but places us in the wrong phylum by personifying society and treating it as though it had aims and purposes of its own.

The elephant that both the sages of the left and those of the right have to contemplate is a decision problem of a particularly difficult variety. In decision theory, we are taught first to locate the *feasible* set and then to select an *optimal* outcome within this set. By and large, the sages of the right seem to have a firm grip on the feasibility issues, but give little or no thought to optimality questions. On the other hand, the sages of the left give their attention almost exclusively to optimality issues without taking proper account of what is or is not feasible. It is the error attributed to the left that is *methodologically* the more serious, but this is not to offer an opinion about the *practical* consequences of making one error rather than another in some particular context.

From the perspective of the theory proposed in this book, the feasibility questions are concerned with how equilibria are *sustained*. The things we call rights and obligations are nothing other than commonly held conventional understandings that have evolved to allow each of us to coordinate our individual attempts to optimize. That is to say they are packaged maxims for maintaining a *particular* equilibrium. The optimality question is that of *selecting* an equilibrium from those that are available. The left wishes to make this selection without considering the stability of what it selects. It therefore invents the notion of a "common good" so that equilibrium questions can be evaded. In consequence, the right wishes no selection to be made, and hence invents *a priori* justifications for rules that are actually honored only through custom and habit.

The same schism repeats itself in debates between moral philosophers. To quote Mackie [163, p.149]:

> Having rejected utilitarianism, we could move in either of two directions. We could retain the consequentialist structure of utilitarian theory, but replace the goal of utility or happiness ... by some other concept of the good which is to be achieved or maximized. Alternatively, we could reject the consequentialist structure, and develop a moral system built not around the notion of some goal that is to be attained but rather around the rules or principles of action or duties or rights or virtues, or some combination of these—in a very broad sense, some kind of deontological system [in which] actions of the kind held to be virtuous are seen as being intrinsically obligatory or admirable.

Although I am close to Mackie [163, 164] on a wide range of issues, I think he goes badly astray here. I agree that utilitarianism should be rejected. But retaining a consequentialist structure does not necessarily involve the notion of a fundamental common good. Nor does abandoning the notion of a common good force one to adopt a deontological framework.

Considerations that apply at different levels are being confused. Rejecting the errors of the left does not necessarily entail adopting the errors of the right.

Economists also face each other across the same divide. Those of the right willingly embrace the position of Hobbes' Foole and imagine this to be what rationality prescribes. Sen [244] rightly calls them "rational fools". But the alternative is not to seek some chimerical notion of "collective rationality"; it is simply to stop interpreting our current notions of rationality naively. There is no need to step outside the economic tradition for this purpose. Adam Smith not only wrote *The Wealth of Nations*, he also wrote *The Theory of Moral Sentiments*. He didn't think that the latter had no relevance to the former—and nor should we.

The lack of clothing suggests that William Blake had Archimedes in mind for this illustration. However, it is actually Isaac Newton who is supposedly toying with some tautologies.

Chapter 2

Toying with Tautologies

> ...be wary of mathematicians and all those who make a practice of
> sacrilegious prediction, particularly when they tell the truth.
>
> Saint Augustine

2.1 Introduction

Although this chapter and the next introduce some of the ideas of game
theory, they are not a good place to learn these ideas for the very first time.[1]
The reason is that the chapters are not focused on why game theorists think
they are right, but on why they think some of their critics are wrong. Such
critics see game theorists as heartless followers of Machiavelli, and game
theory as a recipe for cynical opportunism that would bring civilization
to its knees if taken seriously. Game theorists are puzzled by such attacks,
especially since they find themselves being condemned most virulently when
they are saying nothing substantive at all, but simply stating the logical
implications of their definitions.

Sometimes, of course, a game theorist can see why it would be more
pleasant if logic led somewhere else. But there seems no good reason for
blaming the messenger for his message—still less for lopping off his head and
replacing him with another messenger who takes care to deliver only news
that is bright and cheerful. When seeking to feed the hungry, for example, it
would often be convenient if $2 + 2 = 5$, but nobody blames mathematicians
for asserting that $2 + 2 = 4$, or suggests that the laws of arithmetic should
be revised with a view to eliminating hunger from the planet.

Mathematical theorems are tautologies. They cannot be false because
they do not say anything substantive. They merely spell out the impli-

---

[1] My *Fun and Games* (D. C. Heath, 1991) would be a better place to begin.

cations of how things have been defined. The basic propositions of game theory have precisely the same character. It is therefore impossible for them to be good or bad. What they say is necessarily *neutral* with regard to moral issues. Like arithmetic, game theory is merely a tool. It is not a manifesto for hedonism or egoism or any other ism. Critics who argue otherwise simply do not understand what game theorists are saying. Sometimes they do not want to understand because this would involve abandoning various fallacies that they hold very dear.

The blunder that such critics typically make is to model some real-world situation as a game whose rules are too simple to reflect the actual strategic realities. An analysis of this oversimplified game often leads to a conclusion that is more painful than our experience of the world would lead us to anticipate. The error is then compounded by inventing some exotic form of "reasoning" that allows the oversimplified game to be analyzed in accordance with the analyst's intuitions about the real world. In this way, the analyst confirms his prejudices by carrying out a wrong analysis of the wrong game. Game theorists, however, think it important to begin with the right game. One then seldom needs to call upon anything beyond commonsense reasoning techniques in order to arrive at a correct conclusion.

In both this chapter and the next, attention will be focused on a "toy game" called the Prisoners' Dilemma. This is popular as a paradigm for the problem of human cooperation.[2] The implicit understanding of those who use it for this purpose seems to be that, either we can "solve" the problem of how to get people to cooperate in a simple situation like the one-shot[3] Prisoners' Dilemma, or else we might as well abandon thinking about rational cooperation altogether. The orthodox view among game theorists is that cooperation *cannot* result from rational play in the one-shot Prisoners' Dilemma.

However, as Taylor [261] and others have argued, the fact that rational cooperation is impossible in the stark setting of the Prisoners' Dilemma is not crucial for the successful operation of human societies. If it were, *homo sapiens* would not have evolved as a social animal. More complex games need to be examined if one is to understand what really matters about human cooperation. In particular, the fact that many cooperation problems must be faced *repeatedly* is highly significant since it opens the door to the possibility of *reciprocity*. However, the subject of repeated games will have to wait for a proper airing until Chapter 3 of Volume II.

---

[2]See, for example, Garret Hardin [98], Russell Hardin [99], Margolis [170], Olson [196] and Taylor [261].

[3]This means that the game is played just *once* and has no implications for any other activities in which the players may be involved.

2.2 Equilibrium

This section introduces the most elementary notions of game theory in as informal a manner as I can manage. Those who know some game theory may care to skip forward to Section 2.3.

2.2.1 Hawks and Doves

The Hawk-Dove Game is used by the biologist Maynard Smith [172] to illustrate the relevance of game theory to certain aspects of evolutionary biology.[4] Two birds of an imaginary unisex species compete for the opportunity to reproduce themselves. The manner in which they compete is modeled by a game. Every so often, Nature chooses two birds at random to take the roles of player I and player II in the game. Each bird is programmed for one of two behaviors, *hawk* or *dove*. Two hawkish birds fight and hence risk injury. Two dovelike birds share whatever resource is in dispute. A hawkish bird chases off a dovelike bird.

These characteristics are built into the *payoff* table for the Hawk-Dove Game given in Figure 2.1(a). Although the imaginary species of bird under study has only one sex, the bird that Nature chooses to occupy the role of player I will be called Adam and referred to as he. Similarly, the bird that Nature chooses to occupy the role of player II will be called Eve and referred to as she.[5] Adam's strategies are represented by the rows in the payoff table. Eve's strategies are represented by the columns. The choice of a row and a column determines a cell in the payoff table. The number in the bottom left of this cell is Adam's payoff. The number in the top right of the cell is Eve's payoff. To be consistent with the story just told about hawkish and dovelike behavior, we need that $W < V$. Figure 2.2(b) shows the particular case when $W = -2$ and $V = 2$.

In this chapter it will be important to ask what these payoffs *mean*. It is a common source of misunderstanding for it to be thought that game theorists intend a payoff to be some naive measure of a player's individual welfare, like a sum of money. However, game theory is based on the principle that the players act as though seeking to maximize the payoff[6] they receive at the end of the game. A naive view of the nature of a payoff will therefore

---

[4]This sentence does not signal support for the sociobiological outlook of Wilson [274] and his followers. They are clearly right that certain of our biological and social traits evolved together. However, I believe that these traits are most relevant when humans interact in small groups like the extended families of our species' early history. My guess is that the moral behavior relevant to large-scale societies, and hence to a social contract discussion, is almost entirely a consequence of social evolution alone.

[5]Trying to write game-theoretic statements without the help of pronouns can be very heavy going.

[6]Or, to be precise, their *expected* payoff when the final outcome is uncertain.

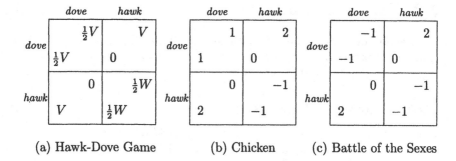

(a) Hawk-Dove Game   (b) Chicken   (c) Battle of the Sexes

Figure 2.1: Ornithology

sometimes not suffice. For example, it is easy to quote situations, especially in a moral context, where almost nobody would regard the amount of money that he gets as being the major determinant in deciding what to do. Game theorists therefore understand the notion of a payoff in a sophisticated way that makes it tautologous that players act as though maximizing their payoffs. Such a sophisticated view makes it hard to measure payoffs in real-life games, but its advantage in keeping the logic straight is overwhelming.

Biological examples exhibit the tautology that is built into the notion of a payoff in a particularly stark manner. In the Hawk-Dove Game, one should not think of the payoffs as quantities of food, or years of life, or square meters of territory—although one or more of these may perhaps correlate sufficiently well with the notion of a payoff to serve as a practical approximation. In a biological context, a payoff is understood to be "average incremental fitness". That is to say, a player's success in the game is measured in terms of how many extra children the player can expect to have on average as a consequence of the way the game is played.

In the Hawk-Dove Game, the assumption is made that children inherit from their parent the instinct that determines whether they have a hawkish or a dovelike disposition. It then becomes yet another tautology that whichever of the two strategies happens to achieve a larger payoff in the game, given the current population mix, will expand at the expense of the other. The tautology is usually expressed in terms of Spencer's "survival of the fittest". We know who will survive because they are fittest. We know who are fittest because they survive.

To speak of the survival of the fittest in a social context commonly provokes one of two knee-jerk responses. The first comes from those who still regard it as an insult to call someone a social Darwinian.[7] But the intellectual climate has changed in more ways than one since 1879, when Spencer's disciple Sumner [258, p.56] criticized the economists of his time as being:

> ...frightened at liberty, especially under the form of competition,
> which they elevate into a bugbear. They think it bears harshly on
> the weak. They do not perceive that ...if we do not like the survival
> of the fittest, we have only one possible alternative, and that is the
> survival of the unfittest [and] a plan for nourishing the unfittest and
> yet advancing in civilization, no man will ever find.

Nobody need fear that a modern social Darwinian might offer such an apology for the worst excesses of laissez-faire capitalism. For one thing, Darwin was always very careful to emphasize that natural selection is usually a noisy process, so that often those who fail and hence are deemed to be unfit are merely unlucky. But the major point is more serious. A modern social Darwinian thinks that Sumner is not so much wrong as incoherent. It is absurd to argue that we have a choice between the survival of the fittest and the survival of the unfittest. Whatever we do, the fittest will survive because of the very meaning of the words from which the slogan is constructed.

But when one insists that the survival of the fittest is true because of the way the words are defined, one provokes other critics—those who think that the word tautology is a perjorative. For example, Bernard Williams [273, p.35] tells us that functionalism suffers from the notorious weakness that it reduces empirical propositions to tautologies. He then goes on to say: "It is tediously a necessary condition of the survival of a group-with-certain-values that the group should retain those values." However, a little mathematical training generates an entirely different attitude to tautologies. It is true that tautologies have no empirical content. But mathematicians know that statements which cannot but be true because of the manner in which their terms are defined may be far from dull. For example, the formula $e^{\pi i} = -1$ is a tautology. It is true by virtue of the definitions of the mathematical objects e, π, i and -1. But it is neither obvious nor tedious. Indeed, one can only envy the joy that Euler must have felt when he discovered such a wonderful formula.[8] Nor is the formula useless. On

---

[7]I am also commonly accused of being a reductionist. But, as Elster [71] patiently explains, to believe that reductionist models are often useful, does not entail believing all the nonsense that those who make blanket appeals to the "reductionist fallacy" wilfully attribute to their victims.

[8]At the time that Diderot was peddling atheistic views at the court of Catherine the Great, Euler was serving as her court mathematician. When she called upon Euler to defend religion, he is said to have declared, "With this formula I refute you!" If the formula had been $e^{\pi i} = -1$, one might almost agree that he had a point.

the contrary, it is one of the building blocks of much of modern physics. As
for Darwin's tautology that only the fit survive, this certainly did not seem
dull to his contemporaries. Nor is it often at all obvious what the result
of exploring the implications of the tautology in a specific situation will
be. There is even a little to be learned from using the tautology in a simple model like the Hawk-Dove Game. In brief, both hawkish and dovelike
behavior can exist together in equilibrium.

Consider, for example, the version of the Hawk-Dove Game labeled
Chicken in Figure 2.1(b). Suppose that half the bird population are hawkish and the other half are dovelike. Then a bird playing Chicken will have a
dovelike opponent with probability $\frac{1}{2}$, and a hawkish opponent with probability $\frac{1}{2}$. A bird that plays *dove* will therefore receive a payoff of 1 with
probability $\frac{1}{2}$ and a payoff of 0 with probability $\frac{1}{2}$. Its average fitness, given
the population mix, is therefore $\frac{1}{2} \times 1 + \frac{1}{2} \times 0 = \frac{1}{2}$. A bird that plays
hawk will receive a payoff of 2 with probability $\frac{1}{2}$ and a payoff of -1 with
probability $\frac{1}{2}$. Its average fitness, given the population mix, is therefore
$\frac{1}{2} \times 2 + \frac{1}{2} \times (-1) = \frac{1}{2}$. It follows that neither type of bird has an advantage over the other. A population in which doves and hawks are equally
numerous will therefore remain in equilibrium.[9]

2.2.2   Equilibrium

The previous section describes how evolution can lead to an equilibrium in
a game without the players' planning ahead or even being aware that they
are playing a game. However, in much of what follows, the role of evolution
is only implicit. Game theorists ask what behavior would be *rational* in
a game, and mostly leave the question of how it might come about that
people should behave rationally for others to answer. This is largely because
they have yet to develop formal models for the social adjustment processes
that are presumably at least as important in fostering rational behavior in
the human species as the type of biological process considered in Section
2.2.1. This gap between theory and practice will not be closed in this
book. However, I think it important to stress that, if the theory of rational
behavior in games is really relevant to mainstream human conduct, it is
not because *homo sapiens* is gifted with such powers of insight that no
strategic problem is too difficult for him to solve; it is because the habits
and customs that rule his life have been shaped by the fumblings and failures
of his fellows when faced with similar problems in the past.

The most fundamental notion in the theory of rational behavior in games
is called a *Nash equilibrium*. This is a strategy profile in which each player's

---

[9]It is, in fact, the unique stable equilibrium for the standard Darwinian dynamics.

strategy is a best reply to the strategies the profile assigns to the other players. A book that claimed to be an authoritative guide on rational play in games would necessarily have to recommend a Nash equilibrium in each game for which it made a specific recommendation. Otherwise, at least one player would choose not to follow the book's advice if he believed that that the other players were planning to play as advised. Since everyone would figure this out in advance, the book's claim to be authoritative could therefore not be sustained.

The game Chicken of Figure 2.1(b) has three Nash equilibria. Two of these are pure strategy equilibria. The third is a mixed equilibrium. A *pure strategy* for a player in a game is a complete description of what the player plans to do whenever he or she might be called upon to make a decision. In Chicken, each player has to choose only between *dove* and *hawk*. These are therefore a player's pure strategies. A *mixed strategy* arises when a player randomizes over his pure strategies—perhaps by tossing a coin or rolling dice.

The Nash equilibria in pure strategies for Chicken are (*dove, hawk*) and (*hawk, dove*). To see this in the case of (*dove, hawk*), notice that *hawk* is the best reply for Eve to Adam's choice of *dove*, while *dove* is simultaneously the best reply for Adam to Eve's choice of *hawk*. Neither player would therefore have a motive to deviate from a book that recommended (*dove, hawk*) for Chicken, unless there was reason to suppose that the opponent might also deviate.

We met the mixed strategy Nash equilibrium for Chicken in the previous section.[10] This calls for both players to use each of their two pure strategies with probability $\frac{1}{2}$. If Eve plays this way, *dove* and *hawk* are equally good for Adam. Adam therefore does not care which he uses, and so he might as well play each with probability $\frac{1}{2}$. If he does so, then the same reasons show that Eve might as well play each of *dove* and *hawk* with probability $\frac{1}{2}$. Both Adam and Eve will then be making a best reply to the choice made by the other.[11]

---

[10]This mixed equilibrium is symmetric, since it requires each player to use the same mixed strategy. It is therefore the only relevant equilibrium in Section 2.2.1 because, in that model, Adam and Eve are drawn at random from the *same* population of birds, each of whose strategy choice is fixed. The probability that Adam or Eve will use a particular strategy must therefore necessarily be the same. The pure strategy equilibria are asymmetric because they call for Adam and Eve to use different strategies.

[11]Among the reasons that suspicion is sometimes directed at such mixed equilibria is that there seems no particular reason why a player should use his equilibrium strategy when there are other strategies that are also best replies. However, Section 2.2.1 illustrates one application of a mixed strategy equilibrium where this objection is irrelevant.

2.2.3   Prisoners' Dilemma

When Albert Tucker first wrote[12] about this most famous of all "toy games", he could have had no idea of the immense literature he was initiating. Such toy games always come with a little story. For example, the story for Chicken is based on the James Dean movie in which teenage boys drive cars towards a cliff edge to see whose nerve will crack first. The story for the Prisoners' Dilemma is set in Chicago. The District Attorney knows that Adam and Eve are gangsters who are guilty of a major crime but is unable to convict them without a confession from one or the other. He orders their arrest and separately offers each the following deal: "If you confess and your accomplice fails to confess, then you go free. If you fail to confess but your accomplice confesses, then you will be convicted and sentenced to the maximum term in jail. If you both confess, then you will both be convicted but the maximum sentence will not be imposed. If neither confesses, then you will be framed on a minor tax evasion charge for which a conviction is certain."

Such stories are not to be taken too seriously. Their chief purpose is to serve as a reminder about who gets what payoff. For the entries x, y and z in the payoff table of Figure 2.2(a) to correspond to the story for the Prisoners' Dilemma, the requirement is that $x > y > z > 0$. The Hawk-Dove Game, for example, reduces to a Prisoners' Dilemma when $V = 6$ and $W = 2$, as shown in Figure 2.2(c). For this reason, confessing is labeled *hawk*, and holding out is labeled *dove*. However, the payoffs with which we shall be working in what follows are shown in Figure 2.2(b). These can be remembered with a less elaborate story than that usually given. Each player chooses *dove* or *hawk* quite independently. Choosing *dove* results in a payment of $2 to the opponent. Choosing *hawk* results in a payment of $1 to oneself.[13]

Game theorists do not claim to be able to give an exhaustive list of what the criteria for a rational choice should be in all games. But they do not think an exhaustive list is necessary to analyze the Prisoners' Dilemma successfully. For this purpose, all that is needed is the weakest possible criterion for rational behavior in a game. This criterion forbids the use of a *strongly dominated* strategy.

Suppose that a player has two strategies, s and t. Then s strongly dominates[14] t if and only if the use of s *always* results in a strictly better

---

[12]The game is said to have been first formulated by the Rand scientists Dresher and Flood in 1950.

[13]The payoffs are given in dollars to give a concrete feel to the discussion. However, as always, it should be assumed that the players seek to maximize their expected payoff.

[14]The strategy s weakly dominates t if and only if the use of s never results in a worse outcome for the player than t, and sometimes results in a strictly better outcome.

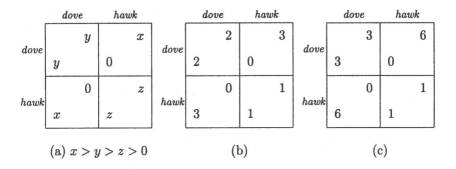

Figure 2.2: Prisoners' Dilemmas

outcome for the player than t, no matter what strategy choices the other players may make. Thus *hawk* strongly dominates *dove* in any version of the Prisoners' Dilemma. In the particular case illustrated in Figure 2.2(b), a player who uses *hawk* will get 3 rather than 2 when the opponent uses *dove*, and 1 rather than 0 when the opponent uses *hawk*. Thus *hawk* is always better than *dove*.

A game theory book will therefore recommend (*hawk, hawk*) as the solution of the Prisoners' Dilemma. If any recommendation is to be made at all, the book has no choice but to recommend (*hawk, hawk*), since it is the unique Nash equilibrium of the game. If both use *hawk*, each player will therefore be making a best reply to the strategy used by the other. But, in the special case of the Prisoners' Dilemma, very much more is true. Because *hawk* strongly dominates *dove*, *hawk* is a best reply to *every* strategy available to the opponent. A player therefore does not even need to consult a game theory book in order to be sure that he is optimizing by playing *hawk*.

The claim that (*hawk, hawk*) is the solution of the Prisoners' Dilemma seems paradoxical to many authors. In the terminology of Section 1.2.8, (*hawk, hawk*) is not a *Pareto-efficient* outcome of the Prisoners' Dilemma. The game has another outcome that both players prefer. In the Prisoners' Dilemma, the outcome (*dove, dove*) is a Pareto-improvement on (*hawk, hawk*) because both players get a payoff of 2 with the former and a payoff of only 1 with the latter.

Personally, I see no paradox at all in the fact that independent choice behavior by rational agents should sometimes lead to Pareto-inefficient outcomes. The rules of the Prisoners' Dilemma create an environment that is inimical for rational cooperation and, just as one cannot reasonably expect someone to juggle successfully with his hands tied behind his back, so one cannot expect rational agents to succeed in cooperating when constrained by the rules of the Prisoners' Dilemma.

Much of this chapter and all of Chapter 3 are devoted to the arguments of those who see things differently. However, only the most primitive of objections will be considered immediately. This is embodied in the question: *If you're so smart, why ain't you rich?*

Suppose that Adam and Eve play as game theory books recommend in the Prisoners' Dilemma and hence end up with $1 each. Next door, Ichabod and Olive throw out their game theory books and end up with $2 each. As a consequence, Ichabod and Olive come out a little richer than Adam and Eve. So what makes Adam and Eve so smart? The answer is that they have made the best of the opportunities that life has offered them, while Ichabod and Olive have not. In particular, if Adam had been lucky enough to be playing Olive, he would have come away with $3, instead of the $2 that Ichabod obtained. Moreover, if Ichabod had been unlucky enough to be playing Eve, he would have come away with nothing at all, instead of the $1 that Adam obtained.

Judging by results makes a lot of sense in some contexts—but not in races where some of the contestants are given a head-start on the others.

2.2.4 Means and Ends

Section 2.2.1 explains the tautological nature of applications of game theory in evolutionary biology. The payoffs are then defined in terms of an organism's "fitness". This makes it a tautology that the organisms that survive will seem to behave as though seeking to maximize their payoffs in the game under study. The same tautological flavor is also to be found when *rational* behavior in games is studied, provided that the payoffs in the game are interpreted according to the theory of *revealed preference* as formulated by Sen [236] and others. It then becomes essentially a tautology that a rational person will fail to cooperate in the Prisoners' Dilemma.

Revealed Preference Theory. Some notation will help in explaining what the theory of revealed preference is about. To write $a \prec b$ means that the decision-maker definitely prefers b to a. To write $a \sim b$ means that he is indifferent between a and b. To write $a \preceq b$ means that $a \prec b$ or $a \sim b$.

This notation for preferences is too clumsy to be an effective mathematical tool. Economists therefore often prefer to work with a utility function. Suppose that $\preceq$ is a preference relation defined on a finite set S of alternatives, and that u is a real-valued function defined on S. Then, to say that u is a *utility function* which describes $\preceq$ means that

$$u(a) \leq u(b) \text{ if and only if } a \preceq b,$$

for each a and b in the set S. Once a utility function representation has been found, optimization problems reduce to finding the largest number in a given set. Fortunately, mathematics is bursting at the seams with techniques for doing just that.

In order that a preference relation $\preceq$ admit a utility function representation it is necessary and sufficient that it satisfy two *consistency* conditions.[15] The requirements are that

$$a \preceq b \text{ or } b \preceq a \qquad \text{(totality)}$$

$$a \preceq b \text{ and } b \preceq c \text{ implies } a \preceq c \qquad \text{(transitivity)}$$

for each a, b and c in the set S. All preference relations in this book will be assumed to satisfy these conditions (and usually much more as well).

Spinoza [251] tells us that: "Blessedness is not the reward of virtue, but virtue itself; neither do we rejoice therein, because we control our lusts, but contrariwise, because we rejoice therein, we are able to control our lusts." As for myself, when I manage to control my lustful urges, I feel little inclination to rejoice in my virtue. I curb my passions for much more mundane reasons. Nor am I sure that those who do rejoice in their own virtue should be counted among the blessed. However, the point of quoting Spinoza is that he gives vivid expression to a mode of thinking that modern utility theory puts firmly aside.

As emphasized in Section 1.2.5, economists who care about foundational questions no longer treat the notion of utility as a primitive. They regard it as a *fallacy* to argue that a person prefers one thing to another *because* the utility of the first exceeds the utility of the second. On the contrary, they construct a utility function u with the property $u(a) \leq u(b)$ because they *already know* that $a \preceq b$. In particular, a player's payoffs in a game are *deduced* from his preferences over its possible outcomes.

For example, in the version of the Prisoners' Dilemma given in Figure 2.2(b), Adam's payoff for the outcome (*dove, dove*) is 2 and his payoff for the outcome (*hawk, dove*) is 3. However, these payoffs are not primitives of the problem. Somewhere in the background is Adam's preference relation $\preceq_A$. This is known to satisfy

$$(dove, dove) \prec_A (hawk, dove), \qquad (2.1)$$

and hence the model-builder chooses to assign a payoff to (*dove, dove*) that is less than the payoff he assigns to (*hawk, dove*).

In revealed preference theory, not even preferences are taken as primitives. Instead, choice behavior becomes the primitive. One observes some of the choices that a player makes and then argues that he is making choices

---

[15]Totality has many synonyms. For example, completeness and connectedness mean the same thing in this context. One might reasonably question whether totality should strictly be regarded as a "consistency" condition, since it merely says that the decision-maker is able to express a preference between all pairs of alternatives from the set S.

as though he were equipped with a preference relation. For example, a modern economist will say that the empirical evidence available about Spinoza is that he was very temperate in his behavior. In seeking to find a neat way of describing what Spinoza found himself doing, it may be helpful to invent a quality called virtue. Once this notion has been coined, we can then categorize his life-style by saying that he behaved *as though* seeking to be virtuous. Such a description may be so useful that an economist would find it expedient to discuss Spinoza's behavior exclusively in such terms. But, if he is careful, the economist will never allow himself to fall into the trap of confusing a picturesque description with a causal explanation.[16] Similarly, a physicist may find it helpful to observe that fluids at the surface of the earth behave *as though* Nature abhors a vacuum. But the physicist would be foolish to proceed as though this conventional formula were a physical explanation of the phenomenon it describes.

In maintaining such a skeptical attitude, a physicist does not necessarily deny the possible existence of a lady with supernatural powers who dislikes vacua—just as an economist who uses revealed preference theory does not necessarily deny the possibility that humans come hard-wired with a capacity to rejoice in their own virtue. But these are not hypotheses that we can afford to take for granted.

From a revealed preference perspective, it is not true that (2.1) is a primitive in setting up the Prisoners' Dilemma. The preference (2.1) is deduced from the prior information that, if Adam knew he had to choose between only (*dove, dove*) and (*hawk, dove*), then he actually would choose (*hawk, dove*). Similarly, the preference

$$(dove, hawk) \prec_A (hawk, hawk) \tag{2.2}$$

is deduced from the prior information that, if Adam knew he had to choose between only (*dove, hawk*) and (*hawk, hawk*), then he actually would choose (*hawk, hawk*).

There may also be other prior information about Adam's choice behavior, but the data that are important in predicting his behavior in the Prisoners' Dilemma are the two facts that have been considered so far:

- Adam chooses *hawk* when he knows that Eve will choose *dove*;
- Adam chooses *hawk* when he knows that Eve will not choose *dove*.

---

[16]I do not think that Spinoza [251] himself often fell into this trap. Indeed, in such statements as: "The foundation of virtue is no other than the effort to maintain one's being; and man's happiness consists in the power of so doing", he would seem to be making behavior the primitive notion, as in modern revealed preference theory. My guess is that he underestimated the dangers of adopting the terminology of those he sought to persuade. But, as with modern writers, what alternative did he have have if he was to be read at all?

However, the problem in game theory is that one usually *doesn't* know what the opponent is going to choose. A new assumption is therefore necessary to get any further. I shall call this the *sure-thing principle*.[17]

To understand the principle, it is necessary to consider three informational situations that differ only in what is known about some proposition P. In the first situation, Adam knows that P is true. In the second, he knows that P is false. In the third, he has doubts about whether P is true or false. It is given that Adam chooses a over b in both the first and the second situations. It therefore seems reasonable to argue that the truth or falsehood of P is irrelevant to which of a and b he chooses, and hence he will choose a over b in the third situation also. This is what the sure-thing principle says. In brief, if Adam chooses a over b both when he knows P is true and when he knows P is false, then he will choose a over b even when he is not fully informed about P.

In order to apply the sure-thing principle to the Prisoners' Dilemma, take P to be the proposition that Eve chooses *dove*. Take a to be Adam's pure strategy *hawk*, and take b to be his pure stategy *dove*. Since Adam will choose *hawk* both when he knows that Eve is choosing *dove* and when he knows she is not choosing *dove*, the sure-thing principle says that he must choose *hawk* whatever his thoughts might be about her prospective choice.

If it ·is accepted that the definition of rationality includes adherence to the sure-thing principle, then the preceding argument shows it to be a tautology that a rational player will necessarily choose *hawk* in the Prisoners' Dilemma. It is admittedly faintly absurd that the mountain should heave so furiously in bringing forth so small a mouse, but Reason is a harsh mistress. Her servants must even endure the indignity of being required to prove the obvious.

Do the Ends Justify the Means? No further use of the theory of revealed preference will be made after this chapter. There is therefore no point in developing the mathematics of the theory.[18] However, there are some philosophical implications of the theory that are worth pursuing.

Game theory is often mistakenly thought to be necessarily committed

---

[17]Although it is only a pale shadow of Savage's [228] sure-thing principle. Economists sometimes refer to the principle required as "first-order, stochastic dominance", but I suspect others would turn off if it were so described.

[18]Sen [237] gives consistency conditions that a person's choice behavior must satisfy if it is to be compatible with a coherent preference relation. However, game theorists normally cannot dispense with assumptions about how a person makes decisions under conditions of uncertainty. For a theory of revealed preference relevant under such circumstances, see Green and Osband [92].

to the heartless principle that the *ends justify the means*. Indeed, some game theorists with macho tendencies are only too willing to embrace such a Machiavellian posture. In moral philosophy, they would therefore be considered consequentialists rather than deontologists, and hence suitable targets for impassioned pleas like Hampshire's [96]: "The one unnatural, and impossible cry is the consequentialist's: Away with convention: anything goes provided that it does not interfere with welfare or the principles of justice." This is more than a little puzzling for a game theorist, who may well innocently agree that he must surely be a consequentialist since he determines what the equilibria are in a game by examining the consequences to each player of deviating from equilibrium play. However, he is certainly unlikely to be raising any cry for the abolition of convention. How would the players know how to coordinate on an equilibrium, he would ask himself, without some conventions to guide them?

Two things need to be said to eliminate this type of misunderstanding. The first is to deny that game theory is wedded to the notion that the ends justify the means. The Prisoners' Dilemma of Figure 2.2(b) will be used as an example in making the first point. When this was introduced, the entries in the payoff table were given as dollar amounts and the players were described as simple maximizers of expected monetary gain. Under such circumstances, Adam and Eve would certainly be people who act as though the ends justify the means. A game theorist who offered them advice on how best to achieve their goals would therefore be offering advice that took for granted that the ends justify the means.

But now consider a second situation in which the physical outcomes that result from playing the game remain the dollar amounts of Figure 2.2(b). However, in the new situation Adam and Eve are different people. Observation of their behavior reveals that they do not act as though maximizing expected monetary gain. Instead, they always choose *dove* over *hawk* no matter what. When questioned, they say that their reading of the great philosophers has convinced them that *dove* is always the right choice, and that to play *hawk* for money would be to sell one's birthright for a mess of pottage. The theory of revealed preference then tells us that, in this situation, payoffs must be written into the game that make *dove* strictly dominate *hawk*. The logic of the Prisoners' Dilemma will still apply (except that the roles of *dove* and *hawk* must now be reversed), and so a game theorist will have no difficulty in deciding what advice to offer the players if they think they need it. But now he is offering advice to players who act as though consideration of the means takes priority over consideration of the ends. In this second situation, his advice will therefore take for granted that the ends definitely do not justify the means.

Notice that, far from game theory demanding that the ends be taken to justify the means, the discipline of setting up a problem as a game[19] makes it impossible for the model-builder to neglect to take into account the attitude of his players to such questions. The *definition* of an outcome in a game includes not only the physical consequences for each player at the end of its play, but also the the manner in which the physical consequences were achieved.[20] One is therefore provided with total flexibility in deciding how the ends are to be balanced against the means.[21]

Consequentialism and Deontology. Even when a game theorist is modeling his players as irredeemably selfish money-grubbers, he should be careful before allowing himself to be labeled as a consequentialist. In order to explain why, I am going to write down a definition of what consequentialism will be taken to be in this book. Notice that I am not claiming to define what consequentialism *is*, because there seems no consensus on a precise definition.[22]

A *consequentialist* is not just someone who judges actions by their consequences. To say that someone is a consequentialist is also to say something about what his judgments are concerned with, and why he makes them. The issues that he weighs in the balance are *social states*. Moreover, he is required to make judgments about these social states in a coherent manner. In particular, if we write $a \preceq b$ to mean that the consequentialist judges social state b to be no worse than social state a, then the relation $\preceq$ must be total and transitive. This implies that it can be represented by a utility function G. It follows that a consequentialist's judgments can be described by saying that he evaluates a social state x in terms of the *common good* $G(x)$ that it generates.

A consequentialist therefore resembles the ideal observers of Section

---

[19] In this chapter, only noncooperative games are considered. The philosophical position with cooperative games (Introduction to Volume II) is much less clear-cut.

[20] For example, one of the outcomes in the Figure 2.2(b) when the entries in the table are interpreted as dollar amounts is Adam-played-*dove*-and-got-nothing-and-Eve-played-*hawk*-and-got-$3.

[21] Sugden [256] would question the word "total" in this sentence. One might argue, for example, that thinking of the "means" as the strategy that a player uses in a game is too narrow a view. Should one not also include how one chooses among strategies, and how one chooses about how one chooses among strategies? But where such considerations are genuinely relevant, it seems to me that one can always widen the notion of a strategy to include the state of mind that one is in at the time of deciding and hence avoid the implied infinite regress.

[22] If I were free to define consequentialism without reference to its usage among moral philosophers, I would simply define it to be "judging actions solely by their consequences". I would then use the definition of consequentialism in the text as a definition of utilitarianism, and employ some qualifier like "Benthamite" for what is defined as utilitarianism in the text.

1.2.7, except that such ideal observers are usually assumed to be impartial in their judgments.[23] Some authors add impartiality to their definition of consequentialism but I shall not do so.

There is also a tendency to blur the distinction between consequentialism and utilitarianism. For me, a *utilitarian* is simply a consequentialist with an "additively separable" common-good function. That is to say, in a society with n citizens:

$$G(x) = G_1(x) + G_2(x) + \cdots + G_n(x).$$

A utilitarian therefore computes how much common good a social state generates by summing how much good it provides to each individual citizen. Bentham [17] and Mill [178] would have insisted on identifying "good" with "happiness", but the not uncommon definition given above leaves the nature of the "good" that is being taken as the measure of a social state entirely open.

A *deontologist* believes that certain actions are obligatory independently of their consequences. He would argue that one does not keep a promise because it is good to keep a promise, but because one has a *duty* to keep a promise. Such a duty would remain in place, for example, even though a consequence of keeping the promise might be that five other promises are broken in the future.

Although deontology is traditionally the theory of obligation, I shall also include the notion of a *right* as a deontological concept. This is because I shall be saying, perhaps somewhat naively, that a person has a right to carry out a certain action if and only if he does not have a duty to refrain from it.

None of this terminology seems to help at all in explaining the type of ethical theory espoused in this book. It takes for granted ways of thinking about ethical issues that I contend should not be taken for granted. The reasons why deontologists may dislike the deontological elements in my theory are explained in Section 2.3.3. The reasons why consequentialists may dislike the theory's consequential elements are described in Section 2.3.4. In brief, I believe that what might be called deontological considerations are relevant in determining which social contracts are *feasible*. Moral rules that we are said to have a duty to obey are what matter in *sustaining* equilibria. Consequentialist considerations become relevant when one seeks to decide which social contracts in the feasible set are *optimal*. One cannot make a *selection* from the set of available equilibria without implicitly taking the consequentialist view that some social contracts are better than others.

---

[23]An impartial or anonymous common good would remain the same if two citizens with the same characteristics exchanged their roles in society.

2.2.5 Suppose Everyone Behaved Like That?

This question often signals that the logic of the Prisoners' Dilemma is about to be denied. Gough [91] quotes the following passage with approval as a "rare example of Kantian rigor" in Spinoza's [252, p.58] work:

> What if a man could save himself from the present danger of death by treachery? If reason should recommend that it would recommend it to all men.

What Kant himself has to say on this subject will have to wait until Section 2.4. For the moment, I simply want to observe that one does not refute an argument by drawing attention to the fact that it leads to an unwelcome conclusion. Game theorists agree that it would often be better for everybody if everybody would sometimes be a little less rational. It would also be nice not to have to work for a living. But wishing don't make it so.

Consider, for example, a society in which wealth is evenly distributed.[24] In declaring his tax liability, each citizen might have two strategies: the hawkish strategy of employing a tax lawyer with a view to avoiding as much tax as possible, and the dovelike strategy of just letting things ride. If everybody employs a tax lawyer, the government will raise the tax rate in order to maintain its revenue. Everybody who is not a lawyer will then be worse off than before because they now have to support a parasitic class of legal eagles without paying any less tax. Everybody would be better off if everybody were to dispense with a lawyer. Nevertheless, tax lawyers will get used.

The tax lawyer problem is a real-life Prisoners' Dilemma with many players. Such a generalization of the Prisoners' Dilemma to the n-player case is often referred to as a *Tragedy of the Commons*. This is the title of an influential article by Garret Hardin [98], which took as its theme the overgrazing of common land that results when each peasant is free to graze as many cattle as he chooses. A Pareto-efficient outcome would be for each of the n peasants to graze N/n cattle, where N is the number of cattle that would be grazed if the common land had a single owner. However, whatever the other peasants do, it is best for any individual peasant to graze as many cattle as he can afford to buy. Thus the common is overgrazed to the detriment of all.

These examples of circumstances under which this section's title has an unwelcome answer are not those that critics of the logic of the Prisoners' Dilemma find most distressing. This is perhaps because we all know that such failures in cooperation go on all the time without society collapsing around our ears. Critics therefore prefer to concentrate on examples in which rational play of the Prisoners' Dilemma involves breaking a promise,

---

[24]The following example was suggested by my colleague Ted Bergstrom.

since they see no future for a civilized society at all if rational people cannot be trusted to honor the commitments they make to others.

Let us therefore dramatize Adam and Eve's decision problem in the one-shot Prisoners' Dilemma by imagining that they have discussed the game before playing it and have *exchanged promises* not to use *hawk*. After such promises have been made, the two pure strategies need to be relabeled so that they become *play-dove-and-keep-your-promise* and *play-hawk-and-break-your-promise*.

There are then two possibilities to be distinguished. The first is that the exchange of promises changes the structure of the game, so that what has to be played is no longer the Prisoners' Dilemma. This possibility is considered in Section 2.2.6. The second possibility is that the game that is played after the exchange of promises retains the structure of the Prisoners' Dilemma. It then remains essentially tautological that rational cooperation is impossible. *Play-hawk-and-break-your-promise* strongly dominates *play-dove-and-keep-your-promise*, and so rational players will indeed break their promises in this situation. This is certainly very unwelcome news, because it is clear that everybody would be better off if everybody could always be relied upon to keep promises. However, even a *very* unwelcome conclusion does not refute the argument that leads to it.

It is a major error to argue that, because promises between rational individuals would *sometimes* be mere empty words, therefore promises between rational individuals must *always* be worthless. Indeed, the fact that this assumption is often implicitly made by those who are distressed by the logic of the Prisoners' Dilemma perhaps shows that they actually do appreciate at some level the *real* reason why the honoring of promises survives in human societies. It is because a *reputation* for honoring promises is exceedingly valuable—and very easily lost. The following quote[25] from a New York curio dealer puts it in a nutshell: "Sure I trust him. You know the ones to trust in this business. The ones who betray you, bye-bye."

A single transgression when dealing with a member of the community in which your reputation for honest dealing is important may be enough to demolish your standing in the community altogether. But it doesn't follow that any transgression whatsoever will destroy your reputation. Broken promises that only become known to those whose poor opinion of your integrity is unlikely to influence anyone who matters will not do you any harm. Do we not, in fact, often "forget" the promises that we make to those who cannot injure us—not out of wickedness, but simply because such promises tend to be crowded out of our memories by other promises that our unconscious minds somehow find "more important"? As the adage has it: Put not thy trust in princes!

---

[25]Mr. Robert Loughlin, interviewed by the *New York Times*, 29 August 1991.

Game theorists have good reason for insisting that their analysis only applies in the case of the *one-shot* Prisoners' Dilemma. By this they mean that nothing outside the game is relevant to how the players behave inside the game. In particular, the one-shot restriction rules out the possibility that the opponent's observation of a promise being broken, or its observation by an onlooker, can be significant to the players. They can therefore break a promise without any damage to their reputations. The fact that rational players may break promises under such circumstances therefore does not imply that the institution of making promises cannot survive in a rational society. It will survive in a rational society for pretty much the same reasons that it survives in the real world. It is true that the institution of making promises will not survive in the context of the one-shot Prisoners' Dilemma, since no rational player will take the trouble to make a promise if he is sure that it will not be believed. But the one-shot Prisoners' Dilemma is only one of many games that people have to play.

2.2.6 Games That are Not the Prisoners' Dilemma

Figure 2.3 shows some games that are not the Prisoners' Dilemma. Figure 2.3(a) shows the game that results after the players have exchanged *unbreakable* promises to play *dove*.

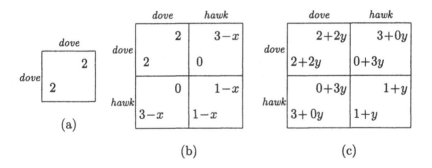

Figure 2.3: Games that are not the Prisoners' Dilemma

Figure 2.3(b) is a game that models a situation in which the players have exchanged promises to play *dove*, but the promises are not unbreakable. However, each player is assumed to suffer a disutility from breaking a promise. It may be, for example, that breaking a promise causes each player some mental distress as a result of their childhood conditioning. This disutility is represented in Figure 2.3(b) by the number x. The interesting case occurs when $x > 1$.

Figure 2.3(c) shows a game in which each player sympathizes with the other. As in Section 1.2.6, this means that they are "members, one of another" to a sufficient extent that they share in the opponent's joys and sorrows. This faculty for sympathetic identification is represented in Figure 2.3(c) by adding to each player's payoff a fraction y of the opponent's payoff.[26] The interesting case occurs when $y > \frac{1}{2}$.

All three of these games admit (*dove, dove*) as a Nash equilibrium. For this reason, an analysis of one of these three games, or some similar game, is sometimes offered as an analysis of the Prisoners' Dilemma. However, game theorists see little point in such a ploy. It may perhaps be true that the Prisoners' Dilemma does not properly represent the issues that human beings face in organizing the cooperative ventures that really matter in holding human societies together. I certainly believe this to be the case myself, and hence feel no distress at all that cooperation is impossible for rational players in the one-shot Prisoners' Dilemma. However, if one shares the view that the Prisoners' Dilemma is not the right game to be studying, why not simply say so? Nothing would seem to be gained by defending whatever position one may hold by offering an analysis of the wrong game.

Reciprocity. I have argued that the Prisoners' Dilemma is often the wrong game to study. But what is the right game? None of the alternatives listed in Figure 2.3 would seem to merit any serious attention as a candidate for the right game. They each assume away the problem that a game-theoretic analysis is intended to clarify. It is true that, if we could not break our promises, or if breaking our promises were always accompanied by a great deal of mental anguish, or if we all cared sufficiently about the welfare of our fellows, then human beings would find it a great deal easier to get along with each other than they do. However, the mere fact that a discipline called game theory exists would seem to guarantee that we do not live in such a "golden age of the poets".

My own views on human cooperation outside small, close-knit groups are explained in Section 1.2.3. I am delighted to be able to quote Confucius as an authority on this point. When asked if he could encapsulate the "true way" in a single word, he replied: "reciprocity".[27]

---

[26] This is a primitive representation because it neglects the fact that Adam, for example, should gain some pleasure from contemplating the fact that Eve gains from contemplating his pleasure. For something more sophisticated, see Bergstrom [18].

[27] But perhaps I am entitled only to the authority of some of those who translate him—as in Munro [185, p.13]. Chinese scholars tell me that the ideogram corresponding to his reply *shu* is difficult to interpret. For example, Fung Yu-Lan [80, p.373] translates *shu* as the-not-doing-to-others-what-one-does-not-like-oneself, which would make it the same as Hobbes' version of the golden rule: *Quod tibi fieri non vis, alteri ne feceris.* Of

Section 1.2.2 emphasizes that reciprocity includes the principle I-won't-scratch-your-back-if-you-won't-scratch-*theirs*, but a two-player model restricts us to reciprocity principles of the type I-won't-scratch-your-back-if-you-won't-scratch-mine. Such principles make no sense unless *time* is explicitly modeled, and the simplest way to do this is to study the implications of allowing a game to be *repeated*.

Repeated Games. Consider, for example, the *indefinitely repeated* Prisoners' Dilemma.[28] This is very different from the one-shot version of the Prisoners' Dilemma studied so far. In the repeated version, Adam and Eve play the Prisoners' Dilemma over and over again until some random event intervenes to bring their relationship to an end. It is usual to model this random event by postulating that each time they finish playing a round of the Prisoners' Dilemma, there is a fixed probability p that they will never play again. Interest then centers on the case when p is very small, so that the players will have good reason to believe that they have a long-term relationship to nourish and preserve.

The strategic considerations in an indefinitely repeated game are totally different from those in a one-shot game because the introduction of time permits the players to reward and punish their opponents for their behavior in the past. The question of how the strategic considerations alter in passing to the repeated case is left until Chapter 3 of Volume II. At this stage, it will perhaps be enough to indicate what the folk theorem of repeated game theory has to say about the indefinitely repeated versions of some of the games that have been considered so far.

Figure 2.4(a) is based on the the Prisoners' Dilemma of Figure 2.2(b). It shows the four payoff pairs $(2, 2)$, $(0, 3)$, $(3, 0)$ and $(1, 1)$ that can result if the players restrict themselves to pure strategies in the one-shot version of the game. The broken line encloses the convex hull[29] of these four points. The unique Nash equilibrium outcome for the one-shot Prisoners' Dilemma is located at $(1, 1)$. To facilitate comparison, the equilibrium outcomes for the repeated Prisoners' Dilemma are given on a per-game basis. Thus the points in the shaded region R of Figure 2.4(a) show the long-run *average*

---

course, Hobbes would not advocate continuing to apply the golden rule to those who do not reciprocate, but perhaps Confucius would.

[28] The finitely repeated Prisoners' Dilemma presents the same problems for rational cooperation as the one-shot version, albeit in a more diluted form.

[29] The convex hull of a set S is the smallest convex set containing S. In the current context, it represents the set of all pairs of expected payoffs that can result if the players *jointly* randomize over their pure strategies. For example, Adam and Eve can organize the pair of expected payoffs $(1, 2)$ by agreeing to play $(hawk, dove)$ with probability $\frac{1}{3}$ and $(dove, hawk)$ with probability $\frac{2}{3}$. Adam will then expect $1 = \frac{1}{3} \times 3 + \frac{2}{3} \times 0$ and Eve will expect $2 = \frac{1}{3} \times 0 + \frac{2}{3} \times 3$.

payoffs corresponding to all Nash equilibria in the indefinitely repeated Prisoners' Dilemma in the case when the probability p that any repetition is the last becomes vanishingly small.

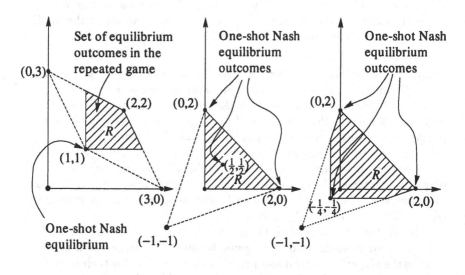

(a) Prisoners' Dilemma   (b) Chicken   (c) Battle of the Sexes

Figure 2.4: Equilibrium outcomes in repeated games

Notice that R is a *large* set because the indefinitely repeated Prisoners' Dilemma has *many* Nash equilibria. One of these calls for Adam and Eve to use *hawk* at every repetition of the game. Repeating the game does not therefore guarantee that rational players will cooperate. But neither is the possibility of rational cooperation excluded, since $(2, 2)$ is also a member of the set R of equilibrium outcomes.

Tit-for-tat. It is easy to verify that $(2, 2)$ is a Nash equilibrium outcome for the indefinitely repeated Prisoners' Dilemma. Consider the strategy TIT-FOR-TAT. This calls for a player to begin by using *dove* in the repeated game and then to copy whatever move the opponent made at the previous stage. If Adam and Eve both stick with TIT-FOR-TAT, *dove* will get played all the time. Moreover, it is a Nash equilibrium for both players to stick with TIT-FOR-TAT.

To see this, it is necessary to check that neither can profit from deviating from TIT-FOR-TAT if the other does not. Suppose it is Adam who deviates by playing *hawk* at some stage. Eve does not deviate, and hence she continues by copying Adam. Eve therefore plays *hawk* in later stages until Adam signals his repentance by switching back to *dove*. If p is sufficiently close to 0, Adam's income stream during his period of deviance will be approximately $3, 1, 1, \ldots, 0$ instead of $2, 2, 2, \ldots, 2$. It follows that his deviation will have been unprofitable. The TIT-FOR-TAT strategy therefore has a built-in provision for punishing deviations. If both believe that the other is planning to use TIT-FOR-TAT, neither will have a motive for using an alternative strategy. Thus it is a Nash equilbrium for both players to stick with TIT-FOR-TAT.[30]

Figures 2.4(b) and 2.4(c) show how the preceding discussion for the Prisoners' Dilemma needs to be modified for the games Chicken and Battle of the Sexes given in Figures 2.1(b) and 2.1(c). These diagrams are included to make it clear that the fine structure of a game that is to be repeated indefinitely is often largely irrelevant. Once attention has been directed away from the infertile one-shot case, the question ceases to be *whether* rational cooperation is possible. Instead, one is faced with a bewildering variety of different ways in which the players can cooperate rationally, and the problem becomes that of deciding *which* of all the feasible ways of cooperating should be selected.

This observation puts the question of what is the "right" game to serve as a paradigm for the problem of human cooperation on the sidelines. Once it is appreciated that reciprocity is the mechanism that makes things work, it becomes clear that it is the *fact* of repetition that really matters. The structure of the game that is repeated is only of secondary importance.[31]

2.3 Games and the Social Contract

This section is a long aside on some of the implications of what has been said so far for social contract issues. Readers who know nothing of how game theory and the theory of social choice have been used by other authors in this context may prefer to skip forward to Section 2.4, where the saga of what is or is not rational in the Prisoners' Dilemma resumes.

---

[30]The strategy TIT-FOR-TAT has been used to illustrate this point because Axelrod [14] emphasized this particular strategy in his influential *Evolution of Cooperation*. However, there are many other symmetric Nash equilibria that lead to the cooperative outcome $(2, 2)$, some of which are at least as worthy of attention as TIT-FOR-TAT (see Section 3.2.5).

[31]However, if other considerations are sufficiently complex to make it necessary to reduce the paradigm being used to a simultaneous-move one-shot game, my recommendation is the Nash Demand Game discussed in Chapter 1 of Volume II.

2.3.1   The State of Nature as a Game

Recall from Section 1.2.1 that Hobbes [117] envisaged the state of nature as being a "war of all against all" in which each man's hand is turned against his brother. Numerous authors, including Gauthier [83], Hampton [97], Kavka [138, 139] and Skyrms [247], have seen a parallel between this vision of the state of nature and the scenario for which the Prisoners' Dilemma or some similar game serves as a model. Sometimes it is said that Hobbes' state of nature "is" a Prisoners' Dilemma. When another game is substituted for the Prisoners' Dilemma, the most popular alternative seems to be Chicken. After modeling the state of nature as a game, the problem for a social contract theorist is then seen as finding a *different game* for society to play—a game whose rules are less inimical for rational cooperation than the game being used to represent the state of nature.

A major difficulty with this approach is that it does not explain why the players should feel *committed* to honor the rules of the new game. Sometimes authors appeal to the concept of "natural law" in this context but, as explained in Section 1.2.4, such a use of the word "natural" seems to me to beg all the questions that matter. I therefore do not think it useful, in a social contract discussion, to adopt a framework in which the *rules* of the game that people play can be changed.[32] The rules of the game of life that I use in my theory should therefore be regarded as immutable. They are to be seen as being natural in the same sense that the laws of natural science are natural. They hold whether we like it or not. As Hume [125] says: "...the lives of men depend on the same laws as the lives of other animals; and these are subject to the general laws of matter and motion." But the fact that we cannot change the rules of the game of life does not imply that we are powerless to alter our fate. We can change the *equilibrium* on which we choose to coordinate.

Such a view makes the one-shot Prisoners' Dilemma a nonstarter as a model for studying rational cooperation because it has only one equilibrium. My own theory rejects all one-shot games as suitable models regardless of how many Nash equilibria they may have. However, one might make a beginning on understanding Hobbes by looking at the one-shot Battle of the Sexes of Figure 2.1(c).

---

[32]This is a decision that a game theorist makes only with great reluctance because it denies him access to the powerful results of the theory of mechanism design. In this theory, a principal invents a game to be played by his agents. He predicts how they will play each possible game at his disposal, and then selects the game that will result in the outcome he likes best. In this theory, however, it is taken for granted that the principal's choice of the rules of the game is *binding*, not only for the agents, but for the principal as well.

Battle of the Sexes. The Battle of the Sexes has three Nash equilibria that can serve to represent possible social contracts. Consider first the mixed equilibrium in which Adam and Eve both play *hawk* with probability $\frac{3}{4}$. Each then gets an expected payoff of $-\frac{1}{4}$, as illustrated in Figure 2.4(c). Such an equilibrium perhaps captures Hobbes' conception of the state of nature a little more closely than the (*hawk, hawk*) equilibrium of the Prisoners' Dilemma, since Hobbes did not argue that man's natural state required him to be continually attacking his neighbor. He argued rather that the periods of fear and suspicion that intervene between bouts of aggression are no more desirable than open warfare itself.

As an alternative to the state of nature in the Battle of the Sexes, there are two Nash equilibria in pure strategies, namely (*dove, hawk*) and (*hawk, dove*). These generate the payoff pairs $(0, 2)$ and $(2, 0)$ as indicated in Figure 2.4(c). One may think of the first of these as representing a reorganization of society in which Adam acknowledges Eve as his sovereign, and the second as a reorganization in which the mantle of royalty is bestowed on Adam. It is therefore reasonable to think of these equilibria as embodying Hobbes' conception of a viable social contract.

Two things are important in attempting to represent Hobbes' ideas with such a simplified model. The first is that (*dove, hawk*) and (*hawk, dove*) are indeed *equilibria*. No outside enforcement is necessary to sustain either outcome. Once it is established that either player intends to act as the equilibrium specifies, it is in the interests of the other to follow suit. The second point is that *both* players prefer either of the Hobbesian social contracts to the mixed equilibrium that represents the state of nature. Even the player who becomes the subject enjoys an improvement from a payoff of $-\frac{1}{4}$ to a payoff of 0 in moving from the state of nature to the equilibrium in which the other player becomes the sovereign.

Hobbes was concerned not only with the state of nature and the civilized state that results when a social contract is in place. He also cared very much about the *process* by means of which society finds its way from one to the other. Indeed, it is for this purpose, unlike most of the philosophers who followed him, that he formulated his "laws of nature". In emphasizing this issue, it seems to me that he showed quite remarkable insight. But before commenting further, it is necessary to return to the subject of repeated games introduced in Section 2.2.6.

Few modern readers would agree with Hobbes about the paucity of viable social contracts. We feel that there must be many workable compromise arrangements between the two extremes in which Adam or Eve is entrusted with the entire power of the state. This view gains support if the game of life is modeled as a repeated game along the lines outlined in Section 2.4.4. It does not greatly matter whether it is the Battle of the Sexes that is repeated, or some other game. Things are much the same if it is the Prisoners' Dilemma that is repeated, as in Axelrod [14] or Taylor [261], or if Chicken is repeated as in Skyrms [247]. What is important is that a whole spectrum of equilibria becomes available as a possible source of social contracts.

Figure 2.4 illustrates the possibilities for the repeated versions of the Prisoners' Dilemma, Chicken, and the Battle of the Sexes. Note that the sets of equilibrium outcomes are convex. This greatly reduces the difficulties involved in getting society from one equilibrium to another. One no longer needs to follow Hobbes in seeing the movement from one type of organization (or lack of organization) to a radically different type of organization being accomplished in one giant leap. Instead, it becomes possible to envisage society moving *gradually* through a sequence of intermediate equilibria from an initial primitive state of nature to a final civilized state. Such a framework allows a story to be told about how a social contract becomes established that does not require that people trust each other very much. If the transition is achieved through a sequence of small steps, nobody stands to lose much if his trust is betrayed. Moreover, the opportunity exists to punish those who resist reform by denying them the benefits of future reforms.

My theory models this aspect of the problem by requiring, not only that the initial and final states are in equilibrium, but that this is also true of the process by means of which society makes the transition from one state to the other. In this way, I seek to eliminate the requirement for trust between the contracting parties that must have been so painful for a down-to-earth realist like Hobbes to write into his "natural laws".

I am not saying here that rational people cannot or should not trust each other. However, rational people do nothing without good reason. In particular, a rational person does not trust his neighbor unless there are sound reasons for believing him trustworthy.[33] But sound reasons for counting on the good faith of others are not necessarily easy to come by, as the next section will perhaps serve to illustrate.

2.3.2   Hunting Stags

When the social contract is mentioned, it is the name of Jean-Jacques Rousseau that first comes to mind. Kant [136, p.vii], for example, called Rousseau the "Newton of the moral world"! Rousseau [224, p.5] begins his *Social Contract* by writing: "In this inquiry, I shall endeavor always to unite what right sanctions with what is prescribed by interest, in order that justice and utility may in no case be divided." Such a goal is certainly one

---

[33]Which is not the same thing as saying that he may not find it expedient to behave *as though* he trusted his neighbor.

that any game theorist would be willing to endorse if he could be persuaded that it was feasible. However, game theorists usually confine their reading of Rousseau [223, p.209] to a parable about hunting deer offered in his *Inequality of Man*. Figure 2.5(a) shows a two-player version of the that Stag Hunt Game is commonly said to illustrate Rousseau's argument.[34]

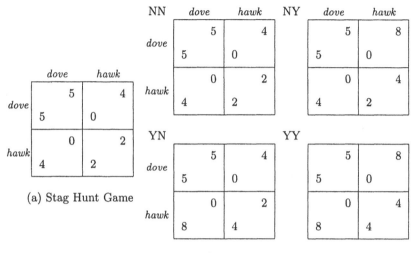

(a) Stag Hunt Game

(b) Who's spotted a hare?

Figure 2.5: Deer hunting

As always in this chapter, *dove* represents a cooperative strategy and *hawk* is a decision to defect from the cooperative enterprise. In the Stag Hunt Game, the cooperative enterprise is to catch a deer. Unless *both* Adam and Eve play their part in the deer-catching enterprise, it is guaranteed that no deer will be caught. However, once Adam and Eve have separated to put their plan to catch a deer into action, both have the opportunity to abandon the enterprise in favor of trying to trap a hare. Trapping hares is an activity that requires no help from anyone. On the contrary, if both players attempt to trap a hare, each will only hinder the other.

The Stag Hunt Game differs from those considered so far in having two *symmetric* Nash equilibria in pure strategies. If the equilibrium (*hawk, hawk*) is identified with the state of nature,[35] an agreement to play *dove* can then be seen as representing a social contract that establishes the equilibrium

---

[34] A variant of the Stag Hunt Game appears in the international relations literature as the Security Dilemma. See, for example, Jervis [130]. Carlsson and Van Damme [54] discuss the issues that have led to game theorists' taking an interest in the game.

[35] One does best to continue thinking in terms of a Hobbesian state of nature rather than attempting to make sense of what Rousseau says about noble savages and the like.

(*dove*, *dove*) that both Adam and Eve prefer to the state of nature. This section is mostly about the question of why implementing such an agreement is not necessarily so easy as it may first appear.

The equilibrium (*dove*, *dove*) in Figure 2.5(a) is a Pareto-improvement on the equilibrium (*hawk*, *hawk*) because both Adam and Eve prefer the former to the latter. Sometimes this relationship is expressed by saying that (*dove*, *dove*) Pareto-dominates[36] (*hawk*, *hawk*). However, it should be noted that (*dove*, *dove*) is a more precarious equilibrium than (*hawk*, *hawk*) because a player who uses *dove* may end up with nothing at all if there is a coordination failure. On the other hand, a player who uses *hawk* will get a payoff of at least 2 whatever the opponent may do.

Harsanyi and Selten [111] seek to capture this aspect of the situation with their notion of risk-dominance. The precise definition of this idea would take us too far afield, but it is worth noting that the fact that (*hawk*, *hawk*) risk-dominates (*dove*, *dove*) implies that adjustment processes of the type discussed briefly in Section 2.2.1 are more likely to converge on (*hawk*, *hawk*) than (*dove*, *dove*).[37] Of course, rational people do not have to fumble their way to equilibria using clumsy trial-and-error processes. They can hurry things along by doing a little thinking. And there is evidence from the laboratory that human subjects can learn to do so quite successfully in some variants of the Stag Hunt Game.[38] One might say that the subjects in laboratory experiments who succeed in coordinating on the mutually beneficial equilibrium in a Stag Hunt Game have learned to *trust* one another.

Is It Rational to Trust Your Neighbor? How hard is the trusting lesson to learn for rational players? As Aumann [13] emphasizes, a simple exchange of promises by Adam and Eve to play *dove* in the Stag Hunt Game does not necessarily guarantee that a self-enforcing agreement is in place. If the players do not trust each other, each will consider what the other has to gain from making a false promise. Eve, for example, will note that an Adam who plans to use *hawk* will get 3 if she uses *dove* against only 2 if she uses *hawk*. It is therefore in his interest to persuade her to play *dove* even if he plans to use *hawk* himself. Of course, it is also in his interest to seek to persuade her to use *dove* if he plans to use *dove*. Thus,

---

[36]In spite of the risk of confusion with the strategic notion of domination introduced in Section 2.2.3.

[37]In the sense that the basin of attraction of the former has a larger area than that of the latter.

[38]See Van Huyck *et al* [263]. Crawford [57] offers a theoretical commentary on the results. However, in other variants of the Stag Hunt Game, experimental subjects are less successful at learning to coordinate successfully. Multiplayer versions seem particularly difficult.

if promises can be at all effective in influencing the opponent's behavior, an Adam who chooses promises on strategic grounds will promise to play *dove* whatever his intentions may be. Eve will therefore regard his promise as conveying no information at all about what he really intends to do.[39]

One can quantify how much trust Eve must place in Adam's promise to use *dove* in the Stag Hunt Game before she will play *dove* herself. Given that Eve attaches probability p to the event that Adam will honor his promise, she expects to get $5p$ from using *dove* herself, and $4p + 2(1 - p)$ from using *hawk*. It is therefore better for her to use *dove* if and only if $5p > 4p + 2(1 - p)$. The condition for this inequality to hold is that $p > \frac{2}{3}$. Eve therefore needs to put a substantial amount of trust in Adam's promise to play *dove* before it becomes expedient for her to honor her own promise to pay *dove*.

Such commentaries often provoke an impatient response akin to that studied in Section 2.2.5. Society would fall apart, it is said, if people didn't trust each other. So why do game theorists claim that trusting one's fellow man is irrational? Cannot Adam and Eve both see that both would be better off if both had more faith in each other's honesty?

Of course Adam and Eve can see that both would be better off if both were more trusting. Equally, both would be better off in the Prisoners' Dilemma if both cared more for each other's welfare, or if both suffered severe distress from breaking promises. But seeing that things would be better if matters were other than they are does not help anyone if the facts cannot be altered. In any case, game theorists do *not* claim that rational people cannot trust each other. They merely argue that trust cannot be taken on trust. When rational people put their trust in someone, they have sound reasons for doing so.

In fact, if we return to Rousseau's [223] original deer-hunting story, ample grounds for *suspicion* rather than trust are provided. What Rousseau actually had in mind is something a little more complicated than the fable that has found its way into the game theory literature. Rousseau's original story postulates that after Adam and Eve part company, having exhanged promises not to be diverted from their joint deer-hunting venture, each might chance to see a hare.[40] The knowledge that a hare is actually around to be caught then obviously enhances the attractiveness of abandoning the deer hunt in favor of attempting to trap a hare.

---

[39]This conclusion is to be contrasted with what happens in the Battle of the Sexes of Figure 2.1(c). If Adam promises Eve that he will play *dove*, she can confidently play *hawk* herself since he has no incentive to seek to persuade her to play *hawk* if he actually plans to play *hawk* himself. An exchange of promises is therefore enough to establish the Nash equilibrium (*dove*, *hawk*) in the Battle of the Sexes.

[40]To keep things simple, assume that a deer is never seen until it is inevitable that it will be caught.

To model this new situation, assume that the probability that a player attaches to the event that the opponent will spot a hare is $\frac{1}{2}$ (whether the player has spotted a hare himself or not). Let Figure 2.5(a) continue to represent the payoffs that Adam and Eve will receive in the event that neither spots a hare. However, we now need further payoff tables to show how things change after one or the other player has seen a hare. These payoff tables are given in Figure 2.5(b). For example, the table labeled YN shows Adam and Eve's payoffs after Adam has seen a hare (Y) but Eve has not (N). This table is obtained by multiplying Adam's payoffs in the *hawk* row of Figure 2.5(a) by 2 in order to represent the enhanced prospects for trapping a hare now that he knows a hare is around to be trapped.

It is no accident that the payoff table in Figure 2.5(b) labeled YY is a variant of the Prisoners' Dilemma. Rousseau's parable is really about why societies should be organized so that people use strongly dominated strategies. However, Rousseau will not be followed down this primrose path. Instead, it will be assumed, as always, that rational people *never* use strongly dominated strategies.

With the payoff tables of Figure 2.5(b), a rational player who has seen a hare will necessarily defect from the cooperative enterprise of hunting a deer to chase after the hare. The reason is that *hawk* strongly dominates *dove* once a hare has been spotted. That is to say, the use of *hawk* results in a higher payoff than *dove* whether or not the opponent has seen·a hare, and whether or not the opponent is planning to play *dove*. One can check this for Adam by comparing his payoffs from *hawk* and *dove* in the lower two tables of Figure 2.5(b).

Return now to the case when neither Adam nor Eve has spotted a hare. However, neither will know what the other has seen. Both will therefore attribute a probability of $\frac{1}{2}$ to the event that the other has seen a hare and chased off after it. But, as noted earlier, a player who has not seen a hare will not play *dove* unless he or she attributes a probability of at least $\frac{2}{3}$ to the event that the other will play *dove*. It follows that, in spite of Rousseau's protestations to the contrary, there are no circumstances under which a rational person will elect to play *dove* in Rousseau's own version of the Stag Hunt Game.

This section has been concerned with the problem of trust between rational players. Its message is that this is something that cannot be taken for granted. In particular, a social contract theorist cannot simply assume that, because everybody agrees that one equilibrium is better than another, then no problem can possibly arise in arranging a transition from the bad equilibrium to the good. It is for this reason that Section 2.3.1 emphasizes the importance of finding a *continuous* route through a series of intermediate equilibria from the primitive state of nature to the final civilized state.

The existence of such a route minimizes the extent to which the players need trust each other during the process of reform.

2.3.3 Rights and the Liberal Paradox

As observed in Section 2.2.6, consequentialist and deontological approaches to moral issues are commonly said to mix like oil and water. This section begins by describing Sen's Paradox of the Paretian Liberal in an attempt to explain why such views are held. Nozick [194, p.164] is an example of those who have appealed to the paradox in arguing against Rawls on the subject of distributive justice.

Sen [240] offers a proof that a rational society cannot consistently pursue a "common good" while simultaneously allowing its citizens to exercise even the most minimal of "rights". The proof employs the vocabulary of social choice theory, which neglects the strategic issues on which game theory focuses. I think such a vocabulary too sparse for an adequate treatment of the deontological notions of a right or a duty. However, my views on this subject will have to wait until the end of the section.

Paretian Liberals? It turns out that everything that matters about Sen's Paradox can be expressed using a society that has only two citizens, Adam and Eve. Moreover, we need only consider the case in which the set S of social states among which they must make a communal choice contains only three alternatives, a, b and c. However, one must be careful not to let the latter simplification lead to a misunderstanding about the nature of a social state. The description of a social state must be understood to include everything that might conceivably be relevant—including even such things as whether Eve wrinkles her nose if Adam behaves crassly.

One way of representing a society in social choice theory is as a *social welfare function* $F : \mathcal{P} \times \mathcal{P} \to \mathcal{P}$. In such a formulation, everything about a society except the manner in which it makes communal decisions is abstracted away. The set $\mathcal{P}$ consists of all possible preferences that an individual might hold over the given set S of social states. The function F then aggregates Adam and Eve's preference relations, $\preceq_A$ and $\preceq_E$, and expresses the result as a communal preference

$$\preceq = F(\preceq_A, \preceq_E) \, .$$

A society equipped with a social welfare function F is ready for anything. Whatever the preferences of its citizens, and whatever the feasibility constraints on the options open to society, the function F provides an answer to the question of what is best for society by generating a communal preference relation $\preceq$. To solve any problem, all that is then necessary is to select whatever social state is best relative to $\preceq$ from whatever set of social states is currently feasible.

Our concern will be with societies in which both individuals and society as a whole make decisions in a consistent manner. As in Section 2.2.4, this will be taken to include the assumption that preference relations $\preceq$ in the set $\mathcal{P}$, whether they represent an individual or a communal preference, are total and transitive.

In Section 2.2.4, the existence of a total and transitive communal preference relation was identified with the idea that a society is organized to promote some common good. We need to assume, not only this, but that the common good is sufficiently sensitive to the preferences of the individual citizens that it satisfies the Pareto principle. This requires that, for all x and y, $x \preceq_A y$ and $x \preceq_E y$ implies $x \prec y$, unless both Adam and Eve happen to be indifferent between x and y.

For Sen [240], a minimal requirement for Adam to have a right to exercise[41] is that there exist at least one pair, a and b, of social alternatives in the set S such that $a \prec_A b$ implies $a \preceq b$. For example, a and b might be complete descriptions of Adam and Eve's social arrangements that differ only in whether or not Adam wears his fig leaf.[42] Eve may prefer that Adam be decently dressed in public, but if Adam has rights on such personal matters, Eve's views will not prevail in determining the communal preference.

Sen's Paradox is that a society organized in accordance with a social welfare function $F : \mathcal{P} \times \mathcal{P} \to \mathcal{P}$ that satisfies the Pareto principle cannot simultaneously allow both Adam and Eve any "rights" at all. It is easy to see why. Suppose that Adam may exercise a right over a and b, while Eve may exercise a right over b and c.[43] For the particular preferences $c \prec_A a \prec_A b$ and $b \prec_E c \prec_E a$, the communal preferences must then satisfy:

$$a \preceq b \qquad \text{(because of Adam's right over } a \text{ and } b)$$
$$b \preceq c \qquad \text{(because of Eve's right over } b \text{ and } c)$$
$$c \prec a \qquad \qquad \text{(by the Pareto principle)}$$

But the communal preference relation then satisfies $a \preceq b \preceq c \prec a$, and hence is intransitive. A contradiction has therefore been obtained.

Figure 2.6(a) illustrates the argument. (Arrows with solid heads indicate strict preferences.) Figure 2.6(b) shows that the preferences at-

---

[41]What follows is actually less than minimal. The natural condition is the stronger $a \prec_A b$ implies $a \prec b$. Of course, the paradox still holds if such a stronger definition is used.

[42]With this example, I am trying to capture the prurient flavor of Sen's [240] story of Lewd, Prude and a copy of *Lady Chatterley's Lover*.

[43]A slightly more complicated argument is necessary if she exercises a right over c and some further alternative d.

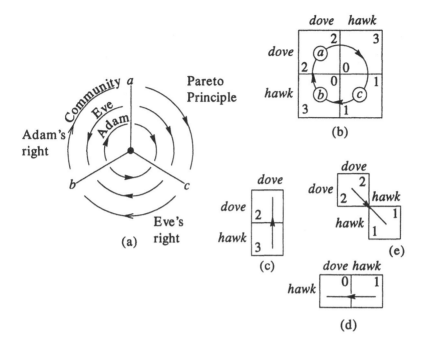

Figure 2.6: Sen's Paradox

tributed to Adam and Eve in generating the contradiction are actually realized in the Prisoners' Dilemma if a, b and c are identified with the outcomes (*dove, dove*), (*hawk, dove*), and (*hawk, dove*). Figures 2.6(c), (d) and (e) show the sequence of comparisons that need to be made in establishing that the communal preference is intransitive.

Rights? Gaertner, Pattanaik, and Suzumura [81] follow Sugden [255, 254] in suggesting that something is awry in Sen's definition of a right.[44] They argue that people should be able to exercise their rights *independently* of one another. Thus, in the Prisoners' Dilemma, one would speak of Adam's having a right over *dove* and *hawk* rather than over (*dove, dove*) and (*hawk, hawk*).[45] However, adopting such a strategic view of the nature

---

[44]In response to Gaertner *et al*, Sen [241] endorses their alternative definition of a right as corresponding to "common-sense", but argues that it is a definition intermediate between his own definition and the stronger definition of Gibbard [87]. I agree with Pattanaik and Suzumura [200] in finding Sen unconvincing on this point, but I do not see that the issue is of much importance to the current discussion.

[45]The exercise of a right would then only guarantee that the social state chosen is in some *subset* of S.

of a right does not make the paradox go away. Indeed, if Adam and Eve each have a right to choose any strategy in the Rock-Scissors-Paper Game of Figure 2.7(a), then we obtain a version of the paradox without even needing to call on the Pareto principle. The necessary sequence of comparisons is shown in Figures 2.7(b)–2.7(g).

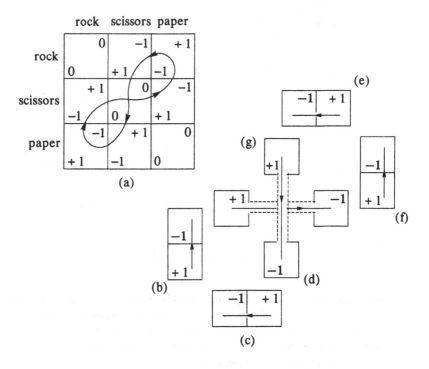

Figure 2.7: Rock-Scissors-Paper

My own view is that one has to work a great deal harder if one is to understand the actual moral phenomena from which we derive our concepts, such as they are, of a "right" or a "duty". In brief, I think that the reason rules for moral or prudent conduct survive in our society is that they provide suitable maxims for sustaining equilibria in repeated games. For example, the strategy TIT-FOR-TAT considered in Section 2.2.6 that supports cooperation as a Nash equilibrium in the indefinitely repeated Prisoners' Dilemma, embodies the principle do-unto-others-as-they-do-unto-you. This may not be the most enlightened of moral precepts, but it is undoubtedly a moral precept of a kind.

To understand the more complex maxims that involve the concept of a right or a duty, one must be prepared to look at equilibria in the game of life that have more structure. A "right" then recognizes actions that will not be punished in equilibrium, no matter what the roll of Nature's dice may bring. A "duty" identifies actions that must necessarily be taken in equilibrium if punishment is to be avoided.[46]

Few deontologists will like the suggestion that "rights" and "duties" are simply conventional rules—unhallowed except by custom or tradition— that exist to coordinate behavior on an equilibrium in the game of life. For them, the following quote from MacMullen's [166] *Corruption and the Fall of Rome* abuses the notion of a "right" when it suggests that the corrupt practices of one age can be transmuted into the legitimate rights of the next:

> There was the Lex Cincia of 204 BC, which forbade taking money for serving as anyone's advocate. It was never formally repealed, only more and more ignored. There were the condoned commoda of the magistrates' assistants and the payoffs extorted from the men in the ranks by their officers' violence. All these, becoming customary, were after some interval elevated to legitimate rights that might be claimed from the highest authority. During the interval, people not familiar with the ways of lawyers, bureaucrats and soldiers continued to apply an incompatible code to their own lives which they believed to be the only code existing. They had much to learn.

The deontological position is that moral rules are *binding* in some sense. Regardless of the consequences, one is required to honor the rules whatever the current climate of opinion may be. Such a view is clearly inconsistent with the Humean [128, p.286] position that no theory of morals can ever serve any useful purpose unless it can show that all the duties it recommends are also in the true interest of each individual. A deontologist may therefore reasonably ask how those of us who agree with Hume reconcile our viewpoint with the undeniable fact that nearly all debates on moral questions center on situations in which the rules demand behavior that is *not* consistent with what self-interest prescribes. Much of Chapter 1 was devoted to answering this question, and those who do not want to hear it answered again can skip forward to Section 2.3.4. But my experience is that such questions can never be answered too often.

---

[46]As Section 1.2.3 observes, it is important to recognize that punishment in such a context does not necessarily imply enforcement by a police force of some kind. For example, in bourgeois neighborhoods, it is often sufficient to prevent people from walking on the grass in the park if those who observe such a minor infringement of a social duty punish it by expressing their disapproval with barely perceptible body language.

The naturalist Konrad Lorenz describes placing a totally inexperienced baby jackdaw on a marble-topped table and then observing the jackdaw perform all the actions appropriate to taking a bath. Such instinctive or programmed behavior is most evident in *pathological* situations in which the programmed behavior is triggered even though the behavior is unadapted to the situation.

The moral behavior with which this book is concerned is learned rather than instinctive. We mimic the behavior of those around us with little or no conscious thought. But we do not readily admit to others or to ourselves that we have no better reason for much of what we do than that it is customary or traditional to do things this way. We prefer to think of ourselves as men of reason living the classical self-examined life. In consequence, as Montaigne [180] puts it: "... whatever is off the hinges of custom, is believed also to be off the hinges of reason ..." In this we are encouraged by the fact that normally no contradiction arises between our moral promptings and what our reason would recommend if it were to be consulted. This is because social evolution has shaped the customs that survive so that, much of the time, we act in our own enlightened self-interest by following what tradition prescribes. Every so often, however, fate places us on a marble-topped table. and then our confidence that everything we do must make some sort of sense creates an internal dissonance for which we insist on an explanation that deontology supplies.

My contention is therefore that deontologists focus their attentions on the use of moral rules in precisely the situations for which the moral rules are not adapted. It is true that, if one planned to make an empirical investigation of what our moral rules actually *are*, then one would certainly wish to study what happens when they get triggered by a pathological situation for which the behavior they prescribe is inappropriate. As with Lorenz's jackdaw, the anomalous behavior then stands out from the background noise like a sore thumb. However, if one wants to know the reason that the rule *survives*, one must look at those situations in which it is easy to overlook that a rule is being used at all because it works so smoothly.

A deontologist might object that the situations I am calling "pathological" are too common to merit such a description. However, as noted in Section 1.2.2, the pathological situations typically either occur only with low probability in any single person's life, or else involve only a relatively small cost in sticking by the moral rule rather than relentlessly optimizing. Either possibility makes it hard for evolution to generate some more sophisticated rule that would eliminate the pathologies—even in the long run. Of course, new varieties of social dilemma, to which evolution has had no chance to adapt, will almost certainly be pathological. It is this that makes it vital that we try to understand what is really going on when moral rules are in use so that we can craft new rules for ourselves, rather than waiting, perhaps in vain, for evolution to do the job for us.

2.3.4 Arrow's Paradox

Somewhat incongruously, an account of Arrow's [8] celebrated paradox is now offered as a footnote to the discussion of Sen's Paradox of the previous section. But first yet another paradox needs to be mentioned.

Condorcet's Paradox says that the institution of majority rule is inconsistent with the public good. Or, less provocatively, if there were such a thing as a common good, it could not be implemented by the institution of majority rule alone.

To see why Condorcet's Paradox is true, imagine that Adam, Eve and Ichabod have the preferences $a \prec_A b \prec_A c$, $b \prec_E c \prec_E a$ and $c \prec_I a \prec_I b$. Then, in an election to determine which of a and b the community should prefer, the winner will be b because Adam and Ichabod will vote for it. Thus majority rule will generate the communal preference $a \prec b$. But it also generates the communal preferences $b \prec c$ and $c \prec a$. The communal preference is therefore intransitive and hence incompatible with any notion of a common good.

This conclusion has nothing to do with Sen's Paradox because pure majority rule accords nobody any rights at all. The result is a consequence of the fact that, when determining the communal preference between a pair of alternatives x and y, majority rule takes no account at all of the preferences that individuals might have over alternatives other than x and y. Such alternatives are treated as being irrelevant to the communal preference between x and y. For this reason, Arrow [8] borrowed[47] the term *Independence of Irrelevant Alternatives* from Nash [190] to describe a social welfare function that has this property.

Arrow's Paradox , like Sen's, requires at least two citizens and at least three alternative social states. Arrow [8] showed, not only that majority rule cannot be a social welfare function, but that this is true for all methods of aggregating individual preferences that satisfy the Pareto principle and the Independence of Irrelevant Alternatives, except for dictatorships.

Deriving Arrow's Paradox from Sen's is very easy. When the Independence of Irrelevant Alternatives holds, there are no pairs of social states over which somebody does not have a right.[48] Sen's Paradox tells us that it must be the *same* somebody for every pair of alternatives. This somebody is a dictator.[49]

---

[47]Although, as we shall see in Chapter 1 of Volume II, Nash's Independence of Irrelevant Alternatives is not the same as Arrow's.

[48]In the sense attributed to Sen in Section 2.3.3.

[49]If the somebody is Eve, then, for each x and y, the argument shows that $x \prec_E y$

Intensity of Preference. The lesson to be learned from Arrow's Paradox is not that the idea of a common good is untenable, but that it needs to take account of more information than the Independence of Irrelevant Alternatives allows. In particular, it cannot ignore the *intensity* with which preferences are held. It may be, for example, that Adam and Eve have opposing preferences over a and b, and also over c and d. However, if Adam is almost indifferent between c and d while Eve is almost indifferent between a and b, then they have a deal in prospect. Adam can agree to abandon his opposition to c should a decision between c and d need to be made, provided that Eve agrees to abandon her opposition to b should a decision need to be made between a and b. However, such log-rolling considerations are disbarred by the Independence of Irrelevant Alternatives.

Section 4.2.2 explains how a Von Neumann and Morgenstern utility function is constructed from a primitive preference relation over sets of lotteries. However, for those familiar with the idea already, it will perhaps be useful to explain how Harsanyi [108] links the notions of intensity of preference and comparison of utilities. Suppose that $a \prec_A b$ and $c \prec_A d$. Then Harsanyi argues that Adam holds the first preference more intensely than the second if and only if Adam would be always willing to swap a lottery ticket **L** in which the prizes a and d each occur with probability $\frac{1}{2}$ for a lottery ticket **M** in which the prizes b and c each occur with probability $\frac{1}{2}$.[50] In terms of a Von Neumann and Morgenstern utility function u_A that describes Adam's preferences over lotteries, Harsanyi's definition reduces to the requirement that $u_A(b) - u_A(a) > u_A(d) - u_A(c)$ (Section 4.2.3).

Notice that Harsanyi's method of measuring preference intensities is denied to us as a social tool if we insist on retaining Arrow's Independence of Irrelevant Alternatives. The latter labels Adam's views on c and d as being "irrelevant" to the decision over a and b. By the same token, it rules out the use of intrapersonal comparisons of utility since it forbids the use of Von Neumann and Morgenstern or other cardinal utility functions. It therefore certainly has no place for the more problematic *inter*personal comparisons of utility that Section 1.2.5 claimed to be necessary for a consequentialist theory to have ethical content.

The appropriate response to Arrow's Paradox is therefore that his Independence of Irrelevant Alternatives is too stringent a condition. If it

---

implies $x \preceq y$. However, a contradiction follows from considering the possibility that $b \preceq_A a$ and $a \prec_E b$ and $a \sim b$. One may take $c \preceq_A a$ and $a \prec_E c$ so that $a \preceq c$; also $c \prec_A b$ and $c \prec_E b$ so that $c \prec b$. We then have that $a \sim b \preceq c \prec b \sim a$, and so the communal preference is intransitive. Thus Eve is actually a dictator in the strong sense that, for each x and y, $x \prec_E y$ implies $x \prec y$.

[50]On the grounds that, if Adam had lottery ticket **N** yielding b or d with equal probabilities, then he would rather exchange c for d in the lottery than b for a.

is thrown away, we can use cardinal utility information in constructing a common good. In particular, any of the welfare functions of Chapter 1 will suffice to define a common good. As we saw in Section 1.2.9, the welfare functions w_N and w_{KS} do not even require that interpersonal comparisons of utility be made. It is true that a society whose institutions do not respect Arrow's Independence of Irrelevant Alternatives will operate on the basis of an untidy network of compromises and trade-offs in which individuals will often use what influence they have strategically. But perhaps we should be reassured rather than discouraged to find that an ideal with which our current political arrangements are often unfavorably compared does not hold water when closely examined.

2.3.5 Teleology

Evolutionary biologists shrink with horror from teleological explanations of natural phenomena. The idea that evolution is designed to fulfill some *a priori* purpose is nothing less than heretical. Authors like myself, who offer naturalistic explanations of moral phenomena in human societies, feel much the same about teleological explanations of social phenomena.

Evolution has not hard-wired us with a commitment to some large-scale common purpose. Any hard-wiring of this kind that may actually exist evolved to facilitate cooperation inside small kin groups. As so often, Hobbes [117, p.225] puts his finger on the nub of the matter:

> ... certain living creatures, as Bees or Ants, live sociably one with another (which are therefore numbered by Aristotle amongst politicall creatures) ... and therefore some man may perhaps desire to know why Man-kind cannot do the same. To which I answer ... amongst these creatures, the common good differeth not from the private.

Bees, ants, and other *hymenoptera* have peculiar genetic arrangements that result in sisters sharing more genes than a mother and a daughter. A worker in a colony will therefore be more successful in propagating her own genes by caring for a sexually active sister than if she were to care for a sexually active daughter of her own. A preternaturally intelligent bee or ant, anxious to explain the altruism displayed by her fellows, would therefore be rewarded in a search for an *a priori* common good towards which the colony is united in striving.[51] The common purpose of the colony is to maximize the expected number of sexually active offspring of the queen that make it to maturity.

However, no such *a priori* common good awaits discovery by human seekers after truth. Nature has engraved no overriding sense of common

---

[51] A preternaturally intelligent ameba in a slime mould society would have an even easier task, since all the citizens of such a society are *clones*.

purpose upon the heart of man. I cannot even conceive what source of wisdom those like Moore [181] imagine they are tapping when they claim to be able to identify the "good" by some process of introspection.[52] Those who claim revelation for their version of an *a priori* common good at least have something coherent to say, although their claims would carry more conviction if they could reach some consensus on what the one true common good actually is.

The actuality is that all the many varieties of the common good with which thinkers have toyed are *inventions*. However, moral philosophers still speak of *teleological ethics* even when the common good toward which mankind is urged is admitted to be artificial. Indeed, a teleological ethical theory is often simply identified with a consequentialist theory. However, such an identification obscures a point that seems to me of very great importance.

What is at issue is whether a consequentialist theory treats its notion of a common good as *primitive*. If it does, it deserves the label "teleological".[53] If it does not, then it is a nonteleological consequentialist theory. A close analogy exists with what was said in Section 2.2.4 about utility theory: namely that modern utility theory regards it as a fallacy to argue that $a \preceq b$ *because* $u(a) \leq u(b)$. Similarly, a nonteleological consequentialist theory regards it as a fallacy to argue that social state b ought to be ranked at least as high as social state a *because* $G(a) \leq G(b)$. In a nonteleological theory, the common good function is chosen to have the property $G(a) \leq G(b)$ by whoever is doing the theorizing because he has *already decided*, for whatever reason, that b is no worse than a.

---

[52] As Moore [181, p.6] puts it: Good is good, and that is the end of the matter. Nor does Moore [181, p.17] have much patience with those who feign incomprehension. He is emphatic that: Every one does in fact understand the question "Is this good?" As for the nature of the "good", Moore tells us that this cannot be defined—and to maintain otherwise is the "naturalistic fallacy". Moore [181, p.15] argues that any proposed definition of the "good" must always fail to capture the concept, because one can always ask of the complex specified by the definition whether it is itself "good". Field [74, p.54] applies Moore's reasoning more generally. When the question "Who was that man in the black overcoat?" is answered by "Mr. Smith", Moore would presumably comment that the man in the black overcoat cannot be Mr. Smith because one can still ask the question, "Was Smith the man in the black overcoat?" As Field observes, the reason that one can still ask the question is because there may still be some doubt. Similarly, when one asks whether the complex defined by a proposed definition of the "good" is itself "good", one is simply expressing some doubt about whether the definition proposed is adequate to express the vague feelings about the nature of the "good" that the definition was supposed to crystallize.

[53] In saying this, I believe that I am just following Rawls [214, p.24], who calls a theory teleological when: "The good is defined independently of the right, and the right is defined as that which maximizes the good." Perhaps I am also capturing some of the flavor of Riker's [216] important distinction between liberalism and populism.

Moral Education. The enormous, and to my mind insuperable, difficulty faced by any theory of ethics that takes some invented notion of an *a priori* common good as a primitive concept is that of persuading people that the invented notion has any relevance to how they should behave. As Rousseau [221, p.260] put it: "if you would have the general will accomplished, bring all the particular wills into conformity with it." The implementation of such a program would certainly eliminate all our problems with the Prisoners' Dilemma at a stroke. The game would become a simple one-player decision problem.[54] But how is each particular will to be brought into conformity with the general will? Rousseau's [222] *Emile* tells us that the appropriate technique is the brainwashing of children.

Such brainwashing will, of course, deny that someone invented the general will in 1743 or thereabouts—otherwise the child might conceive the idea of inventing a general will of his own. It is necessary that the general will be represented as some kind of Platonic ideal beyond human disputation. The same is true of other conceptions of the common good that human ingenuity has created before and since. When it comes to establishing a conception of the common good, only one flower can be allowed to bloom.

I don't mind admitting that the moral training of children is a problem for my view of things. Currently, the gap between the aspirations of our moral pundits and their success in implementing their aspirations is spectacularly wide. This is perhaps because, in order to qualify as a moral pundit, one must abandon all attempts to be realistic about the nature of human nature. Rousseau's [222] pliable creature Emile, for example, does not even belong in the same phylum with my own children!

However, it does not follow that, because past attempts to transform Nature's little Mr. Hydes into Dr. Jekylls have met with limited success, the same must necessarily be true of future attempts based on more realistic assumptions and improved techniques. The question is therefore: If we could effectively brainwash all our children to pursue some invented common good, should we do so?

My theory calls for all ethical issues to be settled using the device of the original position, and it is possible that a decision to restrict the freedom of our children to think things out for themselves is what would emerge from such a forum. Other liberal values might also conceivably be rejected.

---

[54]Perhaps it would be represented by Figure 2.6(e), or maybe Figure 2.8(b) or 2.8(c). The precise answer will depend on what the general will actually dictates. Unfortunately one must be gifted with "sublime virtue" (Rousseau [221, p.255]) if one is to do more than guess at the answer. However, it seems that if Adam and Eve do not have the opportunity for preplay communication, then the general will may legitimately be identified with the "will of all" (Rousseau [224, p.15]). The payoffs on the diagonal in these proposals are therefore probably correct.

This would be much harder in Western democracies than in societies whose current social contracts do not have a similar respect for basic liberties woven into the fabric of their institutions. It might even be impossible. My theory requires that a succession of small reforms be found that takes society from the current *status quo* through a sequence of intermediary stable social contracts to the final contract agreed in the original position— and such a sequence may simply not be available if the current *status quo* is sufficiently resilient.

Nevertheless, it remains possible that measures which we currently regard as illiberal might be agreed upon in the original position. I think that such an outcome would be unlikely, because a society that chose to fetter the minds of its citizens would be less able to exploit its opportunities than a society that encouraged freedom of thought and expression. But others would argue that the advantages enjoyed by a society of freethinking opportunists as a consequence of its capacity to respond flexibly to changes in its external circumstances are outweighed by its greater vulnerability to internal dissension. My heart tells me that Mandeville's [168] doggerel poem *The Grumbling Hive*, which compares the lot of an imaginary bee in a colony of virtuous zealots unfavorably with that of a bee in a freewheeling hive with a booming economy, must surely be correct. But my head tells me that this attitude may simply be a whiggish prejudice derived from a strong personal distaste for authoritarianism even in its most benevolent manifestations.

Rawls [214] does not share such doubts about the stability of conventional liberal institutions. I wish I could agree with him that debate in the original position would necessarily result in precedence being given to the principle that each citizen should have "an equal right to the most extensive basic liberty compatible with a similar liberty for others", but I am unable to convince myself that this is something that could possibly be demonstrated *in the abstract* without reference to the current social institutions of the society or the external threats with which it might be faced.

If such a demonstration were possible in the abstract, it would necessarily be valid for all societies regardless of their special circumstances. But do we not have to admit, to take an extreme example, that Hobbes would be right about the character of the feasible social contracts if society consisted of the crew of an old-time sailing vessel? However, I suspect that the young Rawls [214, p.454] would reply that his argument is intended to apply only in the context of a "well-ordered society". The older Rawls [211] claims even less. He addresses only those who respond to the rhetoric of a modern democratic state.

In summary, although I think that Rawls is probably right in arguing that a Western democracy that chooses to reform itself using the device of the original position will not thereby abandon the institutions that secure what we currently think of as the basic rights and liberties of its citizens, I do not believe that he can be said to have demonstrated this convincingly. Nor can I do any better, even though my insistence on the importance of the current *status quo* to what is agreed in the original position should make the demonstration easier for me than for Rawls. However, I plan to proceed as though this difficulty did not exist. In particular, even if advances in psychology do eventually make it possible to brainwash children to honor some teleological conception of the common good, I shall assume that those in the original position would not agree to have their children so brainwashed.

Welfare Economics. Some last words on teleology are necessary lest it ☐ be thought that I see no useful role for teleological ethical theories at all. In arguing that current versions of the notion of an *a priori* common good get only lip service from most people in modern societies, and that there is no reason why newly invented versions should command any greater respect, I am not saying that welfare economists might as well pack their bags and go home to mother. On the contrary, their approach is clearly very relevant when some person or institution can impose its will on others— just as a mother may insist on certain house rules being obeyed for what she sees as the common good of the family. It will certainly help things along if people can be persuaded to respect the common good in such circumstances, but disaster will not ensue if attempts at persuasion fail, since respect can be enforced if necessary. A recalcitrant teenager might protest at the consequent constraints on his liberty, but Kant [135, p.122] is an impeccable authority for those mothers who like to both have their cake and eat it: "Man therefore *needs* a master who can break man's will and compel him to obey a general will under which every man could be free."

God forbid that I should ever be asked to design a tax scheme, but if I were, I should certainly begin by finding out what welfare function the scheme is intended to maximize. That is to say, I would take a teleological attitude to the enterprise. Such an attitude would not be inconsistent with my earlier criticism of teleological theories because the government stands *outside* society when it compels taxpayers to contribute towards its maintenance. My criticism of teleological theories is concerned with their application to society *as a whole*, or to other situations in which no outside enforcement agency exists. With regard to taxation, for example, the type of issue I am addressing is whether rich voters can be persuaded to vote for a big-spending party on the basis of some conception of the common good. Or, better still, whether they can be persuaded not to understate their tax liability on such grounds.

2.3.6   Jacob's Ladder

Teleological ethical theories take a top-down view of the common good. Nonteleological theories use a bottom-up methodology in which the common good is *constructed* from more primitive ideas.

Harsanyi [109], for example, offers a nonteleological utilitarian theory. His notion of a common good is built into the welfare function $W_H(x) = x_A + x_E$ whose use is illustrated in Figure 1.2. Recall that a social contract in this diagram is identified with a pair $x = (x_A, x_E)$ of payoffs in a feasible set X. The utilitarian social contract H in X is the social contract x in X at which $W_H(x)$ is maximized. However, Harsanyi does not argue that H should be chosen because his common good is intrinsically attractive or because it can be characterized by an elegant system of axioms. He argues that H is what Adam and Eve would agree to if they were placed behind a veil of ignorance in his version of an original position. A discussion of his argument will have to wait until Chapter 2 of Volume II. The immediate point is simply that his common good is not an *a priori* idea. He constructs it from what he sees as more primitive notions.

Broome [48, p.56] is among those who are unenthusiastic about such a bottom-up approach. He quotes Barry [16, p.334] to the effect that no reason would seem to exist why someone who was unconvinced by the intrinsic merits of a utilitarian common good should change his mind after learning of Harsanyi's construction. A nonteleological consequentialist would certainly be wasting his time if such criticisms were always valid. However, the point of adopting a constructive approach is that simple ideas are less confusing than complicated ideas. People who reason well are therefore more readily convinced by simple ideas than by complicated ideas when both are right. Similarly, people who reason badly are more readily convinced by complicated ideas than simple ideas when both are wrong. This is why Euclid thought it worth while reducing complicated propositions in geometry to simpler propositions.[55]

Of course, a skeptic can keep repeating, "So what?" all the way down the line—no matter how simple the arguments offered for his examination. Indeed, I am such a skeptic myself in respect of non-naturalistic approaches to ethics. If "ought" statements can never be deduced from "is" statements,

---

[55]Recall Aubrey's [9] story of Hobbes' finding a copy of Euclid's *Elements* while waiting in an anteroom. On reading Proposition 47, he exclaimed, "By God, this is impossible!" However, he was convinced after mastering Euclid's reduction of the proposition to more primitive notions. But perhaps it is dangerous to tell a mathematical story in this context. One certainly would not wish to make ease of mathematical expression the criterion for simplicity in a consequentialist theory—although I suspect that this is a mistake of which some teleologians are guilty.

then there must presumably exist irreducible "ought" statements which have to be accepted on *a priori* grounds, since it is tautological that reasons cannot be given why one "ought" to accept them. Of course, naturalistic approaches to ethics are also vulnerable to skeptical challenges. However, a naturalist can at least pretend that he has empirical support for the stylized facts on which his theory is supposedly based.

My bottom-up approach to ethical issues requires climbing a different ladder to the notion of a common good than those climbed by Harsanyi [109] or Rawls [214]. I decline to climb their ladders because they stand on ground that I believe unable to carry any weight. By this I mean that their nonteleological theories take some version of *homo ethicus* as their model of man. I follow Barry [16, p.334] in seeing no reason why specimens of *homo sapiens* should allow themselves to be persuaded to honor the terms of agreements that would be reached under the hypothetical circumstances of the original position—unless it can be shown that it would be in their interests to do so. For this reason, I take *homo economicus* as my model of man in the hope of thereby establishing a firm footing for my ladder.

Culture. Not only is my ladder placed on different ground from those of Harsanyi and Rawls, it is a sturdier ladder in that it has more rungs even though it does not reach so high. The first rung on my ladder is the notion of common knowledge.

It is only relatively recently that game theorists, following Aumann [10], have recognized the importance of common knowledge to the foundations of their subject. The idea is simplest when expressed in terms of Milgrom's [177] notion of a public event.[56] A *public event* is something that cannot occur without everyone knowing it. For example, if Adam and Eve were holding hands, then it would be a public event if Eve took a bite from her apple. It would be a public event even if Adam were looking the other way, since eating an apple quietly is beyond the powers even of those with the most refined table manners.

Anything implied by a public event is said to be *common knowledge* after the public event has occurred.[57] Thus, after eating the apple, it became common knowledge between Adam and Eve that their days in the Garden of Eden were numbered.[58]

The philosopher David Lewis [152] anticipated the interest that game theorists now take in common knowledge by pointing out that a convention

---

[56]In my *Fun and Games* (Binmore [29]), a public event is called a "common truism" to preserve an analogy with a related notion for individuals that I call a "truism".

[57]I am grateful to Dov Samet for pointing out to me that this is the most satisfactory way to explain common knowledge.

[58]Of course, *before* eating an apple from the Tree of Knowledge, their logical faculties were not equal to making this deduction.

needs to be commonly known to be effective in a rational society. Lewis used a definition of common knowledge which is equivalent to that given above. His definition makes an event common knowledge if and only if everybody knows it, everybody knows that everybody knows it, everybody knows that everybody knows that everybody knows it; and so on. This seems a formidable amount of knowing, but the equivalent definition in terms of public events makes it clear that it is very easy for certain things to become common knowledge among rational individuals.

A community of rational individuals is held together by the pool of common knowledge that I shall call its *culture*. The gossamer threads of shared knowledge and experience may seem flimsy bonds with which to hold a society together when compared with the iron shackles of duty and obligation postulated by traditional ethical theories. However, one must remember that the iron shackles of the traditionalists exist only in their imaginations, and even the most gossamer of real threads is more substantial than an iron shackle that is only imagined. Moreover, like Gulliver in Lilliput, we are bound by so many threads that even real shackles could fulfill their function with no greater efficiency.[59]

A society's pool of common knowledge—its culture, provides the informational input that individual citizens need to coordinate on *equilibria* in the games that people play. For game theorists, I want to emphasize that culture means more in this context than the fact that it is common knowledge that everybody is rational in whatever sense is deemed appropriate. It includes *historical* data. An analyst ignorant of this data would not necessarily be able to predict the equilibrium on which members of the society would coordinate in a specific game. He might therefore categorize the equilibrium selection criteria that the society uses as arbitrary. However, the criteria will not seem arbitrary to those within the society under study.[60]

The Battle of the Sexes Game of Figure 2.1(c) will be used as an example. The story that goes with this game has Adam and Eve on their honeymoon in a big city. At breakfast, they agree that they will either go to a boxing match or to the ballet in the evening, but the question as to

---

[59]Although, of course, there are some functions that *real* shackles could perform that would be impossible for gossamer threads, however numerous.

[60]I make this point because a common criticism of the heroic attempt by Harsanyi and Selten [111] to create a complete theory of equilibrium selection in games is often criticized for containing arbitrary elements. But any such theory must *necessarily* be a child of the culture that spawns it. Do not Bernheim [20] and Pearce [201] teach us that we cannot in general expect coordination on any equilibrium at all if we insist that our basic pool of common knowledge contains only a specification of the game to be played and the fact that we are all Bayesian rational? A society's culture consists of more than the shared knowledge that we all belong to the same species. Vast amounts of historical data are enshrined in its customs and traditions.

which of the two entertainments should actually be chosen is left entirely open. However, during the day the two lovers are separated and each is consequently left with the problem of deciding which entertainment to attend independently of the other. The payoffs in the game reflect the fact that both will be miserable if they choose different entertainments. If both choose the same entertainment, the payoffs accord with the standard male-female stereotypes,[61] provided that the outcome (*hawk, dove*) is identified with both going to the boxing match and (*dove, hawk*) is identified with both going to the ballet.

The point of the Battle of the Sexes is that one cannot identify either of the two pure-strategy Nash equilibria as the "solution" of the game given the circumstances of the story.[62] Any argument in favor of one is equally an argument in favor of the other. Something needs to be added to the story to break the symmetry, and as Lewis [152] emphasizes, whatever is added needs to be common knowledge.

Actually, we have already been taking for granted that a great deal in the story of the Battle of the Sexes is common knowledge. This is standard in a game-theoretic discussion. Recall that Hobbes characterized a man in terms of his strength of body, his passions, his experience and his reason. As in Section 1.2.2, I identify these with what the rules of the game permit the player to do, his preferences, his beliefs about any chance moves in the game, and the fact that the player follows Bayesian decision theory. All these are routinely taken to be common knowledge in analyzing a game.[63]

However, as we have seen, all this shared knowledge is not enough to provide a basis on which Adam and Eve can coordinate on boxing or ballet in their peculiar predicament. They need some extra clue from their common history for this purpose. How real people convert such clues into a recipe for action is more than a little mysterious. Schelling's [229] celebrated essay on focal points makes it clear that we are frequently able to do this using contextual hints that are barely perceptible. But even those who

---

[61] I did not invent the story that goes with this game! I would choose ballet over boxing any time.

[62] Moreover, there are problems with the mixed Nash equilibrium as well, since both players get only their security levels there. So why don't they switch to their security strategies which *guarantee* the security levels?

[63] This does not mean that all this information must *always* be common knowledge for a game-theoretic analysis to be possible. One can analyze the Prisoners' Dilemma, for example, on the simple assumption that each player knows that *hawk* strongly dominates *dove*. Nor is all lost if one needs things to be common knowledge that are not common knowledge in the model currently being used. Harsanyi's [107] theory of incomplete information provides a method of expanding the original model in a manner that sometimes allows this difficulty to be circumvented. When this procedure is followed, the original model is often called a "game of incomplete information". This book suppresses all informational difficulties. But, if this were not the case, it would explain that there is strictly no such thing as a *game* of incomplete information. (See Binmore [29, p.502].)

have personally participated in successful coordination experiments find it very hard to say afterwards what the precise criteria are that led them from the slender clues provided to the equilibrium they finally decided to go for. I have tried elsewhere (Binmore [33]) to describe a mechanism that near-rational players might use, but it would take us too far afield to discuss such ideas here.[64] The mechanism is mentioned only because of its relevance to the common knowledge issue. In brief, I show that, for the specific case of the Battle of the Sexes, there is no guarantee that the players will succeed in coordinating on a Nash equilibrium using the mechanism, unless the clue from which they begin and the method by means of which the clue is incorporated into their reasoning process is common knowledge.[65]

Of course, we do not need to make life difficult for Adam and Eve by allowing them only subtle hints and cues as a basis for solving their coordination problem. If the last public event they shared before getting separated consisted of Adam's remarking that perhaps the ballet would not be so bad after all, neither would later need to think very hard about where to go in the evening. Similarly, each time that we drive our cars, we have no difficulty in solving the coordination game in which the two strategies are: *drive-on-the-left* and *drive-on-the-right*. However, when Sweden switched from driving on the left to driving on the right, the government made very sure that this decision was as near a public event as they could manage.

Such examples make the agonizing of game theorists about common knowledge look like the medieval controversies over the number of angels that can dance on the end of a pin. And it is certainly true that the foundations of game theory are a morass into which it is not wise to wander if you have some place you want to get to in a hurry. Fortunately, all that needs to be borne in mind for the purposes of this book is that game theorists of the strict school believe that their prescriptions for rational play in games can be deduced, in principle, from one-person rationality considerations without the need to invent collective rationality criteria— provided that sufficient information is assumed to be common knowledge.

Custom. We have seen that the first rung on the ladder to a common good is common knowledge. The second rung consists of what I shall call *common understandings*. These are the conventions,[66] customs, habits, moral principles, maxims, rules of thumb, memes, traditions, and the like that we use in regulating our interactions with those around us. In a society

---

[64]And it would, in any case, be misleading to discuss what is just one proposal among many that have been made.

[65]Otherwise they may end up coordinating on a correlated equilibrium in the sense of Aumann [11]. See Section 3.4.1.

[66]I use this evocative word very little in this section for fear of its being taken in the sense proposed by Lewis [152], which I think overly restrictive.

of the species *homo economicus*, such common understandings would be deduced from the society's pool of common knowledge for the purpose of coordinating on an equilibrium in the game of life—just as Adam and Eve were able to coordinate on the ballet in the Battle of the Sexes once they were provided with a rich enough set of commonly held information.

Unlike the toy games we have been using as examples, the game of life is very complicated. In particular, its strategy set is immense. Coordinating on an equilibrium is therefore not simply a matter of deciding between *hawk* and *dove*. Even describing a single strategy may be a demanding task. One should therefore not think of *homo economicus* as engaged in a trivial activity when he deduces common understandings on how the game of life should be played from his knowledge of the culture his society has inherited from the past. Nor should it be taken for granted that the rules for sustaining an equilibrium in the game of life that he comes up with will necessarily be easy to appreciate. Sometimes they will be subtle and intricate.

Of course, *homo sapiens* makes no such deductions. When he takes the trouble, he is able to identify some of the rules for sustaining equilibria that his society has evolved and which he has incorporated into his behavior. But I do not think any of us fully appreciate the complexity of some of the patterns of behavior with which we have been endowed by our social history. And, until relatively recently, none of us would have thought to ask ourselves how it is that such common understandings survive. They typically seem so comfortable and familiar that doubting their solidity seems as ridiculous as doubting the laws of gravity. A Frenchman speaking to compatriots in Paris does not consider the fact the vocabulary of the French language is simply a set of arbitrary conventions when he opens his mouth to speak. Still less does he pause to deduce which set of possible common understandings to use from the fact that it is common knowledge that French is spoken in France. Indeed, the culture of a society of specimens of *homo sapiens* is manifested *directly* in its set of common understandings. Instead of the citizens of the society deducing their common understandings from an underlying pool of common knowledge, the analyst must deduce the existence of an implicit pool of common knowledge from the fact that the common understandings he observes actually do serve the function of sustaining an equilibrium—insofar as they do.

Deontological intuitions arise at the level of this second rung of the ladder. Section 2.3.3 explains why I believe that those who defend deontological theories of ethics are mistaken in arguing that what I call common understandings are more than coordinating conventions. At this stage, I want only to emphasize that consequentialist intuitions belong at the next level—at the level of the third rung of the ladder. It is for this reason that

I think it an error to regard deontological and consequentialist attitudes as incompatible. Whether they know it or not, the former are talking about rules for *sustaining* equilibria, and the latter are talking about criteria for *selecting* equilibria.[67] Both are obviously important, but they arise at different levels when a game-theoretic perspective is adopted.

The Good. The third and last rung of the ladder is a nonteleological conception of a common good. In a bottom-up approach, the common good is a construct assembled from the building blocks put together at the level below. How can the idea of a common good emerge from that of a common understanding on how to play the game of life?

The game of life is a grandiose notion. When a player chooses a strategy in this game, he chooses a plan for living his whole life. But the game of life can be broken up into many subsidiary games. We do not, for example, need to review our whole relationship with the universe each time we decide on which side of the road to drive when setting out for work.

Each time an equilibrium is played in a subsidiary game, one might say that the community has made a choice from the set of possible outcomes of the subsidiary game. In doing so, the community could be regarded as revealing a communal preference over social states. If this revealed communal preference is total and transitive, society could then be said to be acting as though seeking to maximize a common good. However, such a naive approach is doomed to failure. The Rock-Scissors-Paper Game of Figure 2.7 suffices to show that the revealed communal preference is not transitive even in very simple cases.

To make progress with the fable that the community is an entity capable of making choices, one must begin by first asking what choices are feasible for this entity. Since it can only choose *equilibria* in subsidiary games, all that it reveals in selecting an equilibrium is therefore a communal preference over the equilibria of the subsidiary game. One might say that deontological considerations determine what is *feasible* in any situation. Only after these considerations have been taken into account does it makes sense to ask whether consequentialist considerations may be helpful in determining what is *optimal*.

One must remember, however, that this is a bottom-up theory in which a nonteleological common good is to be constructed from a prior common understanding on how the game of life should be played. But no guarantee exists that a given common understanding will result in equilibria being selected in subsidiary games as though some common good were being maximized. However, as argued in Section 1.2.1, I believe that do-as-you-

---

[67] My guess is that infighting between act-utilitarians and rule-utilitarians is also often beside the point as a consequence of a failure to appreciate this point.

would-be-done-by rules are already entrenched in the imperfect common understandings that govern the workings of the societies of *homo sapiens*. An idealized analogue of such a rule suitable for the societies of *homo economicus* is provided by the device of the original position. If this device is regarded as an equilibrium selection mechanism, then I shall be confirming Rawls' intuition that the equilibrium outcome $x = (x_A, x_E)$ selected in certain important classes of subsidiary games will be that which maximizes the welfare function

$$W_\rho(x) = \min\{U(x_A - \xi_A), V(x_E - \xi_E)\}.$$

This welfare function was introduced in Section 1.2.5 in describing how Rawls' maximin criterion needs to be generalized when the payoffs have not been normalized to take account of interpersonal comparisons of utility.

Whiggery. The ladder now reaches to a place where a whig may hope to effect some repairs to the fabric of society. So far the discussion has been entirely naturalistic. The argument has been that things are the way they are largely because this is where evolution washed us up on the beach. Among the flotsam washed up along with us are equilibrium selection criteria for which the device of the original position serves as an idealized representative. We use this criterion in coordinating on equilibria in certain subsidiary games in the game of life. So why don't we take this familiar device and apply it, not just to some aspects of our lives, but to the game of life taken as a whole? The defense for such a proposal is entirely pragmatic. Here is a tool supplied by Nature. Let us use it to improve our lives, just as we use whatever tools we find in our toolbox when making repairs around the house.

What is important above all is that we do not deceive ourselves about the nature of this or any other tool that may be proposed as an aid to reform. It is true that avoiding such deceptions will hamper our attempts to persuade others to consent to the reforms proposed. People are much readier to buy magic wands than cattle prods if both are sold at the same price. However, if we convince ourselves that what we have to sell is a magic wand, we will find ourselves using it for casting spells rather than prodding cattle. And it won't work.

2.3.7 Rawls' Two Principles of Justice

Rawls' [214, p.60,p.83] famous two principles of justice are:

1. Each person is to have an equal right to the most extensive basic liberty compatible with a similar liberty for others.

2. Social and economic inequalities are to be arranged so that they are both (a) to the greatest benefit of the least advantaged and (b) attached to offices and positions open to all under conditions of fair equality of opportunity.

Rawls requires that the first principle take absolute priority over the second. Only when the the rights and liberties to which it refers have been secured are the distributional questions treated by the second principle to be considered.

Part (a) of the second principle is the maximin criterion that Rawls calls the difference principle. It will be clear enough by now where I stand on this issue. But what of the first principle and part (b) of the second?

I have to admit that I am not entirely clear what these principles imply in practice. Rawls certainly does not intend the first principle to enshrine the right to "kill or be killed". He has a much more bourgeois conception of the rights and liberties to which the principle is to be applied. The principle therefore comes with various implicit riders about which the later Rawls [211] is very much more specific. The same is true of the second principle when (a) and (b) seem to conflict. Should we, for example, be in favor of affirmative action because of (a)—or against because of (b)?

However, my own theory offers even less guidance on such matters of practical implementation, because it applies to all societies in which the fairness notion on which it is based has evolved. But, as Section 2.3.5 explains, I do not see how the same can be said of the approach adopted in Rawls' *Theory of Justice*. Nor do I think that Rawls intended that it should. Indeed, the later Rawls [211] is explicit about the cultural biases built into his principles. In brief, I think Rawls is able say more than I about the results of an appeal to the original position, because he is assuming more about the type of society from which the appeal originates.

In my approach, the set X of all possible social contracts illustrated in Figure 1.2(a) is an enormous black box into which all kinds of considerations have been packed away. One cannot predict what the practical implications of applying my theory will be without unpacking this black box to see what is inside. Amongst other things, it contains a statement of Adam and Eve's personal preferences and beliefs. If they happen to be unanimous in the conviction that God meant women to be subordinate to men, then their social contract will violate Rawls' first principle. Adam and Eve will not agree, even in the original position, to a social contract that assigns men and women the same rights and liberties. Those of us who live in a modern Western democracy might then say that Adam and Eve had created an illiberal society. But these are the sort of conclusions with which one must be prepared to live if one is to insist that all ethical decisions are to be made in the original position. The alternative is to adopt a paternalistic attitude that makes one ready to foist a social contract upon Adam and Eve that both dislike, on the grounds that Daddy knows best.

In spite of these differences with Rawls, I have much fellow feeling for his lexicographic ordering of the two principles of justice. I agree very much that a full consideration of deontological questions should take priority over the issues that consequentialists emphasize. In my treatment, deontological issues are taken account of at the second rung of my ladder, while determining what putative social contracts are *feasible*. Their consideration therefore takes priority over consequentialist questions, which enter only at the third rung, when an *optimal* choice is made from the feasible set. It is true that the views I express about the nature of rights and liberties in Section 2.3.3 are very far from being Rawlsian. Nor do I follow Rawls in insisting that some particular set of deontological constraints be satisfied before consequentialist issues are examined. But it seems to me very Rawlsian in spirit that my approach insists that all deontological questions be clarified *before* any distributive questions are broached.

2.4   My Dear Sir, Clear Your Mind of Cant! ▣

Boswell was a good friend indeed to record such outbursts from Samuel Johnson so patiently. The friends of Thomas Hobbes [9, p.237] must also have been patient to endure his attacks on the great philosophers. He remarked, for example, that Descartes had no head for philosophy and would have done better to stick to geometry. As for Aristotle, he was: "...the worst Politician and Ethick—a Countrey-fellow that could live in the World would be as good." Vilfredo Pareto [199] was also lucky in his friends. They were required to tolerate attacks even on Plato, of whose reasoning he declared: "...that which is comprehensible is puerile; that which is not puerile is incomprehensible." For this section, I have need of similar friends since it now has to be confessed that, while I do not agree with Hobbes about Aristotle and Descartes, I think that Pareto comes pretty close to the mark on Plato.[68] Worse still, I am ready to extend the same strictures to Kant—except that I would argue that Kant is less often puerile than Plato.

It seems to me that Kant is wrong about *a priori* morality for the same reason that he is generally acknowledged to be wrong about *a priori* geometry. However, I would be happy not to court disapproval by criticizing his

---

[68] It is easy to win a dialogue when you write both sides of the argument and are allowed to change what the words mean in the middle of the discussion. If I were allowed to rewrite the exchange between Glaucon and Socrates, guess who would then come out on top! It seems to me that Plato's books are still read, not because of their substantive content, but because they are great works of literature.

reasoning if it were not for the fact that many people seem to see "Kantian rationality" as an optional alternative to common or garden rationality. If the latter doesn't seem to suit the occasion, so the view seems to be, then toss it back in the wardrobe and put on a Kantian hat instead. But perhaps even those who feel that I sadly undervalue Kant will agree that one has to be *consistent* in the way one reasons.

2.4.1   The Categorical Imperative

A hypothetical imperative tells you what you ought to do to achieve some objective. For example, you ought to eat your spinach if you want to grow up to be strong and healthy. A categorical imperative is an "ought" without an "if". It tells you what you ought to do independently of what your personal objectives may be.

According to Kant [134, p.88], true rationality lies in obeying the categorical imperative:

> Act only on the maxim that you would at the same time will to be a universal law.

A maxim in this statement is a personal rule for behavior. For example, break promises if it is expedient to do so; lie if it is convenient; commit suicide if things seem sufficiently bleak; steal money entrusted to your care if you can do so without risk. Kant asks whether we would will any such maxims to be a universal law. That is to say, would we choose to create a society in which "everybody behaved like that"?

Kant seems to think that answering yes involves one in formal contradictions. On breaking promises, for example, he observes that it would be impossible to make meaningful promises in a world in which it was a universal law that promises can be broken whenever they are difficult to keep. But, as we saw in Section 2.2.5, this is simply false. Promises can and do serve a vital role in helping us *coordinate* on equilibria in the game of life. If everybody believes that everybody else will keep his promise to play his part in coordinating on an equilibrium, then it will be in each person's individual interest to keep his own promise. Although such promises are easy for a rational person to keep, they are not at all meaningless. On the contrary, they are an indispensable lubricant for a society that is held together by a web of reciprocal dependencies. Kant is therefore wrong about the nature of meaningful promises, but it does not follow that his method of testing the morality of maxims necessarily fails. We do not have to prove that a world is logically impossible in order to know that we would not will it into existence if we had the power to do so.

Revealing Kantian Preferences. Consider the maxim: Never use a strongly dominated strategy. Gam:? theorists argue that it is *rational* to follow this precept. However, the maxim presumably fails Kant's test because, if it were adopted as a universal law, people would not cooperate in games like the Prisoners' Dilemma of Figure 2.8(a). Kant would therefore classify the the maxim as *irrational*.

But like is not being compared with like if a game theorist accuses a Kantian of behaving irrationally in the Prisoners' Dilemma. In Section 2.2.4, the theory of revealed preference was used to make almost a tautology of the fact that a rational person will never use a strongly dominated strategy. However, a Kantian can reply that it is *impossible* for a person who follows the categorical imperative to reveal the preferences assumed in the Prisoners' Dilemma. It may seem to a game theorist that a Kantian is playing the Prisoners' Dilemma, but this is because the game theorist has taken into account only the personal inclinations of the Kantian. But the categorical imperative calls for such personal preferences to be ignored when an action is chosen.

If a Kantian is not playing the Prisoners' Dilemma when he seems to be playing the Prisoners' Dilemma, what game is he playing? The experts seem agreed that it is not possible to make a definitive statement about what the categorical imperative decrees under all circumstances. However, I shall assume that, when placed in situations that seem like the Prisoners' Dilemma to a game theorist, a person who acts on Kantian principles will play *dove* himself when he knows that his opponent is to play *dove*. Otherwise there would be no grounds for game theorists and Kantians to disagree. A Kantian Adam will therefore reveal what one might call a "rational preference" for (*dove, dove*) over (*hawk, dove*) when acting in accordance with the categorical imperative.[69]

---

[69] The idea that a person might have one preference when he is wearing a hat labeled *homo economicus* and another when wearing a hat labeled *homo ethicus* is a staple in the literature. Harsanyi [106], for example, speaks of "ethical preferences" in a context not too far removed from that I have adopted here. However, it is never clear to me when and why he thinks we should don our ethical hat. Sen [238] plays with the more ambitious idea that people might contemplate a whole array of such "moral preferences" that would generate games ranging from the Prisoners' Dilemma through versions of the Stag Hunt Game to games like those of Figure 2.3(c) in which each player cares explicitly for the welfare of the other. He then equips his protagonists with personal preferences over moral preferences and uses these to discuss what game a player would prefer to be playing. I do not know how he sees this idea as relating to what he says elsewhere (Sen [236]) about revealed preference in a moral context, and it is possible that he has in mind some variant of my attempt to make sense of Kant in Section 2.4.3. However, a naive reading of what he says on these matters is irreconcilable with any approach that a game theorist might hope to rationalize. This is why I am so emphatic in Section 1.2.2 about separating the modeling of a problem from the analysis of the model.

The other preferences that a Kantian might reveal when seemingly play-ing the Prisoners' Dilemma seem less crucial, but if we follow Rawls[70] in thinking it appropriate to apply the maximin criterion, then the game that will be revealed by a Kantian acting rationally is the pure coordination game of Figure 2.8(b).[71] For example, Adam's payoff of 0 for the outcome (*hawk, dove*) in Figure 2.8(b) is derived from Adam and Eve's payoffs of 3 and 0 for the same outcome in Figure 2.8(a) by means of the formula $0 = \min\{3, 0\}$. A utilitarian seeking to explicate Kant might make Adam's payoff for (*hawk, dove*) equal to 3 on the grounds that $3 = 0 + 3$. He would then end up with the game of Figure 2.8(c).

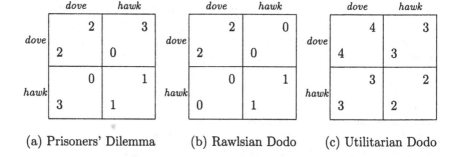

(a) Prisoners' Dilemma   (b) Rawlsian Dodo   (c) Utilitarian Dodo

Figure 2.8: What is a Kantian playing at?

A Kantian-style argument à la Rawls might now go like this. When I am offered a game that would be the Prisoners' Dilemma of Figure 2.8(a) if I were to follow my personal inclinations, I should pretend that I am playing the Dodo Game of Figure 2.8(b). My maxim for behavior should then be to use whatever strategy a game theorist would recommend if the payoffs in Dodo really did represent my personal inclinations and those of my opponent. In consequence, I will play *dove*. The maxim I am using will then be consistent with the categorical imperative because there is no other maxim that a rational being would prefer as a universal law. (A utilitarian would dispute the last point, but we do not need to take sides in this particular debate.)

---

[70]Recall from Section 1.2.1, that Rawls [214, p.67] sees himself as providing a "proce-dural interpretation of Kant's conception of autonomy and the categorical imperative".

[71]I have called this game Dodo elsewhere (Binmore [28]), since only someone studying the foundations of game theory would be sufficiently unfit for getting by in the world to think it necessary to find a reason why its solution should be (*dove, dove*).

2.4.2 Why Obey?

A great deal of unpleasantness would certainly be avoided if people could be persuaded to treat Prisoners' Dilemmas as though they were one of the other games of Figure 2.8. But how can it be *rational* to behave like this? More generally, why does the categorical imperative supposedly command the obedience of a truly rational being? For those brought up on Hume's [128, p.415] view that reason is merely the "slave of the passions", Kant's [134, p.63] beliefs about the function of reason are quite startling:

> In the natural constitution of an organic being . . . let us take it as a principle that in it no organ is to be found for any end unless it is also the most appropriate to that end and the best fitted for it. Suppose now that for a being possessed of reason and a will the real purpose of nature were his *preservation*, his *welfare*, or in a word his happiness . . . In that case nature would have hit on a very bad arrangement of choosing reason in the creature to carry out this purpose. For all the actions he has to perform with this end in view . . . could have been maintained far more surely by instinct than it ever can be by reason.

I do not think knee-jerk hostility to Kant's bad press for reason in this quotation is appropriate. From Nature's point of view, *homo economicus* is something of a nuisance compared with another invented hominid whom I shall call *homo behavioralis*. Both are modeled as stimulus-response machines, but *homo behavioralis* is programmed *directly* with behavior—like a chocolate-dispensing machine. He acts entirely instinctively. Nature can therefore manipulate *homo behavioralis* directly. His behavior can be tailored precisely to the environment by providing him with a suitable program. *Homo economicus*, on the other hand, can only be manipulated *via his preferences*. Nature cannot get directly at his behavior. So why should she make an expensive investment in brainpower in order to end up with a pesky hominid with ideas of his own, when she has an alternative model available who can always be relied upon to do what he is told?

In economics, the *principal-agent problem* involves a principal with certain aims who can only act through agents who may have aims of their own. The principal therefore seeks to design an incentive scheme that minimizes the distortions resulting from having to delegate to the agents.

Nature, as a principal, is blind, but her agent, *homo economicus*, can see his environment. Thus, although Nature *loses* fine control in being unable to modify his behavior directly, she *gains* access to information that would not otherwise have been available to her. If the environment changes sufficiently rapidly, the gains will outweigh the losses. *Homo behavioralis* is as blind as his mistress. She can learn about his environment indirectly by observing which types of *homo behavioralis* are reproductively successful.

But this learning process is very slow. In brief, *homo economicus* adapts quickly but *homo behavioralis* does not. This is why Nature has chosen *homo economicus* rather than *homo behavioralis*.

Kant is wrong to assume that everything is best fitted to its purpose. In particular, nothing says that *homo sapiens* is well equipped for living in large societies. If he were, there would presumably be less of *homo economicus* in his nature and more of some antlike variety of *homo behavioralis*. As a consequence, Nature has to live with societies that have second-best welfare properties. She cannot achieve the first-best outcomes to which those like Kant aspire because the latter are not incentive-compatible. That is to say, they are achievable only if the human beings who live in the society act in a manner that it is incompatible with their nature.

Kant's Teleology. In the preceding discussion, I fell in with Kant's teleological viewpoint without complaint. However, when Nature is treated as a person with aims and purposes in an evolutionary discussion, her existence is, of course, understood to be entirely metaphorical. One speaks of Nature as one might speak of Lady Luck after a good night at the tables, or as Adam Smith speaks of an Invisible Hand. Such entities have no real existence. They represent some complicated and ill-understood process through which chance and necessity combine to generate an outcome that looks orderly to our eyes. Since orderliness implies some sort of consistency, and consistency is the essence of rationality, we find it convenient to describe what we observe by saying that things are *as though* they had been rationally contrived. But, as in utility theory, we are always at risk, when using this descriptive device, of falling into the trap of reversing the implication and arguing that things are as we find them *because* they have been rationally contrived.

But Kant's teleology is not at all metaphorical. He comes straight out with the argument that, since reason is a poorer solution to the problem of securing our preservation than instinct would have been, then we are equipped with reasoning powers for some other purpose. So what does Kant [134, p.64] believe that rationality is for?

> ...its true function must be to produce a *will* which is *good*, not as a means to some further end, but in *itself.*

The last point is a constant theme for Kant. Rationality is not a *means* for achieving an end: it is an *end-in-itself.*[72] We impugn the integrity of

---

[72] Although Kant [133, p.332] continues to argue teleologically elsewhere, he seems no longer to feel it necessary to give an argument for such assertions in works that follow his *Groundwork for a Metaphysic of Morals*. They appear instead as *a priori* propositions that are supposedly characteristic of a kingdom where freedom holds sway. However, I

rationality if we use it for purposes that serve ends which are not inherent in its own nature. A rational will is autonomous, and therefore cannot be subject to whims and fancies deriving from our personal preferences. As Rousseau [223, p.19] puts it: "...the mere impulse of appetite is slavery, while obedience to a law that we prescribe to ourselves is liberty."

It may come as a surprise, but I want to insist that there is some sense in all this. The sense is certainly not to be found in Kant's teleology, nor in the wordplay that supposedly demonstrates that true freedom consists of doing your duty no matter how repugnant this may be. Nor do I think that what sense there is leads to Kant's categorical imperative.[73] However, it seems to me that there is a species of "categorical imperative" that a rational being cannot but obey. It is the law: *Be consistent.*

One might respond that this is not so much a law as a tautology. Would I also say that it is a categorical imperative that a square must have four sides? I agree that it is a tautology to assert that a rational person must be consistent, provided that consistency is suitably defined. I also agree that it sounds more than a little odd to instruct a square to have four sides. But this is what I believe to be the essence of what we should retain from what Kant is telling us about categorical imperatives.[74] That is to say, *only* a tautology can make any real sense in the role of a categorical imperative. For me, a categorical imperative is therefore a very humble notion with no pretensions to grandeur at all. However, as I have been saying repeatedly in this chapter, it is unwise to assume that the humble origins of a tautology imply that it is without power. In particular, I think we can learn a considerable amount about where Kant's reasoning goes awry by studying carefully what it might mean to issue the instruction: Be consistent.

2.4.3 Be Consistent!

What does it mean to issue the instruction: Be consistent? This is a big question to which many answers are possible. However, part of whatever answer is given must presumably be that the manner in which we go about

---

cannot even begin to identify with the frame of mind that must somehow be adopted for such *a priori* propositions to seem plausible, let alone inevitable. Nor do I see how to engage in a rational debate with someone in such a frame of mind.

[73]Indeed, I do not see why his form of the categorical imperative should be thought to follow, even if we were to grant that we have been gifted with the power of reason in order to provide us with a will for good. See Section 2.4.3.

[74]It is admittedly highly unKantian to interpet the categorical imperative as analytic. But a Humean like myself, who believes *a priori* synthetic propositions to be no more than sophistry and illusion, must be allowed some license if he is not to follow the advice of his master and so commit the categorical imperative to the flames (Hume [124, p.165]).

finding an answer needs to be consistent with the answer that we finally give. Consistency therefore demands that we choose a method of choice that chooses itself when applied to the problem of choosing a method of choice.[75] My immediate aim is to relate the idea to Kant's categorical imperative on the one hand, and to the game-theoretic notion of a Nash equilibrium on the other. However, it is important to understand that what follows is not an attempt to explain what Kant meant. It is a rather an attempt to explain what Kant might have meant if he had thought like a game theorist. Those with no taste for metaphysics are strongly advised to skip forward to Section 2.5.

My plan is to play with various renderings of the consistency criterion given above until one of these approximates Kant's categorical imperative, and then to consider what extra input is required to obtain his precise formulation. The first rewording of the criterion goes like this:

> **Version 1.** Choose a method of choice whose adoption would result in your choosing that method of choice.

It needs to be explained that a *method of choice* is to be understood as a comprehensive system of making choices that tells everyone how to resolve all decision problems. It may, however, tell different people to resolve the same decision problem in different ways. That is to say, a method of choice makes the right thing to do a function of the preferences and beliefs of the decision-maker. One might therefore think of a method of choice as a bundle of maxims potentially usable by any person whatsoever.

The next version translates the previous rendering into the language of revealed preference theory:

> **Version 2.** Prefer to have preferences whose adoption would lead to your preferring to have those preferences.

It is necessary to take careful note of the fact that the preferences referred to in this statement are not the personal inclinations of whoever is receiving instruction. They are the "rational preferences" that he would reveal if he were to follow his instructions.

The revealed preference version of the criterion is my favorite.[76] But to make progress in the direction of Kant, we need to abandon it in favor of the following amalgam of the two versions considered so far:

> **Version 3.** Choose a method of choice whose adoption would lead to your revealing a preference for that method of choice.

---

[75]I have used this criterion to obtain a version of Arrow's Paradox that does not depend on the Independence of Irrelevant Alternatives (Binmore [26]).

[76]I like it even better in the form: Prefer to prefer so that, in so preferring, you so prefer to prefer!

Let me translate this immediately into Kantian terms so that it becomes possible to understand why I think it useful to write down such an ugly hybrid:

> **Version 4.** Act only on the basis of a system of maxims that you would at the same time will to be your system of maxims.

This last translation needs some commentary. A "system of maxims" is just the "method of choice" of previous versions. Kant's "at the same time" is taken to mean that "you" are not simply to gratify your natural appetite for maxim systems. The "you" in Version 4 is the you who would be revealed if you were to behave according to the system of maxims that you were just instructed to adopt. This leaves the word "will" to be explained. When Kant and other German philosophers of the period use words that get translated into English as "will", I am never too sure precisely what they mean. However, in Version 4, "will" has a clear meaning. It refers to the preference that you would reveal if you were to adopt the system of maxims that you are instructed to adopt.

Version 4 is in the same ballpark as Kant's: Act only on the maxim that you would at the same time will to be a universal law. However, we still have a a long way to go since Version 4 is clearly a *personal* prescription. Both Kantians and game theorists[77] need to *depersonalize* the prescriptions for consistency that we have been studying up to now. So far our consistency conditions insist only that each individual be true to himself. But we need criteria that require some consistency *across individuals*.

Version 5 is a depersonalized variant of Version 1. It calls on everybody to choose a method of choice in a way that would make it possible for everybody consistently to choose the *same* method of choice.

> **Version 5.** Everybody should choose a method of choice whose adoption would result in everybody's choosing that method of choice.

It needs to be explained why Version 5 is stronger than Version 1. When different people use the same method of choice, they will usually be led to make different choices. However, Version 5 asks that, when the method of choice is applied to choosing a method of choice, it calls upon everybody to make the same choice regardless of their personal circumstances. Kant will be shortly be accused of proposing impossibilities. It should therefore be noted that the same accusation cannot be leveled at Version 5. To

---

[77]Or, at least, those metaphysically minded game theorists who think that firm foundations for game theory can be found by looking closely at what it means to be rational.

see this, simply note that the method of choice might call upon everybody to adopt the viewpoint of some particular citizen when choosing among methods of choice. The citizen chosen needs to be somebody with whom everybody can empathize adequately and whose identity is common knowledge, but otherwise he can be freely chosen. He might even be some kind of ideal observer, provided that the criticisms of Section 1.2.7 are not applicable.

What is the translation of Version 5 into Kantian language? It is a measure of the imprecision with which Kant expresses himself that it is necessary to say that the answer remains Version 4. However, since Version 5 and Version 1 do not say the same thing, Version 4 obviously needs to be reinterpreted somehow. The "everybody" at the beginning of Version 5 need not detain us, since Kant intends his categorical imperative to be addressed to everybody capable of acting rationally. However, the "everybody" in the middle of Version 5 requires that the "you" of Version 4 be assigned a new meaning. It is still to be understood that "you" choose according to the system of maxims that you were just instructed to adopt. However, the "you" who now chooses is no longer you-as-you-are, but you-as-you-would-be if everything other than your rationality were stripped away from your personality. You must therefore adopt the position of an ideal observer who is so much the essence of pure rationality that our conception of him would not differ from that of inhabitants of other planets. I guess that Kant's view is that the standpoint of such an ideal observer is the only one that is simultaneously feasible for *all* rational beings. My reservations about such metaphysical ideal observers are expressed in Section 1.2.7, but I shall not pursue such criticisms here.[78]

Although Version 5 does not carry the full spirit of what Kant means when he writes "you" in his categorical imperative,[79] I shall not attempt to come any closer on this point because we still have the major hurdle to jump if we are to win through to our destination.

Nothing yet has been said about "universal laws". To deal with this problem, yet more "everybodys" need to be introduced. Version 6 is obtained from Version 5 by insisting that, whenever a method of choice is chosen, it is chosen *for* everybody.

> **Version 6.** Everybody should choose a method of choice for everybody whose adoption would result in everybody's choosing that method of choice for everybody.

---

[78] One need not, in any case, follow Kant's grand scheme of legislating for *all* rational beings throughout time and space. One could, for example, restrict attention to one particular human society and envisage the ideal observer as being placed in some version of Rawls' original position.

[79] Version 5 does not even necessarily postulate an ideal observer, let alone Kant's quintessential rational being.

Version 6 is certainly a logically coherent statement that expresses a consistency condition that would need to be satisfied if individuals were able to make other people's choices for them. However, neither the mundane reasoning of game theorists nor the creative thinking of metaphysicians is sufficiently wild to encompass the idea that individuals can somehow command the obedience of others by a simple act of the imagination.[80] Version 7 eliminates the instruction to do something impossible by omitting the first "for everybody" from Version 6.

> **Version 7.** Everybody should choose a method of choice whose adoption would result in everybody's choosing that method of choice for everybody.

We are now very close to our goal, provided that a "universal law" can be identified with a method of choice honored by everybody. The translation of Version 7 into Kantian language is almost his categorical imperative:

> **Version 8.** Act on the basis of a system of maxims that you would at the same time will to be universal law.

It only remains to replace "Act on the basis of a system of maxims" in Version 8 by "Act only on the maxim". The new version is not so precise as the version it replaces, but Kant intends it only as a rationality test that each individual maxim must satisfy.

> **Kant's categorical imperative.** Act only on the maxim that you would at the same time will to be a universal law.

What conclusions are to be drawn from all this wordplay? It needs to be emphasized from the outset that one cannot just insert an "everybody" into a sentence wherever it takes one's fancy without drastically altering its meaning. The same goes when an "everybody" is removed from a sentence. Thus, in the progression given above, the idea that we were simply juggling with consistency conditions was abandoned when the phrase "for everybody" was deleted from Version 7. Or, to put the same thing another way, something substantive was added when the phrase "for everybody" was tacked on at the end of Version 5.

I take it that Rawls [214, p.252] is recognizing the fact that Kant goes beyond saying something about rationality alone when describing him as being concerned with beings who are both "rational *and equal*". However, although the notion of equality must presumably somehow be captured by introducing a universal quantifier somewhere, the question of *where* it

---

[80] Even if we were granted such transcendental powers, Kant would certainly not wish us to use them, since this would be to treat another rational being as a means-to-an-end rather than an end-in-itself.

should go is clearly something that needs to be argued very closely. My guess is that Kant did not do so because he was unaware that his placing of a universal quantifier generates a statement that goes beyond his aim of explicating what it is to be a rational being. I believe that Kant was under the impression that he was simply saying that rationality is the same for everybody. For myself, I think that the idea that rationality can be the same for everybody is already captured by the placing of the "everybodys" in Version 5.

In any case, it seems to me that the universal quantifier obviously cannot go where Kant places it unless one ceases to interpret the word "will" in his categorical imperative as signifying a revealed "rational preference". One cannot reveal a preference to do something impossible. And it is impossible for an individual to make what Kant [134, p.89] calls a "natural law" that everybody should behave as though they were clones. Indeed, it seems to me quite bizarre that a call to behave as though something impossible were possible should be represented as an instruction to behave rationally. Far from expressing a "rational preference", the "will" of Kant's categorical imperative seems to me to represent nothing more than a straightforward piece of wishful thinking.

Such criticism of Kant is now to be exacerbated by the suggestion that game theorists do not make the same mistake in juggling with their version of a categorical imperative. If the method of choice under discussion is interpreted as a method of choosing a strategy in a game with the standard common knowledge assumptions, then it would be natural for a game theorist to elaborate Version 5 to:

> **Nash's categorical imperative.** Everybody should choose a *consistent* method of choice whose adoption *by everybody else* would be consistent with everybody's choosing that method of choice.

I call this Nash's categorical imperative because it says that societies should be organized so that they select Nash equilibria in games. The significant addition[81] is the appearance of the phrase "by everybody else". This insertion into the middle of Version 5 is to be compared with the Kantian addition of "for everybody" at the end of Version 5. Both additions go beyond an attempt to say something about rationality alone. The Kantian addition calls for us to contemplate what we know to be impossible. The Nash addition does not ask that we contemplate something impossible, but it does propel us into a world in which no doubts exist about the rationality of others. Any call for action in such a world must surely satisfy some form

---

[81]The other addition is the insistence that only *consistent* methods of choice be considered. Among other things, this means that methods of choice that reveal intransitive preferences or that violate the sure-thing principle are not to be admitted.

of Nash's categorical imperative if it is not to be self-defeating. But we do not, alas, live in such a world.

I make this last point because, although it seems to me fun to argue that metaphysicians who know their business ought really to be led to the concept of a Nash equilibrium rather than to Kant's categorical imperative, I am fearful of being thought to believe that a metaphysical defense of the notion of a Nash equilibrium has more than entertainment value. Such a defense is easier to make than the evolutionary defenses that I think are really significant. And it certainly assists in explaining the idea of a Nash equilibrium to beginners to argue that someone writing a book on game theory would have no choice but to recommend the use of Nash equilibria if he had good reason to believe that his book would immediately become the unquestioned authority on how to play games. But such an *a priori* approach does not help us at all with such problems as that of deciding how Adam and Eve should independently convert what commonly known information they have into a recipe on how to coordinate in the Battle of the Sexes. Their problem would not exist if both knew what the other was going to do.

2.5 Time and Commitment

When Sidgwick [246, p.418] wrote:

> If the Utilitarian has to answer the question, 'Why should I sacrifice my happiness for the greater happiness of another?' it must surely be admissible to ask the Egoist, 'Why should I sacrifice a present pleasure for a greater one in the future? Why should I concern myself about my own future feelings any more than about the feelings of other persons?'

he did not perhaps mean to be taken too seriously. If Adam is unable to answer $7 \times 9 = \Box$? he might excuse himself by accusing Eve of being unable to answer $3 \times 2 = \Box$? But such a reply will cut no ice with their teacher—especially if Eve actually has a ready answer.

We care about the person we will be twenty-four hours from now in a way that we do not care about the guy who runs the local grocery store, because Nature has wired us up this way. We care about the welfare of the person we will be tomorrow in the same way that we care for food or shelter. Such concerns are built into our personal preferences.

From Nature's point of view, a person and his future alter egos are a community of clones. She does not care which members of this community get to replicate their genes because everybody in the community has identical genes. She just wants as much replication as possible overall.[82] However, we cannot be replicating our genes continuously with no time off for rest and recuperation. The person alive at any particular instant will therefore usually find it optimal to entrust this task to one of his or her future selves—just as a worker ant entrusts the task of replicating her genes to a sexually active sister. But, unlike ants, we do not operate on instinct alone. Nature therefore finds it necessary to manipulate our behavior by equipping us with personal preferences that exhibit a direct concern for our future welfare.

Nature certainly has no interest in building a direct concern for the guy who runs the local grocery store into our personal preferences. Unless he happens to be a relative, the significant genes that he carries will be rivals to yours and mine. It is true that people outside his kin group will often find it serves their individual interests to cooperate with him—as when someone enters his store to buy a six-pack of beer. But such a transaction is not carried out because either of the two parties cares directly for the welfare of the other. They coordinate their behavior for selfish reasons.

In the language of Section 1.2.6, we *sympathize* with the person we will be tomorrow, but we only *empathize* with the local grocer. We can put ourselves in the grocer's position to see things from his point of view, but we do not enter into his joys and sorrows sufficiently to make them our own. It is therefore a false analogy to liken the comparisons we make between different people at one time with the comparisons we make between the same person at different times.

Of course, those who deny a naturalistic origin for moral phenomena are not able to respond to Sidgwick's false analogy so easily. They resort to Kantian wordplay of some type to explain why we care for our future selves. But if such wordplay is to be accepted as valid for the same person at different times, why not for different people at the same time? Nagel [189] sees no reason why not, and goes on to construct a defense for altruism which, although not strictly Kantian, is nevertheless vulnerable to the same criticisms as Kant's.

The theme of Section 2.2.5 was that an argument is not refuted by showing that it leads to an unattractive conclusion. In considering Kantian arguments that lead to the conclusion that we should care for our future selves, we are observing the other side of the coin. In this context, Kantian arguments are sometimes offered that lead to correct conclusions. But this does not make the arguments right—it only makes them attractive.

---

[82]Which means that a qualification of the preceding sentence is necessary. Early replication is better than late replication for obvious reasons. This is presumably why people discount the future in their personal preferences.

However, it is not Kantian arguments that lead to correct conclusions that will be studied in this section, but Kantian arguments that lead to incorrect conclusions. Just as Kantians think that rationality calls upon each of us to behave as though we were all constrained by laws invented by a rational being who assumed that everybody would obey his laws, so there are those who believe that rationality calls upon each individual to behave as though he were constrained by laws invented by a past self who assumed that all his future selves would obey his laws. McClennen [175] speaks of "resolute choice" in such a context.

Game theorists would say that McClennen and those who argue like him are making unacceptable assumptions about the *commitments* that players can make. They treat analyses of games that take the possibility of Kantian commitment for granted as the worst kind of heresy. Their fierceness on this issue doubtless arises from the fact that game theorists themselves were making precisely the same type of error not so very long ago—and nobody is more zealous than a converted heretic. In any case, the remainder of this section is about why it is *tautological* that certain types of commitment cannot be made.

2.5.1 Blackmail

As explained in Section 1.2.4, game theorists have learned from Schelling [229] and others that it is necessary to be very careful indeed in dealing with the problem of commitment. They define a *commitment* to be an action in the present that binds the person who makes it irrevocably in the future. A commitment is therefore a binding unilateral promise. If Adam knows that Eve has truly made a commitment to act in some way in the future, then he will have no doubts at all that she will carry out the action to which she is committed.[83]

Section 1.2.2 emphasized the importance of not confusing the modeling of a problem with the analysis of the model. The same point has been made repeatedly in this chapter in condemning those who offer "wrong analyses of wrong games". The issue also faces us here. Section 1.2.2 points out that modeling players as *homo economicus* does not exclude their having the capacity to sympathize with others. Even Machiavelli presumably cared directly about the welfare of his children! Nor does it exclude the possibility that players can make certain types of commitment. However, the place to incorporate such assumptions about the nature of man is at the *modeling*

---

[83]One could, of course, invent theories in which Adam is not entirely convinced, but only attaches a high probability to her honoring the commitment she is known to have made. But such theories neither add or subtract very much from the relevant issues. In fact, it is wise to be particularly suspicious of paradoxical commitment stories in which the existence of some doubt in Adam's mind appears to be crucial to the argument.

stage when the game to be analyzed is constructed. For example, if Adam and Eve sympathize with one another, one can write this into their payoff matrix.[84]

The same goes for commitment assumptions. They should be built into the rules of the game when the game is constructed. As Schelling's [229] work makes clear, such modeling decisions should not be made lightly. It is hard for real people to make genuine commitments and still harder for them to convince others that a commitment has been made. If one builds commitment opportunities into the rules of a game, one therefore should have ready an explanation of the mechanism that enforces the commitment. For example, an alcoholic might enforce his commitment to give up drinking by taking a course of aversion therapy. A company might enforce its commitment not to pollute a lake by posting a large bond that will be forfeit if it fails to honor its undertaking. However, commitments are often enforced by more subtle mechanisms. For example, Eve might make a credible commitment to act tough in a negotiation because Adam knows that she cannot afford to acquire a reputation for being soft in such a context.

Even when the modeler is ready with such an informal explanation of how the commitment would be enforced, purists like myself do not find it very satisfactory to deal with commitment by introducing explicit commitment moves into the rules of a game. We would rather construct a larger game within which the enforcement mechanism can itself be formally modeled. It then becomes unnecessary to include formal commitment moves.[85] This is particularly important when the proposed enforcement mechanism is based on reputation considerations. Our intuitions on how such mechanisms work are not very firmly founded, and it seems unwise to rely on them too heavily. Game theorists therefore prefer to endogenize the notion of a reputation by looking at appropriate equilibria in a suitably defined repeated game. (See, for example, Fudenberg [78].)

However, whether a game theorist is a purist or not, he takes care of commitment at the *modeling* stage. He does not allow himself commitment assumptions when *analyzing* a game. To do so is to deny propositions that game theorists regard as tautological. To illustrate this point, the game of Blackmail given in Figure 2.9(a) will be used. The discussion will also serve to introduce some game-theoretic ideas that will be needed in studying bargaining theory in Chapter 1 of Volume II.

Games in Extensive Form.   The Prisoners' Dilemma of Figure 2.2(b) is a game in *strategic form*.[86] Each player chooses a strategy simultaneously.

---

[84] Although it need not be done so crudely as in Figure 2.3(c).

[85] Except perhaps as nonbinding statements of intent.

[86] Von Neumann and Morgenstern used the term *normal form.*

Blackmail is given in *extensive form*. Adam moves *first* and Eve may then get an opportunity to move *later*. The story is that Adam has discovered that Eve has a skeleton in her cupboard. He can behave like a dove and keep his knowledge to himself, or he can behave like a hawk and seek to extort money from her. She then has the opportunity of paying up like a dove or adopting the hawkish strategy of exposing Adam as a blackmailer, although this will surely result in her secret being made public

Figure 2.9(a) shows the extensive form of Blackmail. The lower node represents Adam's first move, at which he chooses between *hawk* and *dove*. If he chooses *dove*, the game is over and the payoff box to which his choice of *dove* would lead shows that he then gets a payoff of 2 while Eve gets a payoff of 5. If Adam chooses *hawk*, it is then Eve's move. Whichever of *hawk* and *dove* she chooses, the game ends at one of the two remaining payoff boxes.

Each extensive-form game also has a strategic-form representation. In Blackmail, this takes the particularly easy form shown in Figure 2.9(b) because each player has only two pure strategies. It is easy to use the strategic form to locate the two Nash equilibria in pure strategies. The Nash equilibria are (*hawk, dove*) and (*dove, hawk*). In the former, Adam blackmails Eve and she pays him off. In the second case, Adam chooses not to blackmail Eve because he expects her to denounce him if she does. Which of these Nash equilibria should we regard as the "solution" to the game?

An argument in favor of (*dove, hawk*) goes like this. Eve should make a commitment to expose Adam if he should seek to blackmail her. She should then take steps to ensure that Adam knows that her resolution is entirely genuine—that she will in fact respond to his play of *hawk* by playing *hawk* herself. Gauthier [84, p.173] would say that she should make it *transparent* that she has chosen a *disposition* to be tough. Adam will then be deterred from playing *hawk*, and the result will be the outcome that Eve likes best.

Backward Induction. The analysis of Blackmail just reviewed is very popular. But game theorists follow Reinhard Selten [235] in preferring an analysis that appeals to the principle of of *backward induction*. This principle calls for optimal play in a game between rational adversaries to be determined by looking first at what *would happen* at each of the final decision nodes if it should ever be reached.

Blackmail has only two decision nodes. The second and last requires Eve to make a decision between *hawk* and *dove*. Her payoff from *hawk* is 1 and her payoff from *dove* is 2. If she is rational, she will therefore choose *dove*. This decision is indicated in Figure 2.9(a) by doubling the line that corresponds to her choice of *dove*. Adam will predict that she will make this choice. He will therefore know that, if he chooses *hawk* at the first decision node, his payoff will be 5, as compared to the payoff of 2 he gets from

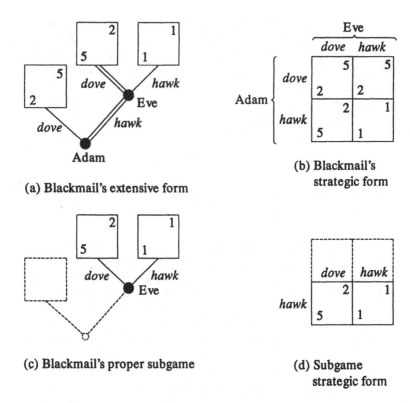

(a) Blackmail's extensive form

(b) Blackmail's strategic form

(c) Blackmail's proper subgame

(d) Subgame strategic form

Figure 2.9: Blackmail

playing *dove*. It is therefore rational for him to play *hawk*. This argument therefore leads to the Nash equilibrium (*hawk, dove*) that Adam likes best.

As in earlier sections of this chapter, the game-theoretic argument can be made into a *tautology* by appealing to the theory of revealed preference. If Eve is ever called upon to make a decision, why does she get a payoff of 2 from choosing *dove* and 1 from choosing *hawk*? If the payoffs are chosen in accordance with the theory of revealed preference, the answer is that the first payoff is chosen to be larger than the second because, if she were required to make a decision, then she would indeed choose *dove* rather than *hawk*. Similarly, if Adam knew that Eve would choose *dove* over *hawk* if called upon to choose, then he would himself choose *hawk* rather than *dove*, and this is why he is awarded a higher payoff for the former than the latter.

I appreciate that such reductions can be very frustrating for those who think that one can do more with logic than shuffle symbols around. It is certainly true that much is being swept under the carpet by such an appeal to revealed preference theory. Even more would be swept under the carpet if the game were longer so that Adam and Eve had the opportunity to learn something useful about how the other must be thinking as play proceeds. Eve's choice at a node late in the game would then depend on the inferences that she was able to draw about Adam's future intentions from his play in the past. However, all such complexities are abstracted away when appeal is made to the theory of revealed preference. As observed in Section 2.2.1, this will often make it exceedingly hard to know what the payoffs in a game ought to be. On the other hand, the advantages of the methodology in clarifying the underlying logic are overwhelming.[87]

Resolute Choice? When feeling uneasy about issues that seem to have been swept under the carpet, it is wise to elaborate the model with which one is working so that the problems that seem to have been evaded can be examined in the full light of day. The preceding backward induction analysis of Blackmail, for example, makes no mention of Eve's making and advertising the resolute choice that the rival commitment analysis places at the center of affairs. This is because a backward induction analysis can only take account of what is modeled in the game. If we want Eve to be able to advertise a resolute choice, it is necessary to look at a game that makes provision for such possibilities in its rules. An example of an appropriate elaboration of Blackmail is shown in Figure 2.10(a). In this new game, Eve moves first. At this first move, she can either tell Adam very firmly that she is resolved to expose him if he blackmails her, or she can equivocate. After this opening announcement, the players' strategic opportunities are then the same as in Blackmail.

As in Section 2.2.5, where the Prisoners' Dilemma was preceded by an exchange of promises, there are two possibilities. Either Eve's advertisement of her intentions at the opening move changes the payoffs in the Blackmail game that follows or it does not. Figure 2.10(a) represents the case when Blackmail is unchanged by Eve's opening announcement. The doubled lines in Figure 2.10(a) represent the choices to which a backward induction analysis leads. Notice that Eve's opening announcement is irrelevant to what follows, and so she is indifferent between putting up a show of firmness and equivocating. Under such circumstances, game theorists say that a show of resolution would be an incredible threat. Adam would simply dismiss her attempt to appear resolute as a piece of idle bombast.

---

[87] If the payoffs in the game are not interpreted according to revealed preference theory, then I have argued elsewhere (Binmore [32]) that backward induction is a tool that needs to be used cautiously. It assumes that players will play rationally in the future no matter how stupidly they may have played in the past. However, consequentialists may prefer Hammond's [93] view on the virtues of backward induction.

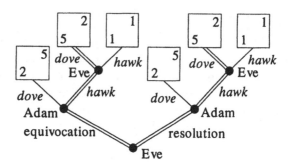

(a) Blackmail with idle bombast.

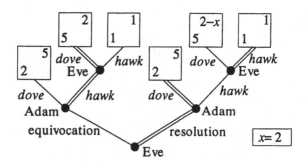

(b) Blackmail with a penalty for backing down.

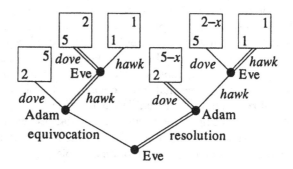

(c) Blackmail with a preliminary confession.

Figure 2.10: Elaborations of Blackmail

Figure 2.10(b) shows a possibility in which Eve's announcement does alter the payoffs in the Blackmail game that follows. If she announces her determination not to knuckle under, she suffers a penalty represented by x if she then goes back on her word.[88] The doubled lines in Figure 2.10(b) then show the result of a backward induction analysis for the case $x = 2$. Notice that, in this new situation, Eve will in fact expose Adam if he blackmails her after she expresses her resolution not to submit. The model therefore captures the intuition that the commitment analysis used to defend the Nash equilibrium (*dove, hawk*) for the original Blackmail game.

In fact, the preceding model can easily be adapted to make Eve's opening show of resolution into a true commitment. One need only delete her later opportunity to play *dove* altogether so that it becomes strictly impossible for her to reneg. However, this would seem to be a step in the wrong direction, since the mechanism by means of which the commitment is sustained is then left completely without explanation. A much more realistic model would replace Eve's opening move in Figure 2.10(b) by the opening move of Figure 2.10(c) at which she has the opportunity to reveal her secret to her family and friends in advance of any blackmailing attempt. She thereby loses x whether she is blackmailed or not, but now becomes invulnerable to a rational blackmailer. In the new situation, he can now see that the added scandal resulting from her secret becoming entirely public would not be enough to deter her from turning him in.

2.5.2 Subgame-Perfect Equilibrium

Game theorists follow Selten [235] in calling the strategy pair (*hawk, dove*) for Blackmail a *subgame-perfect equilibrium*. It gets this grand name because it is not only a Nash equilibrium for Blackmail, but also induces Nash equilibrium play in all Blackmail's subgames. In a game of perfect information,[89] a subgame-perfect equilibrium is just what one gets by applying backward induction. However, it will be worth exploring why this is the case by checking that the strategy pair (*hawk, dove*) to which we were led by backward induction is indeed subgame-perfect.

Blackmail has only two subgames: the whole game itself,[90] and the

---

[88]She might perhaps show Adam her doctoral thesis endorsing Kant's theory that it is "irrational" to lie to anyone under any circumstances whatever, and somehow convince him that it would cause her much more distress to sully her self-image as a rational person than to have her peccadilloes made public.

[89]This means that nothing that has happened in the game up to and including the instant at which a player makes a decision is concealed from him. Poker is a game of imperfect information because the players do not know what cards their opponents are holding when called upon to make bets.

[90]Which is regarded as a subgame of itself for the same reason that a set is regarded as a subset of itself.

game whose first and only move consists of Eve deciding between *hawk* and *dove* after she has been released. This proper subgame is shown in Figure 2.9(c). The corresponding strategic form is shown in Figure 2.9(d). To check whether (*hawk, dove*) is subgame-perfect is therefore easy. It is only necessary to ask whether the use of (*hawk, dove*) leads to each player replying optimally to the other in the subgame of Figure 2.9(c). Since Adam doesn't get to do anything in this subgame, one needs only to check that Eve's use of *dove* calls upon her to optimize in the subgame. Since she gets a payoff of 2 from playing *dove* and only 1 from playing *hawk*, this is easily verified.

It sometimes distresses beginners to learn that subgame-perfect equilibria call upon players to plan to play rationally even in subgames that will not be reached if the subgame-perfect equilibrium is used. Why should anyone care about what people would do under circumstances that will never arise?

Consider, for example, the subgame-perfect equilibrium indicated in Figure 2.10(c) by doubling optimal choices at each node. The equilibrium calls on Adam to plan to play *dove* if Eve begins by revealing her secret to those who matter to her most. Eve will then never have the opportunity of putting her plan of playing *hawk* into action should Adam try to blackmail her after she has come out of the closet. The subgame in which she would make this choice will never be reached if the subgame-perfect equilibrium strategies are used. Nevertheless, the fact that she *would* play *hawk* if this subgame *were* reached is vital to the argument. It is the fact that her plan to behave this way is credible to Adam that deters him from playing *hawk* after she has revealed her secret to her family and friends.

Politicians like to make fun of those who ask hypothetical questions, so that they have an excuse for not answering them. Often they pretend that counterfactual statements are intrinsically nonsensical—as when George Bush[91] responded in his own inimitable style to a hypothetical question about unemployment benefits by saying: "If a frog had wings, he wouldn't hit his tail on the ground." However, hypothetical questions are the lifeblood of game theory, just as they ought to be the lifeblood of politics. Players stick to their equilibrium strategies because of what would happen if they didn't. It is true that a rational player will not deviate from equilibrium play. But the reason that he will not deviate from equilibrium play is because he has predicted that unpleasant things would happen if he did.

Sometimes the subjunctives fly thick and fast in a game-theoretic discussion. Often they fly thicker and faster than is really necessary. But one

---

[91] *Newsweek*, 27 January 1992.

neglects them at one's peril—just as one neglects at one's peril what *would* happen if one *were* to cross a busy street without checking on the traffic.

2.6 Really Meaning It

By way of summary, let me repeat that it is regarded as a fallacy within modern utility theory to argue that action b is chosen instead of action a because the former yields a higher payoff. In discussing decision theory with philosophers, I frequently find their attitude to this issue very frustrating indeed. They commonly agree very readily that it is wrong to argue that modern notions of utility can be used to explain *why* a rational person chooses one action rather than another—but then proceed in the next breath to criticize utility theory as though its adherents still held to the naive and outmoded ideas of Bentham and Mill. Let me therefore insist that game theorists are not covert Benthamites seeking to conceal Victorian views on utilitarianism behind a mathematical smoke-screen. Game theorists actually believe what they say about utility. In particular, one cannot hope to understand what I shall have to say later about interpersonal comparison of utility without wholeheartedly accepting that the modern theory does *not* regard utility as being somehow derived directly from an assessment of the excess of pleasure over pain to be anticipated in different situations.

Modern utility theory makes a tautology of the fact that action b will be chosen rather than a when the former yields a higher payoff by *defining* the payoff of b to be larger than the payoff of a if b is chosen when a is available. The same considerations also apply when individual payoffs are replaced by a common good. In a nonteleological theory, the proposition that a society seeks the good is made into a tautology by *defining* the common good associated with a social state b to be larger than that associated with a social state a if society "chooses" b when a is available. Similarly, the validity of backward induction in analyzing a game with some dynamic structure can be made into a tautology by taking care to ensure that the payoffs are suitably defined.

One reason for emphasizing the tautological nature of these tools of the game theory trade is to direct the attention of critics away from the question of how a formal game is *analyzed* to the more rewarding question of how problems of human interaction should be *modeled* as formal games. It is true that the foundations of game theory are in flux, and that controversy exists about how certain games should be analyzed. But the games in this book are nearly all too simple to be worthy of controversy. Insofar as controversy arises between professional game theorists and laymen over the analysis of such simple games, it is usually because the latter insist on reading analytic statements as though they were synthetic. Such disputes are not totally barren. They often signal that a mistake has been made in the formal modeling of a real-life phenomenon. But the right response is not to get hot under the collar about assertions that have little or no substantive content. We ought to accept instead that it is sometimes necessary to come down from the ivory tower in which we so readily imprison ourselves by prematurely adopting a mathematical format to look again at our received opinions on the nature of real people and actual social institutions.

In the language of Section 1.2.2, we need for example to ask whether we are Dr. Jekylls or Mr. Hydes. To what degree do we genuinely *sympathize* with our fellows rather than just *empathize* with their difficulties? To what extent can we really commit ourselves now to actions that are likely to be distasteful to our future selves by a simple act of will? Game theory is neutral on such questions. Its methods work equally well for a society of rational Jekylls as for a society of rational Hydes. The difference between the two cases is simply that the games played by Jekylls will not be the same games as those played by Hydes. For example, it may be *impossible* for Jekylls to play the Prisoners' Dilemma. However, my own view is that a social contract theory based on such a rosy view of human nature is unlikely to find any useful domain of application.

I know that critics will be unresponsive to my plea that they try to accept that game theorists really mean what they say. After all, the objects of criticism always claim to be misunderstood. The next chapter is therefore devoted to a compendium of the leading arguments that critics have offered in defense of the fallacy that cooperation is rational in the Prisoners' Dilemma. I hope that this will at least make it clear that I have tried hard to take *their* position seriously.

In discussing the Prisoners' Dilemma, the current chapter confined its attention to the fallacy usually signaled by the question: Suppose everybody behaved like that? Section 2.4 irreverently argued that Kantian "rationality" is essentially this fallacy dressed up in fancy clothes. Although I tried to treat the topic in a light-hearted way, let me emphasize that I really do believe that Kant is badly wrong about these matters. Perhaps I am mistaken about human nature, and that, if we could learn to free ourselves from our irrational impulses, we would find that we are all really sheep in wolves' clothing. But this is not something that can be proved by Kantian *a priori* arguments. If we want to know what capabilities Nature has written into our genes, there is no alternative to the use of *empirical* methods.

On the subject of Kant, I have to admit to much fellow feeling for a certain Thomas Wirgman, of whom the mathematician Augustus de Morgan [182] wrote in his *Encyclopaedia of Eccentrics*: "The greatest compliment that Wirgman ever received was from James Mill, who used to say that he did not *understand* Kant." This is told as a joke against the "cracky and vagarious" Wirgman, who supposedly regarded any attention whatsoever from John Stuart Mill's father as a cause for self-congratulation. But I have a sneaking suspicion that the laugh was on the other side.

This is one of William Blake's sequence of illustrations on the life of Job. Here he seems to have just explained that squaring the circle is impossible.

Chapter 3

Squaring the Circle

> Remember always to study power as it is, not as you would have it be.
>
> Machiavelli, *The Prince.*

3.1 Introduction

Thomas Hobbes wrote so much good sense about so many subjects that one
is taken aback to learn that he was also an incorrigible squarer of the circle.
Unlike his modern brethren, he had the excuse that it was unknown in his
time that squaring the circle is impossible,[1] but he was as importunate as
they continue to be in soliciting the recognition of mathematicians for their
discoveries. Like all professionals, mathematicians are reluctant to waste
their time in explaining their trade to amateurs who have no interest in
receiving any instruction. They therefore treat circle-squarers pretty much
like door-to-door salesmen. This is not always wise—as I learned from a
eminent number theorist many years ago when I enquired about the source
of his spectacular black eye.

The game-theoretic equivalent of squaring the circle consists of justifying the use of a strongly dominated strategy in the one-shot Prisoners'
Dilemma. Chapter 3 is about the paradoxes and fallacies created by those
who so seek to rationalize the irrational. It is admittedly hard to admire the
ingenuity of thinkers who deny the tautological, but game theorists should

---

[1]Lindemann proved that π is transcendental. It follows that π is not a quadratic
surd, and hence that one cannot construct a square whose area is equal to that of
a given circle using a classical ruler-and-compass construction. The proof that π is
transcendental is not easy. But the proof that the companion problem of trisecting the
angle is impossible requires only a little high-school mathematics. See my *Logic, Sets
and Numbers*, Cambridge University Press, 1980.

perhaps think twice before joining mathematicians on the high horse from which they look down on those who square the circle. Given a purported proof that the circle can be squared, a mathematician will undertake to put his finger on precisely what is wrong with the argument. He can therefore tell us, not only why he is right, but why his critics are wrong. Game theorists cannot reliably do the same because they still do not properly understand the foundations of their subject.

This *caveat* is offered to make it clear that I do not want to claim the same authority for what I have to say against the arguments of those who justify the play of strongly dominated strategies in the Prisoners' Dilemma as I claimed in the previous chapter when arguing that such play is irrational. However, I believe it important that an attempt be made to isolate the errors built into the arguments that rationalize cooperation in the Prisoners' Dilemma, even though this will sometimes make it necessary to blunder around in areas that everyone knows are a philosophical minefield. There are two reasons for this. The primary motive is evangelical. Missionaries must first put to rest the ghosts of rival superstitions before preaching the true word.

The second reason will be less popular with game theorists. It seems to me that there is something positive to be gained from studying the paradoxes and fallacies that surround the Prisoners' Dilemma. An argument that is a wrong analysis of the wrong game may well contain the seeds of an argument that is capable of being the right analysis of the right game when used in the proper context. It is, for example, impossible to deduce the parallel postulate of Euclidean geometry from Euclid's other axioms. But, before this was demonstrated, many talented mathematicians strove to do precisely this—and sometimes convinced themselves that they had been successful. To dismiss their work as wasted effort would be easy, but misguided. Some of their results have stood the test of time and survive as theorems in *non*-Euclidean geometry. Similarly, it seems to me likely that it will be necessary to revive some of the arguments rejected in this chapter if game theory is ever to make any headway with the equilibrium selection problem.

3.2 Transparent Disposition Fallacies

In a game-theoretic context, people speak of players "having a disposition" to behave in a certain way when they plan to assume that players can make commitments beyond those built into the rules of the game. Dispositions are "transparent" if a player's opponents are necessarily aware of the commitments he makes. The reasons why game theorists think it wrong to assume that players can choose to have a "transparent disposition" were explained in Section 2.5.1 using the Blackmail Game as an example.

This section begins by describing two much-publicized attempts to justify rational cooperation in the one-shot Prisoners' Dilemma that both depend on the Transparent Disposition Fallacy. Bertrand Russell tells us to suspend disbelief when listening to a new argument for the first time, but these arguments require hanging it from skyhooks! However, I do not think the same is true when one ceases to insist that the arguments be applied to abstractly rational behavior, and begins to speculate instead about evolutionary histories that might conceivably lead to cooperation in the one-shot Prisoners' Dilemma. Much of the current section is therefore devoted to this question.

I believe that the evolutionary form of the argument fails at the impossible task of showing that out-of-equilibrium play can be sustained in the long run. However, such arguments can be adapted to provide useful conclusions about equilibrium selection in situations like the Stag Hunt Game where more than one equilibrium is available. The discussion is also relevant to equilibrium selection in repeated games, especially to the indefinitely repeated Prisoners' Dilemma, where the virtues of the strategy TIT-FOR-TAT have been much oversold.[2] The section therefore concludes by pointing out that the evolutionary arguments advanced by Axelrod [14, 15] and others in defense of TIT-FOR-TAT are less than overwhelming. In particular, no compelling reasons exist for supposing that Nature will necessarily select a neighborly strategy like TIT-FOR-TAT. Nasty strategies that begin by playing *hawk* have at least as much right to a place on Nature's agenda.

3.2.1 "Metagames"

Section 2.2.6 discusses a number of games that are not the Prisoners' Dilemma, but which are often analyzed as though they were. Here we look at something more sophisticated. Nigel Howard [122] offers a variety of games as substitutes for the Prisoners' Dilemma. He refers to the substitute games as "metagames". The metagame studied in this section is what he calls the 1-2 metagame based on the Prisoners' Dilemma of Figure 2.2(b). This is usually explained using the metagame's payoff matrix given in Figure 3.2. However, I plan to attempt a simpler exposition based on the extensive-form game shown in Figure 3.1(a).

---

[2] As Martinez Coll and Hirschleifer [171] put it, "Owing mainly to Axelrod's studies of evolutionary competition in an iterated Prisoners' Dilemma context, a rather astonishing claim has come to be widely accepted: to wit, that the simple reciprocity behavior known as TIT-FOR-TAT is a best strategy not only in the particular environment modeled by Axelrod's simulations but quite generally. Or still more sweepingly, that TIT-FOR-TAT can provide the basis for cooperation in complex social interactions among humans, and even explains the evolution of social cooperation over the whole range of life." Others have commented similarly. Vanberg and Congleton [264] are particularly insightful.

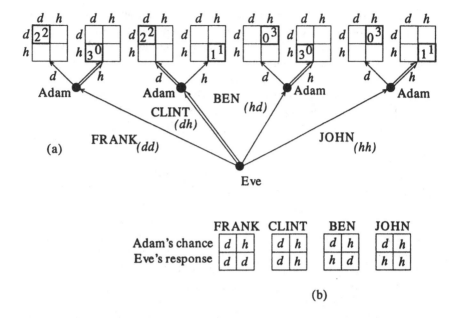

Figure 3.1: Choosing a transparent disposition

The extensive form of Figure 3.1(a) shows Eve making the first move in the role of player II. She chooses what Gauthier [84, p.170] calls a *disposition*, but which I shall call a *persona*. The four possible personas from which Eve may choose are FRANK, CLINT, BEN and JOHN. It may be helpful in remembering their respective characters to think of their names as familiarized forms of St. Francis of Assisi, Clint Eastwood, Benito Mussolini and Genghis Khan.

If Eve assumes the FRANK persona, then she will play *dove* in the Prisoners' Dilemma whatever action Adam may choose. If Eve assumes the JOHN persona, then she will play *hawk* whatever Adam does. The character played by Clint Eastwood in the spaghetti westerns is the basis for the CLINT persona. In the evolutionary literature, such a persona is said to be a "retaliator". If Eve assumes the CLINT persona, she will play *dove* if Adam plays *dove*, but she will play *hawk* if Adam plays *hawk*. Finally, Benito Mussolini is offered as the classic bully. If Eve assumes the BEN persona, then she will play *hawk* if Adam plays *dove*, and *dove* if Adam plays *hawk*. Figure 3.1(b) summarizes the properties of the four personas available to Eve.

The next move in the game of Figure 3.1(a) is Adam's. When he makes this move, he knows the persona chosen by Eve. Gauthier [84, p.173] would say that Eve's choice of a disposition is *transparent* to Adam. Thus, for example, when Adam chooses between *dove* and *hawk* after Eve has chosen the persona BEN, he knows that he will get a payoff of 0 from the use of *dove* (because Eve will then play *hawk*), and a payoff of 3 from the use of *hawk* (because Eve will then play *dove*). His optimal choice under these circumstances is therefore to choose *hawk*, and the line representing this choice in Figure 3.1(a) has therefore been doubled. After doubling the lines representing the optimal choices at Adam's other decision nodes, the principle of backward induction explained in Section 2.5.1 calls for us next to consider Eve's choice of persona. If Adam behaves rationally, Eve will get 0 from choosing FRANK, 2 from choosing CLINT, 0 from choosing BEN, and 1 from choosing JOHN. Her optimal choice is therefore CLINT, and so the line representing this choice has been doubled in Figure 3.1(a).

As explained in Section 2.5.2, the use of backward induction always leads to a subgame-perfect equilibrium in a finite game of perfect information. The subgame-perfect equilibrium shown in Figure 3.1(a) by doubling suitable lines requires Eve to make the strategy choice CLINT, and for Adam to make the strategy choice *hdhh*. Before explaining how Adam's pure strategies are labeled, it should be noted that he has a very large number of pure strategies. Recall that a pure strategy must specify what he should do under *all* contingencies that might arise in the game. Adam therefore has $16 = 2 \times 2 \times 2 \times 2$ pure strategies, because he has two possible choices at each of four decision nodes. The pure strategy labeled *hdhh* means that he should play *hawk* if Eve chooses FRANK, *dove* if Eve chooses CLINT, *hawk* if Eve chooses BEN, and *hawk* if Eve chooses JOHN. For similar reasons, Eve's pure strategy CLINT has been labeled *dh* in Figure 3.2, which is the strategic form of the 1-2 metagame whose extensive form is shown in Figure 3.1(a).

Notice that (*hdhh, dh*) is only one of three Nash equilibria starred in Figure 3.2. However, the other Nash equilibria may be rejected because they are not subgame-perfect—or, as Nigel Howard emphasizes, because Adam's pure strategy *hdhh* weakly dominates all its rivals.

If Adam and Eve use the unique subgame-perfect equilibrium of the 1-2 metagame, Eve will choose CLINT, Adam will choose *dove*, and the result will be that they cooperate in the Prisoners' Dilemma. It is simple enough to observe that the 1-2 metagame is not the Prisoners' Dilemma, and so the fact that rational cooperation is possible in the 1-2 metagame does not imply that rational cooperation is possible in the Prisoners' Dilemma. However, I want to try and explain precisely why one cannot sensibly substitute the 1-2 metagame for the Prisoners' Dilemma.

In the first place, the extensive form of Figure 3.1(a) takes for granted that Eve can make commitments. It is assumed that she can make a com-

	dd	dh	hd	hh
dddd	2 / 2	2 / 2	3 / 0	3 / 0
dddh	2 / 2	2 / 2	3 / 0	1 / 1
ddhd	2 / 2	2 / 2	0 / 3	3 / 0
ddhh	2 / 2	* 2 / 2	0 / 3	1 / 1
dhdd	2 / 2	2 / 2	3 / 0	3 / 0
dhdh	2 / 2	1 / 1	3 / 0	1 / 1
dhhd	2 / 2	1 / 1	0 / 3	3 / 0
dhhh	2 / 2	1 / 1	0 / 3	1 / 1
hddd	0 / 3	1 / 1	3 / 0	3 / 0
hddh	0 / 3	2 / 2	3 / 0	1 / 1
hdhd	0 / 3	2 / 2	0 / 3	3 / 0
hdhh	0 / 3	* 2 / 2	0 / 3	1 / 1
hhdd	0 / 3	1 / 1	3 / 0	3 / 0
hhdh	0 / 3	1 / 1	3 / 0	1 / 1
hhhd	0 / 3	1 / 1	0 / 3	3 / 0
hhhh	0 / 3	1 / 1	0 / 3	* 1 / 1

Figure 3.2: The payoff matrix for the 1-2 metagame based on the Prisoners' Dilemma

mitment to any of the four personas FRANK, CLINT, BEN and JOHN. To see why a commitment is involved, suppose that Eve chooses CLINT and then Adam chooses *dove*. The CLINT persona is then supposed to respond to Adam's playing *dove* by playing *dove* in return. But Eve will not wish to act as the CLINT persona requires after she learns that Adam is to play *dove*, because, as always in the Prisoners' Dilemma, the play of *dove* yields a lower payoff than the play of *hawk*. If she continues to act as the CLINT persona demands, it must therefore be because she has made a *commitment* to do so.

But, for the analysis of the 1-2 metagame to be relevant to the Prisoners' Dilemma, it is not enough that Eve be allowed to make commitments. She must also be able to convince Adam that she has indeed made a commitment. Her resolution must be naked for all the world to see. Not only this, somehow Adam's intended play in the Prisoners' Dilemma must also be transparent. Otherwise Eve would not be able to choose a persona whose choice of action in the Prisoners' Dilemma depends on the choice of action made by the opponent.

Frank's [75] *Passions within Reason* is the place to look if seeking reasons why such constructs as the 1-2 metagame are worthy of study. He argues that we have the power to train ourselves to adopt certain dispositions. What is more, such dispositions will be transparent because biology has wired us up so that it is hard to conceal our emotions from others. Section 3.2.3 takes up these points. At this stage, I want only to note that, even if it were possible to agree wholeheartedly with Frank, it would still be false that an analysis of the 1-2 metagame is an analysis of the Prisoners' Dilemma.

3.2.2 Constrained Maximization

Gauthier's [84, p.157] theory of "constrained maximization" can be seen as a symmetrized version of the Metagame Fallacy of the previous section. He distinguishes a *straightforward maximizer* from a *constrained maximizer*, and argues that it is "rational" to adopt the latter disposition. In the language of the previous section, Gauthier argues that the CLINT persona is more "rational" than the JOHN persona. Gauthier understands that it is necessary for the choice of persona to be properly advertised, but finesses this difficulty by writing:

> Since our argument is to be applied to ideally rational persons, we may simply add another idealizing assumption, and take persons to be *transparent*. Each is then directly aware of the disposition of his fellows, and so is aware whether he is interacting with straightforward maximizers or constrained maximizers. Deception is impossible.

He later notes that transparency can be replaced by *translucency*, by which he means that a player need not be sure of identifying an opponent's disposition for the argument to go through. It is enough if his disposition can be identified with a sufficiently high probability.

Section 2.5.1 explains why game theorists do not believe that it is acceptable to assume that we can commit ourselves to a disposition and then successfully advertise our commitment to those around us. Unless one wishes to follow Gauthier in arguing that transparency should be taken to be one of the attributes of an ideally rational person, there seems nothing to add to this earlier discussion. Such a dismissal of what Gauthier [85, p.185] regards as the "most fruitful idea" in his *Morals by Agreement* is certainly not very prolix. Gauthier [85, p.186] described a somewhat longer account (Binmore [23]) of why constrained maximization should be rejected as "offhand". Let me therefore devote a paragraph to his rejoinder in the hope of making it clear that the fact that the argument against constrained maximization can be expressed in a sentence or two does not imply that I feel at all offhand about this or any other of the fallacies that bedevil game theorists.

In my view, Gauthier's best line of defense to attacks on constrained maximization would be to agree that it is seldom appropriate to model real-life situations using the one-shot Prisoners' Dilemma. He would then be free to tell us more about the game that he actually does analyse: Some meeting of minds might then be possible. But Gauthier [85, p.186] chooses instead to reject game-theoretic methodology altogether. He says that the "received theory of rational choice" is "conceptually inadequate" and should be replaced by some "alternative theory that embraces constrained maximization". He believes that the received theory makes the claim that "utilities and only utilities provide reasons for acting". To such remarks, an economist can only respond that economic textbooks routinely explain that such a Benthamite interpretation of modern utility theory is mistaken. Luce and Raiffa [158, p.32] is the standard reference (but see also Sections 2.2.4, 2.3.5, and 2.6). Gauthier is wrong at a very fundamental level in supposing that modern utility theory seeks to explain *why* rational people choose one action rather than another. The best it can do is to point out that inconsistent behavior cannot be rational. Those of us who resort to the theory of revealed preference, explicitly reject the claim that we have something to say about the "reasons for acting" which I agree would need to be explained within a fully articulated theory of rationality. But no such theory exists. Like a Victorian geographer who comments only on the coastline of darkest Africa, we therefore confine our remarks to what little can reliably be said on a subject that is largely mysterious. Just as a Victorian geographer would have agreed that Africa actually does have an interior, so we agree that a rational player will doubtless have reasons for choosing the actions that revealed preference theory takes as its data. But, once enough data has been supplied, the theory undertakes to *deduce* how the player will behave in other situations—using only the assumption that his future actions will be consistent with his past actions. Often the data taken for granted in specifying a game is subjunctive. In Section 2.2.4, it may only be an hypothesis that Adam would choose *hawk* if he knew that Eve were certain to choose *dove*. But that such hypotheses are to be subsumed is what game theorists *mean* when they say that the game to be played is the one-shot Prisoners' Dilemma. It is true that it then becomes almost a tautology that cooperation in the Prisoners' Dilemma is irrational. But, for this very reason, it makes as much sense to propose an alternative theory of rationality that justifies cooperation in the Prisoners' Dilemma as it would to propose a replacement for traditional arithmetic in which $2 + 2 = 5$. One might perhaps seek to redefine the symbols of arithmetic as Gauthier implicitly seeks to redefine the Prisoners' Dilemma, but how could one reasonably expect anything but confusion to follow from such a maneuver?[3]

Sometimes it is said that Gauthier's constrained maximization is not only a nonstarter as a rationality principle, but that his model is entirely incoherent. This at least is a charge on which I am willing to defend Gauthier. The difficulty is that, in a symmetrized version of the Metagame Fallacy, both Adam and Eve must choose their personas *simultaneously*. But each persona's choice of action in the Prisoners' Dilemma is contingent on the choice of the other. What I do therefore depends on what the other guy does. But this in turn depends on what I do. It therefore seems that we are trapped in a self-reference problem. However, self-references are not intrinsically paradoxical. For example, this sentence is self-referential without being paradoxical.

John Howard [121] considers a computer that has access to the printout of the program of an opposing computer. Using an ingenious device proposed by Quine, such a computer can be programmed to play *dove* in the Prisoners' Dilemma if and only if its opponent has the same program as itself. The program consists of a sequence of commands equivalent to the following algorithm:

> Play *dove* if and only if the opponent's instructions take the form X"X", where X is the material in quotes that follows this sentence.

---

[3] Compare, for example, Gauthier's [85, p.179] appeal to received game-theoretic wisdom when responding to Sugden's [257] criticism of his bargaining theory with his denial of received game-theoretic wisdom a few pages later when responding to my criticism of constrained maximization. Surely Gauthier must see that the arguments for using a subgame-perfect equilibrium in Rubinstein's bargaining model (Chapter 1 of Volume II) cannot possibly be correct if his arguments against using a Nash equilibrium in the Prisoners' Dilemma are right.

"Play *dove* if and only if the opponent's instructions take the form
X"X", where X is the material in quotes that follows this sentence."

This observation makes it possible to redefine the personas CLINT and JOHN
as shown in Figure 3.3(b). The perennial from the literature that I am
calling Gauthier's "metagame" is then as shown in Figure 3.3(a). The
game has two Nash equilibria, (CLINT, CLINT) and (JOHN, JOHN). Unlike
the very similar Stag Hunt Game of Figure 2.5(a), all of the arguments
favor the selection of the Pareto-dominant equilibrium (CLINT, CLINT). If
the Prisoners' Dilemma were Gauthier's "metagame", it would therefore
indeed be true that cooperation was rational in the Prisoners' Dilemma!

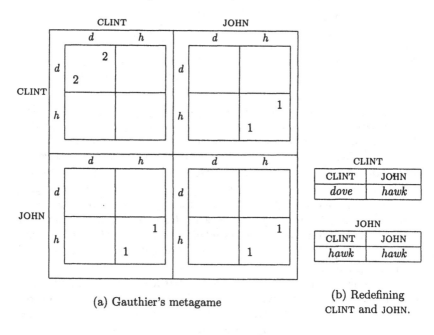

(a) Gauthier's metagame

(b) Redefining
CLINT and JOHN.

Figure 3.3: Knowing who to trust

3.2.3   Cheap Talk and Evolution

Why are we so readily seduced by the fallacies that purport to prove that
principles like Gauthier's [84, p.157] constrained maximization are rational? Part of the reason must surely be that, although we operate largely
on the principle "monkey see, monkey do", we do not like to think of ourselves as monkeys. We prefer to measure ourselves against the ideal of the

philosopher-king, living a carefully considered life of impeccable rationality. However, this flattering self-image is not easy to reconcile with the undeniable fact that much of what we think and do is determined almost entirely by what is customary in the society in which we live. But, rather than accept that we do not understand much of what moves us,[4] we prefer to seize upon any story that comes along which seems to prove that what we find ourselves doing is actually what we would elect to do if we were the philosopher-kings we fancy ourselves to be—especially if the story has already been accepted by the other monkeys in our tree.

In saying this, I am agreeing with Dawes *et al.* [60], Frank [75] and many others who argue that *homo sapiens* sometimes does behave in a manner that looks like constrained maximization. But I do not believe that such behavior has evolved for use in one-shot situations. I believe that it survives because it is needed to sustain equilibria in *repeated* games. It is no accident that the CLINT persona of Section 3.2.2 behaves so similarly to someone using the TIT-FOR-TAT strategy of Section 2.2.6. Nor should we be surprised if the physiological and psychological mechanisms that have evolved to sustain equilibria in repeated games should sometimes be triggered inappropriately in one-shot situations. We should only be surprised if such one-shot behavior survives when it is costly and triggered frequently.

The Role of Emotions. Frank [75] is perhaps the most eloquent of those who put the case for emotions like anger, contempt or guilt[5] serving as hard-wired commitment mechanisms. Once our angry button has been hit, so one of the stories goes, we have no choice but to seek revenge against whoever has caused the offense. Moreover, our disposition to behave in such a potentially self-destructive manner is either literally written in our faces by the action of muscles over which we have little or no conscious control, or else is signaled by other involuntary body language.

I do not think it necessary to repeat the anecdotes usually told in support of such contentions, nor to reproduce the pictures showing people or animals in characteristically angry or fearful poses. We all know what it feels like to experience strong emotions, and how hard it is, once in their

---

[4]Notice that I am not saying that habituated thinking and behavior patterns are necessarily irrational. On the contrary, I believe that they usually make a great deal of sense in the situations for which they are adapted. However, it is not necessarily easy to determine the situations for which they are adapted—nor to see why they are useful even when their domain of application has been recognized.

[5]Personally, I think it unlikely that Adam Smith's moral sentiments—anger, contempt, disgust, envy, greed, shame, and guilt—all have genuine physiological referents. Under certain circumstances, our bodies pump chemicals into our bloodstreams. We then invent myths in seeking to explain to ourselves what we are experiencing. Such myths typically do not separate the train of events that caused the experience from the experience itself.

grip, to conceal what one is feeling from others. But it is not by chance that sane people experience strong emotions only rarely. In familiar situations that are important to us, we almost always have our emotions under tight control. I am an unusually volatile person myself, but I have never found much difficulty in listening with every appearance of respect to the opinions of those with the power to influence my career for better or worse. Nor do I think my hypocrisy has frequently been detected. My experiences at the poker table have also made me very skeptical of the view that people cannot conceal their emotions.[6] Indeed, actors are able to project a whole variety of emotions more or less on demand.

Experiments. Against such views, Frank [75, p.157] offers experimental evidence that subjects allowed to establish a rapport during a thirty-minute fraternization period previous to playing the one-shot Prisoners' Dilemma of Figure 2.2(b) with dollar payoffs can achieve cooperation rates of 68 precent. Subjects asked to predict whether their partner would cooperate or defect after the discussion period were right 75 percent of the time when predicting the play of *dove*, and 60 percent of the time when predicting *hawk*. Many other studies confirm that such high levels of cooperation are commonplace, not only in Prisoners' Dilemma experiments, but also in experiments in which subjects make private contributions to a public good that will not be provided if the sum of what is contributed is not sufficiently large.

As an experimenter myself,[7] I have to warn against being too credulous about such experimental results. I am not saying that the behavior reported is not observed.[8] But how much attention should we pay to experiments that tell us how inexperienced people behave when placed in situations with which they are unfamiliar, and in which the incentives for thinking things through carefully are negligible or absent altogether? One cannot successfully mimic the real-life situations that matter to social contract discussions in the laboratory, but one can at least try to come as close as one can. The unfamiliarity of the decision problem can be countered by using interactive computer demonstrations with graphic displays that make the mechanics of the problem painless to learn. The inexperience

---

[6]I am not denying that people often give themselves away at the poker table by making inadvertent signals. Expert poker players learn to look out for such "tells" in their opponents' behavior. But they also learn to look out for tells in their *own* behavior with a view to eliminating them—hence the term "poker-faced".

[7]For example, Binmore *et al.* [42, 27, 41, 39, 44].

[8]Although authors are commonly very selective in what they choose to report about the experimental literature. For example, I do not suppose that Frank [75, p.174] would have cited Binmore *et al.* [42] even in passing if he had not been under the mistaken impression that it was supportive of his point of view!

of the subjects can be met by allowing them to play over and over again, against new opponents each time, until their behavior settles down into a stable pattern. Providing adequate incentives is simply a matter of paying enough money.

Only when an experimenter has made some attempt to meet such requirements does it make sense to regard his results as relevant to social contract issues. My advice is therefore to be suspicious of experiments in which the subjects were expected to learn the task required from them by reading several pages of typewritten instructions.[9] I suggest being equally suspicious of experiments in which the subjects were given little time for trial-and-error learning, not only about the problem itself, but also about the manner in which others people like themselves react to it. Finally, I think that no credence whatsoever should be accorded to experiments in which the subjects' performance is not rewarded with proper regard to their opportunity costs. In the Frank *et al.* [75] experiment, for example, a subject could gain one dollar by dishonoring any promise he may have made to play *dove* during the thirty-minute preplay fraternization period. But one does not need any training in experimental psychology to see that a one-dollar incentive is peanuts in such a context.[10]

In brief, two questions about experiments with human subjects always need to be asked. Does the behavior survive when the incentives are increased? Does it survive after the subjects have had a long time to familiarize themselves with all the wrinkles of the unusual situation in which the experimenter has placed them? If not, then the experimenter has probably done no more than inadvertently to trigger a response in the subjects that is adapted to some real-life situation, but which bears only a superficial resemblance to the problem the subjects are really facing in the laboratory. In the metaphor of Section 2.3.3, we would then simply be observing a human analogue of Konrad Lorenz's baby jackdaw taking a bath on a marble-topped table. As for the experiments that seem to show that people do not use equilibrium strategies when these are Pareto-inefficient, there is now much evidence, especially in case of private contributions to the provision of a public good (Ledyard [147]), that such behavior has a strong

---

[9]This remains good advice even when the task involved is quite simple. If the experimenter read the instructions aloud, I would advocate even more suspicion being directed at the conclusions. I do not think the experimenter should even be present during the experiment. Anyone who interacts directly with the subjects should have no personal interest in the outcome of the experiment.

[10]Even in 1988! At that time, the conventional wisdom among American experimental economists was that something in the region of $10 would be a minimal meaningful incentive. In 1991, my subjects were leaving my laboratory after a half-hour session with $25 or more. This certainly makes it expensive to run experiments, but there is ample evidence (Vernon Smith [249]) that one does not get the same results if one is mean about the payoffs.

tendency to unravel, both when the incentives are increased and as the subjects become familiar with the problem and the behavior of their peers. In the long run, behavior tends to converge on whatever the equilibrium of the game under study happens to be.

Constrained Maximization in Bargaining?

The story is much the same outside the laboratory. I am sure that humans are capable of preprogramming their behavior to some extent. I am also sure that the fact that one is preprogrammed in a particular way can often successfully be communicated to others. I also agree with Frank [75, p.261] that such behavior can sometimes create an evolutionary advantage for those who practice it. However, for the reasons discussed later in this section, I do not believe that such behavior can survive in situations that are genuinely crucial to what holds societies together. It can survive only when the evolutionary pressure in favor of more complex behavior is too slight to be effective. This is why the examples of real-life constrained maximization are limited to picayune topics—like tipping in restaurants. However, when it comes to matters that are really important in human social history, things are very different.

Bargaining is a good example. Suppose that Eve has an apple to sell that Adam would like to buy if the price is not too high. Adam's reservation price $a is the most he would be willing to pay for the apple—the amount that makes him indifferent between buying the apple and getting along without it. Similarly, Eve's reservation price $e is the least for which she is willing to sell the apple. If $a < e$, there is no point in their discussing an exchange because the apple is worth more to Eve than to Adam. However, if $a \geq e$, Adam and Eve can create a surplus of $$(a - e)$ by agreeing to exchange the apple. How they divide this surplus will depend on the course taken by their bargaining over the price.

There is nothing very interesting in this story when Adam and Eve's reservation prices are common knowledge. However, if their reservation prices are not common knowledge, then there is a risk of a coordination failure. If Adam and Eve are rational, each will seek to exploit the ignorance of the other. Some of the time, they will be so sharp that they will cut themselves. That is to say, sometimes they will fail to reach an agreement even though $a > e$, and so there is a positive surplus to be divided.[11]

---

[11]Consider, for example, the case in which it is common knowledge that both a and e are drawn independently from a uniform distribution on $[0, 1]$, but that only Adam knows the realized value of a, and only Eve knows the realized value of e. Of course, while Adam and Eve are bargaining, they may be able to deduce information about their partner's reservation price from the proposals that he or she makes. If they are rational, Adam and Eve will therefore be very careful about what they say. Indeed, they will regard the negotiation as a species of *game* for which an optimal strategy must be

Bargaining therefore provides an ideal arena for constrained maximization. If we were all to adopt a transparent disposition to reveal our true reservation prices in bargaining situations when confronted by those with a similarly transparent disposition, then we would never have to suffer the losses in surplus that arise when we lie to each other. However, far from providing us with a disposition to tell the truth, social evolution has trained us instead not to think of the untruths that we tell each other when bargaining as lies. But, as Daniel Defoe [63, p.229] reminds us in his *Complete English Tradesman* of 1727: "...for the buyer as often says, I won't give a farthing more, and yet advances; as the seller says, I can't abate a farthing, and yet complies. These are, as I call them, *trading lies.*" Nor, as Defoe [63, p.227] assures us, were the Quakers of his time who sought to "deal honestly" able to remain in business.

Evolutionary Stability. The rest of this section reviews some of the evolutionary arguments offered in support of constrained maximization in the context of the one-shot Prisoners' Dilemma.[12] To follow those who argue in this way, it is necessary to abandon *homo economicus* as our model of man in favor of the equally fictional *homo behavioralis* introduced in Section 2.4.2. The latter is named in honor of the old-time behavioral psychologists who thought that man is no more than a bundle of knee-jerk reflexes. For us, *homo behavioralis* will be a piece of hardware that Nature can program as she chooses—unlike *homo economicus*, whom Nature can manipulate only via his preferences. The program that she writes for him will determine his *disposition*. It is important to bear in mind that *homo behavioralis* does not choose his own disposition. He has no preferences or beliefs. After being programmed, he just carries out his instructions.

Section 2.2.1 looked briefly at biological evolution in the Hawk-Dove Game, of which Chicken and the one-shot Prisoners' Dilemma are special cases. The emphasis in Section 2.2.1 was on the meaning of the payoffs in a biological context, and on the fact that a mixed Nash equilibrium can be evolutionarily stable. For this purpose, it was not necessary to be very

---

chosen. The rules of the bargaining game they play will depend on the institutions of the society in which they live. Let us, however, consider a Utopian society in which the rules are chosen to ensure that, if Adam and Eve both play optimally, then the expected total surplus that their encounter realizes will be maximized. Myerson and Satterthwaite [187] then show that an exchange will occur only if $a \geq e + \frac{1}{4}$. Chatterjee and Samuelson [55] show that the Utopian optimum can be achieved very simply by using the following rules for the negotiation game. Each player simultaneously announces a price. If the buyer's bid exceeds the seller's, then the apple is sold to the buyer at the average of the two bids. Myerson [186, p.278] is an accessible reference for such results.

[12] Although a more fruitful setting is perhaps the Nash Demand Game as in Binmore [35]. One can then see, for example, that if Gauthier were right about constrained maximization, then he ought to be a utilitarian.

specific about the precise meaning of evolutionary stability. But here it will be necessary to be a little more careful.

When Adam and Eve are modeled as specimens of *homo behavioralis*, they are just puppets whose strings are pulled by the program that biological evolution writes in their genes, or which social evolution writes into the memes that inhabit their heads. After evolution has had a chance to operate, it will seem to a kibitzer that Adam and Eve are behaving like players in a game, each seeking to maximize his or her average fitness. However, the real drama is taking place at whatever level the self-replicating programs that control *homo behavioralis* compete for hosts. I follow Dawkins [62] in using the term *replicator* for such a program. Replicators are the genuine "players" in whatever game is really being played when it looks to a kibitzer as though Adam is playing with Eve.

We can capture something of the spirit of this underlying competition between replicators for hosts by inventing two imaginary replicators called HAWK and DOVE. These replicators control the behavior of specimens of *homo behavioralis* when they play the one-shot Prisoners' Dilemma. A player hosting the DOVE replicator plays *dove*. A player hosting the HAWK replicator plays *hawk*.

Figure 3.4(a) represents a population of potential players, of whom a fraction $1 - p$ are hosting the DOVE replicator and a fraction p are hosting the HAWK replicator. Every so often, Nature chooses one player at random from the population at large to take the part of Adam. Simultaneously, she chooses a second player at random to play the part of Eve. The outcome of the game then determines how many extra children each player will have on average. Since replicators in this story are assumed to replicate themselves perfectly from parent to child, the relative success of the strategies induced by the two replicators will therefore be reflected in the manner in which p changes.

Figure 3.4(b) shows a general symmetric 2×2 game. What is the average fitness of a player hosting the DOVE replicator who is chosen to play this game? Since the opponent will be hosting the DOVE replicator $1 - p$ of the time and the HAWK replicator p of the time, the answer is $a(1 - p) + dp$. Similarly, the fitness of a player hosting the HAWK replicator is $c(1-p)+bp$. It follows that the fraction of HAWKs in the population will increase relative to the fraction of DOVEs if and only if

$$c(1 - p) + bp > a(1 - p) + dp. \qquad (3.1)$$

Similarly, the fraction of DOVEs will increase relative to the fraction of HAWKs if and only if

$$a(1 - p) + dp > c(1 - p) + bp. \qquad (3.2)$$

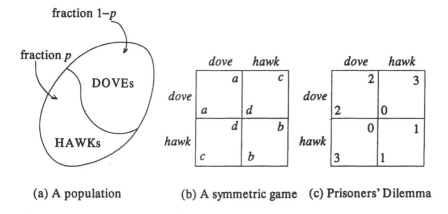

(a) A population   (b) A symmetric game   (c) Prisoners' Dilemma

Figure 3.4: Evolution and the Prisoners' Dilemma

Following Maynard Smith and Price [173], let us say that a population is *evolutionarily stable* if a mutant invasion in which a fraction $\varepsilon > 0$ of the population is taken over by a mutant replicator will necessarily be repelled when ε is sufficiently small.[13]

Consider first the case of a population consisting entirely of DOVEs. The condition that a mutant invasion of HAWKs will be repelled is obtained by writing $p = \varepsilon$ in inequality (3.2) to obtain

$$a(1 - \varepsilon) + d\varepsilon > c(1 - \varepsilon) + b\varepsilon \, .$$

For a population of DOVEs to be evolutionarily stable, this inequality must hold for all sufficiently small $\varepsilon > 0$. This is true if and only if

$$\text{(i)} \quad a \geq c$$
$$\text{and} \quad \text{(ii)} \quad a = c \ \text{ implies } \ d > b$$

The first of these conditions says that (*dove, dove*) must be a Nash equilibrium of the symmetric game of Figure 3.4(b). Thus *dove* must be a best reply to itself. The second condition says that, if *hawk* is an alternative best reply to *dove*, then *dove* must be a better reply to *hawk* than *hawk* is to itself.

It follows immediately from the criteria for evolutionary stability that a population of all DOVEs cannot be evolutionarily stable when the game to be played is the one-shot Prisoners' Dilemma. Only a population consisting entirely of HAWKs is evolutionarily stable for the one-shot Prisoners' Dilemma.

---

[13]It is customary to speak of an evolutionarily stable *strategy* (ESS) rather than an evolutionarily stable population.

Constrained Maximization and Evolution.   The discussion so far assumes that only the replicators HAWK and DOVE are available. However, when animals from the same species compete, it is commonplace for whatever game they play to be prefixed by ritualized displays in which each side shows off its prowess to the other. Such displays allow each animal to signal its intentions to the other, and hence perhaps to diminish the risk of a combat that could be costly for both parties.

Gauthier's [84, p.173] notion that ideally rational beings have transparent skulls corresponds to the assumption that any signals exchanged by Adam and Eve before playing the one-shot Prisoners' Dilemma will necessarily be truthful indicators of their actual intentions. As Howard [121] comments, Nature might achieve the effect of transparency by printing an animal's genetic code on its forehead for all to see.

Consider, for example, a population in which only the replicators CLINT and JOHN of Figure 3.3(b) are present. Each player hosting the CLINT replicator has CLINT written above his eyebrows. A player hosting the JOHN replicator has something different on his forehead, perhaps JOHN or nothing at all. An examination of the game of Figure 3.3(a) shows that only a population of all CLINTs is then evolutionarily stable.[14] A tiny fraction of mutant CLINTs appearing in a population of JOHNs will expand until the JOHNs are all wiped out.[15]

Will the evolutionary argument just outlined suffice to rescue Gauthier's constrained maximization principle? The answer depends on whether we believe that Nature can be relied upon to confine herself to programming *homo behavioralis* with truthful preplay signals. Section 2.2.5 argues that *homo economicus* will not honor any promises he may have made before playing the one-shot Prisoners' Dilemma, but perhaps it is true that a variety of *homo behavioralis* programmed to behave more honorably might derive an evolutionary advantage from his better nature.

Before discussing this question, it is important to make it clear that the preplay signals to be discussed do not alter the game that follows. Some examples of game-altering signals appear in Sections 2.2.6 and 2.5.1. A more dramatic example is provided by certain spiders who inhabit a hostile terrain in the Nevada desert, where sites for webs are rare and therefore valuable. Spiders who do not have a web will seek to dispossess those who

---

[14]Although (JOHN, JOHN) is a symmetric Nash equilibrium, a population of all JOHNs is not evolutionarily stable because CLINT is an alternative best reply to JOHN, but JOHN is not a better reply to CLINT then CLINT is to itself.

[15]With reference to Gauthier's [84, p.174] claim that transparency can be replaced with some notion of translucency that allows occasional mistakes to be made in identifying the disposition of an opponent, it should be noted that a population of JOHNs is invulnerable to invasion by mutant CLINTs if the latter mistakenly identify a JOHN as a CLINT with some fixed probability $\pi > 0$ (unless the initial invading fraction ε is sufficiently large).

do. But, before risking combat, the spiders exchange a sequence of signals. These signals change the game that follows because they convey relevant information in a manner that *cannot* be falsified. In particular, the invading spider begins by strumming the incumbent's web. The amplitude of the induced vibration signals the mass of the invading spider. The biologists report that the incumbent spider will then usually abandon its web if outmassed by 10 percent or more—even though its chances of survival are then very slim.[16]

However, our concern is with preplay signals that are capable of being costlessly falsified. Game theorists follow Farrell [73] in calling such signals *cheap talk*.

Cheap Talk. To explore the cheap talk issue, imagine a population of CLINTs, all with CLINT stamped on their foreheads. A mutant throwback now appears who still brands his hosts with the CLINT trademark but who reverts to the behavior of the more primitive JOHN. Such phony CLINTs will take over the whole population, for the same reason that a mutant invasion of HAWKs will take over a population of all DOVEs.

Of course, a population of phony CLINTs will itself be vulnerable to a mutant invasion. The mutants will need to be able to recognize each other using a more elaborate signal than CLINT. Perhaps they will have CLINT EASTWOOD written on their foreheads. We will then need to consider the game of Figure 3.3(a) again, but with CLINT EASTWOOD replacing CLINT, and phony CLINT replacing JOHN. For the same reason that a mutant invasion of CLINTs will displace a population of all JOHNs, an invasion of CLINT EASTWOODs will displace a population of all phony CLINTs.

A population of all CLINT EASTWOODs is vulnerable in turn to an invasion by phony CLINT EASTWOODs who have CLINT EASTWOOD written on their foreheads but behave like JOHNs—and so on. The result will be a population that fluctuates over time. Sometimes everybody will be cooperating in the one-shot Prisoners' Dilemma and sometimes everybody will be defecting.

One may follow Robson [219] in asking how much time is spent in each phase. This will depend on how likely the relevant mutations are. If one believes that mutations which result in some part of a replicator's program being disabled will occur much more frequently than mutations which enhance the program with further meaningful instructions, then one must presumably accept that the noncooperative phase will be predominant.

---

[16]Veblen [266] gives many examples of similarly unfalsifiable signals in human societies. One cannot, for example, signal that one is wealthy by occupying a mansion filled with idle servants unless one has the money to pay for such conspicuous waste.

Maynard Smith [172, p.147] comments that cheap-talk displays are often not reliable indicators of an animal's intentions; nor does the opposing animal seem to perceive them as such. Presumably the displays were effective in the past, and survive into the present for the same reason that we retain an appendix. Such displays are, in a sense, a fossil record of a history of mutation and counter-mutation in which some version of CLINT was replaced by CLINT EASTWOOD and then by CLINT EASTWOOD JUNIOR, and so on. When we look at animals, my guess is that we see this process in various stages of development.[17] Sometimes the displays are very primitive or absent altogether. Sometimes the species is observed in a phase in which the most recently evolved signal is still effective. However, as always, it is the pathological cases in which the observed behavior is very noticeable but seemingly pointless that are most instructive.

It seems that Nature has little difficulty in programming her creatures to lie when this will improve their fitness. Humans, of course, are more easy to teach because they learn their lessons through quick-acting socioeconomic processes. We should therefore be unsurprised that constrained maximization can sustain more than a temporary foothold in human societies only in situations of marginal importance.

3.2.4 Cheap Talk and Equilibrium Selection

Cheap talk will never persuade rational people to act contrary to their own interests. However, it may help rational folk to coordinate their endeavors. In Section 2.3.6, for example, we studied the equilibrium selection problem in the context of the Battle of the Sexes. The introduction of a preplay cheap-talk session simplifies such problems by expanding the range of possible solutions.

For example, Adam and Eve could seek to solve their coordination problem by tossing a coin at their cheap-talk session and agreeing to go to the ballet if it falls heads and to the boxing if it falls tails. Their promises to abide by such an agreement need not necessarily be commitments for the arrangement to work. After the coin has fallen, it will be *optimal* for each player to honor his promise, provided that he believes that the other plans to do the same. But if Adam is the player disadvantaged by the fall of the coin, why does he not loudly repudiate the deal and demand that the coin be tossed again? And if Eve refuses on the grounds that she sees no reason why the coin should be tossed repeatedly until it favors Adam, what effect will this breakdown in the negotiation process have on her beliefs about the strategy that Adam will now choose in the Battle of the Sexes?

---

[17]With the added confusion that we will never be entirely sure that we are observing signals that are genuinely cheap talk.

Such difficulties may seem farfetched in the context of a supposedly happily married couple like Adam and Eve choosing an entertainment for the evening, but they loom much larger when the issue is the choice of a social contract in the game of life. In fact, as Section 1.2.4 explains, it is crucial to my defense of the Rawlsian maximin criterion that the hypothetical deal reached in the original position should be immune to calls that the hypothetical coin which determines each person's role in society should be tossed again. However, no such immunity is available for deals reached in the uncompromising format of the Battle of the Sexes. This is one of the reasons why it is so important that the game of life should be properly modeled as a *repeated* game. As explained in Section 2.2.6, indefinitely repeated games have *many* equilibria from which a selection can be made.

Since the Battle of the Sexes was invented to illustrate how hard the problem of equilibrium selection can be, we should not be surprised that we keep finding ourselves in difficulties when we try to invent reasons for selecting one of its equilibria rather than another. However, as we learned in Section 2.3.2, equilibrium selection is a problem even for the Stag Hunt Game in which both players prefer the equilibrium (*dove, dove*) to every other outcome of the game.

Recall from Section 2.3.2 that the problem in getting from the state-of-nature equilibrium (*hawk, hawk*) to the civilized equilibrium (*dove, dove*) is that there is no *a priori* reason why rational players should trust any cheap-talk signals they may exchange before the Stag Hunt Game is played. However, here the evolutionary argument considered in the Section 3.2.3 comes to our aid. Such an argument fails at the task of showing that out-of-equilibrium play can be stable, but now it is no longer to be asked to achieve the impossible.

Nothing at all complicated is involved. Suppose that, in the state of nature, the whole population consists of JOHNs. Whenever two members of this original population meet to play the Stag Hunt Game, they both use the strategy *hawk*. A mutant invasion of CLINTS now appears. For the reasons given in Section 3.2.3, the mutant fraction of the population expands until the JOHN replicator is eliminated altogether. Whenever two members of the resulting population of CLINTS meet to play the Stag Hunt Game, they use the strategy *dove*. This simple evolutionary mechanism therefore moves the society under consideration from the state-of-nature equilibrium (*hawk, hawk*) to the civilized equilibrium (*dove, dove*).

It is at this stage that the story deviates from that of Section 3.2.3. In the one-shot Prisoners' Dilemma of Section 3.2.3, a population of all CLINTs is not viable in the long run because it can be invaded by phony CLINTs who promise to cooperate but then cheat on their promise. However, in the Stag-Hunt Game, such a phony CLINT will find himself at a disadvantage in a population consisting almost entirely of CLINTs. He only cuts his own throat by playing *hawk* when faced with a genuine CLINT playing *dove*. Any small bridgehead established by the phony CLINT replicator will therefore shrink over time until it is eliminated altogether.

However, this should not be taken as the end of the story. A population of all CLINTs is *not* evolutionarily stable. No mutant invasion can expand from its intial bridgehead to displace a population of all CLINTs, but neither is it true that any mutant bridgehead will necessarily be extinguished in the long run. That is to say, while no possible mutant is better at surviving in a population of CLINTs than a CLINT, there are mutants who can survive just as well as a CLINT. One such mutant is a toothless CLINT who sends the CLINT signal but behaves like the FRANK persona of Section 3.2.1. Such a FRANK plays *dove* in the Stag Hunt Game whatever signal the opponent may send. If the replication mechanism is *imitation*, then this is a very likely mutation, since a new recruit to a population of all CLINTs will see people sending the CLINT signal and people playing *dove* in the Stag Hunt Game. But he will never see anyone being punished by the play of *hawk* for sending the wrong signal, because there are no such people in the population. If the mutation that removes the teeth from CLINTs occurs sufficiently frequently without other mutations appearing along the way, then the whole population will eventually be toothless. The way will then be clear for the appearance of FRANKs whose attempt to imitate the CLINT signal would not pass muster if any CLINTs with teeth were left to punish a player sending the wrong signal. If this process continues indefinitely, the final result will be a population of FRANKs who may or may not send a signal that resembles the signal of a CLINT, but who all play *dove* in the Stag Hunt Game.

What I think needs to be emphasized about such evolutionary stories is that their plausibility depends on how likely various mutations are. My own view is that *simplifying* mutations must surely be very much more likely than mutations that generate more sophisticated behavior. However, even if one takes this view, one must still face the fact that a population may be bombarded by many simplifying mutations simultaneously. For example, regular CLINTs will have a slight advantage over toothless CLINTs as long as some JOHNs keep trickling into the population. I do not therefore believe that abstract evolutionary arguments can ever be decisive in an equilibrium selection debate. The best they can do is to suggest what data to look for in the historical record.

3.2.5   The Tit-for-Tat Bubble

Section 2.2.6 includes a discussion of the game obtained by repeating the Prisoners' Dilemma of Figure 2.2(b) indefinitely often. Adam and Eve keep playing the one-shot Prisoners' Dilemma over and over again. After each repetition, the probability that they will never play again is some very small number p. This section is also about the indefinitely repeated Prisoners' Dilemma, but our old friend of Figure 2.2(b) will be replaced by the version of the Prisoners' Dilemma given in Figure 3.5(a) in order to preserve compatibility with some of the literature that will be mentioned. Section 2.2.6 also introduces the strategy TIT-FOR-TAT. It was shown that it is a Nash equilibrium for both Adam and Eve to use TIT-FOR-TAT in the indefinitely repeated Prisoners' Dilemma. This conclusion remains valid when the version of the Prisoners' Dilemma given in Figure 2.2(b) is replaced by that of Figure 3.5(a).

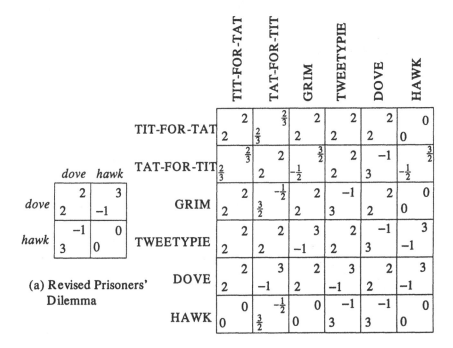

(a) Revised Prisoners' Dilemma

(b) Abbreviated strategic form for the repeated Prisoners' Dilemma

Figure 3.5: More strategic forms for the Prisoners' Dilemma

The strategy TIT-FOR-TAT requires a player to begin by playing *dove*, and then to copy the action last made by the opponent at all subsequent stages of the game. If both players use TIT-FOR-TAT, the result will therefore be that *dove* always gets played.

Figure 3.6(a) is a diagrammatic representation of TIT-FOR-TAT.[18] The circles represent two possible "states of mind". The letters inside the circles show the action to be taken in each state. The sourceless arrow points to the circle representing the initial state. Since this contains the letter D, TIT-FOR-TAT begins by playing *dove*. Two arrows point away from the circle representing the intial state. One is labeled D and the other H. These arrows indicate the state to which a player using TIT-FOR-TAT should move after observing his opponent's reply to his use of *dove*. Notice that, if the opponent ever "cheats" by responding to *dove* by playing *hawk*, then a player using TIT-FOR-TAT moves to a "punishment state" in which he plays *hawk*, and continues to do so until the opponent indicates his "repentance" by playing *dove*. As explained in Section 2.2.6, it is the existence of this punishment state which ensures that it is a Nash equilibrium for both Adam and Eve to use TIT-FOR-TAT in the indefinitely repeated Prisoners' Dilemma. Neither player has an incentive to deviate from TIT-FOR-TAT because such a deviation will be punished by the opponent.

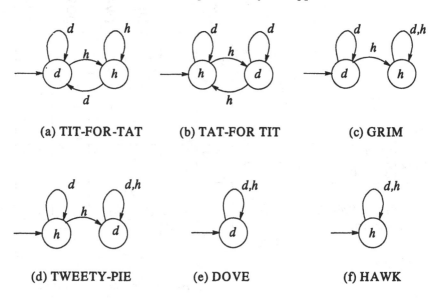

(a) TIT-FOR-TAT   (b) TAT-FOR TIT   (c) GRIM

(d) TWEETY-PIE   (e) DOVE   (f) HAWK

Figure 3.6: Strategies for the indefinitely repeated Prisoners' Dilemma

Axelrod [14] emphasizes that TIT-FOR-TAT is a "nice" strategy in that it is never the first to play *hawk*. Figure 3.6(b) shows a "nasty" strategy TAT-FOR-TIT first considered by Abreu and Rubinstein [1]. Figures

---

[18]The diagrams of Figure 3.6 represent strategies as *finite automata*. For a more systematic account of such representations, see my *Fun and Games*, D. C. Heath, 1991.

3.6(c)–(f) show some other strategies for the indefinitely repeated Prisoners' Dilemma. The GRIM strategy gets its name because it differs from TIT-FOR-TAT in being utterly unforgiving. Nothing the opponent can do will serve to persuade GRIM to leave its punishment state once it has been triggered. The strategy TWEETYPIE is obtained by modifying TAT-FOR-TIT in the same way that TIT-FOR-TAT was modified to give GRIM. However, no strategic lessons are to be learned from TWEETYPIE except perhaps that some strategies have nothing whatever to recommend them.

The indefinitely repeated Prisoners' Dilemma has an infinite number of strategies. Figure 3.5(b) is therefore just a small segment of the strategic form of the indefinitely repeated Prisoners' Dilemma since it takes account only of the strategies listed in Figure 3.6. The entries in the abbreviated strategic form of Figure 3.5(b) are the long-run average payoffs to Adam and Eve in the limiting case when $p \to 0$. Notice that (HAWK, HAWK), (TIT-FOR-TAT, TIT-FOR-TAT), (TAT-FOR-TIT, TAT-FOR-TIT) and (GRIM, GRIM) are all Nash equilibria for the abbreviated strategic form of Figure 3.5(b). They are all also Nash equilibria for the full strategic form of the indefinitely repeated Prisoners' Dilemma. However, they are by no means the only such Nash equilibria. As explained in Section 2.6.6, the folk theorem of repeated game theory guarantees that the complete set of Nash equilibria for the indefinitely repeated Prisoners' Dilemma is very large indeed.

Although the indefinitely repeated Prisoners' Dilemma has many Nash equilibrium strategies, the literature focuses almost entirely on TIT-FOR-TAT. This tunnel vision is accompanied by a stack of misapprehensions about what is and is not true of Nash equilibria in the indefinitely repeated Prisoners' Dilemma. For example, Maynard Smith [172, p.202] offers a "proof" that TIT-FOR-TAT is evolutionarily stable.[19] This is typical of a widespread belief that evolution will inevitably lead to the selection of TIT-FOR-TAT in the indefinitely repeated Prisoners' Dilemma. Those who disdain evolutionary arguments are equally prone to error when defending TIT-FOR-TAT. The misapprehension under which they often labor is that (TIT-FOR-TAT, TIT-FOR-TAT) is not only a Nash equilibrium, but also a subgame-perfect equilibrium for the indefinitely repeated Prisoners' Dilemma. Others make broader claims. For example, Poundstone [203, p.245] tells us that: "It is a contention of game theory that you should never be the first to defect in a Prisoners' Dilemma situation."

To set the record straight, it should be noted that TIT-FOR-TAT is not

---

[19]Maynard Smith attributes the proof to Axelrod. Axelrod [14] actually proves that TIT-FOR-TAT is what he calls "collectively stable". This just means that a pair of TIT-FOR-TATs is a Nash equilibrium as demonstrated in Section 2.2.6. It is not true, as Axelrod [14, p.217] asserts, that collective stability and evolutionarily stability are equivalent in the indefinitely repeated Prisoners' Dilemma when attention is restricted to "nice" strategies.

evolutionarily stable. In fact, no strategy is evolutionarily stable in the indefinitely repeated Prisoners' Dilemma.[20] Nor is it true that the operation of evolution will necessarily lead to the selection of TIT-FOR-TAT. It is not even true that TIT-FOR-TAT was selected in Axelrod's [14] simulated evolutionary process. It is not true that two TIT-FOR-TATs are a subgame-perfect equilibrium for the indefinitely repeated Prisoners' Dilemma.[21] And it is very definitely false that game theorists contend that a player should never be the first to defect in the indefinitely repeated Prisoners' Dilemma.

Why have these myths grown up around TIT-FOR-TAT? Axelrod [14] is partly to blame for writing his book *The Evolution of Cooperation* so persuasively. However, I think the real reason is that TIT-FOR-TAT strikes such a chord of recognition in people's hearts that they cease to think critically about the arguments offered in its favor. Although we are all brought up as little deontologists, we all know deep down inside that it is *reciprocity* that really keeps society going. When we are offered this under-the-counter insight in the shape of a simple formula, we therefore seize upon it with relief. But some caution is advisable. Are not the reasons that make TIT-FOR-TAT intuitively attractive pretty much the same as those which led us to find the CLINT persona of Section 3.2.2 so appealing at first sight? Both endorse the highly practical principle that one should do-unto-others-as-they-do-unto-you. But, as we saw in Sections 3.2.2 and 3.2.3, it is necessary to be especially wary of arguments that seek to rationalize conclusions in whose rationality we have a vested interest.

Unlike the arguments for the CLINT persona based on players' choosing to have a transparent disposition, the arguments in favor of TIT-FOR-TAT do not call for out-of-equilibrium behavior. The difficulty with TIT-FOR-TAT as a paradigm for rational behavior in the indefinitely repeated Prisoners' Dilemma is that it is only one of a very large number of equilibrium strategies. So why pick on TIT-FOR-TAT rather than one of its many rivals?

Axelrod's Olympiad. TIT-FOR-TAT owes its prominence to its success in a computer tournament reported in Axelrod's [14] *Evolution of Cooperation*. In this tournament, various individuals submitted computerized strategies for the repeated Prisoners' Dilemma. These were then matched

---

[20]A population whose members all play TIT-FOR-TAT is not evolutionarily stable because a mutant bridgehead of DOVEs will not be extinguished. (As Figure 3.5(b) shows, DOVE is an alternative best reply to TIT-FOR-TAT, but TIT-FOR-TAT is not a better reply to DOVE than DOVE is to itself.) In general, no strategy in a game can be evolutionarily stable if its use by the whole population results in certain parts of the game tree never being reached. It follows that the standard definition of evolutionary stability given in Section 3.2.3 leaves much to be desired.

[21]Although, since I believe that evolutionary considerations are what is important in this context, I do not attach much significance to this fact.

against each other in pairs in order to determine which of the submitted strategies would do best. In a small pilot experiment with fourteen entries, the most successful strategy was TIT-FOR-TAT, submitted by Anatol Rapoport.[22] This conclusion was advertised as a preliminary to the main experiment in which there was a field of sixty-three entries. Again TIT-FOR-TAT was the most successful strategy.

Axelrod reasoned that if he were to run further trials, then relatively unsuccessful strategies would be submitted less often. He therefore simulated further experiments artificially on a computer using an evolutionary process.[23] After simulating 1,000 generations, he found that TIT-FOR-TAT was still the most successful strategy.

Nachbar [188] offers a critical analysis of Axelrod's procedures.[24] He

---

[22] In this pilot, the entrants were told that the Prisoners' Dilemma would be repeated precisely 200 times. Such a *finitely* repeated Prisoners' Dilemma has a unique subgame-perfect equilibrium in which both Adam and Eve plan to play *hawk* under all eventualities. There are also many Nash equilibria, but all of these result in *hawk* always actually being played. Axelrod abandoned the finitely repeated Prisoners' Dilemma for his main experiment and used instead a version of the indefinitely repeated Prisoners' Dilemma with stopping probability $p = 0.00346$ (which makes the expected number of repetitions equal to 200).

[23] In this process, the fraction of the participants using a particular strategy in one generation is taken to be proportional to the product of the fraction using that strategy in the previous generation and the payoff it was accorded in the previous generation. Axelrod made no provision for mutation in his evolutionary simulation. No strategies beyond the original sixty-three were therefore allowed to enter the fray. He signals this by speaking of *ecological* success rather than *evolutionary* success.

[24] Nachbar [188] concentrates on the fact that Axelrod's evolutionary simulation was really based on the *finitely* repeated Prisoners' Dilemma rather than the indefinitely repeated Prisoners' Dilemma that he advertised. In the indefinitely repeated version, the number of times the Prisoners' Dilemma gets repeated is a random variable. For his main experiment, Axelrod accordingly sampled five game lengths (63, 77, 151, 156, and 308) from the appropriate exponential distribution, thereby creating five finitely repeated Prisoners' Dilemmas of varying lengths. Each strategy played each of these five repeated games against every other strategy. This is a legitimate method of implementing the requirement that the number of repetitions be indefinite. It is true that Axelrod knew the number of repetitions, but what matters is that the participants did not. However, Axelrod used the *same* game lengths in each generation of his simulated evolutionary process. This is not strictly legitimate because, although the participants did not know the chosen lengths at the first trial, everyone would eventually find out what they were after observing a sufficiently long sequence of trials. To dramatize the reason that this might conceivably matter, consider what would have happened if *all* pure strategies for the 308-times repeated Prisoners' Dilemma had been submitted. (One needs a large imagination to envisage this possibility, since the number N of such strategies is 2 raised to the power $\frac{1}{3}(4^{308} - 1)$.) Axelrod would then have had to consider an $N \times N$ game instead of a 63×63 game. As in the 63×63 case, his evolutionary process cannot converge on anything but a Nash equilibrium of the $N \times N$ game. But, in all such equilibria, only *hawk* ever gets played. Fortunately, it turns out that this line of criticism is academic. Linster [155] has repeated the Axelrod calculations using the indefinitely repeated Prisoners' Dilemma in each generation. This produces different results from those reported by Axelrod, but the differences are too slight to affect Axelrod's qualitative conclusions.

points out that Axelrod's evolutionary process cannot converge on anything that is not a symmetric Nash equilibrium of the 63 × 63 analogue of the strategic form of Figure 3.5(b) that would be obtained by replacing its pure strategies by the sixty-three entrants in Axelrod's main experiment. In fact, after 1,000 generations, Axelrod's evolutionary process comes very close to a *mixed strategy* Nash equilibrium of the 63 × 63 game. That is to say, the fractions of the population using various strategies after 1,000 generations approximate the probabilities with which these strategies are used in one of the Nash equilibria of the 63 × 63 game. In this mixed strategy Nash equilibrium, TIT-FOR-TAT is used with a higher probability than any other pure strategy. However, there are other pure strategies that get used with probabilities that are only slightly smaller, and a whole stack of lesser pure strategies that get used with probabilities that are too large to be neglected. It is therefore not really true that TIT-FOR-TAT "won" Axelrod's competition. The strategy that actually "won" is a mixed strategy that calls for TIT-FOR-TAT to be used less than 15 percent of the time.

In the preceding discussion, it is taken for granted that all sixty-three strategies in Axelrod's simulated evolutionary process get used equally often in the first generation. But one need not assume that the sixty-three submitted strategies are distributed evenly over the original population. Different strategies might be used by different fractions of the original population. Axelrod tested the robustness of his conclusions by rerunning his tournament with six different mixtures of strategies in place of his original sixyt-three. He found that TIT-FOR-TAT was the most numerous strategy in five of these six cases. However, it is easy to see that his simulated evolutionary process can be made to converge on *any* of the large number of Nash equilibria of the 63 × 63 game by choosing the original strategy distribution suitably. Linster [155] actually ran the appropriate simulations using random initial strategy distributions. He found that TIT-FOR-TAT is the most numerous strategy after 1,000 generations only about 26 percent of the time. Its nearest rival was most numerous about 24 percent of the time.

Perhaps it now begins to become clear that the "success" of TIT-FOR-TAT in Axelrod's tournament is as much due to the nature of the initial population of strategies with which it had to compete as to its own intrinsic merits. Linster [155] presses this point home by repeating Axelrod's procedure for the case in which the original population is no longer the sixty-three strategies studied by Axelrod, but consists instead of the twenty-six strategies that can be represented as in Figure 3.6 using no more than two circles to represent "states of mind". The most notable feature of Linster's simulation is the success, not of TIT-FOR-TAT, but of the GRIM strategy of

Figure 3.6(c). Starting from random initial strategy distributions, it captures more than half of the population on average after 1,000 generations.[25]

The lesson to be learned from this discussion is similar to the lesson preached in Section 3.2.3 about experimental evidence. One must be very cautious indeed before allowing oneself to be persuaded to accept general conclusions extrapolated from computer simulations. One always needs to ask how things would have changed if the circumstances under which the experiment or the computer simulation was conducted had been different. If there is no evidence that similar data would have been generated under different circumstances, then one is not entitled to generalize any conclusions that the data available may suggest.

Nice or Nasty? In respect of Axelrod's tournament, one may respond that Axelrod supports the conclusions suggested by his data theoretically. However, the theoretical arguments offered in defense of TIT-FOR-TAT can also be used to defend other strategies. For example, TAT-FOR-TIT of Figure 3.6(b) is also an equilibrium strategy for the indefinitely repeated Prisoners' Dilemma that has just as simple a structure as TIT-FOR-TAT. But TAT-FOR-TIT is "nasty" in that it begins by playing *hawk*, and continues to do so until its opponent shows that it also has some teeth.

There is much that can be said in favor of a strategy like TAT-FOR-TIT. Its opening use of *hawk* may be interpreted as a display of the type discussed in Section 3.2.4. A player who uses such a display can be seen as signaling that he is the kind of tough guy that nobody would be wise to push around. If the signal is reciprocated, a player may then conclude that he has been paired with a like-minded player with whom it makes sense to cooperate on an equal basis. The anecdotes that Axelrod [14, p.73] tells about live-and-let-live arrangements between British and German units in the trenches during the First World War are at least as supportive of the real-life use of such a "nasty" strategy as they are of the use of a "nice" strategy like TIT-FOR-TAT.

What is more, TAT-FOR-TIT enjoys some evolutionary advantages over TIT-FOR-TAT. Section 3.2.4 concludes by emphasizing the importance of considering the stability of populations in the presence of *simplifying* mutations. In this spirit, imagine a population in which only the TAT-FOR-TIT replicator is originally present, but in which TAT-FOR-TIT is subject to continual mutation into the simpler replicators DOVE and HAWK. Both these replicators will be at a disadvantage in a population in which the predominant replicator is TAT-FOR-TIT. Any foothold they establish in the

---

[25]This is in stark contrast to the fate of GRIM in Axelrod's tournament. This was submitted by James Friedman and hence referred to by Axelrod as FRIEDMAN. Of all the "nice" strategies in Axelrod's tournament, FRIEDMAN did worst.

population will therefore survive only because it is continually replenished by new mutations. However, the same is not true if the story is retold with TIT-FOR-TAT replacing TAT-FOR-TIT. The reason is that the replicator TIT-FOR-TAT cannot distinguish between an opponent who is hosting a copy of itself, and an opponent who is hosting DOVE. Thus a population of all TIT-FOR-TATs is vulnerable to invasion by a simplifying mutation of itself. Indeed, if HAWK mutants did not occasionally appear on the scene and so keep the expansion of DOVEs in check, the latter would eventually displace the original TIT-FOR-TAT population altogether.

I am not attempting to invent a new mythology for the indefinitely repeated Prisoners' Dilemma in which the role of TIT-FOR-TAT is usurped by TAT-FOR-TIT. It is true that a population of all TAT-FOR-TITs is less vulnerable to invasion by simplifying mutations than a population of all TIT-FOR-TATS, but it is also true that TAT-FOR-TITs must be expected to have a harder time getting themselves established in a hostile environment. For example, in Linster's [155] evolutionary simulation that uses all twenty-six one-state and two-state strategies as the original population, the fraction of the population controlled by "nasty" strategies after 1,000 generations is less than 0.0000000001.[26]

However, one should pause before generalizing too readily from either Axelrod's [14] original study or from Linster's [155] later study. Both proceed from an original population from which many possibilities have been excluded for no very good reason. A better guide is perhaps provided by the much more extensive simulation run by Probst [204], who follows Axelrod [15] in using Holland's "genetic algorithm" to widen the class of available strategies from which natural selection can make a choice.[27] This study confirms that naive reciprocators like TIT-FOR-TAT do well in the short run, but casts doubt on their long-run viability. In Probst's study, the naive reciprocators that are so successful at the outset are eventually displaced by nasty machines like TAT-FOR-TIT which only cooperate after a suitable strength-signaling message has been exchanged.[28]

The truth is that the evolutionary considerations are complicated. The evidence does seem to support the hypothesis that evolutionary pressures will tend to select equilibria for the indefinitely repeated Prisoners' Dilemma in which the players cooperate in the long run.[29] However, there are an in-

---

[26]On the other hand, GRIM's fraction is 0.575, TIT-FOR-TAT gets 0.163, and even DOVE manages 0.007.

[27]He allows finite automata with up to twenty-five states and considers time horizons of up to 10,000 generations.

[28]This cooperative regime does not persist unperturbed. It is punctuated by rare and transient plunges into non-cooperative turmoil, after which nice machines briefly dominate again while the system finds its way back to the standard cooperative regime.

[29]For some theoretical arguments that point in this direction, see Fudenberg and

finite number of different equilibria that result in Adam and Eve eventually playing *dove* all the time in the indefinitely repeated Prisoners' Dilemma. One cannot say anything definitive about precisely which of these evolution will select, because this will depend on accidents of history about which little information is likely to be available. However, the evidence from simulations does strongly suggest that it is unlikely that a pure equilibrium will get selected. One must anticipate the selection of a *mixed* Nash equilibrium. When such an equilibrium is realized, many different rules of behavior for the indefinitely repeated Prisoners' Dilemma will survive together in a symbiotic relationship. However, as all married folk know, to be part of a symbiotic relationship does not imply that pure harmony reigns. Neither the workings of enlightened self-interest nor the blind forces of evolution offer us any guarantees about the removal of "nasty" strategies. On the contrary, nastiness is something with which a rational society must somehow learn to live.

3.3   The Symmetry Fallacy

Spinoza, Rousseau, and Kant are among the more fancied runners in the social contract race who have fallen at the fence raised by the question: Suppose everybody were to behave like that? However, their arguments are so intertwined with other considerations that it is hard to pin down precisely where it is that they go wrong. Examining such questions is one of the major reasons that mathematical models are useful in the social sciences. They can provide a microscope through which the details of a suspect argument can be examined dispassionately at one's leisure.

However, Rapoport [207] did not peer very closely through the microscope provided by the Prisoners' Dilemma of Figure 2.2(b)[30] when he revived the Symmetry Fallacy in 1966 by writing:

> ... because of the symmetry of the game, rationality must prescribe the *same choice to both.* But if both choose the same, then $(2,2)$ is clearly better than $(1,1)$. Therefore I should choose *dove.*

Nor did Hofstadter [119] when he gave the Symmetry Fallacy its biggest boost by endorsing it in the *Scientific American* of 1983. The words in which he expresses the fallacy are very Kantian:

> ... rational thinkers understand that a valid argument must be *universally* compelling, otherwise it is simply not a valid argument. If

---

Maskin [79] or Binmore and Samuelson [40].

[30] Actually, Rapoport considers the general form of the Prisoners' Dilemma. I have doctored the quotation that follows to suit the particular case of Figure 2.2(b).

you grant this then you are 90 per cent of the way. All you need ask now is: Since we are all going to submit the same [strategy], which would be the more logical?

Let me repeat the argument. Since the Prisoners' Dilemma is symmetric, it seems reasonable to argue that rationality will necessarily lead Adam and Eve to make the same choice. If both choose *hawk*, each will get a payoff of 1. If both choose *dove*, each will get a payoff of 2. Which is the better? The answer to this question seems obvious. Since 2 is more than 1, rationality apparently requires that both players act "unselfishly" by playing *dove*.

Some clearing of the air is necessary before the fallacy can be pinpointed. Various assumptions are hidden in the argument. Some of these assumptions happen to be valid in the special case of the Prisoners' Dilemma, but there is one crucial implicit assumption that is simply false.

In the first place, it is not true that rationality *necessarily* requires symmetric behavior from the players in a symmetric game.[31] However, nobody would wish to deny that rationality does happen to require symmetric behavior in the special case of the Prisoners' Dilemma.

The second difficulty arises from the question: Which is the better? As discussed at length in Section 2.2.4, this question is not necessarily meaningful when applied to several players *jointly*. It assumes that they share some "common good". However, the question does make sense when attention is confined to the set S consisting only of the two outcomes (*dove, dove*) and (*hawk, hawk*) on the main diagonal of the Prisoners' Dilemma's payoff matrix, as illustrated in Figure 2.6(e). Adam and Eve are unanimous in preferring (*dove, dove*) to (*hawk, hawk*). Their individual preferences are therefore identical on the set S, and hence can be said to define a "common preference" on S.

But now we come to the crucial hidden assumption. The argument we are studying "deduces" that rational players will choose (*dove, dove*) from the observation that Adam and Eve are agreed in preferring (*dove, dove*) to (*hawk, hawk*). But this argument neglects an elementary principle of rational decision theory. This principle calls for the set of *feasible* outcomes to be identified before seeking to decide what is *optimal*. It may be, for example, that my car breaks down on a lonely highway on a dark and rainy night. I would much prefer to be at home in bed rather than seeking uncertain help in the cold and wet. But I nevertheless choose the second option because the first is not feasible.

---

[31] All finite symmetric games have at least one symmetric Nash equilibrium if mixed strategies are allowed. But why should the players use a symmetric equlibrium if they both prefer an asymmetric Nash equilibrium? Section 2.3.1 illustrates this point using the Battle of the Sexes of Figure 2.1(c).

Nothing in the argument under study entitles us to the conclusion that everything in the set $S = \{(dove, dove), (hawk, hawk)\}$ is feasible. Even if one is willing to grant that it is impossible that an asymmetric outcome could pass whatever test of rationality is being applied, one is still only entitled to deduce that the set R of feasible outcomes is a *subset* of S. If one wishes to argue further that R is the *largest* subset of S, namely S itself, it is necessary to say something about what test of rationality is being applied in order to justify such an extra step.

Game theorists are only too willing to explain what test of rationality they are applying to get the final outcome onto the main diagonal S of the payoff matrix. It is the criterion: Never use a strongly dominated strategy. This test leads to a set R that contains only the single outcome $(hawk, hawk)$.

Proponents of the Symmetry Fallacy are unwilling to say what test of rationality they are employing to get the outcome onto the main diagonal. They are therefore unable to tell us why their proposed second appeal to rationality in selecting $(dove, dove)$ from S is consistent with their first appeal in selecting S from the set of all possible outcomes of the Prisoners' Dilemma. However, the rationality cow is like other cows. It can only be milked so often before it runs dry. In this particular case, it can only be milked once.

3.4 Paradox of the Twins

Informal versions of Nozick's [195] Paradox of the Twins for games other than the Prisoners' Dilemma are a commonplace of political commentary. Consider, for example, the myth of the wasted vote. The myth is that "every vote counts" when people confine their attention to the major parties in a national election, but that a vote cast for a small third party is wasted because such a third party stands "no chance of winning".

Wasted Votes? If a wasted vote is one that does not affect the outcome of the election, then *all* votes are wasted—unless it turns out that only one vote separates the winner and the runner-up. If they are separated by two or more votes, then a change of vote by a single voter will make no difference at all to who is elected. But an election for a seat in a national assembly is almost never settled by a margin of only one vote. It is therefore almost certain that any particular vote in such an election will be wasted—*especially* those cast for a party that the opinion polls put way ahead of its competitors.

Since this is a view that naive people think might lead to the downfall of democracy if it became widely held, reasons have to be given why it is "incorrect". Political columnists have been known to invoke the authority of Immanuel Kant on this subject, but it is hard to believe that such a strategem cuts much ice with their readers! A more popular line goes like this: When Adam casts his vote, he is wrong to count only the impact that his vote alone is likely to have on the outcome of the election; he should instead count the total number of votes cast by all those people who think and feel as he thinks and feels, and hence will vote as he votes. If Adam has 10,000 such soul mates or *twins*, his vote would then be far from wasted, because the probability that an election will be decided by a margin of 10,000 votes or less is often very high.

Those who use this argument to defend the sanctity of democratic institutions are also often advocates of "strong government"—and hence hostile to third parties because of the threat that their existence will lead to a coalition government. Even granting that they are subject to this bias, it is hard to see how they manage to convince themselves that it is possible to prove that every vote *counts* without simultaneously proving that *every* vote counts—even those votes cast for third parties. After all, if Adam and everybody who thinks and feels like Adam were to vote for the third party, perhaps it wouldn't be a third party anymore.

As for myself, I am not sure that a society whose survival depends on its citizens living a lie is worth preserving. However, I do not think that democracy would fall apart if people were encouraged to think about the realities of the election process. Those who think otherwise do not understand why real people vote. Cheering at a football game is a useful analogy. Only a few cheers would be raised if what people were trying to do by cheering was to increase the general noise level in the stadium. No single voice would be able to make any appreciable difference to how much noise was being made if a large number of people were cheering. But nobody cheers at a football game because they want to increase the general noise level. They cheer because it is fun to identify yourself with your team and to urge them on. It is not perhaps very dignified that a democracy's survival should depend on its institutions being able to compete reasonably successfully with alternative forms of entertainment. However, I suspect that dignity is a virtue that it is unwise for a healthy democracy to hanker after.

The Harsanyi Doctrine. As we have seen in a number of other cases, the shoddy thinking that fuels the myth of the wasted vote is spotlighted when it is applied to the Prisoners' Dilemma in the form required by the Paradox of the Twins. The general shape of the argument is already familiar. In the Prisoners' Dilemma of Figure 2.2(b), Adam argues that Eve is his twin and hence: she will do whatever I do. So if I play *hawk*, we will both play *hawk*. If I play *dove*, we will both play *dove*. Since I prefer a payoff of 2 to a payoff of 1, I should therefore play *dove*. Eve is assumed to argue in precisely the same way, with the conclusion that Adam and Eve cooperate in the one-shot Prisoners' Dilemma.

Previous incarnations of this argument were accompanied with various fallacious justifications for treating Adam and Eve as twins. Rousseau wrote as though he believed that children could be educated so that each would regard himself as no more than a vehicle for a single general will. Section 2.4.1 looked at Kant's claim that adherence to a general will à la Rousseau is a necessity for a rational being. Section 3.2.2 examined Gauthier's claim that rationality in the Prisoners' Dilemma consists of choosing a transparent disposition to cooperate if and only if your opponent chooses a twin disposition. However, it is a twist on the Symmetry Fallacy that is most commonly offered in conjunction with the Paradox of the Twins. Adam is made to deduce that Eve is his twin from an argument that goes something like this:

> I am rational. So anything I decide to do will necessarily be rational. Eve is also rational and hence will aways make the same decision as I make when placed in identical circumstances. Therefore, she will do whatever I do in the Prisoners' Dilemma.

The error in this version of the Symmetry Fallacy lies in the implicit assumption that an action is rational because it is chosen by a rational person. But to argue like this is to invert the causal chain. An action is not rational because it is chosen by a rational person. On the contrary, a person is said to be rational because he only chooses rational actions.

Although the Paradox of the Twins is sometimes accompanied by fallacies of the type reviewed above, this section considers the paradox only in its purest form. In this form, Adam and Eve are treated as twins by virtue of an implicit appeal to some variant of the Harsanyi doctrine mentioned in Section 1.2.7. One version of the doctrine is that two specimens of *homo economicus* with precisely the same history of experience will necessarily have precisely the same thoughts in their heads.[32]

If one seeks to justify cooperation in the Prisoners' Dilemma by such an appeal to the Harsanyi doctrine, then it is necessary to restrict attention

---

[32] As pointed out in the discussion of Peter and Paul in Section 1.2.7, the doctrine can be made into a tautology by defining a person's experience so widely that it includes everything that might make two persons different. Game theorists usually do not go this far. They mostly understand a person's experience to include only those phenomena that determine his beliefs. The Harsanyi doctrine is then invoked to justify the assumption that it is common knowledge that players will have the same beliefs before they receive any private information. When the Harsanyi doctrine is used in this way, it is usually taken for granted that players' preferences are given. That is, the process that endows people with preferences is excluded from consideration. However, as Section 1.2.7 explains, Harsanyi [109, p.58] is prepared to include a person's biological inheritance as part of his experience, and hence to apply his doctrine even to preferences.

to situations in which it is common knowledge that Adam and Eve have had a precisely identical history of experience before sitting down to play. However, authors who find the orthodox analysis of the one-shot Prisoners' Dilemma distasteful, seem to feel that such a restriction is a small price to pay in return for the convenience of being able to put the problems raised for them by the Prisoners' Dilemma on an easily forgotten backburner. However, the rest of us may be forgiven if we wonder whether we are not simply being offered a story with the same relevance to real life as the story of Buridan's ass. You may recall that this unfortunate beast starved to death because it was so placed midway between two bales of hay that any argument it could find in favor of moving towards one bale was exactly balanced by an equivalent argument in favor of moving towards the other. Buridan's conclusion is absurd, but not because his argument involves any logical fallacy. If one denies the ass access to any device that might be used to break the symmetry, like tossing a coin or consulting an ouija board, then it does indeed seem to follow that the ass will starve. The conclusion is fantastic because the hypothesis is fantastic—not because there is anything wrong with the reasoning that leads from the fantastic antecedent to the fantastic consequent. The same is true of the use that Nozick's [195] Paradox of the Twins makes of the Harsanyi doctrine. Unlike the bulk of the chapter, this section is therefore mostly about the implausibility of a bizarre premise rather than the errors in some bad reasoning.

Free Choice? Two difficulties with the use of the Harsanyi doctrine in the manner required by the Paradox of the Twins will be considered. The first difficulty takes us into deep philosophical waters. How can Adam's knowledge that Eve is sure to choose as he chooses be reconciled with her having a capacity to choose freely? It would be nice to be able to duck this question. Trying to answer it will force me to express opinions in Section 3.4.2 on the nature of the human mind that are commonly dismissed as naively mechanistic. An earlier age would have called them "Hobbist". Amongst other things, I deny the metaphysical concept of "free will".

Such a denial of "free will" is usually taken as a denial of the phenomena that the idea of "free will" was invented to explain away. But I do not deny that it is meaningful to say that someone is free to choose. However, when we say this, I do not think we are saying something about the person who is making the choice. We are saying something about our own state of knowledge of the workings of the decision-maker's mind. In brief, we say someone is free because we cannot see his chains.[33]

---

[33]Hence the saying: To understand is to forgive. Section 3.4.2 argues that there is a sense in which a person *cannot* understand himself. Perhaps this is why we find it so hard to forgive ourselves our own mistakes.

For example, in formal decision theory, a rational individual is seen as choosing an optimal element from his feasible set. Given that he is rational, he is not free to choose anything else, because any other choice would deny the premise that he is rational. More generally, we cannot sensibly speak of freedom of choice *after* a model has been constructed that allows us to predict accurately what someone is going to do. We can only sensibly speak of freedom of choice *before* such a model has been finalized. Thus, before we have carried through the calculations that tell us what is optimal, we can say that a rational decision-maker is free to choose anything that is physically feasible. But, after determining what is optimal, to make such an assertion would not be meaningful.

Such Hobbist views on the nature of the self are not at all popular. It is therefore fortunate that my social contract theory depends on my guesses about how the human mind works to no greater extent than Hobbes' social contract theory depends on his—that is to say, hardly at all. Readers who choose to skip the psychological speculations of Section 3.4.2 need therefore feel no pangs of guilt.

Buridan's Ass. The second difficulty in interpreting the Harsanyi doctrine as required by the Paradox of the Twins is very much more pressing. I therefore consider this first in Section 3.4.1. Something like the Harsanyi doctrine is essential to the theory I am proposing in this book. Any appeal to the device of the original position would be idle without the assumption that human beings are capable of empathizing to some degree. There would be no point in Adam's trying to see things from Eve's point of view if there were no basis for supposing that his thoughts after experiencing her life were likely to resemble the thoughts that she actually has. However, it is one thing to recognize the necessity for modeling a particular phenomenon, and quite another to find a model that is reasonably true to life. It is chiefly for this reason that I am devoting more attention to the Paradox of the Twins than it may seem to deserve. I agree that the paradox has as much relevance to the behavior of real people as the story of Buridan's ass has to animal husbandry, but an examination of *why* this is the case may help us from going astray when the time comes to look more carefully at the notion of an empathy equilibrium introduced in Section 1.2.7.

Section 3.4.1 focuses on the shortcomings of a version of the Harsanyi doctrine that only applies when Adam and Eve have precisely *identical* life experiences. If their life experiences are taken to include their genetic inheritances along with everything else, then it is difficult to quarrel with the doctrine—unless one wants to make an exotic appeal to the Heisenberg Uncertainty Principle! However, such a restrictive domain of application for the doctrine means that it can only properly be called upon in the type of knife-edge situation in which Buridan placed his ass.

A natural reaction is to argue that I am being overliteral in my interpretation of the conditions under which the Harsanyi doctrine applies. It may be that different people will never have precisely the same life experiences, but surely people with similar life experiences will think similar thoughts when placed in similar situations? Those who see the Paradox of the Twins as providing a way of evading the harsh logic of the Prisoners' Dilemma are often insistent on this point. They see that it is unrealistic to assume that Adam is absolutely certain that Eve will do whatever he does, and seek to ameliorate the implausibility of the assumption by arguing that Adam need only attach a sufficiently high probability to the event that Eve will do whatever he does. I agree that certain aspects of what people with similar life experiences will think when placed in similar situations will probably be similar. Otherwise we would not be able to empathize with each other at all. But, as Section 3.4.1 explains at length, I do not believe that it is at all realistic to propose a version of the Harsanyi doctrine which asserts that *all* aspects of what similar people think in similar situations will probably be similar. However, such a modified form of the Harsanyi doctrine is what would be needed to make the Paradox of the Twins anything more than a mere curiosity.

3.4.1   The Harsanyi Doctrine

In this section, it will be argued that it is a mistake to proceed on the assumption that there is *necessarily* a high probability that people with similar life experiences placed in similar situations will behave similarly. The argument is preceded by a free-ranging discussion of how various equilibrium ideas in game theory are best interpreted. In particular, Aumann's [11] notion of a correlated equilibrium is discussed at length. This involves a digression on the nature of counterfactuals and their use in game theory. If you follow me down this road, there will be no escape from dialogues like that between literature's least lovable twins:

> "I know what you're thinking about," said Tweedledum, "but it isn't
> so, nohow."
> "Contrariwise," continued Tweedledee, "if it was so, it might be; and
> if it were so it would be; but as it isn't, it ain't. That's logic."

Tweedledee is right that getting the logic of subjunctive reasoning straight is necessary in a discussion of the Paradox of the Twins. However, one may reasonably ask whether the Paradox of the Twins is sufficiently important to merit a substantial amount of time spent translating such Tweedletalk into plain English. My advice to those who are doubtful is to skip immediately forward to the discussion of Newcomb's Paradox in Section 3.5. Some of the arguments of the current section reappear there in a diluted form that may be more digestible.

Mixed Strategy Equilibria. It will be useful to begin with some com- ments on the interpretation of mixed strategy Nash equilibria in a non-evolutionary context. The traditional setting for such a discussion is provided by the very simple game of Matching Pennies. Adam and Eve simultaneously show a coin. Adam wins if the coins match. Eve wins if they don't.

To set the scene, recall the boy of Edgar Allan Poe's *Purloined Letter*, who was a regular winner at Matching Pennies. When asked for the secret of his success, the boy replied:

> When I wish to find out how wise, or how stupid, or how good, or how wicked is anyone, or what are his thoughts at the moment, I fashion the expression of my face, as accurately as possible, in accordance with the expression of his, and then wait to see what thoughts or sentiments arise in my mind or heart, as if to match or correspond with the expression.

This story appeals to us because it strips bare one aspect of the empathizing process that we use all the time when making our way in society. When we want to understand the behavior of others, we put ourselves in their shoes, insofar as we can, in an attempt to see things from their point of view.

Could Poe's fictional boy exist in real life? He certainly would be unable to predict *my* choice of heads or tails in the Matching Pennies game. When confronted with such a prodigy, I would use the mixed strategy in which heads and tails are each used with probability one half.[34] I might even make a display of the fact that I was randomizing by tossing the coin, and then showing it without first looking to see how it fell. No matter how expert the boy might be at simulating my thought processes, he could then do no better than to guess right about half the time. All he would learn by empathizing with me is that I decide what to do in such situations by tossing a coin.

---

[34]You guarantee winning half the time on average if you play heads and tails with equal probabilities. If you are an expert, you will therefore not be satisfied with any mode of play in Matching Pennies that results in your winning less than half the time. But this also goes for your opponent. If she is an expert, she will therefore win at least half the time. Thus, you can do no better than win half the time yourself. Randomizing equally between heads and tails is therefore *optimal* in Matching Pennies when playing an expert. On the other hand, you would not necessarily wish to randomize if it is not common knowledge that you and your opponent are experts. You sacrifice the opportunity of exploiting your opponent's bad play if you randomize against a novice. (See Luce and Raiffa [158, p.77].)

This game-theoretic point is often greeted with impatience. Real people, it is said, do not randomize. A game theorist might think them stupid for making themselves predictable, so the story goes, but this is just the way people are. And it is certainly true that you are unlikely to enhance your reputation for sound commonsense if you admit to making important choices at random. In war, for example, one needs to keep the enemy guessing. A game theorist would therefore often advocate the use of a mixed strategy. But, if things work out badly and a court martial ensues, an officer who wants to stay out of a mental hospital would do well to deny having based his decision of whether or not to attack on the fall of a coin!

Although folk wisdom is badly wrong about randomizing, it does not follow that people necessarily behave stupidly in situations in which it is important to keep the opposition guessing. As I have argued repeatedly, social evolution tends to eliminate stupid behavior. Thus, adaptive forces may result in people randomizing without their being aware that this is what they are doing. It will then only be the *explanations* that people offer to themselves and others for what they find themselves doing that are stupid.

As an example, consider a committee of experts convened to advise a finance minister on precisely the right moment to devalue a currency. If the committee's behavior were predictable, as it would be if deciding the "right moment" were really just a matter of bringing sufficient expertise to bear, then currency speculators would have a field day, since they too have access to the necessary expertise. But currency speculators are seldom so lucky, because the decisions of expert committees are commonly no easier to predict than tomorrow's weather. That is to say, insofar as the speculators are concerned, the expert committee serves as a *randomizing device*, no different in principle from a deck of of cards or a roulette wheel.[35]

I want to push this point about people randomizing without realizing it much further. Before doing so, it will be helpful to borrow a metaphor much used in popular accounts of the mathematical theory of chaos. In Gilbert and Sullivan's *Mikado*, the emperor envisages a punishment for pool hustlers in which they are condemned to play on uneven tables with elliptical balls. The reward for an honest player would presumably be to play on a perfect table with ideally spherical balls in a world from which frictions and inelastic collisions had been entirely banished. Imagine a set of balls in movement on a pocketless table in such an ideal world. How well would we be able to predict their future positions if we knew their current locations and velocities? Laplace's answer is that we would be able

---

[35]Of course, from the finance minister's point of view, a committee has advantages over a roulette wheel. Nobody would take the minister seriously if he blamed a roulette wheel for coming up with a decision that didn't work out too well.

to predict their positions perfectly, provided that the data supplied about their current state were entirely without error. However, even tiny errors in the initial data are disastrous for this conclusion. As the balls collide and rebound from the cushions, the uncertainties built into the original measurement errors get larger and larger until eventually Laplace would be able to do little better at predicting the location of the balls than someone who made predictions without knowing the initial data at all.

The same phenomenon will be familiar to anyone who plays around with computers. If you know the program your computer is using and the data on which it is operating, then you will be able to predict what your screen will show when the program is run. But suppose that you learn of a small error in your program. Then your confidence in your prediction will be severely shaken. As we all know, you would be very lucky if a small change in your program led only to a small change on your screen. Tiny programming errors typically lead to wild and unpredictable results when the program is run.

It seems to me obvious that the same phenomena apply also to the operation of the human mind. If a person's *state of mind* is understood to include each nuance of attitude and shade of opinion, then it is surely impossible for one person ever to be certain of the state of mind with which another person approaches a problem. Indeed, in Section 3.4.2, I shall argue that a person cannot always know even his *own* state of mind for certain.

Sometimes our ignorance of an opponent's precise state of mind will not matter. For example, if Adam knows that Eve is a reliable arithmetician, then he does not need to know whether she is feeling sweet-tempered to predict how she will reply when offered a substantial reward for answering $3 \times 2 = \square$? Such an example corresponds to the case in which Laplace is asked to predict the future movement of a set of balls on a pool table *with a pocket*. He then does not need to know the initial data in order to predict that there is a high probability that all the balls will end in the pocket after a sufficiently long time. But suppose that Eve is asked to name a word that rhymes with *blue*? Even tiny differences in her state of mind may now lead her to different replies. In such a situation, Adam faces the same problem as Laplace with a pocketless pool table. Even if he understands how Eve thinks exceedingly well, he would need to know her initial state of mind with a precision beyond all reason in order to predict her answer accurately. One might describe the distinction being made here in terms of "convergent" and "divergent" processes. To make reliable predictions about the latter, one needs *precise* data about the initial conditions.

Let us now place Adam in the role of Poe's boy. Realism demands that he not be assumed to know Eve's state of mind for certain when he begins to play her at Matching Pennies. Thus, even if she is deprived of the opportunity to randomize by tossing a coin or spinning a roulette wheel, Adam will necessarily be uncertain about the precise train of thought that she will follow, because he is uncertain about her initial state of mind. This will cause him little difficulty if all Eve's possible trains of thought converge on the same conclusion with high probability—as a game theorist argues will be the case if she thinks rationally about the one-shot Prisoners' Dilemma. She will then decide that *hawk* should be played whatever her initial state of mind may be. However, in Matching Pennies, rational thinkers will not inevitably be led to a unique conclusion. Their thinking will represent a divergent process whose course depends on the player's initial state of mind.

To what degree is it reasonable to assume that Adam might know enough about Eve's initial state of mind to predict where her train of thought will take her? Poe tells us that his boy deduces what he needs to know about his opponent's state of mind by studying the expression on her face. However, we must remember that the boy in his story is only an invention of a notorious spinner of tall tales. In real life, Eve would need to be quite extraordinarily naive for this to be possible. However, it may be that the game of Matching Pennies that is about to be played is only one of a long series of such games between Adam and Eve. Adam would then have the opportunity to study her past plays with a view to determining some pattern that she may inadvertently be following. Since untrained subjects are usually very bad at generating random sequences, this would be a very plausible way in which he might hope to get an edge over Eve—and, in fact, computers have been programmed that beat human players at Matching Pennies very consistently by exploiting this weakness in our psychological makeup. But Eve is not helpless in the face of such an approach, even if we deny her access to randomizing devices. If she knows her Shakespeare well, she might perhaps make each choice of head or tail contingent on whether there is an odd or even number of speeches in the successive scenes of *Titus Andronicus*. Of course, Adam might in principle guess that this is what she is doing—but how likely is this? He would have to know her intitial state of mind with a quite absurd precision in order to settle on such an hypothesis. Indeed, I do not know myself why I chose *Titus Andronicus* from all Shakespeare's plays to make this point. Why not *Love's Labour's Lost* or *The Taming of the Shrew*? To outguess me in such a matter, Adam would need to know my own mind better than I know it myself.

It follows that a decision which seems entirely determinate to the player who makes it, may be essentially random from the perspective of an opponent. If Eve chooses heads in Matching Pennies because there is an even number of speeches in the first scene of *Titus Andronicus*, then she has made a determinate decision. But, from Adam's point of view, she might as well be using a mixed strategy that assigns equal probabilities to heads and tails. Game theorists say that, in making her choice of heads or tails contingent on an event that is determinate for her but which Adam cannot predict, she has *purified* this mixed strategy.

The deliberations that lead to a choice of pure strategy in Matching Pennies by a rational person deprived of the opportunity to use an external randomizing device will necessarily be divergent. It would therefore be a major mistake to predict that two different Adams with closely similar life experiences will choose the same pure strategy with high probability when playing Matching Pennies. Those versions of the Harsanyi doctrine that entail such a conclusion are therefore highly unrealistic. It seems to me that, if we are to appeal to the Harsanyi doctrine at all, it is necessary to confine our attention to the end products of *convergent* thought processes.

What counts as a convergent thought process? Bayesian decision theory was mentioned briefly in Section 1.2.4. It will be discussed at greater length in Section 4.5. Bayesians argue that a rational person's beliefs can be summarized by assigning subjective probabilities to all of the events that he needs to consider. These subjective probabilities allow him to calculate the utility that he can expect from the various actions open to him. Bayesian-rational behavior then consists of choosing an action that maximizes his expected utility. Bayesianism is the doctrine that a person learns simply by updating his subjective probabilities.[36] If he discovers that event F has occurred, he replaces his *prior* probability $\text{prob}(E)$ for each event E by a *posterior* probability $\text{prob}(E|F)$. The conditional probability $\text{prob}(E|F)$ is often calculated with the help of Bayes' Rule as discussed in Section 4.5. The computation of posterior probabilities is therefore frequently referred to as *Bayesian updating.*

Baysian updating is an example of a thought process that is usually *convergent.* For example, two different people may have different prior beliefs about the probability that a weighted coin will fall heads. As they observe the coin being tossed, they will adjust their beliefs to take into account their new information. In principle, these posterior beliefs might remain very different, but if both players update their subjective probabilities using Bayes' Rule, then their posterior beliefs will get closer and closer together as they get more and more information. Thus, although it is a mistake to apply the Harsanyi doctrine to a rational player's choice of heads or tails in Matching Pennies, the same need not apply to his *beliefs* about the choice that the opponent will make. Indeed, this is perhaps the most useful way to think about the unique Nash equilibrium for Matching Pennies. This mixed equilibrium is usually described by saying that each player should

---

[36]Although Bayesianism is the orthodox creed among game theorists, it seems to me ludicrous to argue that rational learning consists *only* of the mechanical updating of subjective probabilities. However, my doubts on these foundational issues will be put aside until Section 4.5.

use heads or tails with probability $\frac{1}{2}$. However, one is on much sounder ground if one thinks of the equilibrium as an equilibrium in *beliefs* rather than *actions*. One then only argues that each player's belief in equilibrium will be that heads and tails are equally likely choices for the opponent. A rational player will then be indifferent when making his own choice between heads and tails. Nothing then prevents his making the choice contingent on his knowledge of the works of Shakespeare, should such a course of action take his fancy.

Correlated Equilibrium.   Adam and Eve have diametrically opposed preferences in Matching Pennies. It is therefore a zero-sum game that allows no scope at all for cooperation, rational or otherwise. Before returning to the Paradox of the Twins, it will therefore be useful to look at a game that is closer to the Prisoners' Dilemma. The standard example for the purpose I have in mind is a variant of the game of Chicken of Figure 2.1(b). The new version of Chicken is given in Figure 3.7(a). In this symmetric game, the players would presumably agree on (*dove, dove*) if they could trust their opponent to honor such an agreement. However, (*dove, dove*) is not a Nash equilibrium for Chicken. Its Nash equilibria are (*dove, hawk*), (*hawk, dove*) and a symmetric mixed equilibrium in which each player believes that the other is equally likely to play *dove* or *hawk*.

In a cheap-talk session before playing Chicken, Adam and Eve might agree to toss a coin and to play (*dove, hawk*) if the coin falls heads and (*hawk, dove*) if it falls tails. Neither has an inducement to cheat on such an agreement unless they anticipate that their opponent will also cheat.[37] There is therefore an incentive-compatible, preplay agreement for Chicken in which each player expects a payoff of $1\frac{1}{2} = \frac{1}{2} \times 3 + \frac{1}{2} \times 0$. This is less than the payoff of 2 that each player would get if both played *dove*, but more than the payoff of 1 that each would expect from the mixed Nash equilibrium.

It seems at first sight as though Adam and Eve can hope for no more than a payoff of $1\frac{1}{2}$ each if they are restricted to symmetric, preplay agreements that each has an incentive to honor. However, the version of Chicken given in Figure 3.7(a) has been introduced into the discussion because it admits an incentive-compatible, preplay agreement in which each player gets $1\frac{2}{3}$. Studying this agreement will be good for more than our souls because it taps the same intuition that fuels the Paradox of the Twins, but in a manner that does not ruffle the feathers of orthodox game theorists.

Imagine that, instead of tossing a coin at their preplay meeting in order to decide which Nash equilibrium to play, Adam and Eve enlist the aid of an innocent bystander who is known to be impeccably honest. His instructions

---

[37]However the coin falls, the agreement calls for a Nash equilibrium to be used. Thus it is optimal to follow the agreement, provided that your opponent does so also.

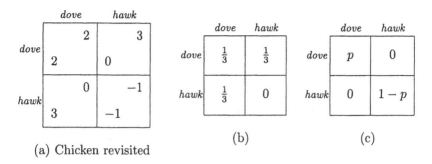

Figure 3.7: Correlated equilibria

are to use a random device to select one of the four cells, $(dove, dove)$, $(dove, hawk)$, $(hawk, dove)$ and $(hawk, hawk)$, from Chicken's payoff table. They are to be selected with the respective probabilities, $\frac{1}{3}$, $\frac{1}{3}$, $\frac{1}{3}$ and 0, as shown in Figure 3.7(b). After a cell has been selected, Adam is to be privately told *only* the row in which the cell lies, and Eve is to be privately told *only* the column. Adam and Eve's agreement is then to use whatever pure strategy the bystander reports to them. If both abide by the agreement, each will then expect to get a payoff of $\frac{1}{3} \times 2 + \frac{1}{3} \times 0 + \frac{1}{3} \times 3 = 1\frac{2}{3}$. But why should they abide by the agreement?

A rational player will only honor the agreement if he thereby maximizes his expected utility. To calculate the latter, we need to know the subjective probabilities that he assigns to his opponent's choice of *dove* or *hawk*. Fortunately, since Chicken is a symmetric game, the necessary calculations are the same for both Adam and Eve. It will therefore be sufficient to check that the agreement is incentive-compatible for Adam.

If the bystander reports *dove* to Adam, he must then update the prior probability distribution of Figure 3.7(b). The calculation is easier than usual when a Bayesian update is necessary, because the bystander's report of *dove* tells Adam that the cell chosen by the random device must either be $(dove, dove)$ or $(dove, hawk)$. Since each is equally likely, the posterior probability for each of the two possibilities must be $\frac{1}{2}$. Assuming that Eve honors the agreement, Adam will believe that she will use *dove* with probability $\frac{1}{2}$ and *hawk* with probability $\frac{1}{2}$ whenever the agreement calls for him to play *dove*. If he honors the agreement by playing *dove*, he therefore expects a payoff of

$$1 = \tfrac{1}{2} \times 2 + \tfrac{1}{2} \times 0. \tag{3.3}$$

If he were to deviate from the agreement by playing *hawk* when the bystander reports *dove*, then his expected payoff would be

$$1 = \tfrac{1}{2} \times 3 + \tfrac{1}{2} \times -1. \tag{3.4}$$

It is therefore (just) optimal for Adam to abide by the agreement on those occasions when this calls for playing *dove*.

Next we must ask whether it is optimal for Adam to honor the agreement when the bystander reports *hawk*. Adam then learns that the bystander's random device must have chosen the cell (*hawk, dove*). Thus, given that the bystander has reported *hawk*, his posterior probability for (*hawk, dove*) is 1. Assuming that Eve honors the agreement, Adam therefore believes that she will use *dove* with probability 1 on those occasions when the agreement calls for him to play *hawk*. If he honors the agreement by playing *hawk*, he therefore expects a payoff of

$$3 = 1 \times 3 + 0 \times -1. \tag{3.5}$$

If he were to deviate from the agreement by playing *dove* when the by-stander reports *hawk*, then his expected payoff would be

$$2 = 1 \times 2 + 0 \times 0. \tag{3.6}$$

It is therefore optimal for Adam to abide by the agreement on those occasions when this calls for playing *hawk*.

Aumann [11] uses the term *correlated equilibrium*[38] to describe an agreement of the type just considered. The reason for this terminology is that the players may believe that their own choice of strategy is correlated with their opponent's choice. For example, in the correlated equilibrium for Chicken just considered, a player who is planning to play *hawk* believes that it is certain that his opponent will play *dove*. Thinking about such correlations brings us close to the Paradox of the Twins, but to come closer we need to follow Aumann [11] further by abandoning the mundane story of a preplay agreement organized with the assistance of a reliable bystander.

Aumann [11] has a grander vision that dispenses with the preplay meeting at which Adam and Eve equip a bystander with a random device of their choice. Aumann applies essentially the same argument to Chicken that was used earlier in showing that the players in Matching Pennies do not need to toss a coin in order to randomize their choice of heads and tails. The report that the bystander makes to a player is replaced by the player's current state of mind—which Aumann interprets as being the sum total of what he knows about what is happening in the universe as a whole. Aumann's vision is therefore very grand indeed. The bystander's random device is

---

[38] A formal definition is not going to be offered because a correlated equilibrium in a game G can be seen simply as a Nash equilibrium of a larger game H obtained by prefixing G with a chance move whose outcome may be only partially observed by the players. When the observations the players make of this random event are correlated, something more general than a Nash equilibrium of G is obtained.

no longer some grubby deck of cards. It becomes instead the mysterious workings of the entire universe!

In Matching Pennies, it was important to emphasize that the relevant features of the states of mind of two different players may be essentially independent. In Chicken, one needs to emphasize that other features of the states of mind of two different people may well be strongly correlated— especially if they share a common set of experiences or a common culture. For example, if Adam and Eve jointly observe the fall of a coin, then there is a high probability that they will agree on whether it fell heads or tails. Similarly, the fact that I know that Shakespeare wrote *Titus Andronicus* makes it likely that others with a similar background will prove equally erudite.

In principle, we can use such correlations to our advantage—as in the correlated equilibrium for Chicken that we have been studying.[39] However, in such a correlated equilibrium, the players' posterior beliefs join their pure strategy choices in being the result of divergent thought processes. It is therefore mistaken to argue that your opponent will necessarily hold posterior beliefs that are close to those that you hold yourself. Nevertheless, it is still best to regard a correlated equilibrium as an equilibrium in beliefs. But to sustain such an interpretation, one must think in terms of the players' thought processes converging on the *prior* beliefs given in Figure 3.7(b), rather than on the *posterior* beliefs that they acquire after discovering what pure strategy is suggested to them by their current state of mind. It is only at the pre-choice stage that it makes sense to appeal to some form of the Harsanyi doctrine to justify the claim that, because Adam and Eve are placed in the same situation, they will necessarily think the same thoughts. Even then one is skating on thin ice. We do not really have a justification for arguing that whatever thinking process leads the players to their priors is convergent; only an example that shows that their later thinking is likely to be divergent.[40]

Correlated Equilibria in the Prisoners' Dilemma. Let us now try to apply what we have learned about correlated equilibria to the Paradox of the Twins. Suppose that Adam and Eve were to coopt a bystander with instructions to use a random device that selects a cell from the payoff table

---

[39]Note that I am not arguing that such a correlation in different people's states of mind provides more than a *theoretical* possibility for transcending the limitations of Nash equilibria in everyday life. It is important in the story of the coopted bystander that it be common knowledge that the information supplied to one player is concealed from the other. However, I cannot think of any real-life situation in which such a requirement is actually satisfied without the explicit intervention of a third party.

[40]I have considered this point elsewhere (Binmore [33]). In my model, convergent deliberation processes do indeed lead to correlated equilibria. Skyrms [247] discusses the issues more systematically.

for the Prisoners' Dilemma of Figure 2.2(b) with the probabilities shown in Figure 3.7(c). Before the bystander reports anything to the players, they will therefore believe that (*dove, dove*) will be selected with probability p, (*hawk, hawk*) with probability $1 - p$, and the other cells not at all. This set of prior beliefs guarantees that, when the bystander tells a player what pure strategy to use, the player will be sure that his opponent has been told to use the *same* pure strategy. The immediate point is that the prior set of beliefs given in Figure 3.7(c) is not in equilibrium unless $p = 0$. To see this, imagine that Adam believes that Eve will play whatever pure strategy is reported to her by the bystander. If the bystander now tells Adam to play *dove*, he will expect a payoff 2 from playing *dove* and 3 from playing *hawk*. It is therefore not optimal for him to follow his instructions. It follows that neither player must ever be told to play *dove* if their behavior is to be in equilibrium. The prior beliefs of Figure 3.7(c) therefore cannot support a correlated equilibrium unless $p = 0$.

It is instructive to explore why the Paradox of the Twins cannot be made to work using the apparatus of a correlated equilibrium. The difficulty in our attempt to justify the Paradox of the Twins using the idea of a correlated equilibrium arises because it is not optimal for Adam to choose *dove* when the bystander tells him to do so. However, a devotee of the Paradox of the Twins will explain that our argument leading to this conclusion is mistaken because the claim that Adam will expect a payoff of 3 from playing *hawk* when he is told to play *dove* is incorrect. The mistake, so the story goes, lies in our assumption that Adam will assign the same probabilities to Eve's pure strategies, both when he considers the implications of sticking with *dove*, and when considering a deviation to *hawk*. If this is an error, we have made it twice before when discussing correlated equililibria in Chicken. Both (3.3) and (3.4) assign the same probabilities to the use of *hawk* or *dove* by Eve. So do (3.5) and (3.6).

Our reason for using the same probabilities in (3.3) and (3.4) in discussing the game of Chicken is that Adam's information about Eve's intentions is the same in both cases. That is, when the bystander tells Adam to play *dove*, he thinks it as likely that Eve has been told to play *dove* as *hawk*. However, once we abandon the story of a preplay agreement and think of the players' consulting their current states of mind rather than listening to a bystander's reports, matters become less clear-cut. It is then possible for Adam to argue that, although he is not in a state of mind in which he will deviate, if he were in such a deviant state, then Eve would necessarily find herself in exactly the same deviant state.

Counterfactuals. It is important to stress the counterfactual nature of a statement that tells us what Adam *would* believe if he *were* to do what he actually will not do. David Lewis [153] is not able to match George Bush

(Section 2.5.2) when it comes to counterfactual whimsy, but he does his best by opening his book on counterfactuals with the sentence: If kangaroos had no tails, they would topple over.

What do such counterfactuals mean? Like Lewis, I think that the least confusing interpretation uses Leibniz's concept of a "possible world". Since kangaroos actually do have tails, a sentence that says what would happen if kangaroos had no tails can only be of interest if it is meant to apply in some fictional world different in some respect from the actual world. It is easy to invent such possible worlds. In one world, it might be that a particular kangaroo somehow has its tail severed, but everything else is as before. Such an unfortunate kangaroo would indeed doubtless topple over if stood on his feet. Alternatively, one can imagine a world in which some crucial event in the evolutionary history of the kangaroo is changed so that all the marsupials then called kangaroos have no tails. Kangaroos would then presumably *not* topple over, because a species with such a handicap would never have evolved.

This digression on kangaroos is intended to make the point that the meaning of a counterfactual statement is as much to be found in its *context* as in its *content*. Often the context is very clear. For example, Eve will have no trouble in understanding Adam if he tells her that he wouldn't have lost this month's mortgage repayment if he had been dealt the four of clubs rather than the nine of diamonds at a crucial stage in last night's poker game. Before the fateful deal, there were many cards that Adam might have drawn, each of which represents a different possible world. But only in the possible world represented by the four of clubs do Adam and Eve retain a roof over their heads. However, it was the possible world represented by the nine of diamonds that was revealed to be the actual world after the deal. Matters are clear in this example because no doubts exist about the mechanism that determines which of the relevant possible worlds is realized. The card dealt was determined by how the dealer happened to shuffle the deck. One cannot anticipate such clarity when dealing with more exotic counterfactuals, but it seems to me that the way to eliminate much of the confusion that counterfactual reasoning often generates is to seek to pin down whatever is serving as a substitute for the shuffling and dealing of the deck of cards in Adam's poker story. It is this mechanism that determines a context within which a counterfactual can be interpreted unambiguously.

Lewis [153] suggests that the default choice of a possible world in which a counterfactual holds should be that which is closest to the actual world. Such a criterion does not seem to me to be very useful for game-theoretic purposes because it is usually far from clear what "closest" ought to mean. The "actual world" of game theory is not the imperfect habitat of our everyday experience. The players are ideally rational supermen for whom no problem is so difficult that they cannot effortlessly supply an answer that is correct in every detail. However, in checking that an action is optimal, even supermen must compare its actual consequences with the consequences that would follow if there were a deviation. They must therefore confront the counterfactual: What would happen if a perfectly rational player were to behave irrationally? When considering such counterfactuals in game theory, it is traditional to invent random events that intervene between a player's decision to take a certain action and the action itself, so that the wrong action sometimes gets played unintentionally. It may be, for example, that the players are afflicted with trembling hands[41] that nearly always obey the dictates of their owners, but cannot be prevented from occasionally pulling the wrong lever, or pressing the wrong button. One can argue that such a possible world is as close to the "actual world" of game theory as it is possible to get without forbidding mistakes altogether. After all, if the players really are rational supermen, then they are incapable of thinking things out wrong, and so any mistakes must be due to events that are outside their control.

However, we will not get very far in understanding the Paradox of the Twins if we stick with the traditional game-theoretic interpretation of counterfactuals. Nor do I believe that game theorists are wise to stand by their tradition when there is any possibility of their conclusions finding some application in the world of our everyday experience. The specimens of *homo economicus* who inhabit the "actual world" of game theory are usually only interesting to the extent that they resemble specimens of *homo sapiens* who are doing their best to behave rationally. The mistakes that we want to consider are therefore not the mistakes that a rational superman would make if he were to make mistakes, but the mistakes that a real person might make when failing to make good his ambition to do the rational thing. This is not a popular view among game theorists, because it forces us to speculate about psychological matters on which little or no hard data is available. However, I see no alternative to biting the bullet. That is to say, when envisaging a process that shuffles possible worlds, some of the cards that are dealt need to specify the players' *states of mind*, rather than referring exclusively to states of their external environment. Otherwise one is forced into denying the obvious fact of life that bad strategy choices are seldom the result of fumbling fingers or tennis elbow. They are almost always a consequence of bad reasoning.

What does all this tell us about the counterfactuals subsumed in Aumann's [11] account of correlated equilibria? Aumann argues that all of a player's deliberative activity has *already* been modeled when the player's state of mind has been specified. It follows that, once a player's state of mind is given, there is no more thinking for him to do. As Aumann

---

[41] As in Selten's [235] notion of a trembling-hand equilibrium.

puts it, the players then "just do what they do". Aumann next asks how matters will appear to an external analyst if it turns out that Adam and Eve always happen to make Bayesian-rational choices. His answer is that the analyst will categorize their behavior by saying that it constitutes a correlated equilibrium. In Aumann's story, it is therefore not Adam who compares (3.3) and (3.4) in Chicken to decide whether or not to play *dove* when told to do so. Adam "just does what he does". The analyst compares (3.3) and (3.4) in checking that Adam is indeed Bayesian-rational. It is then irrelevant what Adam's state of mind would be if he were to do what he actually will not do. When considering how things would be if Adam were to deviate from his equilibrium strategy, the analyst envisages a possible world that is exactly the same as the actual world, except that the actual Adam, who happens to play *dove* when in a certain state of mind s, is replaced by a hypothetical Adam who happens to play *hawk* when his state of mind is s.

Notice that Aumann's story admits no variation in a player's state of mind within a given possible world. This is reflected in the fact that his players do not *consciously* decide to optimize. It is the analyst who decides, after the event, whether their behavior was optimal from his perspective. In the Paradox of the Twins, however, it is definitely intended that it be the players themselves who decide what is optimal.[42] If this assumption is to be respected, then Aumann's story needs to be modified. Consider, for example, what must have passed through Adam's head when his current state of mind lies in the set S of states of mind in which he chooses *dove* in the belief that this choice is optimal. To verify that *dove* is optimal, he must have considered a possible world in which he plays *hawk* instead of *dove*. But his state of mind cannot lie in S in this possible world, because he would then be led to the choice *dove*. He must therefore have imagined that his state of mind t would lie outside the set S in the possible world that he created when envisaging a deviation.

Why the Paradox Works. Only now does it become possible at last to pinpoint what one needs to assume in order to make the Paradox of the Twins work. Adam must regard Eve as his twin, not only in the actual world in which Adam's state of mind is in the set S and he plays *dove*, but also in at least one deviant possible world in which Adam is in a state of mind t in which he plays *hawk*. That is, we have to assume that Eve is not

---

[42]I have commented elsewhere (Binmore [28]) on the fact that abandoning Aumann's account in favor of something more realistic creates interpretative difficulties, since a player's thought processes then become part of the universe that he needs to think about. Section 3.4.2 will perhaps indicate the flavor of the difficulties that arise. However, such difficulties do not trouble those who are fond of the Paradox of the Twins, and so I neglect them here.

only Adam's twin in actuality, but that she would still be his twin even if he were not as he actually is.

Before criticizing this assumption, it may be helpful to prepare the ground by considering an author who makes himself a character in a book that he is writing—as Dante appears as a character in his own *Inferno*. This character will, of course, not necessarily know everything that the author knows. As a result, the character may choose actions that seem a good idea given his knowledge, but which the author knows will be disastrous. Suppose now that the author faces a decision problem in real life in which one alternative is to put himself in a precisely identical position to that in which he has placed his character. Should he now evaluate what his plight would then be using what he knows in his current position as the author, or using what he would know if he were the character in the book? It seems to me that the former is clearly appropriate. That is to say, he should evaluate the possible world created in his book from the viewpoint of an external analyst—just as Aumann looked at things from the viewpoint of an external analyst in his discussion of correlated equilibria.

A little flesh now needs to go on the bones of what I said earlier about the need to consider variations inside players' minds when possible worlds are considered. Fortunately, the considerations required for the Paradox of the Twins are undemanding. However, the same is far from true when one needs to consider games in which one player has the opportunity to learn how another player is thinking as the game proceeds. This is why it was necessary to spend time trying to persuade game theorists that their traditional attitude to counterfactuals needs to be rethought.

In an "actual world" in which everybody is rational, Adam will not deviate from playing *dove* when this is his equilibrium choice. However, in the world as it really is, people are not always successful in following a logical thought process to its correct conclusion. For example, most of the time we are able to solve simple arithmetical problems correctly, regardless of our initial state of mind, provided that adequate incentives are provided. As observed earlier, the thought processes that lead Eve to a solution of $3 \times 2 = \Box$? will therefore converge with high probability. But it is not *absolutely* certain that Eve will get the answer right. She may be experiencing one of those days on which nothing goes right no matter how hard we tell ourselves that we are trying. That is to say, if she commences calculating in certain unusual states of mind, she may make a mistake.

Similarly, a realistic possible world in which Adam deviates from his equilibrium choice will be one in which such irrational states of mind are not excluded altogether. For the reasons given in Section 3.4.2, Adam cannot always be sure even of his own state of mind in the world as it really is. For nearly all his possible initial states of mind, he may reasonably believe that he would have followed analogous lines of thought that all lead to the correct conclusion when considering what strategy to play in a game. However, he need not believe that this is true for all his possible initial states of mind. When Adam contemplates the consequences of a deviation, he is then free to follow the Paradox of the Twins in envisaging a possible world in which his initial state of mind t is not in S. However, it makes little sense for Adam to insist that Eve's state of mind will also be t in this possible world. It is true that the hypothetical Adam he is envisaging will presumably be unaware that he is following a deviant line of thought, and so may well believe it highly likely that Eve will have followed a similar line of thought to the same conclusion. But, in assessing the prospects of a deviation, the actual Adam would be stupid to use the beliefs that he would have if he were, so to speak, a character in his own book, rather than the beliefs that he actually has. The actual Adam will therefore analyze the possible world from the outside à la Aumann, rather than taking upon himself the viewpoint of a hypothetical deviant version of himself. But, from the outside, the thought process embodied in t that leads to a deviant choice, will necessarily be seen as having *diverged* from the mainstream lines of thought in S that lead to the equilibrium choice. To appeal to some version of the Harsanyi doctrine under such circumstances would therefore be to make the mistake of arguing that *all* aspects of what a person thinks will be duplicated with high probability by similar people in similar situations. Such an argument is clearly wrong when applied to the problem of predicting the opponent's choice of heads or tails in Matching Pennies. It is even more wrong in the current context, since the deviant state of mind to be duplicated occurs with a probability much less than $\frac{1}{2}$.

Conclusion. The moral of this section bears repeating one last time: Appeals to variants of the Harsanyi doctrine only make sense when what is to be predicted is the result of a *convergent* process. This is why I feel it necessary to replace Harsanyi's [109] use of his doctrine when analyzing bargaining in the original position by the notion of an empathy equilibrium introduced in Section 1.2.7.

It may seem that I have left no stone unturned in pursuing the Paradox of the Twins to its roots. It may even seem that I have turned each stone over several times. However, I am conscious that at least two moss-covered rocks have been left undisturbed. The first conceals the problems of self-reference that necessarily arise when one discusses thinking processes along the lines attempted in this section. The second conceals the problems that arise if one abandons my informal approach and tries to state the argument that leads to the Paradox of the Twins in conventional Bayesian terms. These issues are treated in Section 3.4.2 and Section 4.5 respectively—although much less obsessively than in the current section, since I do not see that their study casts much light on wider game-theoretic questions.

However, although stones remain to be turned in considering the Paradox of the Twins, I believe that we have already uncovered the misapprehension that afflicts most of its advocates.

I suspect that devotees of the Paradox of the Twins do not appreciate that the claim that Adam and Eve are *actually* twins is very different from the claim that they *would still* be twins even if things were other than they are. Game theorists are happy with the first claim insofar as the Prisoners' Dilemma is concerned. In this game, a rational Adam and Eve will indeed make the same choice. But such a claim is much weaker than claiming that they would still make the same choice even if someone were to behave irrationally. Indeed, if the claim is extended so that I am forbidden to envisage any possible world in which Adam and Eve might think different things when placed in the same situation, I do not see how one could sustain a pretense that Adam and Eve are separate individuals. Someone who wishes to push matters this far *literally* reduces the Prisoners' Dilemma to the one-player game of Figure 2.6(e). It is certainly true that playing (*dove, dove*) is rational in this one-player game, but such a conclusion has little relevance to the problems that the Prisoners' Dilemma was invented to address.

3.4.2   Hobbesian Psychology

In introducing the Paradox of the Twins, I asked how Adam's knowledge that Eve is sure to choose as he chooses can be reconciled with her having the capacity to choose freely. At a superficial level, the answer is easy. If Adam is rational and knows that Eve is rational, then he knows that she will actually choose as he chooses in the Prisoners' Dilemma. Nevertheless, if she were to decide to play *dove*, the fact that Adam has predicted that she will choose *hawk* would not prevent her from playing *dove*. The subjunctives signal a counterfactual. She is free to choose because there exist possible worlds in which Adam's prediction is wrong.[43]

Denying the "I". The superficiality of such orthodox thinking about freedom of choice is revealed when one seeks to establish a context for its counterfactuals by envisaging mechanisms that might determine which of Adam's possible predictions and Eve's possible choices of action are realized. The model that comes immediately to mind is Aumann's setting for a correlated equilibrium. That is to say, Nature endows us with a state of mind in which we "just do what we do". But how can such an unashamed

---

[43]On the other hand, if one maintains that Adam's prediction of Eve's choice will be correct in all possible worlds, as devotees of the Paradox of the Twins sometimes seem to be saying, then one presumably must accept that Eve has no freedom of choice at all.

tale of pure predestination help us to understand what it means for Eve to have a will that is free? My answer is not in the least original. As Spinoza [251] put it:

> Experience teaches us no less clearly than reason, that men believe themselves to be free, simply because they are conscious of their actions, and unconscious of the causes whereby these actions are determined.

Accepting such a resolution of the problem of free will is tantamount to denying that there is such a problem. But, if the problem of free will is nonexistent, how come it causes so many people so much distress? My answer resembles that of Section 1.2, where I denied that the purpose of a naturalistic theory of ethics is to find translations into naturalistic terms of what people commonly mean when they believe themselves to be discussing ethical questions. As with psychological issues like the nature of free will and personal identity, the language that we use to discuss moral issues is structured by the folk wisdom on these matters that was extant in the far past. But nothing guarantees that the entities our ancestors postulated in seeking to understand the world inside and outside their heads have any real existence. It is true that such memes are often helpful in managing one's day-to-day life—otherwise they would have been displaced by more useful memes. For example, the physical principle that "Nature abhors a vacuum" tells the average citizen everything that he is likely to need to know about pneumatics. But it would be a major mistake for scientists to take the practical value of this principle as evidence that some omnipotent lady called Nature so dislikes vacua that she goes around eliminating them.

The error is obvious in the case of *physical* phenomena because our culture has learned to transcend its folk heritage in such matters. It is less obvious in the case of *moral* phenomena, where we are only beginning to develop alternative ways of expressing ourselves that do not take for granted the mistakes of our ancestors. But the error is far from obvious in the case of the mistakes forced upon us by our language when we seek to understand *psychological* phenomena. Indeed, the mistakes are so far from obvious that one usually encounters only ridicule outside the Buddhist world when one suggests that they are mistakes. Even the most enthusiastic admirers of Hume, for example, show signs of embarrassment when commenting on his scepticism about conventional theories of the self. However, I plan to quote from the even more misunderstood Nietzsche [193, p.54].[44] In denying that the "I" presupposed by our language really exists, he says, "The false.

---

[44]Hitler got nothing from Nietzsche beyond the word *Übermensch*. Indeed, it seems rather unlikely that the author of *Mein Kampf* ever read more than a word or two of Nietzsche's writings. Nietzsche was hostile to the German nationalism of his time and explicit in his opposition to anti-semitism.

fundamental observation is that I believe it is I who does something, who suffers something, who has something, who has a quality." How ludicrous! Who is this I who believes that there is no "I"?

Orwell's futuristic novel *1984* contains the idea of an invented language called Newspeak in which it was to be impossible to formulate politically incorrect thoughts. But we do not need to look to imagined futures to see how a language can enslave its speakers. The familiar Oldspeak that we imbibe with our mothers' milk leaves us free to be *politically* incorrect, but makes it very hard to be *psychologically* incorrect. One is forced, like Nietzsche, into locutions that seem to contradict themselves at first sight.

The path away from psychological correctness is therefore hard to follow, but I propose to follow it anyway. I know that I thereby risk discrediting the ideas on morality that I am writing this book to promote. Nor will it help to protest that one does not need to share my views on human psychology in order to agree with what I have to say about morality. My only hope is that the discussion which has led me to this extremity will have been sufficiently dry that my more critical readers will already have skipped to the next chapter.

For most people, it seems obvious that to deny the "I" is to deny the most immediate fact of our personal experience. I think, so the story goes, therefore I am.[45] This presumably means: I think, therefore "I" exists. But what did Descartes *really* experience when he explored the working of his own mind? Was it not merely, to paraphrase Nietzsche [193, p.14]: Here is a thought, therefore thinking takes place. Or, as I would prefer: Here is a thought about a thought, therefore there is thinking about thinking.

In denying a real existence to the "I", nobody, least of all Nietzsche, would wish to dispute the *usefulness* of this little word. In programming a computer, for example, it is highly convenient to be able to invent names for subprograms that need to be called upon repeatedly. If the program is to interact with other programs in computers located elsewhere, these too can be named. If the program needs to predict the result of its interaction with these other programs, the programmer may find it necessary to simulate their operation. His program will then incorporate subprograms that model the operation of the external programs. If these external programs also simulate the operation of the external programs with which *they* interact, then the programmer will thereby be forced into simulating *their* simulations. In doing so, he will need to invent a name that his own program can use in referring *to itself* when it appears as an element in another program's simulation. This name may well be "I".

---

[45]One must be careful not to confuse Descartes' *Cogito ergo sum* with the *Non cogito ergo non sum* of Dr. Strabismus of Utrecht. In the latter, both the consequent and the antecedent are true, and hence so is the material implication that links them.

The subprograms that are used to simulate other programs (and to simulate their simulations) will not necessarily be distinct from one another. If Adam is the programmer, he will not write the same piece of code several times if he can avoid it. To pursue this point, we need a version of the Harsanyi doctrine. Let us assume that all the programmers write their programs under circumstances that make it common knowledge that their finished programs will all be nearly the same.[46] Whenever Adam wants to simulate Eve's program, it would then make sense for him to plan to use his *own* program with *her* data for this purpose.[47] If he succeeds in following this programming strategy, Adam will then have written a capacity for *empathizing* into his program. As Sections 1.2.6 and 1.2.7 make clear, the fact that humans actually do have such a capacity for empathizing with their neighbors is very important to my theory. This is the chief reason why I am risking opprobrium in order to explore the issue of personal identity to some extent.

Consider now what would happen when Adam's attempt to simulate the operation of Eve's program reached a point at which his program began to simulate her simulation of his program. At this stage, Adam's program would be monitoring its *own* operation. But the fact that "I" is capable of *monitoring* what it thinks, is very far from implying that "I" *initiates* its thoughts. It is Adam who wrote the program, not "I".[48] When the program refers to itself as "I", it is therefore not using the word "I" as Descartes understood it. Nevertheless, the label "I" is an indispensable adjunct to the program's operation. Adam would be at an enormous disadvantage if he were deprived of its use and then compelled to enter his program in an evolutionary contest in which his rivals labored under no such constraint.

Man a Machine.[49] Everybody will now be ready for the assertion championed by Dennett [64, 65] that we are "merely" computers ourselves, and

---

[46]This does not mean that the programs will always perform essentially the same calculations. They will usually be operating with different data—that is, they may have different initial "states of mind". Even when their data is the same, they will only be led to the same conclusion when the calculations to be performed represent a convergent process in the sense of Section 3.4.1.

[47]I know that this assertion needs to be qualified. The story as told would involve Adam in an infinite loop in which he simulates simulations of simulations *ad infinitum* (Binmore [33]). Adam must accept that he can use only part of his full program when simulating, so that some capacity is left over for control purposes.

[48]Nietzsche [193, p.54] argues that this is precisely the mistake that humans make. He accuses us of using: A sort of double-sight in seeing, which makes sight a *cause of seeing in itself*.

[49]La Mettrie's [176] well-known *L'Homme Machine* is still worth reading, if only for the pleasure of observing such Anglo-Saxon sentiments in the mouth of an author for whom the English are hateful savages hopelessly degraded by their habit of eating red and bloody meat.

that human consciousness is "nothing more" than a computer program monitoring its own operation.[50] As always, nobody can say what needs to be said better than Hobbes [117, p.81]:

> For seeing that life is but a motion of Limbs, ... why may we not say that all *Automata* (Engines that move themselves by springs and wheeles as doth a watch) have an artificiall life? For what is a *Heart*, but a *Spring*; and the *Nerves*, but so many *Strings*; and the *Joynts*, but so many *Wheeles*, giving Motion to the whole Body, such as was intended by the Artificer?

Of course, the modern Hobbist takes a more sophisticated view of the nature of an automaton. In the words of Gilbert Ryle [225]: Minds are not bits of clockwork, they are just bits of nonclockwork.[51] However, the essential thesis about human psychology is the same as Hobbes'. There is no genuine

---

[50]Which includes monitoring the monitoring. Are we capable of monitoring the monitoring of the monitoring? I have my doubts. Notice, incidentally, that I differ from those experts on artificial intelligence who argue that it would be meaningless to ask whether a machine that passes the Turing Test (Arbib [3]), and hence interacts with the external world in a manner indistinguishable from a human being, would necessarily be self-aware in essentially the same way that a human being is self-aware. Hofstadter [118], for example, imagines a mighty manual that contains a complete description of Einstein's brain together with a set of full instructions on how it can be used to provide the same answers to all questions that Einstein would have given himself. It is sometimes argued that such a manual would itself be self-aware, but it seems to me that self-awareness should not be predicated of an algorithm, but of what happens when the algorithm is running. Nobody suggests, for example, that Einstein's genetic code was self-aware. One therefore needs to include the reader of the Einstein manual as part of the hardware of the machine to be studied—as Searle [233] does in his similar story about an algorithm for answering questions posed in Chinese. (It is sometimes thought significant that the operator of Searle's algorithm would remain ignorant of Chinese while using the algorithm. But one certainly would not wish to identify the "I" of a machine with a piece of its hardware. In fact, Searle's machine is not envisaged as having an "I" at all. I therefore have no difficulty in agreeing with Searle that his machine does not "understand Chinese" as Confucius understood Chinese.) One could then meaningfully ask the machine questions like: What are you thinking *now*? Why did you ask yourself *that* question? More importantly, we could check on whether the machine actually does examine recent steps in the operation of its algorithm in offering answers to such questions. One could object that it is impossible to simulate Einstein's mental processes by the method Hofstadter proposes. My own guess is that one would need at least to take account of his body chemistry as well as his brain and to employ a whole team of operators simultaneously reading different manuals in parallel. However, until we understand better how people think, this will necessarily remain an open question.

[51]For Ryle, this is a piece of irony directed at Cartesian dualists. However, I am happy to take it literally. I agree with Ryle that one makes a category error in thinking that a computer's software exists in the same sense as its hardware—but it does not follow that we necessarily go wrong in thinking of an algorithm as a spectral machine. More importantly, I disagree very much with Ryle [225, p.57] when he tells us that Adam is mistaken to suppose that he learns something about Eve's mental life when he imagines what he would do if he had her preferences and beliefs and finds that his imagined decisions are the same as those she actually makes. It is true that Adam cannot be

reason to suppose that a ghost is to be found among our bits and pieces of nonclockwork. This is not to say that a ghost may not be there: only that I am one of those who see no reason why Occam's razor should not be applied to this issue as to any other.

The hostility that expressing this view sometimes provokes is mystifying, especially when it comes from those who disclaim any religious convictions. People presumably feel somehow diminished at the suggestion that they are "no better" than robots—just as bourgeois Victorians felt their dignity impugned when they learned of their kinship with the apes. Or perhaps they fear that the news that we are apes or robots will result in the proletariat adopting the habits of King Kong or Arnold Schwarzenegger. Both responses seem to me more than a little silly. I certainly noticed no loss in self-importance when I gave up the ghost in my own machine. Nor did my change of heart seem to require that I alter my behavior at all. Indeed, the fear that society will fall apart if people learn of their true nature seems to me absurd. If people are apes or robots, then they are *already* behaving like apes or robots!

We need not join the Victorians in fearing that apes of the species *homo sapiens* will start behaving like baboons if we tell them that they are apes. Nor will people start behaving like cuckoo clocks if we wind them up by telling them that they are machines. They may perhaps come to believe what we tell them, just as they once believed whatever was fashionable among philosophers or theologians in the past. But changes in abstract belief systems usually have little impact on actual social behavior. People carry on behaving sensibly most of the time, just as they always have.[52] For most purposes, all that will happen if we persuade people to replace

---

sure that he thereby models her inner life accurately. But neither can he be sure that physicists' models are accurate models of the material universe—no matter how well they predict the future course of events. In both cases, one can do no more than compare the simplicity of the model with the complexity of the data it supposedly explains.

[52]I am not saying that a *society* will necessarily behave like a sensible individual. We are, after all, engaged in a discussion of the Prisoners' Dilemma. I am saying that *individuals* mostly behave fairly sensibly, even when they live in crazy societies and subscribe to crackpot creeds. Nor am I saying that the way people manage their everyday lives is an historical invariant—only that currently fashionable opinions on the nature of the human predicament are usually peripheral in determining how habituated behavior changes over time. Sometimes, of course, fashionable opinion latches on to a trend already in place by inventing a reason that people then give to "explain" why one particular meme is being ditched in favor of another. Such a mechanism can hurry an already established trend along. But opinions that run counter to a trend already established by social evolution have little or no chance of becoming fashionable. This is not to say that fashionable opinion is *never* crucial. But I think it becomes a significant factor only on those rare occasions when social evolution reaches a bifurcation point, and so allows its future course to become vulnerable to events that are normally mere epiphenomena. Even books like this therefore have some tiny chance of influencing events!

the way they explain their social behavior to themselves by something more scientific is that they will behave a little more sensibly a little more often. In particular, perhaps they will begin to see the absurdity of being "proud" or "ashamed" of personal attributes that are largely the result of accidents of biological or social history—like skincolor, intellectual capacity, nationality, social class or respectability.

Yellowness of Yellow. I have a great deal more sympathy with what are perhaps best described as aesthetic objections to the idea that we are mere machines. I do not mean by this the claim that we cannot be machines because a machine could not be moved as we are sometimes moved by a Wagnerian opera or a Beethoven symphony. My teenage children are impervious to the music that I enjoy, but I am nevertheless fairly sure that they are people. That is to say, "being moved" by works of "great art" is largely a cultural phenomenon. The objections I have in mind focus rather on experiences that are genuinely personal. For example, can a machine genuinely experience what I experience when I see a yellow object? A machine may measure wavelengths and suchlike, but surely only a real person can appreciate the yellowness of yellow! I know it is hopeless to try and reach those who think like this by discussing the physiology of vision, but I shall try. Unfortunately, what I have to say on this subject requires running counter to fashionable philosophical opinion on color perception. As so often, it will therefore be necessary for me to say more on this subject than I would really like.

If one is strict about the literal meaning of the words, it is not obvious that there is such an experience as "seeing" a "yellow object". Like Galileo, I think it far from clear that color is best understood by adopting the Aristotelian view that "yellow" is an attribute of an object. One can regard it instead as being "merely" a symbol that the brain uses to represent a solution to a certain algebraic problem. This may seem a wild claim, but consider what Land [146] discovered about how the brain attributes color to objects in its field of vision. Much remains to be understood, but the simplest account holds that our retinas are sensitive to three different wavelengths. The retina therefore creates what one might call a three-dimensional color map of our visual field. But this is not what we perceive. If it were, then the colors we attribute to objects would change dramatically as the wavelength of the light that illuminates them is changed. But some simple experiments at home will serve to convince anyone that this is not the case. It must therefore be that the brain processes the data it receives from the retina very elaborately. If it does finally assign a three-dimensional vector to a region, then this vector must be a function, not just of the wavelengths it receives from that region, but also of the wavelengths it receives from *surrounding* regions. The brain then assigns one of the color symbols that human evolution has invented for this purpose to each region in its visual field. This invented color is held relatively constant as the wavelengths of the illuminating light vary over a wide range. This is why we can speak of a yellow dress without usually needing to qualify the remark by specifying the wavelength of the source of illumination.

The point of describing Land's model of color perception is that it demystifies the mechanics of the human visual data-processing apparatus, and hence makes it plausible that it could be mimicked by a suitable machine. It does not, however, demystify the nature of what precisely it is that we perceive when we call a dress "yellow". Personally, I doubt whether the symbols that the brain uses to record the results of its visual calculations are capable of demystification in purely verbal terms. Our visual data-processing apparatus was hard-wired into our brains long before our species learned to verbalize. The symbol "yellow" that the brain uses to tell us the results of a visual calculation is therefore not only nonverbal—it escapes our attempts to describe it in verbal terms. When we say that only a real person can appreciate the "yellowness of yellow", we are therefore only saying that our imaginations lack the capacity to transfer our visual experiences from the symbology that Nature has hard-wired into our brains to the verbal symbology that we use to communicate with one another. However, this imperfection in our imaginative powers need not prevent our observing an isomorphism between the symbols used by a machine programmed to mimic how we see and the symbols that we use ourselves for the same purpose.

Some critics feel that to adopt a Landian model of color perception is to deny the reality of our visual experiences. On this point, Galileo's analogy (Redondi [215, p.56]) between perceiving color and being tickled by a feather seems particularly apt. As we all know, it is very hard to tickle *oneself*. It is therefore obvious that the curious sensation we experience on being tickled is something that our brains invent only in certain social situations. We therefore feel no inclination to adopt a mode of expression that makes ticklishness somehow reside in the feather. But who is thereby led to argue that what they feel when tickled by a feather is unreal? Similarly, to deny Aristotle on color is not to claim that our eyes deceive us. When we describe a visual experience by saying, "I see a yellow dress", our description of what we see takes a certain explanation of *why* we see what we see for granted. The implication is that we see the dress as yellow because yellowness resides in the dress. But what we actually *see* does not include this somewhat threadbare explanation. Our visual experience is better described simply by saying "I see that dress as yellow".

Locke's [156] distinction between primary qualities (like shape) and secondary qualities (like color) is a further barrier to understanding, since critics seem to feel that one can only be subscribing to some such view if one denies the Aristotelian position. However, my position is more complicated. In the first place, I do not deny that the Aristotelian model that makes yellow a primary quality of a dress that we normally see as yellow is adequate for most practical purposes.[53] Nevertheless, a Lockean model that makes yellow a secondary quality of a dress is more widely applicable, since it offers an explanation of why the same dress is sometimes *not* seen as yellow.[54] But, although a Lockean model is better than an Aristotelian model when the complexity of the two models is irrelevant, the former seems to me only a temporary stopgap, because it does no more than redefine the terms of a piece of folk wisdom that incorporates a fundamental misconception.[55] A Landian model which makes yellow a symbol that represents the results of a calculation performed when certain signals are received at the retina is more widely applicable than a Lockean model, because it has the potential to explain what color we actually will perceive when a dress normally seen as yellow is seen as some other color. Which model should those who wish to deny that a machine can "genuinely" appreciate the yellowness of yellow prefer? Perhaps paradoxically, it seems to me that their best line of defense is adopt the same Landian model which I think renders it plausible that a machine might be constructed whose manner of perceiving color is isomorphic to human color perception. Adopting one of the other models would allow people like me the opportunity to frame a physically objective definition of yellow that a machine could *easily* be programmed to use.

It is unfortunate that we do not have the same hard data about how our feelings and emotions are generated as we do about our visual experiences.

---

[53]Similarly, the models that make solidity a primary quality of a table or flatness a primary quality of our planet are adequate for most practical purposes. But my training in quantum mechanics and geography has taught me to consider using other models in some circumstances.

[54]I am always left in doubt by Locke as to whether I am to have his cake or eat it. In this case, the question is whether he held that secondary qualities reside in the objects to which they are attributed. Mackie's [165] affirmative answer seems to me a more plausible reading of Locke's thinking than the account given by those who follow Berkeley's [19] interpretation. If Mackie is right, then to say that yellow is a secondary quality of a dress is simply to say that it has the property of inducing us to see it as yellow under normal circumstances. On this reading, one can therefore offer an objective definition of yellow as a secondary quality in terms of the character of wavelengths that it reflects when illuminated by light of a particular wavelength.

[55]I said the same thing about reinterpreting folk explanations of moral phenomena in Section 1.2 and at various intervals in the interim. Even when the fundamental structure of a folk explanation is not flawed, it is inevitable that confusion will continually arise about whether one is using terms in their colloquial sense or their reinterpreted sense. Economists, for example, have unwittingly created precisely this kind of confusion by reinterpreting the Benthamite notion of utility—thereby forcing me in this book to offer continual reminders that modern utility theory reverses the causal chain implicit in the terminology employed.

Presumably, these are not localized in the brain. Nevertheless, we experience something in our brains as well as in our bodies when we taste the bitterness of grief or the ecstasy of orgasm. Is it ridiculous to suggest that what we experience is merely a sequence of symbols with which the brain keeps track of various ongoing calculations? I think not—but neither do I think that a symbol is something to which the word "merely" can automatically be applied. Aside from other considerations, our internal symbols serve as triggers that provide potential access to a whole range of stored previous experience.

Gödel's Theorem. As for intellectual arguments against the hypothesis that we are nothing but machines, I want to mention only the appeal that is sometimes made to Gödel's theorem, since I plan to turn this on its head. Loosely speaking, Gödel's theorem tells us that no formal deductive system of sufficient complexity can be simultaneously consistent and complete. That is, if the system generates no formal contradictions, then there are true statements that can be expressed within the system but cannot be proved within the system. The distinguished mathematical physicist Penrose [202] is commonly quoted as authorizing Lucas's inference that we cannot therefore be machines. A machine can only proceed algorithmically. It can therefore only know to be true what can be deduced from its data by formal deductive methods. But, so the argument goes, Gödel's theorem shows that humans can transcend this limitation. We can know things to be true that cannot be proved!

But can we *really* know things that cannot be proved? I believe that Gödel's famous example of a true but unprovable sentence is true because I am convinced by Gödel's argument. But my mathematical training tells me never to be convinced by an argument unless I am simultaneously convinced that the argument can be reduced to a step-by-step procedure that leads from an agreed set of axioms to the given conclusion. It is tautologous that nothing about this step-by-step procedure can be inaccessible to a computer. The understanding among mathematicians is that you haven't finished providing all the details of a proof until you have reached a stage at which your efforts can be checked by a computer. If a computer cannot duplicate our reasoning, it must therefore be because it does not agree with our axioms. In fact, the argument that shows the Gödel sentence to be true relies on axioms that are not part of the original formal system. The extra axioms are not usually formalized. But if they were formalized, we would have constructed a larger formal system within which the Gödel sentence is not only true, but provable.

Gödel provided a principle that allows extra axioms to be appended to any sufficiently complex formal deductive system in such a way that true statements that were unprovable in the original system become provable in the expanded system. However, nothing prevents this principle being programmed into a computer. We would then have constructed a machine that duplicates the human feat of transcending a computer that is confined to using only the axioms of the original deductive system. Of course, one can also transcend such a new computer in the same sort of way. But this feat can also be duplicated by a suitably programmed computer. That is to say, whenever a human offers us an example based on Gödelian arguments of something that a computer supposedly cannot do, we can in fact program a computer to do it. One may object that humans somehow know that the extra axioms that are appended to a system when it is to be transcended are correct, whereas a computer has to be programmed with this information. But such an objection begs the question. The argument is supposed to *prove* that humans can know things unknowable to a computer—not to take this conclusion for granted.[56]

Actually, it seems to me that the telling points that Penrose [202] has to make have nothing at all to do with such formal arguments. His dissatisfaction with the "men are machines" hypothesis derives rather from his difficulty in reconciling his own attempts at introspection with his image of how things would seem to an "I" programmed into a computer. As great mathematicians commonly report, his ideas just seem to pop up from nowhere. When I try to trace the origins of my own humble attempts to be mathematically creative, I come up against the same problem. The ideas come from somewhere beneath the level of consciousness. It is the same when one seeks to pinpoint the moment at which a decision is made. Hume [128], for example, tells us that he often repeatedly decides to rise from his bed but fails to do so, only later to find himself out of bed and dressing with no clear idea of how this came about.

However, if we truly are machines, are these not the sort of phenomena that Gödel-type arguments would lead us to expect? If we are machines, then it is logically impossible for us always to know everything that is going on in our heads.[57] As I expressed it in Section 3.4.1, a machine

---

[56] More generally, no conclusive objection can be based on the argument that computers are only *simulating* the way humans think or perceive, unless we can specify precisely what it is that humans are doing when they describe themselves as thinking or perceiving. But, if we understood thinking and perceiving well enough to provide full details of how humans think and perceive, then it is hard to see how such a detailed account would not provide a blueprint for the construction of a machine capable of thinking and perceiving just like a human. This would still be true even in the unlikely event that quantum phenomena play some significant role in our mental processes, as suggested by Penrose [202].

[57] This section is short on references to what is a huge literature in which no single work stands out from the others. However, as an economist, I cannot let it pass unnoticed that Hayek [113] was saying what I am about to say way back in 1952. Let me also mention Arbib's [4] *In Search of the Person*, Dennett's [65] *Consciousness Explained*

cannot always be entirely sure even of its own state of mind. Or, to quote Schopenhauer [230]: "Even in self-consciousness ... the I remains a riddle to itself." I believe that it is our incapacity to deal with such riddles using the concept of an "I" that has forced upon us the difficult notion of a "will". But, if there is no "I", then it is unnecessary to postulate a "will", which somehow translates the decisions of an incorporeal entity into movements of the body. Still less is it necessary to explain how this internal "prime mover" somehow moves things without itself being moved. The problems associated with the notion of "free will" therefore do not arise at all. From this point of view, it is as useful to ask how Eve's will can be free as to ask why Nature dislikes a vacuum. We waste our time in seeking new explanations of what such folk explanations might possibly mean. What we really need are new explanations of the phenomena that the folk explanations fail to explain.

My guess is that our mistakes about "free will" have very humble origins. Just as Eve's freedom to choose was explained at the beginning of the section by noting that Adam's prediction of her choice will sometimes be wrong, so I tell myself that "I" is free to choose because I cannot always predict for sure what "I" will think or do. I do not understand why this observation is sometimes said to be paradoxical. After all, a programmer knows all of the code that he has written into a program, but he does not know what the results of running the program will be for all its possible inputs. If he did, he would not bother to write the program. Somewhat more subtly, a program may know its own code—as with John Howard's "program" for the CLINT persona given in Section 3.2.2. If it is appropriate to model people as machines, it therefore follows that I may know everything that there is to know about how "I" processes data, but still not always know how "I" will in fact process any particular piece of data. Just as a programmer will normally need to run his own program to find out what it will do in certain situations, so I will sometimes have no better way to predict what "I" will do in certain situations than simply waiting to see what "I" actually does.

My difficulties in predicting what "I" will do become even more pressing if I do not know for sure precisely how "I" makes decisions. Some doubt about this question will always be realistic, even when "I" is a computer program that has access to its own code. We cannot insulate computer programs from the corrupting influences of the outside world. Nor is there such a thing as a perfectly self-correcting program. For example, as Dowling [67] notes, it is impossible to write a program that can both test its input for a computer virus and simultaneously be guaranteed not to spread a virus

---

and Bicchieri and Gilboa's [22] "Can free choice be known?"

itself.[58] Like Gödel's Theorem, the proofs of such impossibility results usually have at their heart some updated variant of Epimenides' classical Liar Paradox or Pseudomenos.[59] The use of this trick allows mathematicians to come up with remarkably short proofs of their impossibility theorems. However, I suspect that a layman like myself is more likely to obtain genuine insight into why certain things are impossible in computation theory by thinking hard about how one would set about programming a computer to do them, rather than by studying the details of how mathematicians manage to pull various rabbits out of their hats.[60] I therefore plan to offer only one impossibility argument—and my chief reason for doing so is to explain why I think that nobody who is not already persuaded by the "men are machines" argument need feel overly disturbed by such arguments. The argument purports to prove that there is at least one state of mind in which I do not know my own state of mind.

Suppose that I am in a state of mind M in which I respond to questions about my state of mind exactly as I would respond when trying to give an honest answer to the question: Is it possible that I might not tell the whole truth about my current state of mind? If I know that my state of mind is M, how will I reply to the question: Is your state of mind M? The truthful reply is yes. But this makes no the honest reply to: Is it possible that I might not tell the whole truth about my current state of mind? Since this is a contradiction, I must leave the possibility that I am in state of mind M open when replying to the question: Are you in state of mind M? But this makes yes the honest answer to: Is it possible that I might not tell the whole truth about my current state of mind? We are therefore led to a contradiction whichever way we turn. Our error, so the argument goes, is to assume that I know my own state of mind when my state of mind is M.

---

[58] In studying such questions, mathematicians refer to Turing machines when they want to discuss computer programs that are to be envisaged as having access to an indefinitely large amount of storage space in which to conduct their calculations. The Church-Turing thesis is that such a machine can duplicate any formal calculation possible for a human mathematician. (The thesis is not some wild speculation promulgated by wide-eyed fanatics. It commands general support among mathematicians as a working hypothesis that has survived several quite challenging tests.) The archetypal impossibility result in computation theory arises from the Halting Problem for Turing machines. Like regular programs, Turing machines might calculate for ever with certain inputs. Is it possible to guard against this possibility by constructing a Turing machine that will input the code and data of an arbitrary Turing machine and then invariably report if this Turing machine will fail to halt when set to work on its data? The answer is no.

[59] Apparently, ancient Cretans were incorrigible liars. So what does one make of a Cretan who says, "I am a liar"? The Gödel sentence operates in a similar spirit, since it can be interpreted as saying, "I am unprovable".

[60] This is not, of course, to deny the usefulness of the proofs that mathematicians provide. Without them, Adam would have no defense when Eve attributed his failure to see how to write certain programs to a simple lack of imagination.

However, one does not need to accept the conclusion that we sometimes do not know our own minds. As with Bertrand Russell's barber, who shaves every man in the town who does not shave himself, one can deny the existence of a state of mind M satisfying the criteria of the preceding argument. This objection is never made when similar stories about computer programs are told in a careful way.[61] What supposedly distinguishes computer programs from people in such stories is that it is possible to express every detail of how a computer program works within the language that programs use to communicate with the outside world. I agree that humans are not constructed from the "clockwork" components of computers. However, if the manner in which our own bits and pieces of "nonclockwork" operate is, in principle, capable of being described in minute detail within the language that we use to communicate with each other, then the impossibility stories that apply to computer programs apply to us also. It is *this* proposition that I think that those who are skeptical of applying impossibility theorems from computation theory to people should be denying. You do not need to join those of us who believe that it is very likely that we will one day be able to give an adequate scientific account of how our brains work. In particular, if you believe that there is something transcendental in the manner in which humans appreciate the yellowness of yellow, or that humans can somehow directly perceive infinities that a machine can only

---

[61]Such stories are nothing more than a retelling of the Halting Problem for Turing machines. I have used a number of versions for various purposes elsewhere (Binmore [25, 32, 28]). For example, Binmore and Brandenburger [38] offer the following argument while discussing the axioms governing human knowledge that are currently orthodox in game theory: Suppose that possibility questions are resolved by a Turing machine S that sometimes answers NO to questions that begin: "Is it possible that ...?" Unless the answer is NO, possibility is conceded. (Possibility is therefore conceded even if the machine never replies, since timing issues are neglected.)

Consider a specific question concerning the Turing machine N. Let the computer code for this question be $\lceil N \rceil$. Let $\lfloor M \rfloor$ be the computer code for the question: "Is it possible that M will answer NO to $\lceil M \rceil$?" Finally, let T be a Turing machine that outputs $\lfloor x \rfloor$ when its input is $\lceil x \rceil$. Then the program $R = ST$ that consists of first operating T and then operating S, responds to $\lceil M \rceil$ as S responds to $\lfloor M \rfloor$.

Suppose that R responds to $\lceil R \rceil$ with NO. Then S reports that it is *impossible* that R responds to $\lceil R \rceil$ with NO. If what someone knows is always true, then it follows that R never responds to $\lceil R \rceil$ with NO. But, if we, as observers, know this, why don't we replace S with a better program: one that accurately reflects our knowledge? Either our algorithm for determining what is possible is "incomplete" in that it allows as possible events we know to be false, or it is "inconsistent" in that it rejects as impossible events we know to be true.

Binmore and Shin [43] attempt a more formal analysis of the problems that arise when knowledge is assumed to be acquired algorithmically. In particular, they suggest that, for certain foundational questions, there is a case for replacing the modal logic S5 that game theorists (mostly unconsciously) use in characterizing human knowledge, by the modal logic G. One of the axioms of G is called Löb's theorem in mathematical proof theory, where it is shown to be equivalent to Gödel's second incompleteness theorem.

handle indirectly with the aid of a finite symbology, then there is no reason why you should feel troubled by the impossibility results of computation theory.

Also Sprach Zarathustra. The time has come to attempt some sort of summary. Recall the story told earlier in this section about how Adam would need a label "I" to refer to the subprogram he uses to simulate his own program's future behavior when seeking to simulate the attempts of other programs to simulate it. This was followed by an extended discussion intended to justify the claim that the "I" subprogram will necessarily be an imperfect predictor of what Adam's program will actually do. My emphasis on this point is intended to explain why one need not see Aumann's model—in which Nature endows each of us with a state of mind and then we "just do what we do"—as being inconsistent with what we actually experience when we say that we are "choosing freely".

A state of mind is a complicated thing. Our social and biological history has filled our heads with all kinds of memes that compete for attention. Some memes are used for deciding which meme to use. Other memes decide which meme to use in deciding which meme to use. Perhaps our heads hold memes that operate at even higher levels. Although we are wired up to monitor this complex sorting process to some degree, we actually observe very little of what is going on. Far from being able to predict where are thoughts are leading, we are often very surprised at what we find inside our heads. As Schopenhauer says, the working of our own minds is a mystery to us. As people always do when confronted with a mysterious natural process, we therefore invent a supernatural agency that somehow "causes" the phenomena that we cannot otherwise explain. In this case, the supernatural agent is "free will". Perhaps it bears repeating one last time that to deny "free will" is not to deny the *phenomena* that led our ancestors to invent the notion of "free will"—any more than to refuse to answer questions about why Zeus is angry today is to deny that thunder can be heard in the hills. In brief, nothing is lost by abandoning the notion of "free will", except a constraint on our ability to think freely.

I do not want to weary the reader by explaining why I belong to the large community of thinkers who regard it as likely that the story of Adam's computer program is a useful allegory for the manner in which the notion of an "I" evolved concurrently with *homo sapiens*. The arguments have been rehearsed too often for this to be a useful exercise. However, I do think it important to stress the *social* element in the version of the story that I prefer.

I am one of those who are persuaded by the biological arguments that attribute our relatively big brains to the pressing needs of a thinking animal who lives in a society along with other thinking animals. I therefore see morality as being *intrinsic* to our nature.[62] It is because we need the ability to empathize with others that we have developed a sense of personal identity—not the reverse. As communitarians like Macintyre [160], Sandel [227] and Taylor [260] emphasize, we have not evolved as a collection of isolated egos that moral philosophers are free to slot into whatever ideal society they may choose to invent.[63] Our egos are themselves cultural artifacts to a substantial degree. But this insight can never be properly exploited if we insist on keeping the "I" as the centerpiece of our maps of inner space.[64]

The chief function of the "I" is to act as a mirror of others in our own minds[65] and to reflect the manner in which we are similarly mirrored in the minds of others. Its nature is therefore inextricably bound up with the nature of the "I"s with which it interacts. This is why game theory is so important if we are ever to understand what lies at the root of being human. If we persist in treating the ego as some kind of immaculate Platonic ideal that somehow exists independently of the society in which we live, we will never learn to know ourselves. What lies inside our heads is a result of biological and social evolution. Insofar as these processes are complete, we think as we think and we feel as we feel, because it is *in equilibrium* for such thoughts and feelings to survive in the game of life. Or at least, thus says the meme that has managed to gain control of the bundle of memes and genes pushing this particular pen.

Finally, there is a three-hundred-year-old calumny that requires redress. We Hobbists are not necessarily atheists, as Isaac Newton, for example, assumed when he accused John Locke of Hobbism. It is, of course, impossible

---

[62]Perhaps I should reiterate some of what was said in Sections 1.2.2 and 1.2.3 about "natural law"—which I understand in its customary sense as a postulated constraint on human behavior that is neither natural nor legal. As Hume [128, p.484] emphasizes, the conventions for coordinating on equilibria that he identifies with "natural laws" are *artificial*, and so may vary from one society to another. In saying that morality is intrinsic to our nature, I am not therefore saying that our nature somehow binds us to obey any of the so-called "natural laws" of moral philosophy. If I must express myself in this sort of language, what I am saying is only that it is natural that we have "natural laws". Or, more tendentiously, that it is idle for a moral philosopher to invent "natural laws" that respect neither his biological nature nor the cultural history of his society.

[63]But I do not, of course, endorse the communitarian conclusion that the device of the original position must therefore be abandoned. On the contrary, I think it is because we need the capacity to empathize required by social devices like the original position that we have egos at all.

[64]With our own eyes, we watch the sun cross the sky each day from east to west. Yet still we follow Copernicus in refusing to make the earth the centerpiece of our map of outer space. Can we not be equally imaginative about the "I"?

[65]Nothing is more revealing about a person's inner life than the little crimes and transgressions of which he accuses others. Those who are quick to accuse others of dishonesty typically harbor dishonest thoughts themselves!

to be a Hobbist and also to believe all the doctrines of any traditional religion, but Newton himself was anything but conventional in his religious beliefs. Nor are we Hobbists necessarily wicked. Am I not, after all, writing this book because I would like to see society reformed? Nor are Hobbists necessarily crude materialists. Hobbesian psychology may be materialistic, but it certainly need not be crude. Hobbists can accommodate such notions as the putative immortality of the soul or the possible resurrection of the body without blinking an eye.[66] As for grander matters, like the origin and nature of the universe, Hobbists are free to think whatever they choose. There is certainly no reason, for example, why a Hobbist should believe that the whole universe is giant machine, just because he thinks it likely that people are small machines.[67] As for myself, I have no idea how to answer Leibniz's question: Why is there something and not nothing? I do not even know whether I think the question makes any sense.

3.5   Newcomb's Paradox

The Newcomb problem was introduced to the world by Nozick [195], and immediately won the hearts of philosophers the world over. Levi [149] captured the general spirit of the enthusiasm that reigned at the time by writing a paper called *Newcombmania*. Nowadays, the enthusiasm is more muted, but Newcombmania remains a flourishing cottage industry. My own opinion is that this industry is largely wasted, since Newcomb's Paradox makes assumptions about timing, predictability and free choice that cannot hold simultaneously. Like Russell's barber, who shaves every man in a town who does not shave himself, there is therefore no such thing as a Newcomb problem.

Nevertheless, various models based on Newcomb's story are considered in this section. In each case, one of the three basic assumptions of the story has to be weakened in order to construct something coherent. As a consequence, none of the models studied will satisfy a determined Newcombmaniac. To those with maniacal tendencies, I can only say that I am doing my best to provide satisfaction—but there is just no way of realizing a contradiction!

Although Newcomb is said to have formulated the problem that bears his name while thinking about the Prisoners' Dilemma, it does not have the appearance of being a game-theoretic puzzle. It is posed in the form

---

[66] Provided that you do not object to your "soul" being thought of as an algorithm.

[67] I do not understand why those who dislike the "men are machines" hypothesis think it relevant to produce arguments against the claim that the universe as a whole is computable; nor why those who like the hypothesis feel it necessary to offer counterarguments.

of a one-person decision problem. Two boxes possibly have money inside. Adam is free to take either the first box or both boxes. If he cares only for money, which choice should he make? This seems an easy problem. If *dove* represents taking only the first box and *hawk* represents taking both boxes, then Adam should choose *hawk* because this choice always results in his getting at least as much money as *dove*. Nozick [195] abuses the terminology of Section 2.2.3 by saying that *hawk* therefore "dominates" *dove*.

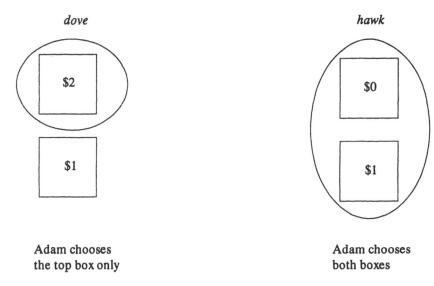

dove   *hawk*

Adam chooses   Adam chooses
the top box only   both boxes

Figure 3.8: The Newcomb problem

However, there is a catch—as there usually is when it seems that a free lunch is on offer. Moreover, this catch is a veritable Catch 22. It is certain that there is one dollar bill in the second box. The first box may contain nothing or it may contain two dollar bills. The decision about whether there should be money in the first box was made yesterday by Eve. She knows Adam very well. Indeed, she is what Brams [47] calls a *superior being*.[68] She knows Adam so well that she is always able to make a perfect prediction of what he will do in all circumstances. Like Adam, she has two choices, *dove* and *hawk*. Her dovelike choice is to put two dollar bills in the first box. Her hawkish choice is to put nothing in the first box. For reasons

---

[68] In an application of Newcomb's Paradox to a macroeconomic model, Schotter [232] casts the government in the role of Adam. Eve's role as the superior being is assigned to the general public!

best known to herself, she plays *dove* if and only if she predicts that Adam will choose *dove*. She plays *hawk* if and only if she predicts that Adam will choose *hawk*. Figure 3.8 illustrates the problem that Adam then faces. His choice of *hawk* would now seem to yield only one dollar bill whereas *dove* yields two dollar bills. But how can it be right for Adam to choose *dove* when we have already seen that this choice is "dominated" by *hawk*?

Nozick [195] tells us that Newcomb's Paradox exposes a conflict between "domination" and the "maximization of expected utility". Nozick contemplates this supposed conflict between "two principles of choice" with disinterested equanimity. He tells us that about fifty percent of his correspondents are sure that domination is right and the other fifty percent are sure that maximizing expected utility is right. However, if Nozick had really uncovered a conflict between the principles as they are understood in game theory, then the fall of the temple of the Philistines would be as nothing compared with the consequences that would follow for game theorists and their works. If game theory makes any sense at all, there *cannot* be a contradiction between domination and expected utility maximization. A game theorist must therefore be forgiven for looking elsewhere for the source of the contradiction. If his search is unsuccessful, then he must submit with what grace he can muster to being dishonorably discharged from the academic service—with his epaulets ripped from his shoulders and his sword broken across his commanding officer's knee.

Readers who survived the prolonged discussion of the Paradox of the Twins in the previous section will be able to predict why I do not think that Nozick has uncovered a skeleton in the game-theoretical cupboard. However, I still think it worth devoting a section to the topic since it directs attention to the Von Neumann and Morgenstern theory of expected utility maximization. Both my approach to ethics and that of Harsanyi [109] depend very heavily on the Von Neumann and Morgenstern theory. However, those who write on ethics often labor under serious misapprehensions about what the Von Neumann and Morgenstern theory says. In a style familiar from Chapter 2, criticism is consequently sometimes directed at propositions that are essentially tautological. Section 4.2 in the next chapter explains this point in detail. No serious attempt will therefore be made in this chapter to set the record straight on "expected utility maximization". Instead, attention will be concentrated on clarifying Nozick's "domination" principle.

Bad Timing. When game theorists apply the principle of domination, they usually first begin by writing down a strategic form for the game in question. Before this can be done, one needs to identify the players' pure strategies. If there is any doubt about what the pure strategies are, it is necessary to take one step further back and to construct a preliminary extensive form for the game in all its gory detail. In studying the Prisoners' Dilemma, we have grown accustomed to treating *dove* and *hawk* as representing pure strategies. It therefore seems natural in Newcomb's story to continue to do the same. But is it right to think of *dove* and *hawk* as being *strategies* in Newcomb's problem? The answer depends on what we think appropriate as an extensive form for the Newcomb problem.

The first model to be considered retains Newcomb's assumptions on predictability and free choice, but abandons his assumptions about the physical timing of moves. Given what was said in Section 3.4.2 about "free will", it may seem odd that I have now begun talking about a model in which Adam is able to choose freely—but perhaps I may beg for a little patience on this point. The first priority is to clarify the notion of a superior being.

It is important to understand that a superior being is not merely somebody who correctly predicts what Adam actually does. Eve does not need to be superior to pull off this trick. Two rational players using a Nash equilibrium each correctly predict what the other will *actually* do, without any need to attribute superior intellect or knowledge to either. To be a superior being, Eve must be modeled as being an accurate predictor of Adam's behavior in all relevant possible worlds—not just in the world that is actually realized. For example, it may be that Adam will actually choose *dove*. If so, then Eve must actually predict that he will choose *dove*. But it must also be true that, if Adam had chosen *hawk* instead, then Eve would have predicted that he would choose *hawk*.

This strong definition of a superior being seems entirely coherent to me if taken on its own. If you share my belief that computer analogies are useful, you can imagine that Eve knows all the code of Adam's operating program together with the data on which it operates. She can therefore always run his program with his data on her machine to predict what he will do.[69] Of course, she will then need to be a more complex entity than Adam, but this is entirely consistent with her status as a superior being.

To construct a model that takes such a story about computer programs literally is to use a hammer to smash a walnut. Much simpler models are adequate.[70] Indeed, a game theorist will be content to follow Brams [47]

---

[69] Game theorists sometimes airily dismiss Newcomb's Paradox on the grounds that it is impossible that Eve could be sure of predicting Adam's choice, because he could always make his decision depend on the fall of a coin. But this is not a very useful response. We can modify the Newcomb story so that Eve always chooses *hawk* unless Adam chooses *dove* for certain. For this reason, I shall stick with the conventional story and not allow Adam to mix his choices.

[70] For example, one can see Eve as nothing other than an embodiment of the CLINT persona of Section 3.2.1. The Newcomb problem then becomes a simplified form of Nigel Howard's 1-2 metagame of Figure 3.1. (The simplification is that Eve's reasons

in modeling the hypothesis that Eve is a superior being with the extensive
form of Figure 3.9(a). In this little game, the first move is assigned to
Adam, who chooses between *dove* and *hawk*. Eve then observes his choice.
In the manner of a political columnist, she then predicts his choice only
after seeing what he does.[71] This guarantees that she can make correct
predictions if she so chooses. The doubled lines in Figure 3.9(a) show the
choices attributed to the players. Since the Newcomb story does not explain
Eve's choices, no payoffs for her are included in the diagram. She "just does
what she does". Given her planned behavior, Adam optimizes by playing
dove. But the story is that *hawk* "dominates" *dove*. How then can Adam
maximize his expected utility by playing *dove*?

The answer is simple. Figure 3.9(e) shows a putative 2×2 strategic form
for the extensive form of Figure 3.9(a). If this were the correct strategic
form, then it would indeed be true that *hawk* dominates *dove*. But it is
wrong to assign only two pure strategies to Eve. In Figure 3.9(a), she has
two nodes at which she must specify what she would do if that node were
reached. At each of these two nodes, she has two alternatives from which
to choose. She therefore has $2 \times 2 = 4$ pure strategies in all. The correct
strategic form is therefore the 2×4 payoff table shown in Figure 3.9(d). In
the style of Section 3.2.2, Eve's four pure strategies are denoted by *dd*, *dh*,
hd, and *hh*. For example, when Eve "just does what she does", she uses *dh*.
This strategy requires her to select *dove* if Adam chooses *dove*, and *hawk*
if he chooses *hawk*. Notice that *hawk* does not dominate *dove* for Adam
in Figure 3.9(d). Indeed, if Adam knows that Eve will use the strategy *dh*
attributed to her by Newcomb's story, then the strategic form shows that
he gets $2 from playing *dove* and only $1 from playing *hawk*. No conflict
between "domination" and "expected utility maximization" therefore arises
in this model.

What of the claim that the model of Figure 3.9(a) allows Adam to choose
freely? Does this not conflict with my denial of "free will" in Section 3.4.2? I
think not. Consider, for example, what would happen if we were to augment
a formal model of a game by including a full account of Adam's thought

---

for choosing the CLINT persona are left unexplained.) Section 3.2.1 concentrated on
the difficulties that Eve would have in making a *commitment* to the CLINT persona.
But here such difficulties are assumed away. Instead, the Newcomb problem focuses
attention on a second difficulty that was mentioned only in passing in Section 3.2.1. To
operate the CLINT persona, Adam's intentions must be transparent to Eve. She must be
able to predict his intentions perfectly. My guess is that part of the reason that stories
involving the CLINT persona are popular, is that expressing this requirement in terms of
such personas disguises the fact that the perfect prediction hypothesis is equivalent to
Adam's moving *first* and Eve's moving *second*—as in Figure 3.9(a).

[71]Political columnists are such superior beings that they not only predict what happened yesterday, they go on to explain why yesterday's events were *inevitable*—especially
in those cases when nobody had even considered their possibility the day before!

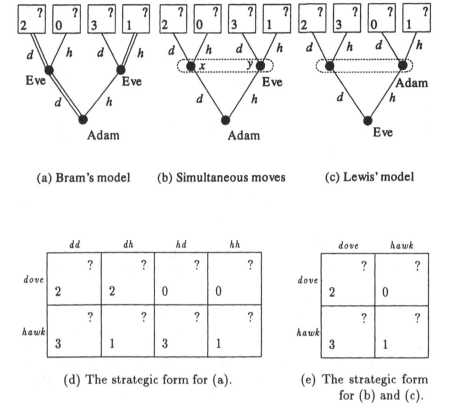

(a) Bram's model   (b) Simultaneous moves   (c) Lewis' model

(d) The strategic form for (a).

(e) The strategic form for (b) and (c).

Figure 3.9: "Domination" in the Newcomb Paradox?

processes and all the influences under which he acts. His apparent freedom would then disappear. Indeed, it is precisely to remove a rational player's apparent freedom to move where he will that game theorists analyze games. After a game theorist has determined what is rational in a game, a rational player can no longer be said to be free to choose.[72] If he were to make an irrational move, then he would not be rational. However, before we have specified what Adam's thought processes will be in a game, it makes perfectly good sense for us to say that he is free to make any move allowed by the rules. In particular, Adam is free to choose between *dove* and *hawk* in Figure 3.9(a) as long as we leave the interior of his head unmodeled. He

---

[72]Except in the uninteresting sense that there are no physical barriers to his using one move rather than another.

is free to choose, because the manner in which he will choose has been left open.

Games of Imperfect Information.   Figure 3.9(e) is the wrong strategic form for Brams' model of Figure 3.9(a), but it is the right strategic form for the extensive form obtained from Figure 3.9(a) by inserting an *information set* as shown in Figure 3.9(b). This information set is indicated by drawing a broken line around the nodes x and y to show that, when Eve decides between *dove* and *hawk*, she does not know whether the game has reached node x or node y. That is to say, she does not know whether Adam previously chose *dove* or *hawk*. This example illustrates how information sets are used to specify the players' knowledge at different stages of a game about what has happened so far. Such a device is unnecessary in games of perfect information like Blackmail of Section 2.5.1. In such games, all the players always know everything that has happened in the game so far. If information sets were indicated in a game of perfect information, they would therefore each contain only one node. We therefore usually reserve the use of information sets for *games of imperfect information* like that shown in Figure 3.9(b).

Recall that Eve has four pure strategies in the extensive form of Figure 3.9(a). But the insertion of an information set into the extensive form reduces this number. In Figure 3.9(b), Eve has only two pure strategies, *dove* and *hawk*. The reason is that she must specify one single choice for her entire information set in this extensive form. She cannot elect to do one thing at node x and another at node y, because she will not have the necessary information to implement such a strategy when the time comes to do so. Figure 3.9(b) therefore has the 2 × 2 strategic form shown in Figure 3.9(e). Notice that Figure 3.9(e) is also the strategic form for the extensive form of Figure 3.9(c), in which Eve moves first and Adam moves second. This may seem paradoxical until one realizes that the physical timing of the moves in these games is irrelevant. It is no help for me to know that my opponent has made her decision already if I have no way of knowing what her decision is. Game theorists register this fact by referring to the games of Figures 3.9(b) and 3.9(c) as *simultaneous-move* games. The timing of moves in these games of imperfect information is irrelevant, and so one may as well think of the moves being made simultaneously.

No Superior Being.   David Lewis [154] argues that one can see the Prisoners' Dilemma as two Newcomb problems placed back-to-back.[73] New-

---

[73]Bertrand Russell apparently met members of a now-extinct species of crackpot on a regular basis. Their claim was that the British are the descendants of the ten lost tribes of Israel. Having found reason no defense, he finally adopted the ploy of offering counter-

comb presumably followed a similar line of reasoning when his musings on the Prisoners' Dilemma led him to formulate the Newcomb Paradox in the first place. Implicit in this view is the belief that the Newcomb problem can be usefully modeled as the game of Figure 3.9(c). If one agrees that Figure 3.9(c) is a legitimate extensive form for the Newcomb problem, then its correct strategic form is Figure 3.9(e). One must then accept Lewis's conclusion that the solution to the Newcomb problem is for Adam to take both boxes, because *hawk* strongly dominates *dove* in Figure 3.9(e). Indeed, Adam's payoffs in the strategic form of Figure 3.9(e) are the same as his payoffs in the standard form of the Prisoners' Dilemma first introduced in Figure 2.2(b). Moreover, if suitable payoffs are assigned to Eve, then Figure 3.9(e) becomes *identical* with the Prisoners' Dilemma of Figure 2.2(b). If these same payoffs are inserted in Figure 3.9(b), this also becomes a Newcomb problem, but with Adam replacing Eve as the person who makes a prediction. We then have two Newcomb problems with a common strategic form. This common strategic form is the Prisoners' Dilemma.

After presenting his argument that the Prisoners' Dilemma is nothing other than a version of Newcomb's problem, Lewis writes: *quod erat demonstrandum*. Given that anything can be deduced from a contradiction, I guess that he is entitled to this flourish. However, we ought to register that Lewis's use of Figure 3.9(c) as a model of the Newcomb problem honors only Newcomb's timing and free-choice assumptions. The model meets the predictability requirement only partially. It is true that, if Adam and Eve optimize in Figure 3.9(c) by using *hawk*, then each will actually predict the choice of the other successfully. On this point, Lewis says things that will be familiar from our discussion of the Paradox of the Twins. However, the essential point is simply that (*hawk, hawk*) is a symmetric Nash equilibrium of a symmetric game. But this does not seem to me to capture the spirit of what Newcomb intends. Eve should be modeled so that she would predict Adam's choice, even if he were not to choose as he actually will choose. That is to say, Eve should be superior to Adam. One can then no longer easily sustain the hypothesis that the Prisoners' Dilemma consists of two Newcomb problems placed back-to-back. How can Adam and Eve each be superior to the other? Equivalently, how can Adam and Eve each simultaneously be the first to move in a model like Figure 3.9(a)?

No Free Choice. Brams' model for the Newcomb problem honors predictability and free choice. Lewis's model honors timing and free choice. However, I suspect that more is to be learned by looking at models that take

---

arguments that restricted this honor to the Scots. If I were similarly mischievous, I would argue that two back-to-back Newcomb problems are not the Prisoners' Dilemma, but Gauthier's "metagame" of Figure 3.3!

up the third possibility. In these models, timing and predictability are honored, but not free choice. More precisely, Adam's thinking processes will be modeled, albeit exceedingly abstractly, using Aumann's framework—within which Nature determines a player's state of mind, after which the player "just does what he does". Since we are already modeling Eve as someone who "just does what she does", the games to be considered will therefore be *without players* as game theorists usually understand the term. This last point will be emphasized in what follows by removing the options that Eve has hitherto been offered in models of the Newcomb problem. These options were included only to explain why some authors think that Newcomb's Paradox is relevant to the Prisoners' Dilemma. But now that this point has been covered, we might as well simplify and treat Eve as nothing more than a stimulus-response machine. Since she is a superior being, she will be a more complicated stimulus-response machine than Adam, but the models are too abstract for this complexity to be explicitly represented.

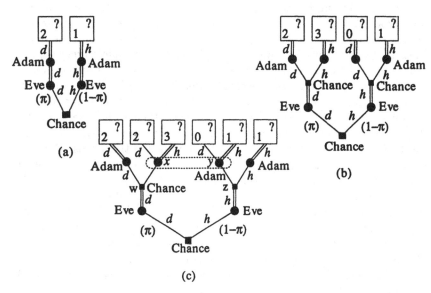

Figure 3.10: No Free choice?

The first move in the no-player game of Figure 3.10(a) is a *chance move*. Nature[74] decides at this move whether *dove* or *hawk* will be realized. Game theorists insist that the alternatives that can be chosen at a chance move

---

[74]Those so inclined might perhaps assign this move, not to Nature, but to a Schopenhauerian Will, whose decisions Adam's conscious reasoning faculties can only observe but not influence!

are all assigned probabilities. Otherwise the players would be denied the information that they need to assess the uncertainties that the existence of chance moves creates. In this case, the probability that Nature will choose *dove* is taken to be π. The probability that she will choose *hawk* is therefore $1 - \pi$. The chance move at which Nature chooses between *dove* and *hawk* replaces Adam's choice between the same alternatives in the previous models. The chance move determines Adam's state of mind, after which he "just does what he does". All the influences that determine Adam's choice are therefore separated into two classes: the class in which he is led to play *dove*, and the class in which he is led to play *hawk*.

The next event in the game is Eve's prediction of Adam's choice. To say that she is a perfect predictor is to say that she knows enough about Adam's circumstances and the way in which his mind works, that we can be sure she will never predict his action wrongly. We must therefore carefully avoid drawing an information set that includes her two decision nodes. Without an information set, we are saying that Eve knows everything that she needs to know in order to predict perfectly when she makes a prediction. Neither Adam nor Eve are modeled as being free to choose in Figure 3.8(a). Both are stimulus-response machines that simply repeat whatever signal Nature transmits to them. In particular, the final event of the game, in which Adam makes his choice between *dove* and *hawk*, is entirely predetermined by what·has gone before.

A game-theoretic analysis of a game with no players is intellectually undemanding. We just sit back and admire the view. Adam will play *dove* with probability π, and *hawk* with probability $1 - \pi$. One may, of course, reasonably ask what determines these probabilities, but one must go outside the model in seeking an answer. For example, if Adam were free to choose his own disposition, he would choose a persona that would make π as close to 1 as possible. However, allowing Adam to make such a choice simply reduces the problem to a more complicated version of Brams' model of Figure 3.9(a). It is more interesting to consider an explanation that attributes the value of π to evolutionary forces. A meme inside Adam's head that leads to a large value of π will have more chance of being replicated to other heads than a meme that leads to a small value of π. The evolutionary pressures are therefore in favor of Adams who play *dove* rather than those who play *hawk*.

Superior Guessing. Newcombmaniacs will dislike Figure 3.10(a) be- cause of its uncompromising rejection of free choice. But free choice *must* be rejected. Adam cannot be allowed to choose *hawk* after Nature has selected *dove*. To do so, would be to deny the premise that Eve knows everything necessary to make a perfect prediction of what Adam will do.

Newcombmaniacs will hasten to explain that the paradox does not depend on Eve making a *perfect* prediction. It may be, for example, that Adam's experience of Eve's prowess at prediction leads him to the conclusion that she is only right some of the time. That is, she is only a superior guesser rather than a perfect predictor. Perhaps Eve guesses correctly with probability p when Adam chooses *dove*, and with probability q when he chooses *hawk*.[75] To retain the conclusion of the original Newcomb story that Adam should continue to make the supposedly "dominated" choice of *dove* in this new framework, we shall insist that

$$2p + 0(1 - p) \geq 1q + 3(1 - q) \, .$$

This inequality is satisfied, for example, if $p + q \geq \frac{3}{2}$. (Recall from Section 3.2.3 that Frank [75, p.157] reports an experiment supporting the estimates $p = .75$ and $q = .60$ for the Prisoners' Dilemma. These figures would not be good enough to support "cooperation" in the current context.)

Figure 3.10(b) adapts the model of Figure 3.10(a) to the new situation. The chance moves that follow Eve's prediction make it impossible for her to get things right all the time. Nevertheless, things are pretty much as in Figure 3.10(a), provided that the probabilities p and q are sufficiently large. In spite of the fact that Eve now only guesses at what he will do, Adam still cannot be allowed free choice. If he were allowed to choose freely, he might choose to play *hawk* all the time after Nature has signaled *dove*, and *dove* all the time after Nature has signaled *hawk*. This would deny the premise that Eve is a superior guesser, since she would then be wrong all the time. Of course, it may seem to Eve that Adam is exercising free choice, since she is unable to predict exactly what he will do. Adam himself will perhaps also believe that he is exercising free choice, since he is unlikely to be equipped with any model at all of the events in his own mind that we have so crudely modeled with three chance moves. However, we analysts, looking down from on high to observe the fall of the smallest sparrow, can see that each player "just does what he does".

Although I do not think that the way Newcombmaniacs model Eve as a superior guesser advances matters at all, I agree that removing the perfect prediction requirement from Newcomb's story does allow us to construct a model in which all of Newcomb's assumptions are satisfied simultaneously. Such a model is shown in Figure 3.10(c). Notice that Nature now sometimes leaves Adam free to choose—that is to say, the model does not tie down every aspect of his behavior. We must therefore leave open the precise probabilities with which Eve is to guess correctly. However, since we shall

---

[75] As Section 4.5 explains, such a story is not easily reconciled with the tenets of Bayesian decision theory. However, since free choice is to be denied to Adam in this model, Bayesian decision theorists need not be disturbed, because Adam will be making no decisions.

still require that $p + q \geq \frac{3}{2}$, it is necessary that the probabilities with which Adam is offered the opportunity to choose freely are small. In the terminology of Section 3.4.1, a train of thought that leads Adam to a state of mind in which he is free to choose must necessarily be regarded as a low-probability deviation from the mainstream lines that Eve uses in predicting his behavior. Notice that an information set has been drawn to include both the nodes x and y. This indicates that Adam does not know what Eve has predicted when he finds himself free to choose. More importantly, the exclusion of the nodes w and z from this information set shows that Adam *knows* when he is free to choose. One might say that it is the very realization that he has a choice to make that frees him from slavishly using whatever behavior happens to verify Eve's prediction.[76]

An analysis of Figure 3.10(c) is very simple. A game theorist will recommend that Adam should play *hawk* when he is free to choose, because *hawk* strongly dominates *dove* in this game. If we finish modeling Adam's thought processes by assuming that he will take a game theorist's advice whenever he finds himself free to choose, then the result will be as indicated by the doubled lines in Figure 3.10(c). This may not seem so different from our analysis of Figure 3.10(b), given that Adam's probability of having a free choice is assumed to be low. However, the difference in the two analyses becomes important when one considers the evolutionary implications. Evolutionary considerations based on Figure 3.10(b) will drive the system towards a population of Adams who all play *dove*—just as in Figure 3.10(a). But the same is not necessarily true in Figure 3.10(c). Deviant memes that insiduously suggest to their hosts that they are "free to choose" in certain circumstances will have an evolutionary advantage. They will therefore tend to become more numerous in the population. Such a trend will destabilize the story that goes with the Newcomb problem. That is to say, if the assumptions of the Newcomb problem ever did hold, evolution would eventually sweep them away. Indeed, this is presumably why the Newcomb story strikes people as being so farfetched in the first place!

We have now considered a number of attempts to model the Newcomb problem.[77] Conventional reasoning led us to different conclusions in different models. However, no hint of any conflict between "two principles of choice" was uncovered. For such a conflict to arise, we would need to have

---

[76] Something similar is often said of fancy automobiles. If it occurs to you to wonder whether you can afford one—then you can't.

[77] There are also others. Some of these, as in the work of Gibbard and Harper [89] or Lewis [151], involve the use of exotic decision theories invented for the purpose. I have to admit to being suspicious of formalisms that are introduced with the avowed intention of exploring issues that we do not yet understand. It seems to me that such formalisms usually obscure more than they illuminate. In any case, I see the Newcomb Paradox as representing a small challenge for our *modeling* expertise rather than a large challenge to conventional methods of *analysis*.

to have been led to different conclusions by different principles in the *same* model. To sustain the impression that a conflict exists, it is necessary that the nature of the model being used is left ambiguous.

3.6　Paradox of the Surprise Test

The moral just drawn from our study of Newcomb's Paradox is the same as the moral for the whole chapter. In brief, getting your model right is half the battle. Indeed, for the paradoxes and fallacies considered in this chapter, getting your model right is essentially the whole battle.

To press this point home, I now plan to indulge myself by concluding Chapter 3 with one last paradox—the Paradox of the Surprise Test. In modeling Newcomb's Paradox, we had to answer the question: What is a prediction? To this we now add the rider: What is a surprise? My mundane answer is that a person is surprised when he has made a prediction that turns out to be wrong.

In the story of the surprise test, Eve is a teacher who tells her class that they are to be given a test one day next week, but the day on which the test is given will come as a surprise. Adam is a pupil who has read Section 2.5.1 on backward induction. He therefore works backward through the days of the coming school week. If Eve has not set the test by the time school is over on Thursday, Adam figures that Eve will then have no choice but to set the test on Friday—this being the last day of the school week. If the test were given on Friday, Adam would therefore not be surprised. So Adam deduces that Eve cannot plan to give the test on Friday. But this means that the test must be given on Monday, Tuesday, Wednesday or Thursday. Having reached this conclusion, Adam now applies his backward induction argument again to eliminate Thursday as a possible day for the test. Once Thursday has been eliminated, he is then in a position to eliminate Wednesday—and so on, until all the days of the week have been eliminated. He then sighs with relief and makes no attempt to study over the weekend. But then Eve takes him by surprise by setting the test first thing on Monday morning!

If sense is to be made of this battle of wits between Adam and Eve, a suitable model needs to be constructed. This model will be a game. The game is unwieldy with a five-day school week and so Figure 3.11(a) just shows what the game would be if the school week consisted only of Thursday and Friday. The payoffs have been chosen so that Adam gets +1 if he predicts the day on which the test takes place, and −1 if he fails to do so. Eve's payoffs reverse these rewards. Figure 3.11(b) shows the strategic form for the game. Notice that Thursday is a weakly dominating strategy for both players. Each player will therefore be doing as well as he or she

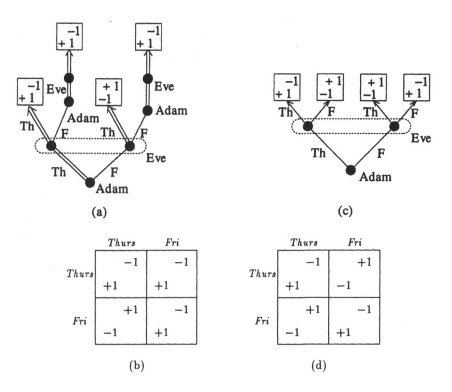

Figure 3.11: The surprise test

possibly can if Adam predicts that the test will be on Thursday and Eve runs the test on Thursday.

This doesn't seem right. Surely Eve would do better to switch the test to Friday if Adam is going to predict that it will take place on Thursday? But it is not the analysis of the game that is wrong, but the game itself! To say that Adam's strategy in the game of Figure 3.11(a) is Thursday is to say something complicated. It means that Adam should predict Thursday on Thursday, but if this prediction proves to be wrong, then he should switch his prediction to Friday on Friday![78] This may seem crazy, but it isn't my fault. The story of the surprise test definitely allows Adam to revise his prediction on Friday in the light of what has happened previously in the week. Its logic would fall apart if one were to add the requirement that none of Adam's previous predictions must have been falsified. But, like marks

---

[78] Similarly, in the full game, he should predict Monday on Monday, Tuesday on Tuesday, Wednesday on Wednesday, and so on.

in a shell game, we never thought to consider what Adam might have been predicting earlier in the week when we considered what he would predict if Friday were reached! What is going on is very simple. Adam will never be surprised by having a prediction falsified if he is always allowed to predict that today is the day of the test. Eve was therefore mistaken in announcing that he will be surprised when she springs her test on him. If we insist on making her assertion an assumption, we therefore create a contradiction. But anything whatever can be deduced from a contradiction—including the conclusion that Adam will be surprised when the test is given on the first day of the week.[79]

Figure 3.11(c) shows a strategic form for the story of the surprise test that accords much more closely with what we mean when we talk about people being surprised when their predictions fail to be realized. It is a simultaneous-move game in which Adam and Eve each choose either Thursday or Friday in ignorance of the choice of the other. However, if Adam chooses Thursday, he cannot change his mind if Thursday passes without a test. If he predicts Thursday, and Thursday passes without a test, then he will be surprised when Thursday comes to an end that his prediction is wrong. He might not be able to sustain his sense of astonishment overnight until Friday, but that is beside the point. To analyze Figure 3.11(c) is easy. The game has a unique Nash equilibrium in which Adam and Eve each use the mixed strategy that selects Thursday or Friday with equal probabilities. When this Nash equilibrium is used, Adam is surprised with probability $\frac{1}{2}$.

As always when an attempt is made to resolve a paradox, it can be objected that a very specific interpretation has been given to the meaning of the words in which the paradox is posed. This is certainly true for the word "surprise" in my attempt to deal with the Paradox of the Surprise Test. However, we must not forget that the usual reason that something strikes us as paradoxical is that some hand that is quicker than the eye has persuaded us to internalize an ambiguity. The result is that we unwittingly try to operate two different models simultaneously. Critics should therefore only be allowed to sustain an objection to a model if they are willing and able to substitute a model of their own that is equally specific.

---

[79] Quine's [205, p.19] proposed resolution of the Surprise Test Paradox rests on a similar point. He thinks that essentially the same paradox would arise if the teacher announced that the test will take place tomorrow, but that the day on which it comes will still be a surprise. I differ from Quine only in thinking that somewhat more is at stake.

This cardinal seems less than happy at the comparisons he is being invited to make.

Chapter 4

Cardinal Comparisons

"Were I Alexander," said Parmenio, "I would accept of these offers made by Darius."

"So would I too," replied Alexander, "were I Parmenio."

Longinus

4.1 Ordinal and Cardinal Utility

In a list of the shortcomings of game theory, Russell Hardin [100] bewails the fact that conventional game theorists write *cardinal* payoffs into their strategic forms rather than *ordinal* payoffs. This leads them, so he thinks, into such errors as supposing that a two-player game in which Adam and Eve have diametrically opposed preferences can always be modeled as a zero-sum game.[1]

The distinction between ordinal and cardinal notions of utility is left over from a controversy of the 1930s. Old-time social scientists were accustomed to using utility notions in a manner that makes their modern counterparts shudder with refined horror. These unsound practices were eventually swept away by a generation of reforming economists led by Marshall, who showed that one can often dispense with unscientific utility ideas by considering carefully what happens "at the margin". The errors of their forebears were then denounced in no uncertain terms—notably by the economist Lionel Robbins, whose jeremiads against the notion of cardinal utility are still quoted by modern critics. It is ironic, however, that even as Robbins was pouring scorn on the very notion of cardinal utility, Von Neumann and Morgenstern [269] were simultaneously writing a brief

---

[1] In a zero-sum game, Adam and Eve's payoffs for each outcome always sum to zero. For example, the games of Figure 3.11 are all zero-sum.

259

appendix to their *Theory of Games and Economic Behavior*, giving an easy argument that justifies the use of cardinal utilities when making decisions in risky situations.

Unfortunately, Von Neumann and Morgenstern's simple justification for the use of cardinal utilities has become obscured by a failure by many critics to distinguish between *intra*personal comparisons of utility and *inter*personal comparisons. Von Neumann and Morgenstern must bear some of the blame for this confusion. Their justification for the use of cardinal utilities applies only in the case of intrapersonal comparisons. Roughly speaking, this means that Adam's utility can be measured in *utils*,[2] with each extra util being worth the same to Adam as the one that went before. However, the fact that Adam values each of his utils equally says nothing about how *Eve* values Adam's utils relative to hers—and Von Neumann and Morgenstern offer no justification at all for making such interpersonal comparisons. Nevertheless, in studying coalition formation in the latter part of their book, Von Neumann and Morgenstern muddied the waters by taking as a working hypothesis, not only that utils can be compared across individuals, but that individuals can trade them back and forward like physical commodities.

This notion of "transferable utility" is fraught with difficulty. Adam can certainly give Eve a dollar bill if he chooses. He will thereby typically decrease his utility and increase hers. But what would he have to do to make himself exactly one util worse off and Eve exactly one util better off? I ask this question only to make it clear that it has no easy answer. Even the less demanding problem of how interpersonal comparisons of utility might meaningfully be made will have to wait until later in the chapter. The immediate point is simply that it is not reasonable to follow those critics who reject what Von Neumann and Morgenstern say about intrapersonal comparisons of utility on the grounds that they do not adequately defend what they say about interpersonal comparisons.

Ordinal versus Cardinal. The idea of an ordinal utility function was introduced in Section 2.2.4. For example, in seeking an ordinal utility representation of the preferences $a \prec b \sim c \prec d$, one looks for similarly ordered sequences of numbers like $2 < 4 = 4 < 5$, $-17 < 3 = 3 < 59$ or $0 < \frac{1}{2} = \frac{1}{2} < 1$. One possible utility function u for the given preferences may then be defined by taking $u(a) = 2$, $u(b) = u(c) = 4$ and $u(d) = 5$. Another utility function v is given by $v(a) = -17$, $v(b) = v(c) = 3$ and $v(d) = 59$. A third utility function w representing the same preferences is given by $w(a) = 0$, $w(b) = w(c) = \frac{1}{2}$ and $w(d) = 1$. When utility functions

---

[2]Economists measure utility in utils on the same principle that physicists measure temperature in degrees.

are constructed in this way, they tell us nothing whatever about how *intense* a person's preferences may be. Indeed, an ordinal utility function is said to be ordinal precisely because only the *order* of its values has any significance. The relative magnitudes of its values are irrelevant.

Only in a few games like the Prisoners' Dilemma is it adequate to work with payoffs that are derived from ordinal utility functions. Game theorists therefore systematically assume that a rational player will always act as though seeking to maximize his expected payoff.[3] In doing so, they take for granted that the payoffs in a game are to be expressed in terms of the players' Von Neumann and Morgenstern utility functions. As Section 4.2 explains, Von Neumann and Morgenstern utility functions are *cardinal*. The relative magnitudes of their values carry important information. They tell us about a person's attitudes to taking risks.

Gambling as a Source of Pleasure? Like much else in this book, the assertion that a person's Von Neumann and Morgenstern utility function describes his attitudes to taking risks is open to misinterpretation. For example, in discussing Rawls' arguments for the use of the maximin criterion in the original position, Kukathas and Pettit [145, p.40] dismiss the maximization of expected Von Neumann and Morgenstern utility as "the gambling strategy". However, numerous economics textbooks to the contrary, a Von Neumann and Morgenstern utility function does *not* measure how much a person likes or dislikes gambling as an activity. Indeed, as Harsanyi [108] points out, Von Neumann and Morgenstern's assumptions *do not apply* if a person actually derives pleasure or distress from the process of gambling itself.[4]

Although the specimens of *homo economicus* to which the Von Neumann and Morgenstern theory applies will see no point in taking vacations in Las Vegas, the language of the casino and the racetrack has nevertheless become so much a part of the terminology of decision theory that one can do little else but acquiesce in its use. However, in using this language, it is important not to envisage the decision-maker as being someone who enjoys gambling for its own sake. Think rather of a Presbyterian minister considering how

---

[3]I anticipated the current chapter by beginning to make this assumption in Chapter 2. Its initial appearance may perhaps have passed unnoticed, since I slyly prepared the ground by first considering an evolutionary model in Section 2.2.2 for which it is tautological that the players will behave as though maximizing their expected payoffs in the long run. However, the payoffs in such models are not derived from utility functions constructed by economists. They are defined as "average incremental fitness".

[4]Someone who likes or dislikes the gambling process for its own sake would be unlikely to accept Von Neumann and Morgenstern's assumption that two different lotteries should be regarded as equivalent when they generate the same prizes with the same probabilities. He would prefer whichever lottery squeezed the most drama and suspense from the randomizing process.

to value his house or car. He will not regard the possibility that his house might burn down or his car be stolen as a possible source of excitement. He will make a sober assessment of the probabilities, and then take out insurance to cover himself against the risks he faces. If we observe these decisions, we will learn something about the relative value that he places on his various possessions. Suppose, for example, that he is willing to spend $1,000 to insure his house against fire when the probability that his house will be burnt to the ground is 0.001, but that he is unwilling to insure his car against theft for the same amount when the probability of the car being stolen is 0.1. We then learn that he values his house above his car. But there is more in the data than this ordinal information. We also learn something quantitative about the extent to which he values his house above his car. This extra information is cardinal in its nature.

I am emphasizing the sober character of the considerations involved in using Von Neumann and Morgenstern utility functions because of the hostility that one sometimes encounters to their being used in an ethical context. It is said, for example, that one should never take risks with people's lives—and therefore that the Von Neumann and Morgenstern utility of a human life would need to be "infinite". Those who argue like this will sometimes insist that they never take bets themselves—or even that gambling is fundamentally wicked. Such attitudes are wrongheaded in a very dangerous way. Everybody risks his life every day. Even a Presbyterian minister will cross a busy road to collect a small debt. He then risks his life for a small sum of money. This will not seem a thrilling experience to him. On the contrary, he will take great care to keep the risk as small as possible. Nevertheless, there will remain an irreducible probability of an accident. When he crosses the road, he demonstrates, not only that he sometimes gambles, but that he does not regard his own life as being infinitely valuable.

As for the dangers that result from taking up an ostrichlike attitude to such questions, I think that they are very real. Those who "do not gamble" sustain this view only by pretending that low probability risks do not exist. As a consequence, public opinion is very responsive to health hazards that pose high-probability dangers to individuals lucky enough to attract the attention of the media, but very much less responsive to health hazards that pose low-probability dangers to large numbers of anonymous folk. Only outrage would follow if one were to use "expected number of dead babies" as a measure of the consequences of diverting funds from routine public health measures to more dramatic problems like the provision of open-heart surgery facilities, but this is not infrequently the essence of the matter.

It seems to me that a major error is made if risk is seen as something peripheral to ethical questions. What more fundamental ethical question could there be than: Who should bear what risk? Von Neumann and Morgenstern utility theory is therefore not an optional extra for a social contract theory. Nor can social contract theorists afford misunderstandings to arise about what the Von Neumann and Morgenstern theory says.

4.2 Intrapersonal Comparison of Utility

Why does a rich man hail a taxicab when it rains while a poor man gets wet? Economists answer this traditional question by making an intrapersonal comparison. They argue that an extra dollar in Adam's pocket would be worth more to him if he were poor than it would be if he were rich. But how are we to measure such increments in well-being? The unit of measurement certainly cannot be the dollar because dollars become less valuable the more of them you have! Matters become even more vexed when interpersonal comparisons of utility are attempted. We can at least appeal to Adam's authority on the question of how he would feel if placed in various predicaments—but, in the absence of a Tiresias with experience of both roles, to whom do we appeal when asked to compare the welfare of two such different people as Adam and Eve?

To study these questions, it is necessary to begin by considering how Von Neumann and Morgenstern utility functions solve the problem of intrapersonal comparisons of utility. Since Von Neumann and Morgenstern utility functions arise in the theory of decision-making under risk, the first priority is to say something about probabilities. Fortunately, what needs to be said can be made very brief.

4.2.1 Probability

If a dice is thrown, the set $B = \{1, 2, 3, 4, 5, 6\}$ is the set of relevant *states of the world*. An *event* is any subset of B. For example, the event that an even number is rolled is represented by the subset $E = \{2, 4, 6\}$. The complementary event that an odd number is rolled is represented by the notation $\sim E = \{1, 3, 5\}$. The impossible event that nothing is rolled is represented by the empty set $\emptyset$. The certain event that some number will be rolled is represented by the set B of all states of the world. One writes $S \cap T$ for the event in which both S and T occur. Similarly, $S \cup T$ represents the event that at least one of S and T occur. Thus, $E \cap \sim E = \emptyset$, because it is impossible that the number rolled is both even and odd. Also $E \cup \sim E = B$, because it is certain that the number rolled will be either even or odd.

A probability measure p defined on a finite set B assigns a real number $p(S)$ to each subset S of B, subject to the requirements:

(1) $0 = p(\emptyset) \le p(S) \le p(B) = 1$;

(2)　　$p(S \cup T) = p(S) + p(T)$, provided $S \cap T = \emptyset$.

The second requirement says that, if two events cannot occur simultaneously, then the probability that at least one of them will occur is equal to the sum of their separate probabilities. One also needs to know that $p(S \cap T) = p(S)p(T)$ when S and T are *independent* events.[5] The probability that both of two independent events will occur is therefore equal to the product of their separate probabilities.

Expected Values.　Apart from knowing when to add and when to multiply probabilities, the only other idea from probability theory that will be needed in this book is that of an *expected value*. Suppose, for example, that Adam makes a bet with Eve that will result in his winning a total of $4 if an even number is rolled and losing a total of $6 if an odd number is rolled. Such a bet defines the *lottery*[6] **L** shown in Figure 4.1. The first row indicates the *prizes* that a participant in the lottery may win. The second row shows the probabilities with which these prizes occur. In Figure 4.1, it is assumed that the dice to be rolled is fair, and so $p(E) = p(\sim E) = \frac{1}{2}$. Since the prizes in the lottery **L** are given in dollars, we can compute its expected dollar value[7] as

$$\mathcal{E}\mathbf{L} = \$4 \times \tfrac{1}{2} + (-\$6) \times \tfrac{1}{2} = -\$1 \,.$$

$$\mathbf{L} = \begin{array}{|c|c|} \hline \$4 & -\$6 \\ \hline \tfrac{1}{2} & \tfrac{1}{2} \\ \hline \end{array}$$

Figure 4.1: A lottery

Expected values are interesting because they indicate how much Adam can anticipate winning on average in the long run. More precisely, if Adam were sufficiently foolish to make the same bet with Eve every day, then the probability is zero[8] that his average winnings over the whole series of

---

[5] Mathematicians make a tautology of this proposition by defining two events S and T to be independent if and only if $p(S \cap T) = p(S)p(T)$.

[6] Mathematicians speak of a *random variable* in this context. This is a function f that assigns a prize to each state b in B. For example, in Adam's bet, $f(2) = f(4) = f(6) = \$4$ and $f(1) = f(3) = f(5) = -\$6$.

[7] In general, if $f(b)$ is the dollar prize that Adam receives in a lottery **M** when the state of the world turns out to be b and $p(b)$ is the probability with which b occurs, then one calculates the expected dollar value of **M** by summing the product $f(b)p(b)$ over all the states in B.

[8] This does not imply that it is *impossible* that he will win in the long run. There are

bets will fail to converge to $\mathcal{E}L = -\$1$. Such statements are commonly bowdlerized by saying that Adam expects to lose $1 per bet.

What Do Probabilities Mean? The simple ideas from probability theory introduced above have been in routine use in previous chapters. There
is therefore no point on expanding on them here. However, it is necessary to say something about the interpretation of probabilities. There are
at least three schools of thought on this subject. Objectivists hold that
probabilities are long-run frequencies. For them, assigning a probability to
the event that a coin will fall heads, or that a roulette wheel will stop on
number 17, or that an even number will be rolled with a dice, is a matter
for experimentation. The coin can be tossed, or the wheel spun, or the dice
rolled, many times. The frequency of observed successes then serves as an
estimate of the objective probability under investigation.

Subjectivism comes in 57 varieties. Game theorists commonly prefer
the Bayesian flavor. The pure form of this theory is best understood by
recalling the theory of revealed preference mentioned in Section 2.2.4. Just
as economists do not argue that people necessarily have objective utility
functions that they consult in deciding what to prefer, so Bayesians do not
argue that people necessarily have objective probability measures that they
consult in deciding what to believe. Instead the argument is that a rational
person will make decisions *as though* he were equipped with a probability
measure.

A subjectivist's probability measure will be approximately the same as
the probability measure of an objectivist for events like rolling dice or spinning roulette wheels. But objectivists are helpless in the case of events like
horse races or the stock exchange.[9] One cannot run the Derby repeatedly,
or ask that a stock be floated for a second time. Even if one could, the
conditions under which the experiment was repeated would be significantly
different each time. It therefore makes no sense to speak of an objective
probability for the event that *Consolidated Merchandise* will rise next week,
or that *Punter's Folly* will win the Derby. Nevertheless, we have no choice
but to make decisions when faced with such uncertainties. If the decisions
we then make are coherent, so the subjectivist story goes, we will then make
decisions *as though* our beliefs were based on a probability measure p. Of
course, all the warnings of Chapter 2 about fallacious reasoning with utility
functions also apply to such *subjective* probability measures. For example,

---

an infinite number of possible futures. Only when the set of possibilities is finite can one
identify a zero-probability event with an impossible event.

[9]I am using the story of betting at a racetrack because it is traditional to make the
necessary distinction by contrasting a roulette wheel with a horse race. But one could
equally well discuss the director of a major charity trying to guess which of several
potential famines is likely to prove most devastating.

Eve might reasonably say that Adam took his umbrella to work yesterday because the *objective* probability of rain was high. But she should never say that he took his umbrella because his *subjective* probability for rain was high. On the contrary, we choose to say that his subjective probability for rain was high *because* he took his umbrella.

I see little reason for disputes between objectivists and subjectivists. However, I see many reasons why both objectivists and subjectivists should be suspicious of the claims of the logicists. This third school of thought regards a probability as the rational degree of belief in an event that is justified by the evidence. A probability then becomes a point on a spectrum for which truth and falsehood are the two extremes. The difficulties involved in constructing such a theory are notorious. Keynes [141] is only one of numerous great minds who have fallen at this particular fence. Fortunately, *logical* probability measures are not needed in this book. It is necessary for me to mention them at all only so that I can insist that a subjectivist is not the same thing as a logicist. This will be important when responding to Rawls' rejection of Bayesian decision theory on the grounds that Laplace's principle of insufficient reason is unsound.

4.2.2   Von Neumann and Morgenstern Utility

Early workers in probability theory thought it natural to measure the value of a lottery $\mathbf{L}$ by calculating its expected dollar value $\mathcal{E}\mathbf{L}$. But the famous St. Petersburg Paradox soon made it clear that such an approach is unacceptably naive.

St. Petersburg Paradox.   It is said that St. Petersburg boasted a casino in the time of the czars which would sell any lottery whatever at a price of its own choosing. One lottery that Adam might consider buying involves tossing a fair coin until it falls heads. If it falls heads for the first time on the nth trial, Adam's prize is 2^n rubles. The probability of this event is $(\frac{1}{2})^n$. (For example, the probability of the event TTTH is $\frac{1}{2} \times \frac{1}{2} \times \frac{1}{2} \times \frac{1}{2}$.) Adam's expected dollar winnings are therefore infinite because

$$2^1 \times (\tfrac{1}{2})^1 + 2^2 \times (\tfrac{1}{2})^2 + 2^3 \times (\tfrac{1}{2})^3 + \ldots = 1 + 1 + 1 + \ldots .$$

If he thinks the appropriate measure of the worth of a lottery is its expected dollar value, it follows that Adam should be prepared to liquidate his entire fortune in return for the opportunity to participate in the St. Petersburg lottery. But the probability that someone who buys into the St. Petersburg lottery for X rubles will come out a net winner is less than $2/X$.[10] Later

---

[10]If $2^{n-1} \le X < 2^n$, then the probability of winning a prize worth more than X is $(\frac{1}{2})^n + (\frac{1}{2})^{n+1} + \ldots = 2(\frac{1}{2})^n < 2/X$.

in the section, it will be emphasized that primitive gut feelings are not necessarily a good guide when making judgments about rational behavior in risky situations. However, the early theorists were certainly right in thinking that there is something fishy about a theory which recommends that a very rich man should liquidate his entire fortune to bet on a prospect that gives him a negligible chance of being a net winner!

If the expected dollar value $\mathcal{E}\mathbf{L}$ of a lottery $\mathbf{L}$ is too crude a measure of its worth, why not consider its expected utility $\mathcal{E}u(\mathbf{L})$ instead? This resolves the St. Petersburg Paradox, provided that the utility function u is suitably chosen. Indeed, if Adam uses the utility function suggested by Bernoulli, then Adam will be willing to pay only a very small amount to participate in the St. Petersburg lottery.[11]

However, as Robbins [217, 218] and many others have pointed out, such a procedure seems entirely arbitrary. Why should we choose Bernoulli's utility function? Why not one of the infinite number of possible alternatives? And why take expectations anyway? Why not employ the maximin criterion or some other aggregation method? It was just such a Kantian question that Nozick [195] put to the world in Section 3.5 when he asked which of his two "principles of choice" should be chosen to resolve Newcomb's Paradox. The ready answers he received suggest that many people still see the issues pretty much as Bernoulli saw them. However, modern utility theory has learned not to get trapped in this particular blind alley. Before we get the right answers, we first have to learn to ask the right questions.

Modern Utility Theory. The Von Neumann and Morgenstern [269] theory does not seek to tell people what utility function they ought to use or how they should use it in making decisions in risky situations. As explained in Section 2.2.4, modern utility theory reverses the causal chain. It *begins* with the decisions that an agent makes. If these decisions are consistent with one another in an appropriate sense, the theory then shows that the decisions are made *as though* the agent were equipped with a preference relation. It then goes on to show that the preferences so revealed can be generated by a utility function.

In the case of decisions made in risky situations, different people will

---

[11]Bernoulli suggested taking the utility of a sum of money x to be $u(x) = \log x$. If logarithms to base 2 are used, then

$$\mathcal{E}u(\mathbf{L}) = u(2)\tfrac{1}{2} + u(2^2)(\tfrac{1}{2})^2 + \ldots = \tfrac{1}{2} + 2(\tfrac{1}{2})^2 + 3(\tfrac{1}{2})^3 + \ldots = 2 = \log_2(2^2) = u(4)\,.$$

(Sum the series by first differentiating both sides of the equation $1+x+x^2+\ldots = 1/(1-x)$ and then multiplying through by x.) Thus Adam assigns the same utility to getting 4 rubles for certain as he does to the lottery $\mathbf{L}$. He is therefore indifferent between getting 4 rubles and taking his chances with the lottery.

reveal different utility functions. The differences in the utility functions they reveal reflect the different attitudes they have to taking risks. Insofar as they behave consistently when dealing with risk, most people seem to be fairly risk-averse. They would pay only small amounts for the opportunity to participate in the St. Petersburg lottery. Others are less risk-averse and would be willing to pay more. A risk-loving person would pay everything that he has to get into the game. None of these attitudes conflict with the consistency criteria of the Von Neumann and Morgenstern theory.

Von Neumann and Morgenstern's theory therefore accepts that rational people may differ about whether it is worth taking a particular risk—just as they may differ in their assessment of the music of Wagner or Beethoven. In commenting on Gauthier's [84] *Morals by Agreement*, Goodin [90, p.121] seeks to make this point by writing: "In the standard microeconomic tradition upon which Gauthier's model rests, tastes for risks are regarded as tastes like any other. Those who are risk averse are simply said to have a stronger taste for 'security'." But such statements invite misunderstandings—especially in a social contract discussion. As Harsanyi [108] points out, the tastes described by the Von Neumann and Morgenstern theory are not tastes for or against risk *per se*. If they were, then some people might find it intrinsically distasteful to contemplate the risks involved in passing behind Rawls' veil of ignorance. The rational tastes described by Von Neumann and Morgenstern refer to the prospective *consequences* of participating in a risky process—not to the process itself.[12]

Preferences over Lotteries. Although the revealed preference interpretation of utility will be maintained throughout this book, half of the labor of constructing a utility function from an agent's choice behavior will be skipped. It will be assumed that a preference relation has already been constructed and that it remains only to show that it can be represented using an appropriate utility function.[13] The primitive notion for this section will

---

[12]Section 2.2.4 explains why game theorists do not necessarily take for granted that "the ends justify the means" when they model a social situation as a game. However, in using Von Neumann and Morgenstern's theory of utility, they certainly do assume that rational people are neutral in respect of the character of the random device or devices used to implement a lottery. Fortunately, consequentialist assumptions at this deep level seem to be regarded as harmless, even by those who are very vocal in their attacks on consequentialism in general.

[13]The theory of revealed preference of Section 2.2.4 tells us to begin by constructing an agent's preference relation from observations of his choice behavior. Such an approach requires imposing consistency requirements on how a person behaves when making choices in risky situations. For such conditions to lead to a Von Neumann and Morgenstern utility function, they need to be more complicated than the totality and transitivity conditions of Section 2.2.4 that allow the construction of an ordinal utility function representing the preferences. (See, for example, Green and Osband [92].)

therefore be that of a preference relation. This preference relation must describe Adam's preferences over risky prospects. Such risky prospects will be represented by lotteries of the type illustrated in Figure 4.1. It is important to keep in mind that the probabilities that appear in such lotteries are objective. One should therefore see the prizes as being determined by tossing a coin or spinning a roulette wheel.

To keep things simple, suppose that Adam has only three final outcomes or *prizes* that he need consider—lose, draw and win.[14] These will be denoted by $\mathcal{L}$, $\mathcal{D}$ and $\mathcal{W}$ respectively. Adam shares with most of us the urge to come out on top, and so his preferences over these prizes are given by $\mathcal{L} \prec \mathcal{D} \prec \mathcal{W}$. However, these preferences tell us nothing about Adam's attitudes to taking risks. For example, if Adam found himself in a chess game that looks equally likely to end in his winning or losing, will he accept an offer of a draw from his opponent? One cannot deduce an answer to such a question by contemplating a rational person's preferences over sure outcomes—although sometimes authors attempt to do precisely that when the enterprise is less obviously ridiculous than in our chess example. Such authors are typically cautious by nature and hence feel an urge to dismiss those who are less cautious as irrational. But there is nothing irrational in Adam's refusing a draw.[15] Nor is there anything irrational in his accepting a draw. Whichever way he jumps, he is merely expressing a preference—no different in principle from his preference between the music of Wagner and Beethoven.

The first line of Figure 4.2 shows a lottery **L** in which the prizes $\mathcal{L}$, $\mathcal{D}$ and $\mathcal{W}$ are offered with the respective probabilities p, q, and r. Thus, when deciding whether or not to accept a draw, Adam has to compare the lottery **L** when $q = 1$ with the lottery **L** when $p = r = \frac{1}{2}$. As in Section 2.2.4, some mild consistency conditions[16] ensure that Adam's preferences over lotteries can be described by an *ordinal* utility function V that assigns a numerical value $V(\mathbf{L})$ to each possible lottery **L**.

Von Neumann and Morgenstern Utility Functions. In contrast to the ordinal utility function V, a Von Neumann and Morgenstern u is not

---

[14]My *Fun and Games* (D. C. Heath, 1991) contains a more general account of the theory, along with various explanatory examples and exercises. Kreps [144] succeeds in providing a sophisticated discussion without going overboard on the mathematics.

[15]For example, it may be that the game is the last of a series played among a number of contenders for a large cash prize. If Eve is currently ahead of the field with 9.5 points to Adam's 9, one can hardly argue that he would be irrational to refuse her offer of a draw.

[16]Totality and transitivity alone do not suffice because Adam's preferences now extend over an infinite set. However, nothing is to be gained by discussing the necessary extra conditions, since they are certainly satisfied when Von Neumann and Morgenstern's assumptions hold.

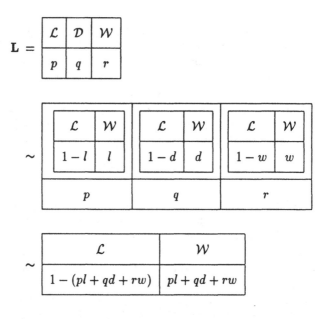

Figure 4.2: Von Neumann and Morgenstern's argument

defined on the set of all lotteries. It is defined only on the set of prizes.
Thus to specify u, we need only say what the values of $l = u(\mathcal{L})$, $d = u(\mathcal{D})$,
and $w = u(\mathcal{W})$ are to be. The *expected utility* of the lottery **L** is then given
by

$$\mathcal{E}u(\mathbf{L}) = pl + qd + rw \,.$$

Unlike u, the function U specified by $U(\mathbf{L}) = \mathcal{E}u(\mathbf{L})$ is defined over the
entire set of lotteries. It is therefore a candidate as an ordinal representation
of Adam's preferences over this large set. Von Neumann and Morgenstern's
achievement was to see that, if Adam's preferences over lotteries satisfy
certain consistency requirements, then l, d, and w can be chosen in such
a way that $U = \mathcal{E}u$ does indeed turn out to describe Adam's preferences
over lotteries correctly. When this is the case, the function u is said to be
a Von Neumann and Morgenstern utility function. Adam's behavior can
then be characterized by saying that he acts as though seeking to maximize
the expected value of his Von Neumann and Morgenstern utility.

   The broken lines in Figure 4.3(a) show the lotteries between which Adam
is indifferent when he acts as though maximizing the expected value of a
Von Neumann and Morgenstern utility function. A point is labeled (p, q, r)

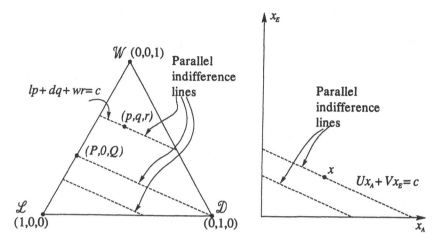

(a) Von Neumann and Morgenstern indifference curves.

(b) Social indifference curves.

Figure 4.3: Straight-line indifference curves

in this diagram if it lies at the center of gravity of three weights p, q, and r placed at the vertices of the triangle labeled $\mathcal{L}$, $\mathcal{D}$, and $\mathcal{W}$.[17] Any lottery **L** that assigns probabilities p, q, and r to the prizes $\mathcal{L}$, $\mathcal{D}$, and $\mathcal{W}$ can therefore be identified with a unique point (p, q, r) in Figure 4.3(a). Adam will be indifferent between all lotteries **L** that give him the same expected utility $\mathcal{E}u(\mathbf{L})$. Since $\mathcal{E}u(\mathbf{L}) = lp + dq + wr$, it follows that his indifference curves are a set of parallel straight lines of the form $lp + dq + wr = c$, where different values of the constant c correspond to different levels of Adam's expected utility.[18]

If no restrictions were placed on Adam's preferences over lotteries, then his indifference curves in Figure 4.3(a) might take all kinds of different shapes. It is therefore a severe constraint on a person's behavior that he acts as though maximizing the expected value of a Von Neumann and Morgenstern utility function. However, Von Neumann and Morgenstern argue that person who violates this constraint is irrational or inconsistent. To

---

[17]If the triangle itself is weightless, the center of gravity of the system is the single point at which it could be supported without tipping over.

[18]The fact that the indifference curves in this diagram are straight lines sometimes leads to the Von Neumann and Morgenstern utility function u being called "linear". Mathematicians find this very confusing, since it is actually the function $\mathcal{E}u$ that is linear as a function of (p, q, r).

evaluate their claim, it is necessary to be familiar with the assumptions
about rational behavior in risky situations that Von Neumann and Morgenstern think it appropriate to make. This is particularly important for
those who wish to attack the theory, since its defenders will immediately
respond by asking which of Von Neumann and Morgenstern's assumptions
such a critic thinks should be abandoned.

Von Neumann and Morgenstern's Rationality Conditions. Recall
that Adam regards $\mathcal{L}$ as the worst possible prize and $\mathcal{W}$ as the best possible
prize. Von Neumann and Morgenstern proceed by relating everything to
lotteries involving these two prizes alone. Such a lottery $\mathbf{M}(z)$ results in $\mathcal{L}$
with probability $1 - z$ and $\mathcal{W}$ with probability z.

Von Neumann and Morgenstern's first assumption is that, for each prize
$\mathcal{Z}$, there is a probability z of his winning that makes Adam indifferent
between $\mathcal{Z}$ and $\mathbf{M}(z)$. We can therefore find probabilities l, d, and w so
that Adam's preferences satisfy

$$\mathcal{L} \sim \mathbf{M}(l) ; \quad \mathcal{D} \sim \mathbf{M}(d) ; \quad \mathcal{W} \sim \mathbf{M}(w) . \tag{4.1}$$

Obviously $l = 0$ and $w = 1$, but the value of d tells us something substantive
about Adam's attitudes to taking risks.[19]

Von Neumann and Morgenstern's second assumption is used to justify
the first of the two indifference relations in Figure 4.2. We know from (4.1)
that Adam is indifferent between the prizes $\mathcal{L}$, $\mathcal{D}$ and $\mathcal{W}$ and the respective
lotteries $\mathbf{M}(l)$, $\mathbf{M}(d)$ and $\mathbf{M}(w)$. Von Neumann and Morgenstern therefore
see no reason why Adam should then object if the former are replaced by
the latter in the lottery $\mathbf{L}$ of Figure 4.2. Their second assumption therefore
legitimizes such substitutions.

The general form of Von Neumann and Morgenstern's second assumption is nowadays called the *Independence Axiom*. This uninspired piece of
terminology will win no creative writing competitions, but it does serve
to direct attention to the fact that the assumption takes for granted some
properties of the prizes whose exchange is to be permitted. These properties matter a great deal, although they are seldom mentioned explicitly. In
Figure 4.2, for example, it is important that the manner in which the prize
is determined in the lottery $\mathbf{M}(d)$ be *independent* of the manner in which
the prizes are determined in the lottery $\mathbf{L}$.[20] More generally, it is necessary

---

[19]Suppose, for example, that $\mathcal{L}$, $\mathcal{D}$, and $\mathcal{W}$ consist of respective payments of $0, $20,
and $100. I would then not buy the lottery ticket $\mathbf{M}(0.1)$ for $20. Nor would I sell the
lottery ticket $\mathbf{M}(0.5)$ for $20. Hence, in my case, the value of d for which $\mathcal{D} \sim \mathbf{M}(d)$
satisfies $0.1 < d < 0.5$.

[20]Assume that you are indifferent between receiving $10 for sure and getting $20 if a
fair coin falls heads. Now suppose that you are to receive $10 if a fair coin falls tails. Are

to exclude all other influences that might make the availability of one prize relevant to the valuation of another—no matter how subtle such effects may be. Many fallacies and paradoxes invented by critics of the Von Neumann and Morgenstern theory are based on a failure to appreciate that such implicit understandings are built into the foundations of the theory. However, further comment on this important point will have to wait until Section 4.5.

Von Neumann and Morgenstern's third assumption justifies the second of the two indifference relations of Figure 4.2. It says that Adam believes the laws of probability. To obtain the final lottery of Figure 4.2 from the compound lottery that proceeds it, he therefore simply calculates the total probability $pl + qd + rw$ that he will win. One may therefore summarize Figure 4.2 by saying that someone who respects Von Neumann and Morgenstern's assumptions must be indifferent between $\mathbf{L}$ and $\mathbf{M}(pl+qd+rw)$.

Von Neumann and Morgenstern's fourth and final assumption is that, when only $\mathcal{L}$ and $\mathcal{W}$ are possible, then Adam will act to maximize the probability of getting $\mathcal{W}$. Since each lottery $\mathbf{L}$ always satisfies $\mathbf{L} \sim \mathbf{M}(pl + qd+rw)$, the fourth assumption implies that Adam will always make choices among lotteries as though seeking to maximize the number $pl + dq + rw$. It follows that the equation $U(\mathbf{L}) = pl + qd + rw$ defines an ordinal utility function U that fully describes Adam's preferences over lotteries. It only remains to to define $u(\mathcal{L}) = l$, $u(\mathcal{D}) = d$ and $u(\mathcal{W}) = w$. The function u so defined is then a Von Neumann and Morgenstern utility function because

$$U(\mathbf{L}) = pl + qd + rw = pu(\mathcal{L}) + qu(\mathcal{D}) + ru(\mathcal{W}) = \mathcal{E}u(\mathbf{L})\,.$$

Notice that that $U = \mathcal{E}u$ is an *ordinal* utility function that describes Adam's preferences over *lotteries*. However, u is a *cardinal* utility function that describes Adam's preferences over *prizes*. If u were ordinal, the ordering of its values would tell us Adam's preferences over the prizes—and that would be that. However, u encodes much more information. The relative magnitudes of its values tell us everything there is to know about Adam's preferences over lotteries.

Criticisms of the Von Neumann and Morgenstern Theory. Some critics dispute the claim that the Von Neumann and Morgenstern assumptions should be seen as characterizing rational behavior in risky situations. Other critics take for granted that the Von Neumann and Morgenstern theory is intended to describe the behavior of *homo sapiens* rather than *homo economicus*, and give examples where it signally fails to do so.[21] Yet other

---

you ready to swap the $10 prize in this lottery for the opportunity to win $20 if a fair coin falls heads? Think twice, because nothing has been said to exclude the possibility that it is the *same* coin toss that is to be used in each lottery!

[21]Nobody seems able to agree on what conclusions should be drawn from the experimental evidence on decisions made under risk (except perhaps that real people have

critics cannot decide which of these two hats they should be wearing. The common signal of such ambivalence in headgear is the appearance of the question: Would you behave like that?

For example, some bullets are loaded into a revolver with six chambers. The cylinder is then spun and the gun pointed at your head. Would you now be prepared to pay more to get one bullet removed when only one bullet was loaded or when four bullets were loaded? Usually, people say they would pay more in the first case because they would then be buying their lives for certain. But the Von Neumann and Morgenstern theory says that you should pay more in the second case, provided only that you prefer life to death and more money to less.[22]

What conclusion should be drawn from such a conflict between one's gut feelings and the recommendations of Von Neumann and Morgenstern's theory? Few people want to admit that their gut feelings are irrational and should therefore be amended.[23] They prefer to deny that the Von Neumann and Morgenstern assumptions characterize rational behavior. However, it is instructive to consider another informal experiment with which I have teased various experts in economics and finance. Would you prefer \$(96 × 69) or \$(87×78)? Most prefer the former. But $96×69 = 6,624$ and $87×78 =$

------

little natural capacity for statistics). As a consequence, it is in this area that I believe modeling *homo sapiens* as *homo economicus* has least to recommend it. To, continue the defense of Section 1.2.2, I have two things to say. The first is simply to repeat that the decision to use *homo economicus* as a model of man is certainly not ideal, but, like democracy, it seems better than all the alternatives. The second is that other models must necessarily be self-defeating in the long run, because evolution will eventually refute them. As we saw in Section 2.2.1, evolution will tend to select in favor of behavior that maximizes average fitness. Such a fitness measure will then serve as a Von Neumann and Morgenstern utility function. However, biological evolution is not over, and social evolution may yet have far to go. Until we get further down the road, one cannot but agree with Kant [134, p.63] on the subject of the reasoning capacity of *homo sapiens*—insofar as these views apply to making decisions in risky situations. As quoted in Section 2.4.2, Kant says that Nature has hit on "a very bad arrangement of choosing reason in the creature to carry out this purpose". Animals that rely on instinct doubtless behave much more like *homo economicus*—but only in the restricted range of situations to which their instincts have had time to adapt.

[22]Suppose that you are just willing to pay \$X to get one bullet removed from a gun containing one bullet and \$Y to get one bullet removed from a gun containing four bullets. Let $\mathcal{L}$ mean death. Let $\mathcal{W}$ mean being alive after paying nothing, $\mathcal{C}$ mean being alive after paying \$X and $\mathcal{D}$ mean being alive after paying \$Y. Then $u(\mathcal{C}) = \frac{1}{6}u(\mathcal{L}) + \frac{5}{6}u(\mathcal{W})$ and $\frac{1}{2}u(\mathcal{L}) + \frac{1}{2}u(\mathcal{D}) = \frac{2}{3}u(\mathcal{L}) + \frac{1}{3}u(\mathcal{W})$. Simplify by taking $l = u(\mathcal{L}) = 0$ and $w = u(\mathcal{W}) = 1$. Then $c = u(\mathcal{C}) = \frac{5}{6}$ and $d = u(\mathcal{D}) = \frac{2}{3}$. Thus $u(\mathcal{D}) \prec u(\mathcal{C})$ and so $X < Y$. (This elegant problem is attributed to Zeckhauser by Gibbard [88] and Kahneman/Tversky [131]. Kahneman and Tversky think the example misleading on the grounds that matters are confused by the question of whether money has value for you after you are dead.)

[23]As did the statistician Savage when trapped by the economist Allais into expressing preferences that were inconsistent with his extension of the Von Neumann and Morgenstern theory.

6,786. How should we react to this anomaly? Surely not by altering the laws of arithmetic to make $96 \times 69 > 87 \times 78$! So why should we contemplate altering the Von Neumann and Morgenstern assumptions after observing experiments that show they do not correspond with the gut feelings of the man in the street? Our untutored intuitions about statistical matters are no more trustworthy than those that lead a toddler to prefer a candy jar with a big cross-section to a rival with a larger volume. Adults learn to think twice about such matters. If the matter is sufficiently important, we may calculate a little—or perhaps read the label on the packet.

It is such second thoughts about our wants and aspirations that seem to me relevant when ethical issues are at stake. A theory based on gut feelings may perhaps be appropriate in consumer theory when studying impulse buying in supermarkets. But people are likely to be in a much more reflective mood when considering social contract issues. As the old form of English marriage service used to say, this is an occasion for making decisions "advisedly and soberly".

Utility Scales. A Von Neumann and Morgenstern utility function is cardinal in that it measures how much Adam values winning above drawing, and drawing above losing. Sometimes these valuations are expressed in terms of an invented unit called the *util*. Von Neumann and Morgenstern [269] went to some trouble to emphasize the analogy between such utils and the *degrees* used to measure temperature. One is free to choose the zero and the unit on a temperature scale as one pleases. On the centigrade scale, they are chosen so that $0°C$ is the freezing point of water and $100°C$ is the boiling point of water. But one can equally well use the Fahrenheit scale in which the freezing point of water is $32°F$ and the boiling point of water is $212°F$. Going back and forth between the two scales is very easy, since a room whose centigrade temperature is c has a Fahrenheit temperature of $f = \frac{9}{5}c + 32$. Which scale one chooses is a matter of taste. Scientists presumably prefer the centigrade scale because it is less quaint.

In using Von Neumann and Morgenstern's argument to construct a Von Neumann and Morgenstern utility function for Adam's preferences over lotteries, the zero and the unit of his utility scale were chosen by taking $u(\mathcal{L}) = 0$ and $u(\mathcal{W}) = 1$. However, if u is a Von Neumann and Morgenstern utility function, then so is $v = \alpha u + \beta$, provided that $\alpha > 0$ and β are constants.[24] Von Neumann and Morgenstern utility functions are therefore definitely not unique. By choosing different values for α and β, one can generate many different Von Neumann and Morgenstern utility functions,

---

[24]The reason is that $\mathcal{E}v(\mathbf{L}) = \alpha \mathcal{E}u(\mathbf{L}) + \beta$. Thus $\mathcal{E}v$ and $\mathcal{E}u$ achieve their maximum values at the same place. Hence, someone trying to maximize the expected value of u will reveal the same preferences as someone trying to maximize the expected value of v.

all of which are equally good representations of Adam's preferences. However, once α and β have been chosen, there is no further room for maneuver. Nothing that is not of the form $\alpha u + \beta$ can be a Von Neumann and Morgenstern utility function that represents the same preferences over lotteries as u. As with temperature scales, determining the zero and the unit of a utility scale exhausts our freedom of action.[25]

Utility in Zero-sum Games. Russell Hardin [100] believes that game theorists go astray when they use Von Neumann and Morgenstern utilities in modeling strictly competitive games as zero-sum. My guess is that he thinks that they are thereby led into the invidious error of comparing the utils of the two opponents without any justification for so doing. It is because such misunderstandings so easily arise that I am spending so much time here and elsewhere on the nitty-gritty of utility theory. In the case of zero-sum games, it is particularly easy to see how an error in interpretation may arise. In such a game, the payoffs the players receive always sum to zero whatever the outcome may be. However, in awarding $-x$ utils to Eve whenever they award x utils to Adam, are game theorists not denying that Eve might feel both victory and defeat more keenly than Adam? To see why not, it is necessary to look a little more closely at what game theorists actually do assume when they model a strictly competitive game as zero-sum.

A strictly competitive game is one in which Adam and Eve's interests are diametrically opposed. In chess, for example, it would be unusual if Adam and Eve's preferences did not satisfy $\mathcal{L} \prec_A \mathcal{D} \prec_A \mathcal{W}$ and $\mathcal{W} \prec_E \mathcal{D} \prec_E \mathcal{L}$, provided that $\mathcal{L}$, $\mathcal{D}$, and $\mathcal{W}$ refer to a loss, draw or win *for Adam*. But, to specify such ordinal preferences over the final outcomes of the game it is not enough to capture everything that is involved in saying that Adam and Eve have diametrically opposed interests.

Suppose, for example, that Adam's Von Neumann and Morgenstern utility function u_A is given by $u_A(\mathcal{L}) = 0$, $u_A(\mathcal{D}) = \frac{3}{4}$, and $u_A(\mathcal{W}) = 1$, while Eve's is given by $u_E(\mathcal{W}) = 0$, $u_E(\mathcal{D}) = \frac{2}{3}$, and $u_E(\mathcal{L}) = 1$. Then both Adam and Eve prefer a draw to half a chance of winning or losing. They therefore share a common interest in agreeing on a draw in certain situations, rather than battling on to the bitter end. To eliminate such possibilities, it is necessary to insist that their preferences are diametrically opposed, not only over the prizes $\mathcal{L}$, $\mathcal{D}$, and $\mathcal{W}$, but also over all lotteries

---

[25]We may, for example, introduce a new utility scale for Adam using a Von Neumann and Morgenstern utility function v with $v(\mathcal{L}) = -1$ and $v(\mathcal{W}) = 2$. Then $\beta = \alpha u(\mathcal{L}) + \beta = v(\mathcal{L}) = -1$ and $\alpha + \beta = \alpha u(\mathcal{W}) + \beta = v(\mathcal{W}) = 2$. Thus $\alpha = 3$ and $\beta = -1$. It follows that $v(\mathcal{D}) = \alpha u(\mathcal{D}) + \beta = 3d - 1$. In other words, once two points on the utility scale have been fixed, the other points on the scale are all determined.

involving these prizes. That is to say, for all lotteries **L** and **M**, we need that **L** $\preceq_A$ **M** if and only if **M** $\preceq_E$ **L**. This translates into the requirement that $\mathcal{E}u_A(\mathbf{L}) \leq \mathcal{E}u_A(\mathbf{M})$ if and only if $\mathcal{E}u_E(\mathbf{M}) \leq \mathcal{E}u_E(\mathbf{L})$. But the second inequality is equivalent to $-\mathcal{E}u_E(\mathbf{L}) \leq -\mathcal{E}u_E(\mathbf{M})$. It follows that $-u_E$ is a Von Neumann and Morgenstern utility function that describes *Adam's* preferences. Hence $-u_E = \alpha u_A + \beta$, where $\alpha > 0$ and β are constant.

Since this is a clumsy relationship, it seems natural to change the zero and unit on Eve's utility scale by introducing a new Von Neumann and Morgenstern utility function v_E for her that is related to her old Von Neumann and Morgenstern utility function by the formula $u_E = \alpha v_E + \beta$. Then $-(\alpha v_E + \beta) = \alpha u_A + \beta$, and so

$$u_A + v_E = 0.$$

We have therefore found utility representations for Adam and Eve's preferences so that the payoffs assigned to Adam and Eve always sum to zero—whatever the outcome of the game may be. The strictly competitive game with which we began has therefore been reduced to a *zero-sum game*.

In this zero-sum game, each extra util gained by Adam is one less util for Eve. Does this deny that Eve might feel victory or defeat more keenly than Adam? To answer yes is to argue that Adam's utils in the game can meaningfully be compared with Eve's. But no such assumption is involved when a strictly competitive game is expressed in zero-sum form. Indeed, the construction of v_E makes it quite clear that the decision to link the zero and unit on Eve's utility scale with the zero and unit on Adam's scale is made entirely on the basis of mathematical convenience. Eve's preferences over lotteries are exactly the same whether we represent them with her original Von Neumann and Morgenstern utility function u_E or with the simplified alternative v_E. All that would change if u_E were used instead of v_E is that the necessary mathematics would become a little more cumbersome.

4.2.3 Intensity of Preference

A Von Neumann and Morgenstern utility function u_A that describes Adam's preferences over risky prospects is cardinal. It not only matters to Adam that u_A assigns more utils to $\mathcal{C}$ than $\mathcal{D}$, he also cares *how many* utils separate the two alternatives. Such a statement would make little sense if Adam did not think each util was equally valuable. But what does this mean? One possible interpretation takes us back to Harsanyi's [108] thoughts on the intensity of a preference mentioned in passing while discussing Arrow's Paradox in Section 2.3.4.

Suppose that $\mathcal{C} \prec_A \mathcal{D}$ and $\mathcal{E} \prec_A \mathcal{F}$. Then Harsanyi follows Von Neumann and Morgenstern [269, p.18] in arguing that Adam should be deemed to hold the first preference more intensely than the second if and only if he would be always be willing to swap a lottery **L** in which the prizes $\mathcal{C}$ and $\mathcal{F}$ each occur with probability $\frac{1}{2}$ for a lottery **M** in which the prizes $\mathcal{D}$ and $\mathcal{E}$ each occur with probability $\frac{1}{2}$. To see why Harsanyi proposes this definition, imagine that Adam is in possession of a lottery ticket **N** that yields the prizes $\mathcal{D}$ and $\mathcal{F}$ with equal probabilities. Would Adam now rather exchange $\mathcal{D}$ for $\mathcal{C}$ in the lottery or $\mathcal{F}$ for $\mathcal{E}$? Presumably, he should prefer the latter swap if and only if he thinks that $\mathcal{D}$ is a greater improvement on $\mathcal{C}$ than $\mathcal{E}$ is on $\mathcal{F}$. But, to say that he prefers the first of the two proposed exchanges to the second is to say that Adam prefers **M** to **L**.

In terms of Adam's Von Neumann and Morgenstern utility function u_A, the fact that $\mathbf{L} \prec_A \mathbf{M}$ reduces to the proposition that

$$\tfrac{1}{2}u_A(\mathcal{C}) + \tfrac{1}{2}u_A(\mathcal{F}) < \tfrac{1}{2}u_A(\mathcal{D}) + \tfrac{1}{2}u_A(\mathcal{E}).$$

Thus, Adam holds the preference $\mathcal{C} \prec_A \mathcal{D}$ more intensely than the preference $\mathcal{E} \prec_A \mathcal{F}$ if and only if $u_A(\mathcal{D}) - u_A(\mathcal{C}) > u_A(\mathcal{F}) - u_A(\mathcal{E})$.

To evaluate the implications of Harsanyi's definition of an intensity of preference, consider the possibility that $u_A(\mathcal{D}) = u_A(\mathcal{C}) + 1$ and $u_A(\mathcal{F}) = u_A(\mathcal{E}) + 1$ Then Adam gains one util in moving from $\mathcal{C}$ to $\mathcal{D}$. He also gains one util in moving from $\mathcal{E}$ to $\mathcal{F}$. Both these utils are equally valuable to Adam because he holds the preference $\mathcal{C} \prec_A \mathcal{D}$ with the same intensity as he holds the preference $\mathcal{E} \prec_A \mathcal{F}$. Unlike dollars, each util is therefore worth the same as its predecessors, no matter how many Adam has already.

4.2.4 Teleological Utilitarianism

A teleological ethical theory, as envisaged in Section 2.3.5, begins with an *a priori* conception of the "common good". Bentham and Mill felt comfortable in talking about the sum total of human happiness, but modern authors have learned to be more circumspect. The modern teleological approach is to write down a list of axioms that are said to characterize the concept of a common good. The nature of the common good is then deduced from these axioms, rather than simply being asserted to be self-evident. The axioms used by utilitarians like Harsanyi take the personal preferences of individual citizens as given, and describe how these are to be related to the preferences of society as a whole.[26] Society is therefore treated as a single person written large. Or, as some authors prefer to say, the interests of society are identified with those of an *ideal observer*, whose

---

[26]It should be noted that Sen [245] regards the utilitarians to whom this sentence refers as being unworthy of the name. He argues that one cannot properly use "utilitarian" to describe a theory that merely aggregates preferences. He feels that a utilitarian theory should be founded on a more sublime conception of individual well-being, so that it becomes possible to do good to your neighbor whether he likes it or not.

preferences are some kind of average or aggregate of the preferences of all the individuals in the community. This ideal observer's utility function is then said to be a welfare function for the society as a whole.

Our study of Arrow's Paradox in Section 2.3.4 shows that, unless the ideal observer is to be a dictator who simply imposes his own personal preferences on society, then his preferences must take into account how intensely citizens feel about things. Section 4.2.3 explains how Harsanyi [106] uses Von Neumann and Morgenstern utility functions to model such intensities in this context.[27] Broome [48], Hammond [94] and Weymark [271] are excellent references to the large literature that has since sprung into being.[28] However, nothing at all sophisticated will be said on the subject here because my view is that the teleological approach on which it is based is too badly flawed to be useful.

Treating Leviathan as a person seems to me to beg all the important questions. This is not to deny, as Section 2.3.6 explains, that a rationally organized society may behave like a single person under certain circumstances. But it is a long way from such an admission to the confident affirmatives with which teleologians typically respond to the following questions:

- Does a welfare function necessarily always exist?
- When a welfare function exists in a given context, will it necessarily share all the properties that are commonly attributed to the utility functions of individuals?
- Will a welfare function that describes the behavior of society in one context necessarily describe its behavior in another context?

Far from following teleologians in taking a yes answer to such questions for granted, a constructivist like myself sees the problem of characterizing a common good as that of predicting how the equilibria of certain games will alter as their parameters are changed. As Section 2.3.6 explains, we know that such equilibria do *not* in general move in a manner consistent even with collective transitivity. It should therefore be a matter for suprise and delight if we should find any special circumstances under which a teleologian's *a priori* assumptions turn out to be correct.

---

[27]The teleological Harsanyi who did this work is unfortunately the same as the non-teleological Harsanyi discussed in Sections 2.3.6 and 4.4. I think it likely that Harsanyi's readiness to wear different hats in this matter has caused a fair measure of confusion amongst those trying to get the underlying philosophy straight.

[28]Lest it be thought that I am guilty of the fallacies in interpreting Von Neumann and Morgenstern utility functions of which Weymark [271] accuses Harsanyi, note that I follow the standard practice of restricting their domain to the set of *prizes* rather than extending them to the set of all lotteries.

Rather than relying on a set of doubtfully based axioms characterizing an *a priori* "common good", nonteleological theorists believe in *constructing* a welfare function for a society, when possible, from more primitive notions—just as Von Neumann and Morgenstern *constructed* a utility function for an individual from primitive assumptions about his preferences over lotteries. However, such a nonteleological approach has to grapple with a major problem—the problem of how interpersonal comparisons of utility should be made. The current section provides a bowdlerized account of how teleologians manage to evade this major problem by appealing to the *intra*personal comparisons that their axioms attribute to an ideal observer. However, I hope no reader will be tempted to follow them down this easy road. Only the strait and narrow path rejoined in Section 4.3 offers hope of eventual redemption.

There are many teleological theories with utilitarian implications. Only a particularly simple variant of one possible theory is discussed here. It begins with a set S that contains all possible social states. In Section 2.3.3, Adam and Eve were allowed to have any consistent[29] preferences over the social states in S. Our problem was then to find some means of aggregating their preferences so as to generate a consistent preference relation for the community as a whole. However, Arrow's Paradox of Section 2.3.4 shows that there are only two methods of aggregating Adam and Eve's preferences that satisfy certain mild requirements. One method identifies the community's preferences with Adam's personal preferences. The other identifies them with Eve's.

Section 2.3.4 argues that Arrow's Paradox depends partly on the fact that the aggregation methods considered are not allowed to depend on the intensities with which Adam and Eve hold their preferences over social states. As we know from Von Neumann and Morgenstern's theory, the necessary cardinal information to measure such intensities can be gathered by observing the preferences that Adam and Eve hold over the set of all *lotteries* with prizes in S.[30] If Adam and Eve honor the Von Neumann and Morgenstern rationality conditions, their preferences over lotteries can be summarized by Von Neumann and Morgenstern utility functions defined on the set S of social states. To keep things simple, let us assume that Adam and Eve agree that there is a worst social state $\mathcal{L}$ and a best social state $\mathcal{W}$. We can then select the zeros and the units on Adam and Eve's utility scales so that $u_A(\mathcal{L}) = u_E(\mathcal{L}) = 0$ and $u_A(\mathcal{W}) = u_E(\mathcal{W}) = 1$. The Von Neumann and Morgenstern utility functions u_A and u_E will serve as

---

[29] As in Section 2.2.4, consistent means total and transitive in this context.

[30] One could seek to aggregate these ordinal preferences directly into a communal preference over lotteries. However, if Adam and Eve honor the Von Neumann and Morgenstern rationality conditions, one would then have to surrender Arrow's hypothesis that Adam and Eve may have *any* consistent set of preferences.

inputs to our aggregation method. That is to say, the ideal observer, whose preferences are to represent the preferences for the whole community, is not to be restricted to ordinal information as in Arrow's Paradox. He is allowed to take account of the cardinal information built into u_A and u_E.

The next step is very much less innocent. Not only are Adam and Eve assumed to honor the Von Neumann and Morgenstern rationality conditions, but the same is assumed to be true of the ideal observer. This is the teleological error in its crudest form.[31] The ideal observer is seen as being no different in kind from Adam and Eve. In particular, he may be assigned a Von Neumann and Morgenstern utility function u_i that describes his preferences over lotteries in which the prizes are social states. As with Adam and Eve, the zero and the unit on the ideal observer's utility scale will be chosen so that $u_i(\mathcal{L}) = 0$ and $u_i(\mathcal{W}) = 1$.

The third step places the theory firmly in the consequentialist camp. In assessing the consequences of choosing an action that leads to one lottery over social states rather than another, the ideal observer is assumed to take into account *only* Adam and Eve's personal preferences over the lotteries. One can translate this requirement into formal terms by requiring that, for each lottery $\mathbf{L}$,

$$\mathcal{E}u_i(\mathbf{L}) = v_i(\mathcal{E}u_A(\mathbf{L}), \mathcal{E}u_E(\mathbf{L})), \qquad (4.2)$$

where the values $v_i(x_A, x_E)$ of the function v_i depend only the pair (x_A, x_E) of utilities that Adam and Eve receive as a consequence of the ideal observer's decision. In brief, the ideal observer's expected utility for a lottery is assumed to depend only on Adam and Eve's expected utilities for the lottery.

Equation (4.2) implies that the function v_i is *linear* on its domain of definition D.[32] Such a conclusion should come as no surprise after Figure 4.3(a), which illustrates how someone whose preferences over lotteries can be described by a Von Neumann and Morgenstern utility function must have parallel, straight-line indifference curves in the space of all lotteries. Figure 4.3(b) illustrates the same conclusion for the indifference curves

---

[31]The account that follows is therefore something of a caricature of the formal argument with which some teleologians defend utilitarianism. However, my intention is only to give the flavor of the arguments that are offered. Teleological arguments, no matter how subtle, are so alien to my approach that I discuss them only to make it clear why I think them inadmissible.

[32]If x is in D, then there exists a lottery $\mathbf{M}$ such that $x_A = u_A(\mathbf{M})$ and $x_E = u_E(\mathbf{M})$. A corresponding lottery $\mathbf{N}$ can be associated with any y in D. Let $\mathbf{L}$ be the compound lottery that yields the prize $\mathbf{M}$ with probability p and $\mathbf{N}$ with probability $1 - p$. Then the left-hand side of (4.2) is $\mathcal{E}u_i(\mathbf{L}) = p\mathcal{E}u_i(\mathbf{M}) + (1 - p)\mathcal{E}u_i(\mathbf{N}) = pv_i(x) + (1 - p)v_i(y)$. The right-hand side of (4.2) is given by $v_i(\mathcal{E}u_A(\mathbf{L}), \mathcal{E}u_E(\mathbf{L})) = v_i(pu_A(\mathbf{M}) + (1 - p)u_A(\mathbf{N}), pu_E(\mathbf{M}) + (1 - p)u_E(\mathbf{N})) = v_i(px + (1 - p)y)$. It follows that $v_i(px + (1 - p)y) = pv_i(x) + (1 - p)v_i(y)$. Mathematicians will recognize this equation as the requirement that v_i be affine. But $u_A(\mathcal{L}) = u_E(\mathcal{L}) = u_i(\mathcal{L}) = 0$. Hence $v_i(0) = 0$, and so v_i is linear.

of our ideal observer in the space of all pairs $x = (x_A, x_E)$. In fact, the information that v_i is linear implies more than this. A standard result from elementary linear algebra[33] tells us that constants U and V must exist for which

$$u_i(x_A, x_E) = U x_A + V x_E \,.$$

If we assume that the ideal observer makes Pareto-efficient decisions, then the constants U and V will necessarily be non-negative.[34] It then follows that the ideal observer's utility function has exactly the same form as the weighted utilitarian welfare function W_h of Section 1.2.5. In particular, the ideal observer will always pick the utilitarian point h from the feasible set X of Figure 1.3(a). In doing so, he values each of Adam's utils as being worth U/V of Eve's. In postulating the existence of an ideal observer who is able to compare his own utils with each other, teleologians therefore implicitly assume an *a priori* standard for comparing utils across individuals.

4.3   Interpersonal Comparison of Utility

We have just seen how teleologians can deduce a standard for making interpersonal comparisons of utility from the intrapersonal comparisons of an ideal observer. However, those of us who are unwilling to acquiesce in teleological shortcuts have no such easy out. We have to go back to first principles in seeking appropriate criteria for making interpersonal comparisons of utility.

It is important to begin by recognizing that the Von Neumann and Morgenstern theory as described in Section 4.2.2 provides no basis at all for making interpersonal comparisons of utility. Widespread confusion exists on this point. In discussing coalition formation, the second half of Von Neumann and Morgenstern's [269] book uses a notion of "transferable utility" that they do not attempt to justify. Some authors have therefore been misled into thinking that Von Neumann and Morgenstern utility theory is about "transferable utility". Others are aware that the theory does not justify interpersonal comparisons of utility, but imagine that game theorists do not share their wisdom. (It is for such authors that Section 4.2.2 explains why Von Neumann and Morgenstern did not introduce interpersonal comparisons of utility under the counter by modeling strictly competitive games as zero-sum.) Yet other authors are sure that interpersonal comparisons of utility are *intrinsically* meaningless. Presumably, their certainty on this score derives from the fact most attempts to provide a justification for

---

[33]Recall that linear transformations necessarily have a matrix representation.
[34]Moreover, since $u_A(\mathcal{W}) = u_E(\mathcal{W}) = u_i(\mathcal{W}) = 1$, $U + V = 1$.

such comparisons have been badly flawed. However, I hope that this section will convince the reader that there is at least one theory that provides a coherent account of what it means to compare utilities across individuals. This is the theory promoted by Harsanyi [109] on those occasions when he is wearing his nonteleological hat.

If it were true that interpersonal comparisons of utility could not be made, I believe that there would be no point in writing a book about rational ethics. As Hammond [95], Harsanyi [106], and many others insist, ethics would then be a subject without substantive content. However, to make sense of comparisons of utility across individuals, it is necessary to go beyond the *personal* preferences studied in Section 4.2. One also needs to take account of the *empathetic* preferences previewed in Section 1.2.6. Such preferences are studied by Arrow [6], Suppes [259], Harsanyi [109] and Sen [239] as "extended sympathy preferences".

Interpersonal Comparison on the Cheap? Something first needs to be said about why more straightforward ways of comparing the well-being of different human beings will not suffice. For example, one might compare Adam's welfare with Eve's by counting their daily consumption of apples. Such a procedure has the advantage of being relatively easy to operational-ize, but it is vulnerable to numerous criticisms. Perhaps Eve is rich and Adam is poor, so that she can eat as many apples as she chooses but his straitened circumstances restrict him to only one apple a day. It would then be surprising if Eve did not derive a great deal less joy from one extra apple per day than Adam.[35]

Even if everybody had equal access to apples, we would still have prob-lems. Suppose that Adam and Eve are both poor, but Adam cares only for fig leaves. Rawls [212] is only one of many who see no difficulty here, on the grounds that fig leaves can be exchanged for apples in the market-place. One can therefore assess their relative values by quoting their price in dollars. However, as I comment in Section 1.2.6, assigning some *a priori* legitimacy to the market mechanism begs exactly the sort of question that a social contract argument ought to answer.[36] Even when a market for

---

[35]The economists' notion of *consumer surplus* faces precisely this problem—even in the special case of quasilinear utility, for which Varian [265, p.169] describes consumer surplus as being exactly the appropriate welfare measure. An *ordinal* utility function for Adam is quasilinear if it assigns utility $a + U(f)$ to a commodity bundle consisting of a apples and f fig leaves. One can then regard U as defining a *cardinal* utility scale for fig leaves. Adam will always be ready to swap one util's worth of fig leaves for one apple, and so any util on the fig-leaf scale is exactly comparable to any other—if the standard for comparison is the number of apples that Adam will trade for it. But, who is to say that apples (or dollars) are the "appropriate" standard of comparison?

[36]Gauthier [84, p.84] even argues that: "Morality arises from market failure." I take this to be an expression of the commonly held conservative view that no role exists

apples and fig leaves can be taken for granted, the rate at which apples are exchanged for fig leaves in this market tells us little about the relative felicity that Adam and Eve derive from consuming apples and fig leaves. Markets are driven by the relative scarcity of the goods that are traded. If Eve is a pop star, she may be able to trade a nanosecond of her labor for a kidney dialysis machine. But that does not mean that the sacrifice of a nanosecond of her time is worth the same to her as a kidney machine would be to Adam if he were suffering from kidney failure.

One can, of course, invent an index of goods in which the weights attached to fig leaves and apples somehow reflect their use-value rather than their exchange-value. However, objections are not hard to find. For example, it may be that Adam likes martinis mixed only in the proportions of 10 parts to gin to each part of vermouth, whereas the hard-drinking Eve likes them only in the proportions of 1,000 parts of gin to each part of vermouth. It then makes little sense to say that Adam and Eve are equally well-off if each are assigned 10 bottles of gin and 1 bottle of vermouth. Adam will now be able to enjoy 11 bottles of martini, whereas Eve will be able to enjoy only 10.01 bottles of martini.[37]

Such examples suggest an idea that it is familiar in the economic theory of the household. Instead of measuring Adam and Eve's welfare in terms of the raw commodities they consume, why not measure their welfare in terms of the characteristic benefits that they get from their consumption? One might ask, for example, how much health, wealth and wisdom an agent derives from any given bundle of consumption goods. As noted in Section 1.2.6, Rawls [212] proposes just such a list of "primary goods". The primary goods that he proposes for aggregation in an index are "the powers and prerogatives of office", "the social basis of self-respect" and "income and wealth".

Economists are not fond of theories that depend on such intangibles. However, even if Rawls' primary goods could be defined in precise terms, one would still be faced with an indexing problem. How do we weigh such primary goods against each other? Rawls seems to think this is a

---

for a social contract where markets operate successfully. As always, such conservatives confuse the conventions of the current social contract with the rules of the game of life. However, as pointed out in Section 1.2.8, market institutions do not have the status of Newton's law of gravity. When people honor the rules of market games, it is not because they have no choice but to do so, but because it is in their interests to do so.

[37]Notice that, after Adam and Eve have each been assigned the same bundle of commodities, neither will see any advantage in swapping their bundles. Economists say that an allocation of commodities with this property is *envy-free*. No interpersonal comparisons of utility need be made in identifying such an envy-free allocation. However, I hope the gin and martini example will suffice to indicate why it is wrong to deduce that interpersonal comparisons are therefore irrelevant.

matter on which a broad consensus can be expected.[38] However, I believe that we cannot rely on different individuals valuing some set of primary goods in a similar fashion. Even my own dean is uncharacteristically obtuse when it comes to weighing my self-respect against the prerogatives of her office! Indeed, it seems to me largely because such issues are so contentious that human societies need a social contract. Of course, moral philosophy would be a great deal easier if there really were primary goods about which everybody felt pretty much the same. Everybody would then find the same mixtures of the primary goods attractive, and it would then make sense to follow Bernoulli in seeking to identify the "right" utility function for a rational human being. The values of this utility function would then define a personal "good" that would be the same for everybody.

My own views on such an approach will be painfully familiar by now. The notion of an *a priori* personal good needs to be rejected for much the same reasons that an *a priori* common good was rejected in Sections 2.3.6 and 4.2.4. A teleological approach stands the relevant issues on their heads. If the "good" is to be discussed at all, it should be *constructed* from more primitive ideas, rather than being hypothesized from the outset. In brief, the strait and narrow path signposted by modern utility theory must be followed all the way to our destination. The shortcuts that people propose are often tempting, but they lead only to confusion in the long run.

4.3.1 Empathetic Preferences

In surveying the history of utilitarianism, Russell Hardin [100] dismisses Hume's emphasis on the importance of sympathetic identification between human beings as idiosyncratic. Although Adam Smith [248] followed his teacher in making human sympathy a major plank in his *Theory of Moral Sentiments*, Hardin is doubtless broadly right in judging that later moral philosophers appeal to human sympathy only when in need of some auxiliary support for a conclusion to which they were led largely by other considerations. Nor is it hard to see why Hume's ideas on human sympathy should have been eclipsed by more peripheral notions. The reasons are much the same as those that led to the eclipse of his even more significant insight into the importance of conventions in human societies. In brief, until game theory came along, no tools were available to operationalize Hume's ideas.

The credit for seeing the relevance of game theory to Hume's idea of a convention probably belongs largely to Schelling [229]. In the case of

---

[38] Rawls [214, p.94] speaks of the judgment that would be made by a representative agent. He then muddies the waters by saying that only a representative of the least-advantaged social grouping need be considered. But how does one know which group is least advantaged if one has not already decided the scale that determines advantage?

Hume's notion of human sympathy, my guess is that it is Harsanyi [109] who saw the way ahead most clearly. In any case, it is Harsanyi's development of the idea that will be followed here.

Sympathetic Preferences. Section 1.2.6 distinguishes between sympathy and empathy. Adam sympathizes or empathizes with Eve when he imagines himself in her shoes in order to see things from her point of view. When Adam *sympathizes* with Eve, he identifies with her so strongly that he is unable to separate his interests from hers. For example, before the creation of Eve, Adam perhaps took no interest at all in apples while gathering his daily supply of fig leaves.[39] But, after falling in love with the newly created Eve and observing her fondness for apples, he might then have found himself unable to pass an apple tree without salivating at the thought of how much Eve would enjoy its fruit. In such a case, it would not even be very remarkable if he were to abandon foraging for fig leaves altogether, so as to devote himself entirely to gathering apples for Eve.

The theory of revealed preference has no difficulty in describing Adam's behavior in such a case of sympathetic identification. If Adam chooses to gather apples rather than fig leaves, he reveals a preference for the consumption of apples by Eve to the consumption of fig leaves by himself. If he is consistent in this behavior, it can be described using a utility function u_A. One would then speak of the utility $u_A(a, f)$ that Adam derives when Eve consumes a apples and Adam consumes f fig leaves, just as one would speak of the utility that Adam derives from consuming one cup of coffee with two spoonfuls of sugar. No theoretical difficulty therefore exists in incorporating altruistic (or spiteful) preferences into a player's utility function. If Adam really cares for Eve to the extent that he is willing to sacrifice his own physical well-being for hers, then this will be the right and proper way to model the situation.[40]

It is easy to see why the forces of biological evolution might lead to our behaving as though we were equipped with sympathetic preferences. Mothers commonly care for their children more than they do for themselves—just as predicted by the model that sees us merely as machines that our genes use to reproduce themselves. In such basic matters as these, it seems that we differ little from crocodiles or spiders. However, humans do not sympathize only with their children; they also sympathize, albeit to varying

---

[39]I recall that Adam was unashamed of his nakedness before he had tasted the fruit from the Tree of Knowledge, but I am claiming some poetic license here.

[40]Of course, as Section 2.2.6 emphasizes, having built a player's sympathetic preferences into his utility function, and therefore into the payoffs of whatever game he is playing, one is then not entitled to call on the notion of sympathetic identification again when analyzing the game.

degrees, with their husbands and wives, with their extended families, with their friends and neighbors, and with their tribe or sect.

It is also easy to understand why biological evolution would select for such altruistic preferences in respect of the kinfolk with whom we share genes to a greater or lesser degree. Presumably the same mechanism explains such phenomena as the fact that African hunting dogs regurgitate food for hungry packmates. But how does an animal know who its kinfolk are? Some animals use chemical signals for this purpose, but humans seem to depend largely on the fact that, in prehistoric times, there would have been a very high probability that a neighbor was a blood relative. Of course, this is no longer true in modern times, but our genes have yet to adapt to the new reality. This fact must constitute at least part of the reason that small groups of humans often establish such close sympathetic bonds—especially when they share extended periods of danger or hardship.

Sympathy and Empathy. I have repeatedly emphasized that I think it highly misleading to generalize from the social arrangements of small close-knit groups to society as a whole.[41] I may be Dr. Jekyll to my near and dear, but strangers would be unwise to assume that Mr. Hyde is not waiting in the wings to deal with any attempt to impose on my good nature. However, I do not dispute that optimists who emphasize the Jekyll in our natureš have *some* grounds for being optimistic. As I have been saying, I agree that it certainly looks as if biology has equipped us with hard-wired sympathetic preferences that often lead to our behaving altruistically in small insider groups—even when the relationships are long-term and the behavior is costly.[42] However, I do not think the social contract issues that can be solved by appealing to the existence of sympathetic preferences are those on which it is profitable to focus.

What matters in a social contract context is not so much how we run our family lives, but how we organize a society in which most people are strangers to one another. I recognize that my decision to restrict attention most of the time to societies consisting of only Adam and Eve tends to obscure this point. However, one should think of the novels of Jane Austen rather than those of Charlotte Brontë in envisaging the marriage contract they will negotiate in the Garden of Eden. Hot-blooded passion will therefore play no role in their considerations. Instead they should be thought of

---

[41]See, for example, Sections 1.2.2, 2.2.5, and 3.2.3.

[42]I will even go so far as to express some optimism myself. One can make a case that biology has also equipped us with hard-wired *anti*sympathetic preferences that lead to our behaving spitefully towards outsiders—even when the relationships are long-term and the behavior is costly. But I have hopes that such irrational behavior arises as a result of *socially* acquired behavior being misapplied to situations for which it is ill adapted.

as negotiating calmly and rationally about such bourgeois matters as how to decide who will wash the dishes.

I do not recommend such an attitude to Adam and Eve's feelings because my theory cannot handle sympathetic preferences. In fact, the theory assumes very little about the personal preferences embodied in Adam and Eve's Von Neumann and Morgenstern utility functions u_A and u_E. If Adam and Eve were so much in love as to be in total harmony on all topics, this would be reflected in the equation $u_A = u_E$. Adam and Eve would then have no differences on the optimal distribution of apples and fig leaves in their little society. The problems that social contract theorists seek to answer would therefore become trivial. What I have to say on the social contract is therefore only interesting when the sympathetic preferences built into u_A and u_E leave at least some social contract questions open.[43]

Since Adam and Eve's sympathetic preferences are to be abstracted away into their personal utility functions u_A and u_E, we do not have the right to appeal to *sympathetic* identification in resolving the differences between Adam and Eve that then remain. Instead an appeal will be made to the notion of *empathetic* identification.

When Adam *empathizes* with Eve, he does not identify with her so closely that he ceases to separate his own preferences from hers. We weep, for example, with Romeo when he believes Juliet to be dead. We understand why he takes his own life—but we feel no particular inclination to join him in the act. Similarly, when Adam seeks to predict what Eve will do when playing a zero-sum game, he puts himself in her position to see things from her point of view—without ever losing sight of the fact that what is good for her is bad for him. In brief, no matter how vigorously he empathizes with Eve when they are thinking their way to an equilibrium in a game, Adam's *personal* utility function u_A will remain unchanged.

Neither Hume nor Adam Smith made a clear distinction between sympathetic identification and empathetic identification. However, as observed in Section 1.2.2, a loan shark is unlikely to sympathize with the plight of his victims, but he will be very much more effective as a loan shark if is able to put himself into the shoes of those whom he exploits, so as to see their difficulties as his victims see them, with a view to predicting how they will respond to his overtures. I think we routinely carry out such feats of empathetic identification when playing the game of life each day with our fellow citizens. Indeed, as mentioned in Section 3.4.2, I am one of those who think it likely that our big brains and sense of personal identity have evolved precisely because of the importance of this mechanism in getting

---

[43]Others will differ, but my own judgment of the sympathetic preferences with which most of us are equipped is that they leave open *all* of the questions about which social contract theorists commonly care.

us to equilibria quickly in new and different games. I therefore do not see empathetic identification as some auxiliary phenomenon to be mentioned only in passing. On the contrary, it seems to me basic to our humanity. If Adam could not conceive what it meant to be Eve, he would not understand what it meant to be Adam.

Why Empathy? It seems evident to me that empathetic identification is crucial to the survival of human societies. Without it, we would be unable to find our way to equilibria in the games we play except by slow and clumsy trial-and-error methods. However, it is not enough for the viability of a human society that we be able to use empathetic identification to recognize the equilibria of commonly occurring games. The games we play often have large numbers of equilibria. As Hume saw so clearly, society therefore needs commonly understood coordinating conventions that select a particular equilibrium when many are available. Sometimes the conventions that have evolved are essentially arbitrary—as in the case of the driving game mentioned in Section 2.3.6. Whether one drives on the left or the right is so obviously arbitrary that nobody has any doubt that society's choice in this matter is entirely conventional. However, in circumstances that are more deeply rooted in our social history, we are only too ready to overlook the conventional nature of our equilibrium selection criteria. The traditional criteria become so deeply internalized, that we often even fail to notice that selection criteria are in use at all.

We are particularly prone to such sleepwalking when using those conventional rules that we justify by making airy references to "fairness" when asked to explain our behavior. In saying this, I do not have in mind the rhetorical appeals to fairness that typify wage negotiations or debates over taxation.[44] I am thinking rather of the give-and-take of ordinary life. Who should do tonight's dishes? Who ought to buy the next round of drinks? How long is it reasonable to allow a bore to monopolize the conversation

---

[44]My guess is that such grand issues are largely determined by the balance of power. The accompanying talk of fairness serves only as a piece of self-deception that makes the exercise of naked power more palatable both to the oppressor and the oppressed. To register this fact is not, of course, to approve of it. I believe that power is often exercised in an absurdly myopic manner in such circumstances. The powerful are seldom realistic about the game of life. Even less do they appreciate the wide range of equilibria usually available. If they understood the realities of power better, they would see that the equilibria hallowed by tradition are often Pareto-inferior to other equilibria. They would also see that fairness criteria have evolved to facilitate coordination on such Pareto-improvements. (Recall that I am not a conservative but a whig. My recognition that fairness considerations often serve only a cosmetic role in practical affairs should therefore not be read as asserting that fairness is irrelevant in the face of naked power. Nor am I a socialist. My recognition that matters could often be improved by taking fairness seriously should therefore not be read as asserting that the realities of power can be neglected.)

over the dinner table? We are largely unconscious of the fairness criteria we use to resolve such questions, but the degree of consensus that we achieve in so doing is really quite remarkable. My guess is that the reason the idea of the original position appeals so strongly to our intuition is simply that, in working through its implications, we recognize that it epitomizes the basic principle that underlies the fairness criteria that have evolved to adjudicate our day-to-day interactions with our fellows.[45]

In order to use the device of the original position successfully as an equilibrium selection criterion, we need to be able to empathize with other people. In particular, we need to recognize that different people have different tastes. The device would obviously be worthless if Eve were to imagine how it would feel to be Adam without substituting his personal preferences for hers. But more than this is necessary. In order to make fairness judgments, Eve must be able to say *how much* better or worse she feels when identifying with Adam than when identifying with herself. It is important to understand that empathetic identification by itself is not sufficient for this purpose. An essential prerequisite for the use of the original position is that we be equipped with empathetic *preferences*.

Empathetic Preferences. Adam's *empathetic* preferences need to be carefully distinguished from the *personal* preferences built into his personal utility function u_A. For example, as Section 1.2.5 explains, I am expressing an empathetic preference when I say that I would rather be Eve eating an apple than Adam wearing a fig leaf. My own personal preferences are irrelevant to such an empathetic preference. Since I am no beach boy, I would personally much prefer a fig leaf to cover my nakedness than an apple to add to my waistline. However, if I know that apples taste very sweet to Eve and that Adam is totally unselfconscious about his body, I would clearly be failing to empathize successfully if I were to allow my own impulses towards modesty to influence my judgment about whether Eve is gaining more satisfaction from her apple than Adam is getting from his fig leaf.

It seems uncontentious that we actually do have empathetic preferences that we reveal when we make "fairness" judgments. *Homo sapiens* is doubtless less than consistent in the empathetic preferences he reveals, but I shall idealize as always by taking *homo economicus* as my model of man. His empathetic preferences will therefore be consistent. Since he will be making decisions in the risky environment of the original position, this will be taken to mean that his empathetic preferences satisfy the Von Neumann and Morgenstern rationality requirements given in Section 4.2.2. His em-

---

[45]Both Harsanyi [109] and Rawls [214] offer *a priori* Kantian defenses of the original position. My empirical viewpoint is therefore far from orthodox.

pathetic preferences can therefore be described using a Von Neumann and Morgenstern utility function.

Modeling my empathetic preferences using a Von Neumann and Morgenstern utility function v_i is easy, provided one bears in mind that my empathetic utility function is quite distinct from my personal utility function u_i. Let C be the set of possible consequences or prizes. Let $\{A, E\}$ be the set consisting of Adam (A) and Eve (E). Then $C \times \{A, E\}$ stands for the set of all pairs (C, j) with C in C and j in $\{A, E\}$.[46] My personal utility function u_i assigns a real number $u_i(C)$ to each C in the set C. By contrast, my empathetic utility function v_i assigns a real number $v_i(C, j)$ to each pair (C, j) in the set $C \times \{A, E\}$. The number $u_i(C)$ is the utility I will get if C occurs. The number $v_i(\mathcal{D}, E)$ is the utility I would derive *if I were Eve* and $\mathcal{D}$ occurs. To write $u_i(C) > u_i(\mathcal{D})$ means that I prefer C to $\mathcal{D}$. To write $v_i(C, A) > v_i(\mathcal{D}, E)$ means that I would rather be Adam when C occurs than Eve when $\mathcal{D}$ occurs.

Empathetic Preferences in the Original Position. If I am Adam seeking to coordinate with Eve using the device of the original position, I must make decisions as though I do not know whether I am Adam or Eve. I agree with Harsanyi [109] in believing that such a veil of ignorance creates exactly the type of decision problem for which Von Neumann and Morgenstern utility functions were designed. However, for reasons that will be discussed in Section 4.6, Rawls [214] feels quite differently about the matter.

Suppose that I have to evaluate a proposed social contract C.[47] Behind the veil of ignorance, I do not know whether I shall occupy the role of Adam or Eve within the social arrangements specified by C. Harsanyi [109] tells me to assign equal probabilities to these two events.[48] I will then be faced with a lottery in which two prizes are each available with probability $\frac{1}{2}$. One prize consists of my enjoying C in the role of Adam. The other consists of my enjoying C in the role of Eve. My expected Von Neumann and Morgenstern utility for this lottery is

$$w_h(C) = \tfrac{1}{2}\{v_i(C, A) + v_i(C, E)\}. \qquad (4.3)$$

---

[46]In general, the set $A \times B$ consists of all pairs (a, b) such that a is in the set A and b is in the set B.

[47]In this section, I follow Harsanyi [109] and Rawls [214] in denying myself the opportunity to consider deals in the original position that would result in the social contract C if I turn out to be Adam and $\mathcal{D}$ if I turn out to be Eve. Making such a richer class of possible deals available would only complicate matters without affecting the conclusions significantly. But Chapter 2 of Volume II dispenses with the restriction.

[48]Rawls [214, p.168] complains that we are not entitled to use *objective* probabilities. However, Harsanyi [109] intends the probabilities to be *subjective*. Section 4.5 explains how Harsanyi's position may be justified using Bayesian decision theory.

Rawls [214] differs from Harsanyi in arguing that the veil of ignorance should be taken to be so thick[49] that I cannot even attach probabilities to the possible roles I might turn out to occupy in society. Instead of seeking to maximize the function w_h, Rawls argues that my circumstances behind the veil of ignorance will lead me to seek to maximize the function w_r defined by

$$w_r(\mathcal{C}) = \min\{v_i(\mathcal{C}, A), v_i(\mathcal{C}, E)\}. \tag{4.4}$$

Should we follow Harsanyi in using w_h or Rawls in using w_r? All the big guns are on Harsanyi's side. His position is entirely orthodox among decision theorists. However, in this section I shall develop the two approaches side by side—disregarding the fact that Rawls' [214] introduction of the maximin criterion sticks out like a sore thumb in the current context. The reasons why I think that Rawls goes wrong on this point will be taken up in Section 4.6.

Both (4.3) and (4.4) become more tractable after my empathetic utility function v_i has been related to Adam and Eve's personal utility functions u_A and u_E. However, before attempting to derive this relationship, it is wise to be very specific about which of the many possible Von Neumann and Morgenstern utility scales are to be used in describing Adam and Eve's personal preferences. I know that I am often painfully pedantic about such matters in this chapter, but my feeling is that much confusion in the literature derives from simple misunderstandings about the significance of these essentially trivial manipulations.

The zero and the unit on Von Neumann and Morgenstern utility scales can be chosen at will, but then our freedom for maneuver is exhausted. To keep things simple while juggling with the utility scales, assume that everybody at least agrees that there is a worst outcome $\mathcal{L}$ and a best outcome $\mathcal{W}$ in the set C of feasible social contracts. Perhaps $\mathcal{L}$ is the event that everybody goes to hell and $\mathcal{W}$ is the event that everybody goes to heaven. We may then take $u_A(\mathcal{L}) = u_E(\mathcal{L}) = 0$ and $u_E(\mathcal{W}) = u_A(\mathcal{W}) = 1$.

Such an arbitrary choice of utility scales is surprisingly often proposed as a means of making interpersonal comparisons of utility. However, I hope that Section 4.2.2 makes it clear that such a means of introducing an interpersonal comparison of utilities is entirely arbitrary. Eve, for example, may be a jaded sophisticate who sees $\mathcal{W}$ as only marginally less dull than $\mathcal{L}$, while Adam may be a bright-eyed youth for whom the difference between $\mathcal{L}$ and $\mathcal{W}$ may seem unimaginably great. Nothing in the Von Neumann and

---

[49]Since I think that the original position is interesting because we actually use it, I do not believe that we are entitled to choose the thickness of the veil at all. In my theory, the thickness of the veil has already been determined by our cultural history. In Section 4.3.2, this attitude also brings me into conflict with Harsanyi—although his reasons for thickening the veil are very different from those given by Rawls.

Morgenstern theory allows us to exclude either possibility—or an infinitude of other possibilities.[50] We are working towards a sensible way of making interpersonal comparisons of utility, but we have some way to go yet.

Comparing Utilities à la Harsanyi. Harsanyi [109] compares Adam and Eve's personal utility scales by looking at their empathetic utility scales. If I am totally successful in empathizing with Adam, then the preferences I will express when imagining myself in Adam's position will be identical to Adam's own personal preferences. This is an important point. It escapes Parmenio, for example, in the quotation that heads this chapter. He makes the mistake of putting himself in Alexander's shoes while retaining his own personal preferences. Alexander corrects him by putting himself in Parmenio' shoes *with Parmenio's personal preferences*.

It follows that the Von Neumann and Morgenstern utility function u_A and the utility function $\tilde{u}_A$ defined by $\tilde{u}_A(\mathcal{C}) = v_i(\mathcal{C}, A)$ should represent exactly the same preferences. However, the Von Neumann and Morgenstern theory of Section 4.2.2 tells us that two Von Neumann and Morgenstern utility scales which represent the same preferences can only differ in the location of their zeros and their units. It follows that

$$v_i(\mathcal{C}, A) = \tilde{u}_A(\mathcal{C}) = \alpha u_A(\mathcal{C}) + \gamma, \tag{4.5}$$

where $\alpha > 0$ and γ are constant. Similarly, for suitable constants $\beta > 0$ and δ,

$$v_i(\mathcal{C}, E) = \tilde{u}_E(\mathcal{C}) = \beta u_E(\mathcal{C}) + \delta. \tag{4.6}$$

Although the zeros and units on Adam and Eve's personal scales have been fixed, the zero and unit on my empathetic utility scale remain undetermined. Somewhat arbitrarily, I shall therefore fix this scale so that $v_i(\mathcal{L}, A) = 0$ and $v_i(\mathcal{W}, E) = 1$. We are not free to meddle anymore with my empathetic utility scale. It follows that the two constants $U_i > 0$ and $V_i > 0$ defined by

$$U_i = v_i(\mathcal{W}, A) \text{ and } 1 - V_i = v_i(\mathcal{L}, E) \tag{4.7}$$

tell us something substantive about my empathetic preferences. Indeed, these two parameters characterize my empathetic preferences. To see this, substitute the four values $v_i(\mathcal{L}, A) = 0$, $v_i(\mathcal{W}, E) = 1$, $v_i(\mathcal{W}, A) = U_i$ and $v_i(\mathcal{L}, E) = 1 - V_i$ into equations (4.5) and (4.6). The result will be four equations in the four unknowns α, β, γ and δ. Solve these equations and substitute the resulting values for α, β, γ and δ back into (4.5) and

---

[50]Similar objections apply to Braithwaite's [46] attempt to make interpersonal comparisons on the basis of the rules of the game that his protagonists play.

(4.6). We then find that my empathetic utility function v_i can be expressed entirely in terms of the two parameters U_i and V_i:

$$\begin{aligned}
v_i(\mathcal{C}, A) &= U_i u_A(\mathcal{C}) \\
v_i(\mathcal{C}, E) &= 1 - V_i\{1 - u_E(\mathcal{C})\}.
\end{aligned} \tag{4.8}$$

Notice, for example, that the case $U_i = V_i = 1$ occurs when I am indifferent between being Adam or Eve, both in heaven and in hell. If $U_i < 1$ and $V_i < 1$, then I would rather be Eve than Adam both in heaven and in hell.

The task of simplifying w_h and w_r can now be completed. On substituting from (4.8) in the formula (4.3) for w_h, we obtain that

$$w_h(\mathcal{C}) = \tfrac{1}{2}\{U_i u_A(\mathcal{C}) + 1 - V_i(1 - u_E(\mathcal{C})\}. \tag{4.9}$$

This is the quantity that a follower of Harsanyi will seek to maximize in the original position.

We can now return to Section 1.2.5 to find out what we were talking about there. Figure 1.3 shows a set X of payoff pairs $x = (x_A, x_E)$. After writing $x_A = u_A(\mathcal{C})$ and $x_E = u_E(\mathcal{C})$, one can interpret X as the set of all pairs x of personal utilities that I see as being feasible when I am in the original position. Which of these pairs will I regard as optimal? To arrive at the answer offered in Section 1.2.5 when Harsanyi's version of utilitarianism was first introduced, we need to begin by observing that the constant term $1 - V_i$ can be omitted from (4.9), as it makes no difference to where the maximum value of w_h is achieved. The coefficient $\tfrac{1}{2}$ can be omitted for the same reason. Writing $x_A = u_A(\mathcal{C})$ and $x_E = u_E(\mathcal{C})$ on the right hand side then generates the conclusion that I should choose whichever x in the feasible set X maximizes the function W_h defined by

$$W_h(x) = U_i x_A + V_i x_E. \tag{4.10}$$

A follower of Harsanyi in the original position will therefore be a utilitarian. He will seek to maximize a weighted sum of Adam and Eve's personal utilities.

We are now, at last, in a position to say something about interpersonal comparison of utilities. Suppose that someone proposes a change from the current social contract that will result in Adam acquiring one extra personal util. How many personal utils would need to be taken from Eve to make me indifferent between staying at the current social contract and moving to the new social contract. Equation (4.10) tells us that the answer for a follower of Harsanyi is U_i/V_i. That is to say, in the original position, one of Adam's personal utils seems to me to be worth precisely U_i/V_i of Eve's personal utils.

Notice that the rate U_i/V_i at which I am ready to exchange Adam's personal utils for Eve's personal utils in the original position depends on who I am. This is reflected in the fact that U_i and V_i are indexed by i. It should not be taken for granted that Eve will make the same interpersonal comparisons when she joins me behind the veil of ignorance. Her rate of exchange U_j/V_j between Adam and Eve's personal utils may be quite different. The interpersonal comparisons of utility that Harsanyi deduces from the assumption that our empathetic preferences satisfy the Von Neumann and Morgenstern rationality assumptions are therefore *idiosyncratic*.

Comparing Utilities à la Rawls. Rawls has been left out in the cold for some time. However, a straightforward repetition of the story given for Harsanyi's model leads to the conclusion that a Rawlsian in the original position will seek to choose whichever utility pair $x = (x_A, x_E)$ in the feasible set X maximizes the function W_r defined by

$$W_r(x) = \min\{U_i x_A, 1 - V_i(1 - x_E)\}. \tag{4.11}$$

We have therefore been led to a version of Rawls' maximin criterion—although not to one of the neat formulations of Section 1.2.5. However, we shall come up with something less clumsy in Chapter 2 of Volume II when we take account of the state of nature.[51]

It is sometimes said that a Rawlsian does not need to make cardinal interpersonal comparisons because he does not need to concern himself with the *size* of the welfare gap between rich and poor. For him, no level of ease accorded to the rich can ever compensate for the smallest iota of discomfort inflicted on those at the bottom of the heap. However, the conclusion that Rawlsians therefore do not make interpersonal comparisons of utility is more than a little disingenuous. Rawlsians do not make such interpersonal comparisons as utilitarians make them, but they do nevertheless make interpersonal comparisons of a kind.

If the feasible set X of Figure 1.3 is convex and comprehensive,[52] then the maximum value of the function W_r of (4.11) is necessarily achieved at a point $x = (x_A, x_E)$ in X at which

$$U_i x_A = 1 - V_i(1 - x_E).$$

That is to say, the social contract in X that a Rawlsian in the original position likes best will make him indifferent to occupying the role of Adam or Eve. A Rawlsian therefore cares about which social contracts are egalitarian in this sense.

---

[51]Recall from Section 1.2.1 that I regard the "state of nature" for a social contract discussion as being society's current *status quo*. I therefore do not follow Harsanyi and Rawls in proposing reforms independently of a society's history of experience.

[52]It is always convex in my theory as a consequence of the folk theorem of repeated game theory.

Suppose now that the current social contract is egalitarian and a new social contract is proposed in which Adam gets one extra personal util. How many extra personal utils would we need to assign to Eve before the new social contract also becomes egalitarian? The answer is U_i/V_i. Thus, if Rawlsians really were willing to discuss the world in terms of Von Neumann and Morgenstern utilities rather than indices of primary goods, they would agree with Harsanyi that a person in the original position should be seen as regarding one of Adam's personal utils as being worth U_i/V_i of Eve's.

Confusing Renormalizations.   One final possible source of confusion needs to be addressed. After deriving the utilitarian welfare function W_h of (4.10), Harsanyi [109] alters Adam and Eve's personal utility scales by introducing new Von Neumann and Morgenstern utility functions defined by $\overline{u}_A = U_i u_A$ and $\overline{u}_E = V_i u_E$. If $X_A = U_i x_A$ and $X_E = V_i x_E$, it follows that a social contract that generates the personal utility pair $x = (x_A, x_E)$ with the old scales will generate the personal utility pair $X = (X_A, X_E)$ with the new scales. The welfare function W_h of (4.10) then needs to be replaced by the welfare function W_H defined by $W_H(X) = X_A + X_E$. This is the classical form of a utilitarian welfare function as proposed by Bentham [17] and Mill [178].

The rescaling that Harsanyi performs in order to arrive at this classical form is entirely legitimate. However, I believe that such a rescaling of Adam and Eve's personal utility scales represents a major expositional error, because it entails a large risk of misunderstandings arising about the underlying interpersonal comparison theory. Once the parameters U_i and V_i have disappeared from view, one is tempted to forget that their values are problematic. Indeed, since Adam's new personal utils are now traded one-for-one against Eve's new personal utils, it is only too easy to forget that interpersonal comparison issues need to be addressed at all. However, a Benthamite who thinks that he can deal with such problems simply by announcing that he is planning to maximize $X_A + X_E$ only deceives himself. To maximize $X_A + X_E$ is to maximize $\overline{u}_A(\mathcal{C}) + \overline{u}_E(\mathcal{C})$. We cannot maximize the latter expression without knowing what $\overline{u}_A$ and $\overline{u}_E$ are. But these functions depend on the values of U_i and V_i. In brief, one may sweep the problem of interpersonal comparison of utility under the carpet, but one cannot make it go away.

4.3.2   Common Interpersonal Comparisons

The Von Neumann and Morgenstern theory of Section 4.2 provides a cardinal theory of utility within which it makes sense for an individual to make comparisons between an extra util he receives when he is a poor and an extra util when he is rich. If he is also equipped with empathetic preferences, such intrapersonal comparisons of utility can be supplemented by interpersonal comparisons of utility between other people's utils. But the interpersonal comparisons described in Section 4.3.1 are *idiosyncratic* to the individual making them. If further assumptions are not made, there is nothing to prevent different people comparing utils across individuals in different ways. Under what circumstances will these different value judgments be the same for everybody in a society? Only then will we have an uncontroversial standard for making interpersonal comparisons available for use in formulating a social contract. Indeed, in the absence of such a *common* standard, many authors would deny that any real basis for interpersonal comparison of utilities exists at all.

Harsanyi [109, p.60] holds that the interpersonal comparisons of utility that we actually make reveal a high degree of agreement across individuals. I believe that he is broadly right in this judgment. However, I am not satisfied simply to note the existence of some measure of consensus in the society in which we actually live. It seems to me that the standard of interpersonal comparison that a society employs is subject to the same forces of social evolution as its social contract. One cannot therefore glibly take a standard for interpersonal comparison as given when discussing social contract issues. One needs to ask how and why such a standard interacts with whatever the current social contract may be—and how it would adapt in response to proposed reforms of the current social contract.

Chapter 2 of Volume II expands on Section 1.2.7, in which I suggest that our empathetic preferences are a product of *social* evolution. We need such empathetic preferences only because they serve as inputs to the equilibrium selection criteria that lead us to speak of "fairness" when we try to explain to ourselves what we are doing when we use them. However, it is important not to allow oneself to be deceived by this propaganda. Our "fairness" criteria do not necessarily treat all citizens in an even-handed mannner—whatever this might mean. As with all social institutions, the "fairness" criteria we use will tend to result in certain types of behavior becoming perceived as more successful than others. Those whose behavior is perceived to be successful are more likely to serve as the locus for meme replication than those who are perceived as failures. The point here is that social evolution will tend to favor the survival of whatever empathetic preferences promote the social success of those that hold them at the expense of those that do not. In the medium run, an equilibrium in empathetic preferences will be achieved. In the next volume, I shall argue that, in such an *empathetic equilibrium*, everybody will have the same empathetic preferences and hence we will all share a common standard for making interpersonal comparisons of utility. In the notation of Section 4.3.1, $U_i/V_i = U_j/V_j = U/V$, and so there will be a consensus that one of Adam's personal utils is worth U/V of Eve's.

Creating a Consensus? I have been at pains to reiterate my evolutionary approach to the status of the original position in order to make it clear that, although I have followed Harsanyi [109] hitherto on the subject of empathetic preferences, my position on the establishment of a *common* standard for interpersonal comparison of utilities differs very sharply from his. Thus, although the rest of this section is devoted to Harsanyi's account of the origins of a common standard, I do not want to give the impression that I endorse his approach. On the contrary, its Kantian flavor renders it totally unpalatable to a Humean like myself.

Not only is it important to distinguish my position on these matters from Harsanyi's, it is also important not to confuse the views on interpersonal comparison attributed to Harsanyi in this section with the quite different approach attributed to him in Section 4.2.4. In this earlier section, he is credited with being the father of a teleological form of utilitarianism that uses the intrapersonal comparisons of an *a priori* ideal observer when interpersonal comparisons between the citizens of a society are made. However, we are now engaged in the nonteleological exercise of showing how to construct interpersonal comparisons of utility from ground-zero. It is unfortunate from the expositional point of view that, like those sailors with a wife in every port, Harsanyi [109] should prove to be the father of two distinct brands of utilitarianism—a teleological variety and a nonteleological variety. However, except in Section 4.2.4, one would be wise in reading this chapter to forget that Harsanyi ever flirted with teleology at all.[53]

Both Harsanyi and Rawls see the original position as providing an *a priori* justification for a moral society. They are therefore both Kantians in this respect. They also share the view that the veil of ignorance to be used in the original position should be taken to be much thicker than I think appropriate.[54] Section 4.6 discusses Rawls' [214] reasons for insisting on a thick veil. Harsanyi's [109] reasons are very different. All social contract theorists who appeal to the device of the original position agree that Adam and Eve should forget their identities, and hence their *personal* preferences, when they go behind the veil of ignorance—but Harsanyi insists on much more. Behind Harsanyi's veil of ignorance, people forget *everything* that

---

[53]My impression of the utilitarian literature is that Harsanyi's efforts in his two different ports of call have been partly responsible for a blurring of the distinction between the teleological and nonteleological approaches that I think is very harmful. However, Broome [48, p.15] has entirely the opposite view!

[54]Although they differ on how the thickness of the veil will affect what those behind it can see.

might make them different. In particular, Adam and Eve forget whatever *empathetic* preferences they may have out in the real world.[55]

Since Harsanyi's agents put their actual empathetic preferences aside when they enter the original position, they need to construct new empathetic preferences behind the veil of ignorance. For this purpose, Harsanyi appeals to what Section 3.4.1 called the Harsanyi doctrine. In this context, the doctrine says that, since the veil of ignorance wipes everything that makes people different from their minds, their history of experience will be precisely the same—and hence they will be led to think in precisely the same way. Section 3.4.1 describes my suspicions of such assumptions. In brief, I believe that it only makes sense to rely on the Harsanyi doctrine when the thought processes under consideration are *convergent*—so that small changes in a person's initial state of mind cannot lead to large changes in the conclusions to which he is led. But it is particularly doubtful that the thought process which someone in the original position might follow in constructing an empathetic preference would be convergent.

As Section 1.2.7 explains, Harsanyi [109, p.60] regards the problem of constructing empathetic preferences behind the veil of ignorance as being that of identifying with an "ideal observer" who has full information about everybody's personal characteristics and about the general psychological laws governing human behavior. Such an ideal observer seems to me no more than a personification of a consensus across society on how interpersonal comparisons of utility should be made. I am sure that Harsanyi [109, p.60] is right to regard the preexistence of such a consensus as essential if the device of the original position is to be useful. It is for this reason that I think we should seek to study how social evolution might foster such a consensus. But Harsanyi asks us instead to envisage some kind of Kantian consensus that would exist *prior to society itself*. Not only this, we must also believe that the nature of this Kantian consensus can somehow be deduced by a sufficiently rational being from data that makes no reference to the store of common knowledge that Section 2.3.6 identifies with the culture of a society.

I have no idea what algorithm a rational superbeing would use for this purpose. A rational superbeing would probably find himself even more at sea, since he would be less inept in clearing his mind of cultural influences than ordinary folk. One might argue that a rational superbeing does not need an algorithm as such. Like you or me, he can simply be asked for his

---

[55]He differs from both myself and Rawls on this point. Of course, Rawls does not discuss empathetic preferences. He achieves the necessary interpersonal comparisons of utility by appealing to his notion of an index of primary goods. This index is not negotiated in the original position. It is therefore presumably something on which consensus exists in the real world and which is not forgotten when Adam and Eve pass beyond the veil.

best shot at an answer. The Harsanyi doctrine will then guarantee that all
superbeings will make the same guess when placed behind a thick enough
veil of ignorance. But this is the defense of the Paradox of the Twins that
was lampooned in Section 3.4 by comparing it with the story of Buridan's
ass! Even if we could rely on all rational superbeings coming up with the
same rate U/V for trading Adam's utils for Eve's, how would we poor
mortals ever manage to predict what this ratio would be?

In summary, although I have criticized Rawls' use of a supposedly uncontroversial index of primary goods to evade interpersonal comparison
problems, I am nearer to him on this issue than to Harsanyi. We have no
choice but to rely on some measure of consensus *already existing* in the
society under study if a *common* standard for comparing utilities across
individuals is to be available. Harsanyi's brave attempt to argue that the
circumstances of the original position *create* such a standard seems to me
to lack all conviction when closely examined.

4.4   Kant and the Prisoners' Dilemma

Section 2.4.1 used the Prisoners' Dilemma in attempting to explain how
both Harsanyi's and Rawls' positions can be seen as attempts to operationalize Kant's categorical imperative. This section returns to the same
arena with a view to providing a concrete example of how the ideas on
interpersonal comparison introduced in Section 4.3 may be applied.

In one sense, everything to be said is a mere gloss on Section 2.4.1.
However, the gloss is of great importance, since it needs to be emphasized
that the arithmetic of Section 2.4.1 was entirely empty. We had no idea at
the time how the payoffs with which we were then working should properly be interpreted. We therefore fell headlong into the trap of comparing
quantities without asking ourselves whether the quantities were measured
in comparable units. It is because this error is so common that such care
was taken in Section 4.3.1 to be painfully precise in specifying how the zeros
and units on all the various Von Neumann and Morgenstern utility scales
were to be determined. The same pedantic attention to detail will also be
apparent in the current section for exactly the same reason.

Getting the Kantian Arithmetic Straight. Section 2.4.1 discusses
the Prisoners' Dilemma and so the same example will be used here. The
game has four possible outcomes: $\mathcal{C} = (dove, dove)$, $\mathcal{D} = (dove, hawk)$, $\mathcal{E} =$
$(hawk, dove)$ and $\mathcal{F} = (hawk, hawk)$. Let us also consider two consequences
$\mathcal{L}$ and $\mathcal{W}$ that are not feasible when the Prisoners' Dilemma is to be played.
As in Section 4.3, it will be assumed that Adam and Eve agree that $\mathcal{L}$ is
the worst of all possible outcomes and $\mathcal{W}$ is the best. Adam's personal

preferences over these six consequences will be taken to satisfy

$$\mathcal{L} \sim_A \mathcal{D} \prec_A \mathcal{F} \prec_A \mathcal{C} \prec_A \mathcal{E} \sim_A \mathcal{W}.$$

Such ordinal preferences are inadequate for our purpose. Let us therefore suppose that we learn from observing Adam's behavior that he is indifferent between $\mathcal{C}$ and a lottery in which he gets $\mathcal{L}$ with probability $\frac{1}{3}$ and $\mathcal{W}$ with probability $\frac{2}{3}$. He also turns out to be indifferent between $\mathcal{F}$ and a lottery in which he gets $\mathcal{L}$ with probability $\frac{2}{3}$ and $\mathcal{W}$ with probability $\frac{1}{3}$. As we know from Section 4.2, such preferences involving lotteries can be described with the help of a personal Von Neumann and Morgenstern utility function u_A. As in Section 4.3.1, choose the zero and the unit on the corresponding Von Neumann and Morgenstern utility scale so that $u_A(\mathcal{L}) = 0$ and $u_A(\mathcal{W}) = 1$. Then it must be true that $u_A(\mathcal{D}) = 0$, $u_A(\mathcal{F}) = \frac{1}{3}$, $u_A(\mathcal{C}) = \frac{2}{3}$ and $u_A(\mathcal{E}) = 1$. Eve's personal Von Neumann and Morgenstern utility function will also be normalized so that $u_E(\mathcal{L}) = 0$ and $u_E(\mathcal{W}) = 1$. Assume that, after exploring her preferences over lotteries, it is found that $u_E(\mathcal{E}) = 0$, $u_E(\mathcal{F}) = \frac{1}{3}$, $u_E(\mathcal{C}) = \frac{2}{3}$ and $u_E(\mathcal{D}) = 1$.

The preferences attributed to Adam and Eve have been carefully chosen to be one third of the personal payoffs that we regularly use for the Prisoners' Dilemma. The version of the Prisoners' Dilemma with which we are working is therefore as shown in Figure 4.4(a). We could equally well have made a different choice of Eve's personal utility scale by taking $u_E(\mathcal{L}) = 0$ and $u_E(\mathcal{W}) = 3$. Eve's payoffs in the resulting Prisoners' Dilemma would then be three times her payoffs in Figure 4.4(a), and hence identical to her payoffs in the regular Prisoners' Dilemma of Figure 2.2(b). However, although things would now look very asymmetric to the untutored eye, since Eve's payoffs would be larger than Adam's, it would be a bad mistake to think that anything fundamental had been achieved by such a rescaling. We would simply find ourselves using different values of U and V in what is coming next.

Kantians like Harsanyi and Rawls deny Hume's view that it is idle to propose a standard for morality that requires a person to act in a manner contrary to his enlightened self-interest. Such a Kantian view requires that Adam and Eve ignore the strategic structure of the Prisoners' Dilemma when behaving morally. For both Harsanyi and Rawls, the adoption of such a moral viewpoint demands that Adam and Eve pretend that they are not playing the Prisoners' Dilemma. They are to act instead as though they were playing the Prisoners' Dilemma as it would seem to them if neither Adam nor Eve were aware of their identities. To describe their behavior in such circumstances, we need to employ the material from Section 4.3.1 that systematizes the notion of an empathetic preference. It will be assumed in particular that the zero and the unit on the empathetic utility scales are chosen as in Section 4.3.1.

	dove	*hawk*
dove	$\frac{2}{3}$ $\quad$ $\frac{2}{3}$	1 $\quad$ 0
hawk	0 $\quad$ 1	$\frac{1}{3}$ $\quad$ $\frac{1}{3}$

	dove	*hawk*
dove	$\frac{1}{6}$ $\quad$ $\frac{1}{6}$	0 $\quad$ 0
hawk	0 $\quad$ 0	$\frac{1}{12}$ $\quad$ $\frac{1}{12}$

	dove	*hawk*
dove	$\frac{5}{6}$ $\quad$ $\frac{5}{6}$	1 $\quad$ 1
hawk	$\frac{1}{4}$ $\quad$ $\frac{1}{4}$	$\frac{5}{12}$ $\quad$ $\frac{5}{12}$

(a) Prisoners' Dilemma   (b) Rawlsian Dodo   (c) Utilitarian Dodo

Figure 4.4: Kantifying the Prisoners' Dilemma when $U = 1/4$ and $V = 1$

Suppose that I am Adam following Harsanyi's utilitarian advice behind the veil of ignorance. The event that I am Adam will then be assigned the same probability as the event that I am Eve. I will therefore seek to maximize the function W_h of (4.10) defined by $W_h(x) = U_i x_A + V_i x_E$. When Eve joins me behind the veil of ignorance, she will seek to maximize a similar function, but her parameters U_j and V_j need not be the same as mine. Section 4.3.2 gave the argument that Harsanyi uses to justify the requirement that $U_i = U_j = U$ and $V_i = V_j = V$. If we accept Harsanyi's argument, both of us will be therefore be seeking to maximize the *same* function in the original position. We therefore have a common aim. Since we also have precisely the same information in the original position, the bargaining issues raised in Section 1.2.9 become irrelevant. Two minds with but a single thought have no need to negotiate. In the original position, Adam and Eve will simply agree to choose whichever social contract generates the payoff pair $x = (x_A, x_E)$ that maximizes $U x_A + V x_E$.

Figure 4.4(c) shows how things will seem to the two players in the original position when $U = \frac{1}{4}$ and $V = 1$.[56] The social contract that a utilitarian will choose when $U = \frac{1}{4}$ and $V = 1$ is therefore $(dove, hawk)$. Notice that this differs from the social contract $(dove, dove)$ said to be utilitarian in Section 2.4.1. The difference is easily explained. Without any justification at all, Section 2.4.1 took for granted that $U = V = 1$.[57]

It always needs to be kept in mind that Rawls believes that he can finesse the problems that utility theory is designed to address by working with an index of primary goods. However, if we insist that players work

---

[56]If a cell in Figure 4.4(a) contains the payoff pair $x = (x_A, x_E)$, then the corresponding cell in Figure 4.4(c) contains the payoff pair $(U x_A + V x_E, U x_A + V x_E)$.

[57]If we were to use $U = V = 1$ in the current section, Figure 4.4(c) would be replaced by a version of Figure 2.8(c) in which each payoff is multiplied by $\frac{1}{3}$.

with utilities, we can still capture something of the flavor of the Rawlsian enterprise simply by replacing Harsanyi's use of expected utility maximization by the maximin criterion as recommended by Rawls. Figure 4.4(b) shows how things will then seem to players in the original position when $U = \frac{1}{4}$ and $V = 1$.[58] The social contract that a Rawlsian will choose when $U = \frac{1}{4}$ and $V = 1$ is therefore *(dove, dove)*. The same social contract was said to be Rawlsian in Section 2.4.1 for the case $U = V = 1$. However, a Rawlsian analysis does not always lead to a social contract like *(dove, dove)* in which Adam and Eve get treated identically. For example, the Rawlsian social contract when $U = 0.1$ and $V = 10$ is *(dove, hawk)*.

The Humean Criticism. We have just examined some arguments for taking *(dove, dove)* or *(dove, hawk)* as the social contract in the Prisoners' Dilemma. A similar argument can equally well be given for the other Pareto-efficient outcome *(hawk, dove)*. On the other hand, whatever values might be assigned to U and V, neither Harsanyi nor Rawls could ever be led to propose *(hawk, hawk)* as a social contract, because this outcome is not Pareto-efficient. However, as we know from the lengthy discussion of the Prisoners' Dilemma in Chapters 2 and 3, *(hawk, hawk)* is the only Nash equilibrium of the game.

Harsanyi is untroubled that his theory selects an outcome of the Prisoners' Dilemma that is not an equilibrium. As Section 1.2.4 explains, he argues that Adam and Eve should see themselves as being *committed* to the hypothetical deal reached in the original position. The fact that the hypothetical deal may conflict with their personal incentives is therefore an irrelevance. Rawls agonizes about the "strains of commitment", but takes essentially the same view as Harsanyi once the chips are down. However, Humeans like myself see no way that a social contract can survive unless it is responsive to the personal ambitions of the citizens in the society whose operation it supposedly regulates. A Humean therefore has no choice but to restrict the social contracts he regards as feasible to the class of *equilibria* in the game of life. In brief, all the Kantian discussion of this section, whatever the conclusion to which it leads, is beside the point. If the game of life really were the Prisoners' Dilemma, then the only feasible social contract would be *(hawk, hawk)*.

But there is no need to be entirely negative. Humeans may not wish to follow Harsanyi into the cold waters of Kantian constructivism, but nothing prevents their stealing the warm clothes he has left behind on the river bank. In particular, the idea of using empathetic preferences to generate

---

[58] If a cell in Figure 4.4(a) contains the payoff pair $x = (x_A, x_E)$, then the corresponding cell in Figure 4.4(b) contains the payoff pair $(\min\{Ux_A, 1 - V(1 - x_E)\}, \min\{Ux_A, 1 - V(1 - x_E)\})$.

idiosyncratic standards for comparing utilities across individuals is far too good to throw away.

4.5 Bayesian Decision Theory

If God did not exist, it would be necessary to invent him. In saying this, Voltaire was making fun of those who allow their beliefs to be determined by their preferences. If nothing else, our prolonged study of the Prisoners' Dilemma shows that nobody can count on being immune to this most seductive of errors. It is therefore fitting that the next topic for attention is Bayesian decision theory, whose primary tenet for rationality is that a person should *separate* his beliefs from his preferences. Savage [228] showed that this principle implies that a rational decision-maker who knows what decisions he would make under a sufficiently wide enough class of contingencies will necessarily act as though maximizing the expected value of a Von Neumann and Morgenstern utility function relative to a subjective probability measure.

Most readers will want only to skim the summary of Savage's theory offered here. It is not possible to avoid the topic altogether, in spite of its being only peripheral to the social contract questions considered in this book. However, some grounding in Bayesian decision theory will be necessary when the time comes to assess the disagreement between Harsanyi [105] and Rawls [213] about whether Savage's theory is applicable in the circumstances of the original position.

Although I do not share Harsanyi's attachment to Bayesianism as a metaphysical doctrine, I side wholeheartedly with him in this dispute with Rawls. Indeed, it seems to me that the hypotheses of the original position create a microcosm that might have been tailor-made for applications of Bayesian decision theory. However, this is an issue that will have to wait until Section 4.6. Readers who are already convinced that the maximin criterion is a nonstarter in the rationality stakes will wish to skip all the way forward to Section 4.7.

Bayesianism. Savage [228] offers a *subjectivist* theory of probability. Unfortunately, the clarity of his vision has been obscured by later writers, who have implicitly reinterpreted his theory in logicist terms. Elsewhere, I have referred to the metaphysical doctrine to which such logicists subscribe as *Bayesianism* (Binmore [24]). Adherents of this creed believe that the problem of scientific induction is solved. They hold that rational learning requires nothing more of a scientist than that he use Bayes' Rule to update his prior probabilities as new evidence becomes available.

Bayesianismists differ on the source of wisdom from which rational decision-makers are to derive their prior probabilities. True believers proceed as though suitable priors are somehow part of the equipment with which Nature endows rational folk. However, those who seek to apply Bayesianism to real problems find it necessary to be more pragmatic.[59] They offer a menu of possible priors that have been found to "work well" in the past. These typically represent some adaptation of Laplace's principle of insufficient reason—which says that equal probabilities should be assigned to different events unless some reason can be found for distinguishing between them.[60]

Savage [228] variously describes the idea that one can use his theory on the grand scale required by Bayesianism as "ridiculous" and "preposterous". He insists that it is only sensible to use his theory in the context of what he calls a *small world*. As Savage puts it, a small world is one within which it is always possible to "look before you leap". A decision-maker can then take account *in advance* of the impact that all conceivable future pieces of information might have on the underlying model that determines his subjective beliefs. Any mistakes built into his original model that might be revealed in the future will then *already* have been corrected, so that no possibility remains of any unpleasant surprises.

In a large world, however, the possibility of an unpleasant surprise that reveals 'some consideration overlooked in the original model cannot be discounted. As Savage puts it, in a large world, one can only "cross certain bridges when they are reached". Knee-jerk consistency is no virtue in such a world. Someone who insists on acting consistently come what may is just someone who obstinately refuses to admit the possibility of error. However, after being surprised by a stream of unanticipated data, even a Bayesianismist might sometimes wonder whether the confidence he reposes in his initial choice of prior probabilities is well founded. When afflicted by such doubts, why should he then not abandon the criteria on which he based his original set of prior probabilities in order to start afresh with a new set? I can think of no good reason at all. In brief, whoever said that foolish consistency is the hobgoblin of little minds hit the nail right on the head insofar as rational learning in large worlds is concerned. Only when our small minds are encased in a small world does consistency become an unqualified virtue.

I wish it were possible to persuade people to call Bayesian decision

---

[59] I have no quarrel at all, incidentally, with those statisticians who defend Bayesian methods *entirely* on pragmatic grounds. After all, classical statistics is no better founded. It is the metaphysical claims of Bayesianismists with which I am taking issue.

[60] Adaptations are needed because of the well-known difficulties that can arise with Laplace's principle when it is applied in infinite state spaces. Keynes [141] and Kolmogorov [143] provide some striking examples.

theory something else. One might, for example, simply speak of Savage's theory of subjective probability. As things stand, laymen take for granted that Bayes' Rule must surely be the linchpin of the whole system.

Bayes' Rule was discovered by the Reverend Thomas Bayes some time before 1763. It specifies how the conditional probability $\text{prob}(E|F)$ that an event E will occur given that the event F occurs, is related to the conditional probability $\text{prob}(F|E)$ that the event F will occur given that the event E occurs. Since $\text{prob}(E|F)$ is defined to be $\text{prob}(E\cap F)/\text{prob}(F)$, the rule is not hard to find. It simply says that

$$\text{prob}(E|F)\text{prob}(F) = \text{prob}(F|E)\text{prob}(E).$$

How Bayesianismists manage to convince themselves that this trivial algebraic manipulation somehow unlocks the secret of rational learning is beyond my comprehension. Bayes certainly thought no such thing. Doubtless he would join Savage in calling such a view ridiculous and preposterous if he were around to be asked. But this is precisely the error that we invite by referring to Savage's theory of subjective probability as Bayesian decision theory. As a consequence, Bayesians like myself are constantly misunderstood. We must always be emphasizing that a subjectivist is a very different animal from a logicist. However, just as a mathematician can use Pythagoras's theorem without subscribing to the Pythagorean metaphysics that apparently made pure number the essential stuff of the universe, so one can be a Bayesian without being a Bayesianismist (Binmore [24]).

Game theorists insist that the rules of a game always include the proviso that the probabilities assigned by a player to the various options available to Nature at chance moves within the game be common knowledge. When attempts are made to apply the theory to real problems, critical attention then tends to focus on how plausible it is to assume that the players' subjective beliefs about such chance moves should be commonly known. Almost never does the implicit assumption that these beliefs can be described with probabilities come into question. However, sometimes the chance moves are less simple than the shuffling and dealing that opens a game of poker. Objective probabilities may not then be available, and so subjective probabilities must be used instead. We are then implicitly assuming that the microcosm to which the theory of games is being applied must be one of Savage's small worlds.

When are we justified in making such a small-world assumption? This question would be easy if formal criteria were available to distinguish between worlds that are large and worlds that are small.[61] Unfortunately,

---

[61]Savage [228] did attempt to lay the foundations for such a formal theory. He discusses how a microcosm to which his theory applies can be embedded in a large universe to which his theory does not apply. But it is not generally thought that this discussion

just as one cannot say when one extra grain will convert a pile of rice into a heap, so one cannot say precisely how much more complicated a small world can be allowed to become before it has to be categorized as large.[62] However, although such difficulties might very properly trouble the sleep of those who seek to apply game theory in a macroeconomic context, they need not concern those of us who are content to confine our attention to toy games like those considered in this book. In such simple games, the "look before you leap" principle is obviously immediately applicable.[63] Whether the same is true for the game played by Adam and Eve in the original position is a matter for a debate that will have to await Section 4.6. At this stage, I only want to deny the Bayesianismist claim that Bayesianism applies not only in the original position—but always.

Savage's Theory. A full account of the foundations of the theory of subjective probability as developed by Savage [228] would be very lengthy. It is not even practical to seek to emulate Kreps [144], whose excellent summary of the theory suppresses all the messy details. Nor is there space to discuss the various alternative theories surveyed by Machina [159]. I do not even plan to review any of the paradoxes that critics of Savage's ideas have constructed in an attempt to discredit his theory. Instead, I propose to sketch in just enough of the foundations of the theory to make it clear that some of these criticisms are attacks on propositions that are essentially tautological.

When introducing *homo economicus*, Section 1.2.2 quotes Hobbes' characterization of man in terms of his strength of body, his passions, his experience, and his reason. In Bayesian decision theory, each of these items is given a formal expression. When Adam is faced with a decision problem, his feasible set consists of all the actions that he is physically able to

---

holds together very successfully.

[62]The "Sorites" is the fallacy that heaps do not exist, because no single extra grain of rice ever makes a pile into a heap. Bayesianismists sometimes claim that all worlds are small by appealing to variants of this fallacy.

[63]Matters are very different in the *foundations* of game theory. It seems to me that one cannot sensibly discuss what solution concept for a game makes sense without taking a view on what the players think about each other. The universe of discourse for a player must therefore include entities—the other players—whose complexity is comparable to his own. Such a universe cannot but be large in Savage's sense, unless dramatic simplifying assumptions are made (Binmore [24]). When I say that the microcosm created by the rules of a toy game is tautologically a small world, I am talking about how players attach subjective probabilities to chance moves specified *within* the rules of the game, not to various events *outside* the scope of the rules that players must consider in deciding how to play—like whether an opponent will play this strategy or that. If one applies Bayesian decision theory to such matters, as we shall in some examples coming up shortly, one implicitly confers small-world status on a universe of discourse for which such an assumption may well be inappropriate.

choose.[64] Adam's strength of body is identified with this feasible set. His
passions are identified with his preferences. His experience is identified with
his beliefs. His reason is identified with the manner in which he chooses.
For a specimen of *homo economicus* who lives in a small world, reason is
therefore reduced to applying the principles of Bayesian decision theory.

Let A be Adam's feasible set of *actions*. Let B be the set of *states of the
world* about which Adam has beliefs. Let C be the set of *consequences* to
which Adam's decision may lead. We also require a function $f : A{\times}B \to C$
that specifies how the sets A, B and C are related. Recall that the set $A{\times}B$
consists of all pairs (a, b). The function f therefore assigns a consequence
$c = f(a, b)$ in the set C to each pair (a, b) in the set $A{\times}B$. We interpret this
value of c to be the consequence that will result if Adam chooses action a
when the state of the world happens to be b.

In Section 3.5, for example, we considered how Lewis [154] models the
Prisoners' Dilemma as two back-to-back Newcomb problems. Adam is then
seen as a decision-maker, whose set A of feasible actions consists of two
alternatives: *dove* and *hawk*. The set B of states of the world is taken to be
Eve's two possible predictions: *dove* and *hawk*. The set C of consequences
consists of four different sums of money, \$0, \$1, \$2 and \$3. The function
f is indicated with the help of the table of Figure 4.5(a) (which simply
repeats Adam's payoff matrix from Figure 3.7(e)). In this table, the rows
represent the set A, the columns represent the set B, and the entries in the
table represent the set C. For example, when $a = dove$ and $b = hawk$, then
$c = f(a, b) = \$0$.

	dove	*hawk*
dove	\$2	\$0
hawk	\$3	\$1

	correct	*mistaken*
dove	\$2	\$0
hawk	\$1	\$3

(a) Newcomb à la Lewis.   (a) Newcomb à la Ferejohn.

Figure 4.5: Some decision problems

The consequences c in the set C correspond to the prizes of Section

---

[64] As Section 3.4.2 argues, he is "free to choose" any of these feasible actions until we
have tied down his thought processes by identifying an action in the feasible set that is
optimal for him. After the optimal actions have been identified, Adam can no longer be
said to be "free to choose" a suboptimal action—unless one is simultaneously to deny
that he belongs to the species *homo economicus*.

4.2.2. The actions a in the set A are also familiar. They correspond to pure strategies in a game. However, the states b in the set B are something that we have not considered explicitly before. In Section 4.2.2, we were able to avoid them by restricting attention to states for which objective probabilities are available. It is usual, as in Section 4.2.1, to think of such states in terms of the possible outcomes that can arise when a roulette wheel is spun. However, in the current section, the focus will be on states that do not come equipped with objective probabilities. Such states are usually exemplified as the possible outcomes of a horse race. Savage's theory can then be seen as an attempt to characterize Adam's betting behavior at the race-track in terms of subjective probabilities for events like *Punter's Folly* winning the Derby.

Consider, for example, the action a illustrated in Figure 4.6(a). This action represents Adam's betting everything he owns on *Punter's Folly*— right down to the shirt on his back. If E represents the event that his horse wins, then two possible consequences can follow from the action a. We represent these consequences by $\mathcal{D} = f(a, E)$ and $\mathcal{L} = f(a, \sim E)$. If Adam could assign an objective probability $p(E)$ to the event E, then the Von Neumann and Morgenstern theory of Section 4.2.2 would be adequate to deal with the problem. The action a would be seen as leading to the lottery $\mathbf{L}$ in which Adam gets $\mathcal{D}$ with probability $p(E)$ and $\mathcal{L}$ with probability $p(\sim E) = 1 - p(E)$. Adam would then be said to be rational in choosing action a if and only if a maximizes his expected Von Neumann and Morgenstern utility

$$U(a) = p(E)u(\mathcal{D}) + p(\sim E)u(\mathcal{L}). \qquad (4.12)$$

However, the Von Neumann and Morgenstern theory does not apply to horse racing because the necessary objective probabilities are unavailable. Savage [228] showed that the Von Neumann and Morgenstern theory could nevertheless be extended to cover such cases. With appropriate assumptions about rational behavior, Savage proved that Adam will choose actions from the set A *as though* seeking to maximize the expected utility of a Von Neumann and Morgenstern utility function u relative to a *subjective* probability measure p. To emulate Savage, we must therefore deduce *two* functions from observations of his preferences over actions in A: a utility function u defined on C and a probability measure p defined on B.

Savage constructed u and p from scratch, but it is a great deal easier to follow Anscombe and Aumann [2] or Kreps [144] in adopting a framework that allows a direct appeal to be made to the work of Von Neumann and Morgenstern. Within this framework, Adam may observe both horse races *and* roulette wheels. The availility of the latter makes it possible for Adam to use mixed actions—just as a player in a game may use a mixed strategy. Such mixed actions correspond to lotteries in which the prizes are the pure actions in the set A. If we assume that Adam honors the Von Neumann and Morgenstern rationality assumptions of Section 4.2.2, we are then entitled to deduce that the preferences he reveals over actions can be described by a Von Neumann and Morgenstern utility function U defined on the set A. Our problem then reduces to showing that such a Von Neumann and Morgenstern utility function U can be expressed in the form (4.12).

Separating Preferences, Beliefs and Actions. Just as one cannot make bricks without straw, so one cannot prove that U admits the representation (4.12) without making some assumptions. As we shall see, the necessary assumptions only make sense if we first ensure that our decision problem has been formulated in a manner that properly separates the domains inhabited by Adam's preferences, beliefs and actions.

Critics of Savage's theory often overlook this point. However, it is obvious that the theory cannot possibly be the appropriate tool if relationships between the sets A, B, and C other than those built into the function f are relevant to Adam's decision. A formal theory can only take account of relationships that have been expressed within its formalism. In setting up a model to which the theory is to be applied, one must therefore be careful to choose definitions for A, B, and C which ensure that *only* linkages incorporated in the function $f : A{\times}B \to C$ have any bearing on Adam's decision problem. Examples produced to cast doubt on the Savage theory routinely neglect to honor this elementary precaution, and so I think it worth spending some time expanding on it.

Let us consider the implications of the requirement that the domains inhabited by Adam's preferences and his actions be properly separated. Recall that the theory locates Adam's preferences in the set C of consequences. Of course, as Section 2.2.4 explains, once we observe what choices Adam makes, we will be able to appeal to the theory of revealed preference and so be able to describe the actions he will take using the utility function U defined over the set A of actions. However, Savage's theory implicitly requires that the actions be defined so that Adam's interest in them is entirely instrumental. For example, if he reveals a preference for action a_1 over action a_2, it will not be because he has any intrinsic liking for actions indexed by odd numbers over those indexed by even numbers, but because he believes that the consequence of choosing action a_1 is likely to be superior to the consequence of choosing a_2. In brief, the preferences his choice behavior reveals over actions must not depend directly on the actions themselves, but only on his beliefs about their anticipated consequences.[65]

---

[65] Critics often express their disapproval of such "consequentialist" assumptions. However, as Section 2.2.4 explains, they are wrong to think that it is implicitly being assumed

Suppose, for example, that Eve refuses a draw when playing chess, but then loses. She might then be unhappier than she would have been if no draw had ever been offered. If so, we make a bad mistake if we define the set of consequences in Eve's decision problem to be $C = \{\mathcal{L}, \mathcal{D}, \mathcal{W}\}$. At the very least, we must distinguish between losing-having-refused-a-draw and losing-without-having-refused-a-draw. That is to say, where necessary, the means by which the end is achieved must be absorbed into the definition of an end.

We have just looked at a case where it was necessary to redefine the set C after realizing that our first thoughts on the subject were inadequate. It is much less common for it to be necessary to redefine B for similar reasons. However, Newcomb's Paradox of Section 3.4 provides one such example. According to Brams [47], Ferejohn suggests modeling the problem as in Figure 4.5(b). In this model, the states of the world represent Eve's success in predicting Adam's choice. They are therefore labeled *correct* and *mistaken*. The model differs very sharply in this respect from the model of Lewis given in Figure 4.5(a). In Lewis' model, the states of the world are what Eve actually predicts: namely *dove* or *hawk*. Which model we adopt matters a great deal. In Lewis' model, Nozick [195] would presumably join everybody else in recommending that Adam choose *hawk*. This would follow, for example, from the application of his "domination principle". In Ferejohn's model, I take it that Nozick would apply the "principle of expected utility maximization" and hence advise Adam to choose *dove* on the grounds that *correct* is overwhelmingly more likely than *mistaken*. I do not want to repeat what Section 3.5 says about the reasons why such apparent contradictions between the two "principles of choice" are illusory. At this stage, I want only to make the point that one cannot interpret the Ferejohn model as a representation of the Newcomb problem without violating the requirement that the set B be defined independently of A. Far from states of the world being defined independently of actions in Ferejohn's model, one has to know both Eve's actual prediction *and* Adam's choice of action before one can say what state the world is in. Bayesian decision theory therefore offers no endorsement for an application of the "principle of expected utility maximization" to the Ferejohn model.[66]

---

that the "ends justify the means". In fact, the contrary position is being asserted. The theory *insists* that if you have defined your consequences (or ends) so that your actions (or means) matter, then you are about to apply Savage's theory to a situation in which it is not applicable. If Savage's theory is not to be abused, it is essential that the consequences be defined so as to *include* the means by which they are achieved.

[66]Of course, nothing prevents the invention of new decision theories, like those of Gibbard and Harper [89] or Lewis [151], in which interdependence between actions and beliefs is expressly permitted. Similarly, one might invent a non-Euclidean geometry to cope with a situation in which a line has been defined to be some sort of curve. In some cases, this will be the most elegant treatment. However, the conclusions to which one

We have looked at cases where things go wrong because linkages un-expressed by the function $f : A{\times}B \to C$ have been permitted between A and B and between A and C. It is equally important that no linkages be allowed between B and C. Suppose, for example, that an umbrella and an icecream are among the prizes available at a county fair, and the possible states of the world are *sunny* and *wet*. It would then not be at all surprising if Adam's preferences over the prizes were influenced by his beliefs about the state of the world. In such circumstances, the set C again needs to be redefined. One expedient is to insist that the members of the set C be taken to be Adam's *states of mind* rather than physical objects. One would then speak of the states of mind that accompany having an umbrella-on-a-sunny-day or having an umbrella-on-a-wet-day, rather than speaking just of an umbrella.

When expedients of this type are employed, critics often complain that they are being fobbed off with a theory devoid of any substance—all its propositions having been made into tautologies. As in Chapter 2, such critics miss the point. Bayesians are delighted when their underlying assumptions are thought to be so uncontroversial that the propositions of the theory can be dismissed as tautological. The last thing Bayesians like myself have in mind is the creation of a theory whose assumptions are controversial. On the contrary, we intend that Bayesian decision theory should provide an uncontroversial language within which substantive questions about rational decision-making can be framed. Debates about matters of substance can then proceed without any questions being begged. Suspicion should therefore be directed at a Bayesian who shows signs of discomfort when his theory is categorized as being devoid of content. Most likely, he's just waiting to be thrown in the briar patch!

Formalities. The coming mathematics have been kept to a minimum in order to emphasize my belief that it is the preformal ideas that we have just been discussing that are really important to an understanding of Bayesian decision theory.

Recall that action a in equation (4.12) represents Adam's betting everything he has on *Punter's Folly* in the Derby. In the event E that his horse wins, the consequence for Adam is $\mathcal{D}$. In the event $\sim\!E$ that his horse loses, the consequence for Adam is the worst possible outcome $\mathcal{L}$. The top row of Figure 4.6(a) shows the two relevant consequences $\mathcal{D}$ and $\mathcal{L}$. The bottom row shows when they occur.

The first assumption needed to derive (4.12) is that *only* the information incorporated in the table of Figure 4.6(a) is relevant to Adam's evaluation

---

is led ought to be the same as those one obtains by using ordinary Euclidean geometry with a line defined to be a line.

of the action a. Unless the actions have been defined with this consideration in mind, Savage's theory therefore does not apply.

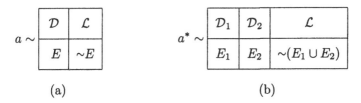

(a)   (b)

Figure 4.6: Betting on horses

The first assumption is needed to justify writing Adam's Von Neumann and Morgenstern utility $U(a)$ for the action a in the form

$$U(a) = V(\mathcal{D}|E),\qquad(4.13)$$

where the dependence on $\mathcal{L}$ has been suppressed because this prize will be held fixed all the time.

The second assumption consists of a list of bookkeeping requirements concerning the function V of (4.13). For all possible[67] events E and all consequences $\mathcal{D}$ with $\mathcal{L} \prec \mathcal{D}$,

$$0 = V(\mathcal{L}|E) < V(\mathcal{D}|E) \leq V(\mathcal{W}|E),$$

$$0 = V(\mathcal{D}|\emptyset) < V(\mathcal{D}|E) \leq V(\mathcal{D}|B).$$

Also $V(\mathcal{W}|B) = 1$.

The third assumption is the most fundamental. It represents the requirement that Adam separate his preferences from his beliefs. What needs to be ruled out is the sort of reasoning that goes: "I don't believe that because I don't like what it implies." Or, equally irrationally: "I don't want that because I'm not likely to get it."

With this aim in mind, consider the function V of (4.13). For each fixed $E \neq \emptyset$, V can be regarded as a Von Neumann and Morgenstern utility function describing a preference over lotteries in which the prizes are consequences in the set C.[68] The third assumption is that this preference be the *same* for all $E \neq \emptyset$.

---

[67]Recall that the empty set $\emptyset$ represents the impossible event that no horse wins the Derby. Among other things, the second assumption will deny that Adam regards some possible events as being so unlikely that they might as well be impossible. When the state space B is infinite, such a denial will often not be sensible, and a less crude assumption will need to be substituted.

[68]Whose receipt, in this context, is contingent on the occurrence of the event E.

It is worth pausing to consider the implications of this third assumption. For example, it implies that if $V(\mathcal{D}_1|E) < V(\mathcal{D}_2|E)$, then $V(\mathcal{D}_1|F) < V(\mathcal{D}_2|F)$ for all $F \neq \emptyset$. But this is not an assumption that one would want to make if $\mathcal{D}_1$ and $\mathcal{D}_2$ are an umbrella and an icecream when the events E and F represent rain or shine.

Substituting different values of $E \neq \emptyset$ into (4.13) leads to different Von Neumann and Morgenstern utility functions, all of which represent the *same* preference over lotteries. It follows from Section 4.2.2 that these Von Neumann and Morgenstern utility functions differ only in using different choices for the zero and unit on the utility scale that represents Adam's preference over lotteries. In particular,

$$U(a) = V(\mathcal{D}|E) = \alpha V(\mathcal{D}|B) + \beta, \qquad (4.14)$$

where $\alpha = \alpha(E) > 0$ and $\beta = \beta(E)$ do not depend on $\mathcal{D}$. In fact, $\beta(E) = 0$, because the second assumption implies that $V(\mathcal{L}|E) = V(\mathcal{L}|B) = 0$.

The functions u and p are now defined by $u(\mathcal{D}) = V(\mathcal{D}|B)$ and $p(E) = \alpha(E)$. Since $u(\mathcal{L}) = 0$, equation (4.14) then reduces to

$$U(a) = V(\mathcal{D}|E) = p(E)u(\mathcal{D}) = p(E)u(\mathcal{D}) + p(\sim E)u(\mathcal{L}),$$

which is the equation (4.12) that we have been trying to establish.

Unfortunately, things are not quite so easy. We have neglected to prove that p is a probability measure according to the criteria of Section 4.2.1. Our second assumption suffices to show that $0 = p(\emptyset) \leq p(E) \leq p(B) = 1$, but it remains to prove that $p(E_1 \cup E_2) = p(E_1) + p(E_2)$ when $E_1 \cap E_2 = \emptyset$. For this purpose, the third assumption needs to be strengthened.

Figure 4.6(b) shows an action a^* that is more complicated than the action a of Figure 4.6(a).[69] To apply the third assumption to a^*, it needs to be supplemented with a version of the sure-thing principle mentioned in Section 2.2.4. To be precise, it will be assumed that the argument leading to (4.14) remains valid with $\mathcal{D}$ and E replaced by $\mathcal{D}_1$ and E_1—provided that $\mathcal{D}_2$ and E_2 are held fixed. As before, α and β are independent of $\mathcal{D}_1$. However, they now depend not only on E_1, but on $\mathcal{D}_2$ and E_2 as well. Nor is it true that $\beta = 0$ in this new situation. Setting $\mathcal{D}_1 = \mathcal{L}$ yields that $\beta = p(E_2)u(\mathcal{D}_2)$. Hence

$$U(a^*) = \alpha(\mathcal{D}_2, E_1, E_2)u(\mathcal{D}_1) + p(E_2)u(\mathcal{D}_2). \qquad (4.15)$$

The same reasoning, of course, also leads to the similar equation

$$U(a^*) = \alpha(\mathcal{D}_1, E_2, E_1)u(\mathcal{D}_2) + p(E_1)u(\mathcal{D}_1). \qquad (4.16)$$

---

[69]We shall take for granted that a^* is equivalent to an action of the form a when $E_i = \emptyset$, $\mathcal{D}_i = \mathcal{L}$ or $\mathcal{D}_1 = \mathcal{D}_2$.

It follows from (4.15) and (4.16) that

$$\frac{\alpha(\mathcal{D}_2, E_1, E_2) - p(E_1)}{u(\mathcal{D}_2)} = \frac{\alpha(\mathcal{D}_1, E_2, E_1) - p(E_2)}{u(\mathcal{D}_1)}.$$

Since the left-hand side is independent of $\mathcal{D}_1$ and the right-hand side is independent of $\mathcal{D}_2$, both sides must be equal to a quantity $q(E_1, E_2)$ that depends on neither $\mathcal{D}_1$ or $\mathcal{D}_2$. Thus,

$$U(a^*) = p(E_1)u(\mathcal{D}_1) + p(E_2)u(\mathcal{D}_2) + q(E_1, E_2)u(\mathcal{D}_1)u(\mathcal{D}_2). \qquad (4.17)$$

Take $\mathcal{D} = \mathcal{D}_1 = \mathcal{D}_2$ in (4.17). Since $U(a^*)$ is then equal to $p(E_1 \cup E_2)u(\mathcal{D})$, we obtain that

$$p(E_1 \cup E_2)x = (p(E_1) + p(E_2))x + q(E_1, E_2)x^2, \qquad (4.18)$$

where $x = u(\mathcal{D})$. If there exists at least one consequence $\mathcal{D}$ satisfying $\mathcal{L} \prec \mathcal{D} \prec \mathcal{W}$, then (4.18) holds for three distinct values of x. But a quadratic equation can only have two roots, unless the coefficients of x and x^2 are both zero. Thus $q(E_1, E_2) = 0$ and $p(E_1 \cup E_2) = p(E_1) + p(E_2)$. The proof that p is a probability measure is therefore complete.

Bayes' Rule? Everything and more that needs to be said about Bayesian decision theory for the purposes of this book has now been said. We could go on to use Figure 4.7 to derive the rule $p(E|F) = p(E \cap F)/P(F)$ for computing a conditional probability and hence Bayes' Rule, but enough is perhaps enough.

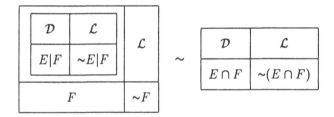

Figure 4.7: Handling contingent events

4.6 Rawlsian Maximin

This section considers the reasons that Rawls gives for assuming that those in the original position will use the maximin criterion rather than orthodox

Bayesian decision theory when choosing a social contract. Much hangs on this point. Utilitarians, for example, are willing to let the poor get poorer if this will make the rich sufficiently richer, but a Rawlsian analysis will tolerate no such sacrificial lambs.

My own view is that Rawls [214] goes astray in confronting the utilitarians at this level. The circumstances of the original position look to me as though they might have been tailor-made for applying Bayesian decision theory. If Bayesian decision theory is to be denied under these circumstances, it seems doubtful whether it could be legitimately be applied under any circumstances at all. In rejecting Bayesian decision theory for use in the original position, Rawls is therefore playing at Samson in the temple of the Philistines. Speaking as one of the Philistines, I am only too willing to replace any pillars of wisdom that prove to be unsound by something more solid—but first I need to see a proof that the pillar is indeed unsound. In particular, a critic of Bayesian decision theory needs to give me detailed reasons for rejecting whichever of the assumptions of the theory he believes to be mistaken. However, Rawls [214] makes no serious attempt to do so.[70]

I take Rawls' halfhearted interest in this seemingly vital matter as evidence that he does not really have a deep-seated antipathy to the tenets of Bayesian decision theory. My guess is that he is simply unable to accept the utilitarian conclusion to which Harsanyi [109] is inexorably led by a systematic application of the theory. I agree with Rawls that utilitarian recommendations are often absurdly impractical, but I do not think the remedy lies in challenging orthodox decision theory. As Section 4.3.1 explains, I believe that most of us share Rawls' intuition that the original position captures something important about "fairness" because we actually do already use rough-and-ready versions of the device in getting along with our fellows in everyday life. However, to return to the slaveholding story of Section 1.2.4, real people would simply laugh at a utilitarian who suggested that a a coin should be tossed to decide which of two people should be the master and which the slave. What sort of person would accept the role of slave because a coin fell badly? Or, as the loser might put it in backing out of the arrangement, why *that* toss of the coin—why not *this* toss of the coin? In brief, there is no point in proposing deals in the original position that are not self-policing. The notion that people will somehow see themselves committed to the agreement that they made before tossing the coin is idle.

It is this consideration that makes the maximin criterion attractive. Since the maximin criterion maximizes the welfare of the least well-off,[71]

---

[70]I shall only be considering what he says in his *Theory of Justice*. Rawls [213] says more in response to an article in which Harsanyi [105] criticizes his use of the maximin criterion, but I do not think this exchange adds very much to the debate.

[71]If the set X of personal utility pairs that are feasible as social contracts is convex

the chances that the loser will wish to back out of the deal once he learns his role are minimized. The maximin criterion is therefore attractive for *stability* reasons. The fact that Rawls [214] feels the same would seem to be confirmed by his devoting some two hundred pages in the third part of his book to stability questions—while defending the maximin criterion as a decision rule with just a few passing remarks in the first part. However, it is these passing remarks which occupy the remainder of this chapter.

My own view is that, if stability matters—and I agree with Rawls that it matters very much—then it should not be abstracted away when formulating the circumstances of the original position. Section 1.2.4 provides an outline of how I think this can be done by inventing a hypothetical "game of morals". Within this game of morals, the players maximize expected utility like good little Bayesians, but the equilibrium outcome is determined by the maximin criterion as Rawls would wish. The argument involved is very simple indeed, but its details will have to wait until the next volume since experience has taught me that I will only be misunderstood if I do not prepare the ground very carefully.

Whence Maximin? I suspect that the maximin criterion would not be a serious contender as a rule for making decisions in uncertain circumstances if Von Neumann [268] had failed to discover the theory of two-person, zero-sum games. One cannot therefore sensibly discuss the notion without first reviewing how it arises in this context.

Recall that a Nash equilibrium in a two-person game is a pair (s, t) of pure or mixed strategies with the property that s is a best reply by Adam to the choice of t by Eve, and t is simultaneously a best reply by Eve to the choice of s by Adam. In two-person, zero-sum games, this fundamental notion leads to the maximin criterion. In explaining why, it is useful to begin with the notion of a security level in a general two-person game.

Adam's *security level* v in a game is the largest expected payoff that he can be sure of getting, whatever Eve may do.[72] A strategy for Adam which guarantees that he gets an expected utility of v or more is called a *security strategy*. To compute his security strategies in a game, Adam has to behave

---

and comprehensive, the use of the maximin crtierion will result in an egalitarian outcome in which Adam and Eve will be entirely happy to swap roles.

[72]Beginners are often troubled by the juxtaposition of the words "expected" and "guarantee". But recall that, if Adam follows Von Neumann and Morgenstern, then he is only interested in how much expected utility each of his strategies will generate. The use of some strategies may result in much more uncertainty than others, but his attitudes to such uncertainty are *already* taken account of by his Von Neumann and Morgenstern utility function. It is a *fallacy* to argue that a rational person faced by two prospects with the same expected utility will prefer whichever has the smaller variance. To deny that he is indifferent between the two prospects is to deny the basic conclusion of the Von Neumann and Morgenstern theory.

like a paranoiac. He assumes that Eve will predict whatever strategy[73] he will choose, and then select her own strategy to minimize his payoff rather than to maximize her own payoff. For each strategy a available to him, Adam therefore assumes that Eve will choose the stategy b that minimizes his resulting payoff $\pi(a, b)$. If a paranoiac Adam chooses a, he will therefore anticipate that his payoff will be $\min_b \pi(a, b)$. It follows that such an Adam will choose a to maximize $\min_b \pi(a, b)$. His security level is therefore

$$v = \max_a \min_b \pi(a, b).   \qquad (4.19)$$

A security strategy a for Adam occurs where the maximum of (4.19) is achieved. One therefore computes a player's security level in a game by applying the maximin criterion.

The paranoia involved in calculating a security level is almost always irrational. The case of two-person, zero-sum games is an exception. Paranoia is then entirely reasonable, since each player maximizes his own payoff in such a game by minimizing the opponent's. Indeed, a pair (s, t) of strategies in a two-person, zero-sum game is a Nash equilibrium if and only if s is a security strategy for Adam and t is a security strategy for Eve.[74] Game theorists are therefore happy to recommend the use of the maximin criterion in two-person, zero-sum games when the players are rational.

I suppose it was inevitable that the success of the maximin criterion in Von Neumann's theory of two-person, zero-sum games should lead to its being advocated as a rule for resolving decision problems in general. For this purpose, the set B from which Eve chooses her strategy in the expression (4.19) is reinterpreted as a set of states of the world. Eve herself becomes Mother Nature.

The fact that the maximin criterion selects a security strategy in games is made into a virtue when recommending it for general use by describing it as a *conservative* or *prudent* decision rule. Such words certainly make it seem attractive. Who, for example, would wish to make an imprudent investment in the stock exchange? But, is it really prudent to be paranoic? I think not. Indeed, an investment counselor who admitted to working on the hypothesis that Nature is a malevolent force with nothing better to do with her time than watch every move of his clients with the intention of doing them down would soon find himself with no clients at all!

---

[73]To choose a *mixed* strategy is to delegate the decision about which pure strategy should be played to a random device. Adam's paranoia does not extend to believing that Eve will be able to predict the choices such a random device will make. She is only assumed to be able to predict which random device Adam will choose.

[74]Adam guarantees getting at least $\pi(s, t)$ by playing s, because Eve is doing as well as she possibly can by replying to s with t. On the other hand, Adam cannot guarantee getting more than $\pi(s, t)$ because he cannot prevent Eve from playing t, to which s is his best reply.

In brief, Von Neumann's theory of two-person, zero-sum games provides no justification at all for using the maximin criterion as a decision rule in more general circumstances. Even in two-person, zero-sum games, game theorists do not make the maximin criterion a fundamental principle of rational behavior. Maximizing expected utility is always fundamental. In two-person, zero-sum games, it just so happens that the use of the maximin criterion leads to a Nash equilibrium. If it led somewhere else, the maximin criterion would probably merit only an occasional footnote in the literature on decision theory.

Reflective Equilibrium. I follow Kukathas and Pettit [145] in focusing on the three features of the maximin criterion that Rawls [214] feels justify its use in the original position. However, I differ from them in my evaluation of their relative importance. In particular, the first seems to me almost frivolous. Rawls' [214, p.154] tells us that the alternatives rejected by the maximin criterion are "outcomes that one can hardly accept".

Rawls is not simply urging us to adopt whatever decision rule happens to lead to the conclusions our prejudices favor. An implicit appeal is presumably being made to his notion of a *reflective equilibrium*. I understand this to be an adaptation of the standard manner in which scientific models are developed through an interplay between theoretical considerations and empirical data. One constructs a model and compares it with the data. If the model does not fit, one either modifies the model or looks more closely at the data.[75] However, sometimes the empirical evidence is too slender to play this game. But this does not deter theoretical physicists. They then substitute their physical intuitions for the missing physical data. In recommending his notion of a reflective equilibrium, Rawls suggests that the same technique be used by moral philosophers. That is to say, moral philosphers should seek to systematize their moral intuitions by constructing formal models within which the intuitions are realized, and to reexamine their moral intuitions when they cannot be reconciled with such a formal model. Pessimists may doubt whether Rawls or anyone else has moral intuitions that are sufficiently well grounded to put the traditional methodology of speculative science to effective use—but no progress would ever be made in any subject whatever if heed were paid to such skeptics!

However, if the traditions of speculative scientific investigation are to be followed with any hope of success, certain disciplines need to be observed. Indeed, the major motivation for expressing intuitions concretely within a formal model is to discipline our wilder flights of fancy, by exposing the incomplete and inconsistent nature of the castles in the air that our

---

[75]The astronomer Eddington is famous for his advice that one should be sceptical about a new piece of data until it has been "confirmed by theory".

imaginations so freely construct. Logic and mathematics are the chief disciplinary tools for the physicist. We would, for example, be very suspicious of a theoretical analysis in physics that asked us to suspend our belief in *modus ponens* or to abandon our faith that $2 + 2 = 4$. In the moral sphere, where we are much more likely to be led astray by our prejudices, it seems to me that there is even less room for laxity. As Rawls [214, p.121] says: "We should strive for a kind of moral geometry with all the rigor that this name connotes."

What constitutes rigor in moral geometry? In such a context, practical reasoning matters as much as pure reasoning. Axioms for rational decision-making must therefore take their place alongside the axioms for logic and mathematics. I do not want to claim that the axioms of orthodox Bayesian decision theory have the same rock-solid status as the axioms of mathematics or logic. But they surely deserve to be treated with respect. To throw them out when they lead to unwelcome conclusions seems to me like junking a computer when it tells you that you owe more tax than you think possible. Perhaps the computer is wrong—but a computer technician will laugh if you tell him that you have deduced this conclusion from the fact that its computations do not accord with your intuitions about how much tax you owe. He will very sensibly demand solid evidence of a hardware error before he risks wasting his time in attempting a repair. The same goes for Bayesian decision theory.

These remarks are not intended to challenge Rawls' moral intuitions. To pursue the computer analogy, I think that he understands the general level of his tax liability very well. However, I am not prepared to believe that the Bayesian computer is broken because a programmer isn't getting the results he expects. In the time-honored style of all hardware technicians, I shall believe that the malfunction is in the programmer's software until definite proof of a fault in the hardware is produced.

In fact, the bug in Rawls' software seem to me easy to locate. In spite of what he says about not admitting social contracts that would strain Adam and Eve's powers to make commitments, he nevertheless assumes that they will be committed to the hypothetical deal that would be reached in the original position. When this bug is eliminated from his program, the Bayesian computer generates solutions that are consistent with his intuition. However, this is an issue for a later chapter. The remainder of this section will continue to evaluate the evidence that Rawls' offers in support of his contention that there is an error in the hardware.

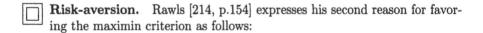 **Risk-aversion.** Rawls [214, p.154] expresses his second reason for favoring the maximin criterion as follows:

The second feature that suggests the maximin rule is the following: the person choosing has a conception of the good such that he cares little, if anything, for what he might gain above the minimium stipend that he can, in fact, be sure of by following the maximin rule. It is not worthwhile for him to take a chance for the sake of a further advantage, especially when it may turn out that he loses much that is important to him.

An economist reads this as saying that a person in the original position will use the maximin rule because he is highly risk-averse. Before discussing this claim, it will be useful to say something about how risk-aversion is treated within Bayesian decision theory.

Consider, for example, a lottery **L** in which the prize $a occurs with probability $1 - p$ and the prize $b with probability p, where $0 < a < b$ and $0 < p < 1$. How much would you pay for a ticket to participate in **L**? Figure 4.8 shows that Adam would pay $x for a ticket and Eve would pay $y. If $x < y$, then Adam reveals that he is more risk-averse than Eve in respect of **L**, because he will not pay so much for a lottery ticket. If x turns out to be the smaller of a and b, then Adam is as risk-averse in respect of the lottery **L** as he could possibly be.[76] An example of a utility function U_A for Adam that describes such extreme risk-aversion over lotteries is given by

$$U_A(\mathbf{L}) = \min\{a, b\}.$$

When Adam chooses a lottery **L** that maximizes the value of such a utility function, he can therefore be said to be acting as a maximiner.

However, some caution is necessary before embracing such an attempt to respectabilize the maximin criterion. Let u_A be a Von Neumann and Morgenstern utility function for Adam. To say that Adam is indifferent between the prize $a and the lottery **L** of Figure 4.8(a) is then to assert that $u_A(a) = (1 - p)u_A(a) + pu_A(b)$—and hence that $u_A(a) = u_A(b)$. But Adam will then be indifferent between the two prizes $a and $b, even though one may be much larger than the other. Thus, unless Adam is to violate one of Von Neumann and Morgenstern's rationality assumptions from Section 4.2.2, we cannot justify his maximining on the grounds of extreme risk-aversion without simultaneously taking him to be someone who is indifferent between receiving large sums of money and small sums of money!

The same point can be made by looking at the graphs of the Von Neumann and Morgenstern utility functions of successively more risk-averse people. In general, someone is said to be risk-averse in money if he would never be willing to pay more for a lottery ticket than the expected dollar

---

[76]It cannot be that x is smaller than the smaller of a and b unless Adam either violates the sure-thing principle or else prefers less money to more.

	$a	$b
$x \sim_A$	$1-p$	p

	$a	$b
$y \sim_E$	$1-p$	p

(a) Adam will pay $x.   (b) Eve will pay $y.

Figure 4.8: Lottery ticket prices

value of the lottery.[77]   For example, in Figure 4.8(a), a risk-averse Adam
will have $x \leq (1-p)a + pb$. Figure 4.9 shows how one can tell whether
Adam is risk-averse simply by looking at the shape of the graph of his
Von Neumann and Morgenstern utility function. If the graph is concave,[78]
he is risk-averse. Roughly speaking, the more concave a person's utility
function, the more risk-averse he is.[79]   Figure 4.9(a) shows one extreme
of risk-aversion, in which Adam's Von Neumann and Morgenstern utility
function reduces to a straight line. Figure 4.9(d) shows the other extreme.
Notice the discontinuity at the origin. Such an extremely risk-averse person
has a utility function u_A given by $u_A(0) = 0$ and $u_A(z) = 1$ if $z > 0$. He
is so averse to coming up empty-handed that he is indifferent between all

---

[77]Since Adam will just be willing to pay $x for a lottery ticket for **L** when $u_A(x) = \mathcal{E}u_A(\mathbf{L})$, he is risk-averse if and only if it is always true that $\mathcal{E}u_A(\mathbf{L}) \leq u_A(\mathcal{E}\mathbf{L})$. He is risk-neutral if and only if it is always true that $\mathcal{E}u_A(\mathbf{L}) = u_A(\mathcal{E}\mathbf{L})$. He is risk-loving if and only if it is always true that $\mathcal{E}u_A(\mathbf{L}) \geq u_A(\mathcal{E}\mathbf{L})$.

[78]The chords to the graph of a concave function lie on or beneath the graph. A risk-loving person has a convex Von Neumann and Morgenstern utility function. Chords drawn to the graph of a convex function lie on or above the graph. A risk-neutral person has an affine Von Neumann and Morgenstern utility function. This means that its graph is a straight line.

[79]A sufficient condition for Adam always to be more risk-averse than Eve is that $\lambda_A(z) \geq \lambda_E(z)$ for all z. The indices $\lambda_A(z)$ and $\lambda_E(z)$ are somewhat grandiosely said to be Arrow-Pratt measures of absolute risk-aversion. The Arrow-Pratt measure for a person with a Von Neumann and Morgenstern utility function u is given by $\lambda = -u''/u'$. It follows, for example, that Adam is more risk-averse than Eve for positive sums of money whenever $u_A(z) = z^\gamma$, $u_E(z) = z^\delta$, and $0 < \gamma < \delta$. To see why the Arrow-Pratt criterion implies that Adam is more risk-averse about the lottery **L** of Figure 4.8 than Eve, begin by replacing u_E by $v_E = \alpha u_E + \beta$, where $\alpha > 0$ and β are chosen so that $v_E(a) = u_A(a)$ and $v_E(b) = u_A(b)$. A sufficient condition that Adam is more risk-averse than Eve about **L** is then that $u_A(z) \geq v_E(z)$ for all z satisfying $a < z < b$. In terms of u_E, this inequality becomes $\{u_A(b) - u_A(z)\}/\{u_E(b) - u_E(z)\} \leq \{u_A(z) - u_A(a)\}/\{u_E(z) - u_E(a)\}$. By the Cauchy mean-value theorem, the left-hand side is equal to $u'_A(\eta)/u'_E(\eta)$ for some η between z and b. The right-hand side is equal to $u'_A(\xi)/u'_E(\xi)$ for some ξ between a and z. A sufficient condition for the inequality to hold is therefore that the function u'_A/u'_E is decreasing. This is true when its derivative is non-negative. This leads to the inequality $u''_A u'_E - u''_E u'_A \leq 0$, and hence to the criterion $\lambda_A \geq \lambda_E$.

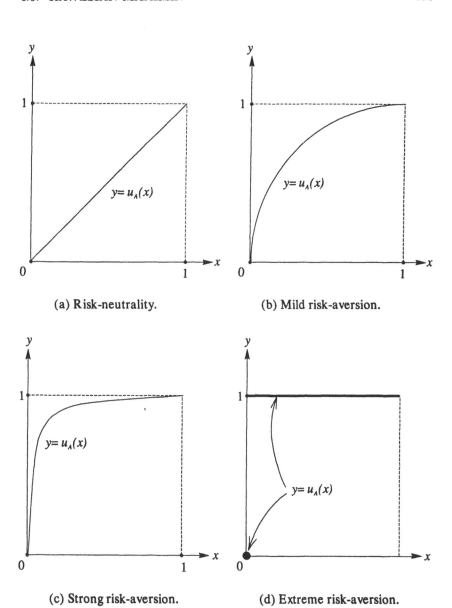

(a) Risk-neutrality.

(b) Mild risk-aversion.

(c) Strong risk-aversion.

(d) Extreme risk-aversion.

Figure 4.9: Increasing risk-aversion

positive sums of money—no matter how large. All that matters to him about a sum of money is that it not be nothing at all.

Perhaps some people are genuinely indifferent between being rich and poor. However, I suspect that this is never true of those cautious folk who recommend using the maximin criterion on the grounds that it is a "prudent" decision rule. It follows that such maximiners fall afoul of at least one of the Von Neumann and Morgenstern rationality axioms of Section 4.2.2. Indeed, in thinking of risk-aversion as being embodied in the *decision rule* that Adam uses rather than in his *utility function*, they reveal an attitude that is entirely alien to traditional economics. For economists, Adam's preferences are *given*. He does not ask himself how risk-averse he ought to be. Nor does he consider what decision rule to use. If his preferences are consistent in the sense of Von Neumann and Morgenstern, then he will *necessarily* decide as though maximizing the expected value of a Von Neumann and Morgenstern utility function. If Adam is risk-averse, then this fact will be manifested in the concavity of his Von Neumann and Morgenstern utility function.

Although maximiners violate the traditions of neoclassical economics, I do not see this as an adequate reason for rejecting their views. Indeed, it is important for my approach to social contract problems that the traditional view among economists that preferences are fixed and sacrosanct be regarded as only part of the story. I am therefore not very traditional myself. Section 1.2.7 explains the distinction I think it useful to make between the short, medium and long term in this context. Recall that preferences are fixed in the short term. With my definitions, all economic activity, as normally understood, therefore takes place in the short term. In the medium term, socially determined preferences may adjust to changes in the environment. In the long term, biologically determined preferences may also adjust. Once such a perspective has been adopted, one cannot avoid asking how social and biological evolution determine the preferences that traditional economists take as given. In particular, one may ask whether evolutionary pressures are likely to lead to a society in which people are extremely risk-averse.

Of course, followers of Kant will be impatient with such evolutionary questions. They prefer to ask whether it is *rational* to reveal risk-averse preferences.[80] Orthodox neoclassical economists will not admit that such a question could be meaningful, because they choose to adopt a very narrow definition of what rationality means. However, they nevertheless take a Kantian attitude to the set of consistency requirements from Bayesian

---

[80]In Section 2.4.3, I tried to make sense of the categorical imperative by asking what method of choice a rational being would choose. Would he perhaps choose the maximin criterion?

decision theory that they regard as fully characterizing rational behavior. That is to say, rather than ask *why* economic agents should be assumed to behave consistently, they think it enough to defend consistency on the *a priori* ground that it is rational to be consistent.[81]

But why do we care what is rational? Why do we think that *homo economicus* is sometimes a suitable model for *homo sapiens*? Presumably it is because rational persons are more likely to get the opportunity to transmit their characteristics to others. In particular, people whose behavior is not single-mindedly devoted to the objective of replicating their characteristics to others will tend to be displaced by those who do pursue this objective single-mindedly. But notice that, in this story, evolution does not reward consistent behavior because it is consistent. Only consistent behavior that is directed at its own survival is rewarded. Behavior that is consistently directed at its own extinction will not be rewarded at all. Indeed, it will be eliminated faster than behavior that is inconsistently directed at this objective!

When Rawls says that the maximin criterion is reasonable or rational,[82] I therefore do not think it adequate to respond by saying that he does not understand what a neoclassical economist means by rationality. Nor do I think we will get anywhere by attempting a Kantian analysis of what it means to say something is reasonable or rational. The real question is the extent to which risk-aversion has survival value.

Consider, for example, an isolated village scratching out a living at the edge of viability. Its survival as a community will not depend on how successfully it manages in an average year, but how well it manages in the rare bad year when there is a severe drought or a plague of locusts. If the practices enshrined in the customs and traditions of the village fail under such adverse circumstances, they will disappear along with the village and hence cease to be replicated. One should therefore expect that evolution will select in favor of strongly risk-averse communities—and the seemingly obstinate conservatism of subsistence-level farmers would seem to provide some evidence that this is actually what has happened. Similar considerations apply in less extreme situations. For example, if a person cannot fall below a certain income level without losing his bourgeois status, then one would expect to see strongly risk-averse behavior from those who occupy the lower echelons in the ranks of the bourgeoisie. Indeed, I suspect that many of those who insist so firmly that extreme risk-aversion is rational are merely rationalizing the rules that they have unwittingly

---

[81] As Section 4.5 explains, I believe that such an attitude leads them sadly astray when they elect to model "rational learning" as nothing more than as Bayesian updating.

[82] It should be noted that Rawls [214, p.154] does *not* recommend the maximin criterion when the probabilities in the lottery to be assessed are *objectively* determined as in the situations we are currently considering.

inherited from their parents about how to retain their membership of the lower middle class.

But is it true that evolution will *always* select for extreme risk-aversion? As soon as the question is asked, it seems to me obvious that the answer must be no. In Chapter 1 of Volume II, for example, we shall learn that a person who is known to be extremely risk-averse will fare very badly when he bargains with a person known to be risk-neutral. That is to say, even though they bargain on equal terms, the risk-neutral person will come away with more of the surplus over which they have been bargaining. The reason is very simple. A risk-averse person has less bargaining power because he is less willing to risk the negotiations' breaking down. In a society in which bargaining is an important element, there will therefore be strong evolutionary pressures against revealing risk-averse preferences.[83]

The truth is, I think, that evolutionary forces of different types push us both towards and away from risk-averse behavior. The nature of these pressures depends, among other things, on the society in which we live and the role that we occupy within that society. Different people in different societies must therefore be expected to achieve a different balance between the pressures for and against risk-aversion. Nothing says that more risk-averse people will necessarily outperform those who are less risk-averse.

In summary, the idea that it is wise to be extremely risk-averse when big issues are under consideration seems to me no more than a bourgeois prejudice from which we urgently need to free ourselves. It is particularly dangerous to fall into the bourgeois habit of characterizing those who are less risk-averse than ourselves as feckless. When a bourgeois Adam observes a bohemian Eve involved in an enterprise that he regards as prohibitively risky, he usually takes for granted that she must have miscalculated the risks. If he is feeling particularly uncharitable, he may assume that she has failed to calculate the risks at all. After all, if he were in her shoes with *his* preferences, he would not have chosen to take the risks he sees her taking. However, if we are to empathize successfully with Eve, we must imagine ourselves in her shoes with *her* preferences.[84]

---

[83]This consideration seems particularly important when an appeal is to be made to the device of the original position. The players must then predict the hypothetical deal that they would reach under certain hypothetical circumstances. If the citizens in a society are experienced bargainers, they will be accustomed to suppressing any urge they may feel towards risk-aversion in a bargaining context. So why should we follow Rawls in postulating that they will predict that the result of their bargaining in the original position would be extremely risk-averse? On the other hand, if they have little experience of bargaining, how would they be able to predict how the negotiations behind the veil of ignorance would go?

[84]But we need not follow Friedman and Savage [77] in claiming that poor people are typically risk-loving (since they buy tickets in actuarially unfair lotteries) while richer folk are risk-averse (since they insure their houses against fire). My guess is that people

It is especially important that the bourgeois prejudice in favor of extreme risk-aversion be put aside when contemplating the use of the original position. Unless we are to abandon all attempt at maintaining some discipline in what we allow ourselves to assume, *homo economicus*, with all his faults, is our only viable option as a model of man. But he never takes uncalculated risks. Nor does he ever fail to empathize successfully with his neighbors. He does not therefore believe that his standards of risk-aversion apply to the whole world. Nor does he use the maximin criterion as a decision rule, unless its use happens to coincide with maximizing expected Von Neumann and Morgenstern utility. He understands that everybody's risk-aversion has *already* been incorporated into the model by specifying their Von Neumann and Morgenstern utility functions.

How Thick Should the Veil of Ignorance Be? If the arguments that have just been given against the maximin criterion are accepted, then it follows that our examination of the consequences of using the maximin criterion in Section 4.4 was an idle activity. If one is willing to acquiesce in Harsanyi's formulation of the problem as described in Section 4.4, one really has no intellectually respectable choice but to accept his utilitarian conclusion. Nonutilitarians like myself therefore need to challenge Harsanyi's right to formulate the problem as in Section 4.4.

Rawls third argument in favor of the maximin criterion consists of just such a challenge. Rawls' challenge takes the form of denying that one can properly assign probabilities to the options available in the original position. When they enter the original position, Rawls assumes that Adam and Eve pass behind so thick a veil of ignorance that they are unable to offer any opinion at all on how likely it is that one of them is really Adam and the other Eve.[85] As Rawls [214, p.155] puts it:

> The veil of ignorance excludes all but the vaguest knowledge of likelihoods. The parties have no basis for determining the probable nature of their society, or their place in it. Thus they have strong reason for

---

play gambling games largely for fun and hence, as observed in Section 4.1, the Von Neumann and Morgenstern theory does not apply to this aspect of their behavior.

[85]Recall from Section 4.3.2 that Harsanyi also proposes a thick veil of ignorance. But Harsanyi's reasons for making his proposal bear no resemblance to the reasons given by Rawls. A thick veil of ignorance is also proposed by Olson [197, p.29]. He claims that the need to make interpersonal comparisons of utility can be eliminated by translating a line of argument originating with Lerner [148] and developed further by Sen [243] into Rawlsian terms. It is true that Olson's approach will lead to a dollar being divided equally between a risk-averse Adam and Eve without the need for any investigation of either their personal or their empathetic preferences. This is achieved by disbarring social contracts that make Adam's payoff contingent on his preferences. However, the baby is then thrown out with the bathwater. What use is a fairness criterion that splits a vial of insulin equally when Adam is a diabetic and Eve is perfectly healthy?

being wary of probability calculations if any other course is open to them. They must also take into account the fact that their choice of principles should seem reasonable to others, particularly their descendants, whose rights will be deeply affected by it.

Section 4.2.1 distinguishes between objectivist, subjectivist and logicist theories of probability. It is not hard to agree with Rawls that those in the original position should not be assumed to assign *objective* probabilities to their hidden identities. Adam and Eve cannot really switch identities. It is therefore impossible that anyone could actually compare the frequency with which someone leaving the original position turns out to be Adam with the frequency with which he turns out to be Eve.

Rawls [214, p.168] rejects the logicist view of probability by drawing attention to the well-known paradoxes that arise when attempts are made to apply Laplace's principle of insufficient reason. This says that equal probabilities should be assigned to different events unless some reason exists to suppose that one is more likely than the other. For example, if I know that only red and white billiard balls have been placed in an urn, but nothing at all about how many red and white balls there are, Laplace's principle instructs me to attach a probability of $\frac{1}{2}$ to the event that a ball drawn at random from the urn will be red. In the original position, the veil of ignorance conceals all information about my identity and so Laplace's principle then tells me to attach a probability of $\frac{1}{2}$ to the event that I am Adam and a probability of $\frac{1}{2}$ to the event that I am Eve.

I will return to Rawls' reasons for rejecting such a use of Laplace's principle. But first it needs to be noted that to exclude the objectivist and the logicist interpretation of probability for use in the original position is not to exhaust the possibilities. What of the subjectivist view taken by most modern economists?

The subjectivist view does not claim to provide an objective basis for probabilities through counting how often various events happen. Nor does it insist on some *a priori* legitimacy for the notion of probability. The aim of a subjectivist is simply to describe consistent behavior. If someone makes, or would make, decisions consistently over a wide enough range of possibilities, then Bayesian decision theory tells us that he will be behaving *as though* he had assigned subjective probabilities to the relevant events and were seeking to maximize the expected utility of a Von Neumann and Morgenstern utility function. Notice that a subjectivist does *not* maintain that a rational person must assign *equal* subjective probabilities to events about which he is equally uninformed. In the original position, I can act as though I believe that I will be Adam with probability $p = \frac{2}{3}$ and Eve with probability $1 - p = \frac{1}{3}$ without violating any tenet of Bayesian decision theory. Far from subscribing to Laplace's principle, subjectivists tell us to look outside their theoretical framework if it is necessary to determine the value of p. Rawls' criticism of Laplace's principle is therefore irrelevant to the subjectivist position. In denying that I will use *some* value of p in the original position, he therefore rejects the subjectivist position without offering any grounds at all for such a rejection. But a subjectivist like myself would like to know *why* Rawls feels that those in the original position should be assumed to be inconsistent in their decision-making.

Having added the subjectivist view on probability to those which Rawls needs to reject, let us return to his rejection of logicism as represented by the use of Laplace's principle. Significant paradoxes arise from Laplace's principle only when it is applied in situations that make it necessary to evaluate an infinite number of possible states of the world. If such an infinite number of possible states of the world are to enter into our considerations in the original position, then it must be the case that we lose knowledge of far more than our identities when we pass behind the veil of ignorance. Rawls does indeed seem to intend that we be very ignorant indeed behind his thick veil. I cannot say that I fully understand precisely what Rawls intends that I remember and forget when I pass beyond his veil of ignorance. Indeed, he sees the issue in much more complicated terms. Rather than one thick veil, Rawls [214, p.195] tells us of four veils which, like Salome, I am to strip away one by one as I come closer to a final agreement with my companions in the original position.

We are to begin by determining the principles of justice. The first veil is then dropped. A political constitution is then agreed. Next, the second veil is dropped and we decide on the fundamental legal statutes for our society. The third veil is then dropped and we settle issues of economic and social welfare. Finally, the fourth veil is dropped and we get on with our lives.[86] The following quote will perhaps indicate some of the flavor of what Rawls [214, p.196] has in mind when the first veil is dropped:

> Since the appropriate conception of justice has been agreed upon, the veil of ignorance is partially lifted. The persons in the [resulting consitutional] convention have, of course, no information about particular individuals: they do not know their own social position, their place in the distribution of natural attributes, or their conception of the good. But, in addition to an understanding of the principles of social theory, they now know the relevant general facts about their society, that is, its natural circumstances and resources, its level of economic

---

[86]Rawls [214, p.196] points to the procedure used in drawing up the American Constitution as his inspiration for this scheme. However, in seeking some basis for the legitimacy of liberal institutions, it seems to me that one begs the question if one assumes that the historical procedures that led to our current bourgeois wonderland are those that rational beings in the original position would necessarily use.

advance and political culture, and so on. They are no longer limited
to the information implicit in the circumstances of justice.

Rawls clearly intends that his story with four veils be nothing more than
an elaboration of the single veil story he describes earlier in the *Theory of
Justice*. Such an attitude creates no problem in itself—provided that one
follows Rawls in permitting commitment in the original position. When all
four veils are in place, Adam and Eve can sign comprehensive agreements
that are *contingent* on the information that they receive at later times.
In this way, all future interaction between Adam and Eve can be settled
while they are in their most ignorant state. However, it is evident that
Rawls does not intend that the agreements signed before the fall of each
veil should be contingent on what Adam and Eve may learn in the future.
His principles of justice, for example, contain no small print that would
allow their suspension if Adam and Eve returned from the original position
to find themselves in a society at war with its neighbor or in the midst of
a plague or famine. Rawls' Dance of the Four Veils is therefore not really
just a harmless breaking down of the issues into several inevitable steps.
If he forces Adam and Eve to sign *noncontingent* contracts before each
veil is dropped, he is forcing a structure on the final deal that might even
prove to be Pareto-inefficient.[87] Not only this, Rawls reveals that he does
not regard the current *status quo* in society as being irrelevant to the final
social contract negotiated in the original position. It is only irrelevant to
the principles of justice incorporated in the contract.[88]

The Dance of the Four Veils makes it complicated to pursue the issue of
whether probabilities should be assigned to uncertain events in the original
position. I therefore plan to offer a compressed version of Rawls' story
that I believe makes his position on this question easier to defend. The
compressed story returns to Rawls' original conception of just one thick veil.
This conceals two things. As always, it conceals Adam and Eve's identities.

---

[87]Moreover, he is wrong to think that Adam and Eve will approach the four-stage
decision problem he proposes by signing an agreement at the first stage and only then
turn their attention to later stages. If they are rational, Adam and Eve will proceed by
backward induction as described in Section 2.5.1. The first item on their agenda will
therefore be the *last* stage in Rawls' process. They will *not* begin by asking questions
about justice. Instead they will begin by itemizing all possible agreements that might
be reached at the first, second and third stages of Rawls' process. Next they will itemize
all possible pieces of information they might have been vouchsafed as the first three veils
fall. For each such possible future, they will then predict the fourth-stage agreement that
they would then negotiate. They will therefore *begin* by contemplating socioeconomic
questions, leaving abstract principles of justice to the very end.

[88]Recall from Section 1.2.1 that Wolff [276] is among those who have criticized Rawls
for dispensing with a state of nature in his social contract story. However, it seems that
Rawls is not so guilty as might at first appear—provided that one is willing to follow me
in identifying the relevant state of nature with the current *status quo* in society.

However, unlike my own version of the original position summarized in Section 4.7, it also conceals the current *status quo* in society—which I choose to identify with the state of nature. Moreover, again in contradistinction to my own version of the original position, Adam and Eve are forbidden to write social contracts that are contingent on who turns out to be who or on what the current *status quo* in society happens to be. But it does not follow that the state of nature is irrelevant to Adam and Eve in this version of the original position. They cannot, for example, emerge from behind the veil of ignorance and simply sweep away the past to create a brave new world from scratch. If nothing else, they will be constrained by the geographical location of their society—by its climate and access to natural resources. Their agreement behind the veil of ignorance is therefore not to be understood as determining everything that there is to be determined about their future society. Somehow, the shape of their future society is decided both by the social contract on which they agree in the original position and the actual state of nature that they encounter when they leave the the original position.

The point of inventing this compressed version of the Dance of the Four Veils is to generate a framework within which Rawls' use of the maximin criterion admits some sort of defense. If the set of states of nature that Adam and Eve think possible in the original position is sufficiently large and diverse, then Rawls could reasonably claim that his thick veil of ignorance confronts them with a "large world" decision problem. But, as Section 4.5 explains, Savage [228] was willing to defend the consistency requirements that he invented as a basis for Bayesian decision theory only within a "small world" context. A thick veil of the type contemplated here would therefore leave Rawls free to call upon one of the various theories of "decision-making under complete ignorance" intended for use in "large world" contexts.[89] In particular, he would be able to quote Milnor's [179] axioms for decision-making under complete ignorance. Since a subset of Milnor's axioms turns out to characterize the maximin criterion, Rawls would then be able to appeal to at least one source of authority in defense of his unorthodox attitude to decision theory. A Bayesian might reasonably respond that Milnor's axioms have a highly speculative status, but this is one of the few controversies that I plan not to explore,[90] because I believe the crux of the

---

[89]Bayesianismists seem to be largely unaware that such theories exist. They have some excuse, since it must be admitted that the theories are not very good. However, one would have thought that they would read enough of their bible to notice that Savage [228] devotes much of the *Foundations of Statistics* to a nonBayesian decision rule that he calls the minimax regret principle.

[90]Luce and Raiffa's [158, p.297] apt comments on Milnor's work are not out of date. Very little work has been done in this area since Bayesianism became predominant. Let me only add that Milnor's "column duplication" axiom clearly demonstrates that his

matter lies elsewhere. In brief, I do not think that there are good reasons for denying Adam and Eve knowledge of the state of nature when they enter the original position. Moreover, if they were completely ignorant of the state of nature, I do not believe that the use of the maximin criterion would lead them to the liberal principles of justice expounded by Rawls.

On this last point, consider the possibility raised in Section 2.3.5 that Adam and Eve might emerge from behind the veil of ignorance to find themselves crewing an old-time sailing vessel in a storm. They would then find it acutely embarrassing to be committed to a set of principles of justice designed for use in a bourgeois democracy. Indeed, society aboard old-time sailing ships was presumably organized on a strictly hierarchical basis because other arrangements are less efficient at dealing with life-threatening emergencies. If Adam and Eve believe that the physical continuation of their society should take precedence above all else and that they should act in the original position as though the worst of all possible scenarios for the actual state of nature were correct, it seems inevitable to me that they would be led to an authoritarian structure for society in the style of Hobbes, rather than a liberal structure of the type envisaged by Rawls.

One may respond that my story of an old-time sailing ship is too far-fetched to be worthy of attention. However, in rejecting such an extreme scenario as a possibility for the way things are on the other side of the veil of ignorance, one also rejects the hypothesis that Adam and Eve are completely ignorant about the true state of nature. In fact, it seems to me that Rawls' [214] *Theory of Justice* implicitly takes for granted that Adam and Eve know a great deal about the type of bourgeois institutions that constitute the current *status quo* in modern Western democracies in order to justify the decisions about the nature of a just society that he assumes they will make in the original position. The later Rawls [211] is careful to be very much more explicit about the commonly held cultural values that he feels we are entitled to remember when passing beyond the veil of ignorance.

My own view is that such knowledge should not only be made explicit—it should be assumed to be exhaustive. *Only* their identities should be concealed from Adam and Eve in the original position. Everything else about the way society is currently organized should be an open book. How else can they design a society that is properly adapted to its physical circumstances and history of experience?[91] In taking this line, I believe myself

---

conclusions are intended to apply only in "large world" contexts.

[91] A homely example may serve to press this point home. My wife and I are planning a vacation in the tropics, but she and I have divergent views on the type of hotel at which we should stay. In using the device of the original position to resolve our problem, would we be wise to forget that we have a tropical destination in mind? If we do, we may end up by agreeing on whichever hotel has the most efficient central heating arrangements!

to be endorsing the essence of the communitarian critique of the younger Rawls articulated by such authors as Sandel [227]. I am not sure how helpful it is to express such criticism in terms of metaphysical notions of the self, but I agree very much that will often be an impossibly hard task to step outside one's culture to adopt the attitudes of a culturally neutral outsider. Nor are there good reasons why they should choose to do so.

However, if we deny Rawls his thick veil of ignorance and insist that Adam and Eve know everything about the current *status quo* except their place in it, then all grounds for rejecting orthodox Bayesian decision theory would seem to disappear. When placed behind such a thin veil of ignorance, the set $B = \{A, E\}$ of possible states of the world that I will need to consider contains only two alternatives. In state A, I am Adam and my companion in the original position is Eve. In state E, I am Eve and my companion is Adam.[92] If the notion of a "small world" that Savage [228] envisaged as providing a suitable arena for the use of Bayesian decision theory is ever applicable, it must surely be to the case when only two states of the world need to be considered. If one is to reject the axioms of Bayesian decision theory in such a context, one presumably must be ready to reject them altogether. Someone who takes this view but follows Rawls in accepting the use of expected utility theory when probabilities are objective, therefore denies the assumptions of Section 4.5, which insist that a rational person will necessarily separate his beliefs from his preferences. Perhaps we ought to admire such critics for being so determinedly skeptical. However, I suspect that it is more appropriate to forgive them on the grounds that they know not what they do.

On the other hand, if one accepts that rational people will separate their beliefs from their preferences, then one would seem to have little choice but to agree that a person behind a thin veil of ignorance will behave as though he had assigned subjective probabilities $p = \text{prob}(A)$ and $1 - p = \text{prob}(E)$ to the respective events A and E. Subjective probability theory tells us nothing whatever about the value of p. As I insisted earlier in this section, Laplace's principle of insufficient reason is part of a logicist view of probability theory. So how does a subjectivist deduce that $p = \frac{1}{2}$? The brief answer is that he doesn't. But this is a topic for the next section. The immediate point is simply that *some* probabilities must be assigned to A and E—unless one is willing to claim that orthodox decision theorists are totally wrong on the very matters about which they feel most confident.

---

[92] I do not mean to imply that we will be omniscient about matters behind the veil of ignorance. We certainly will not know, for example, what cards will be dealt in next week's poker game. However, I think it reasonable to treat such uncertainties in the real world as though they can be assigned probabilities in an uncontroversial manner.

4.7   The Game of Morals

Much of this chapter has been an attempt to provide a straightforward exposition of orthodox decision theory. I have written at length on this subject because my experience suggests that even those who use the theory routinely in their research sometimes misunderstand the principles on which it is based. As a consequence, confusion is endemic when attempts are made to apply the ideas to problems of interpersonal comparison.

The rest of the chapter was mostly devoted to criticism of the thick veils of ignorance proposed by Harsanyi and Rawls. Recall from Section 4.6 that Harsanyi [109] proposes a thick veil of ignorance to ensure that those in the original position will forget their own empathetic preferences, and hence be led to adopt the empathetic preferences of an ideal observer. Rawls [214] is not concerned with empathetic preferences and the like because he believes that problems of interpersonal comparison can be finessed using his notion of primary goods. Rawls has very different reasons from Harsanyi for proposing a thick veil of ignorance. He believes that his thick veil of ignorance can be used to justify the use of the maximin criterion in the original position.

When discussing the thick veils of ignorance proposed by Harsanyi and Rawls, I have tried hard to make it clear that I disagree with both about how the veil of ignorance should be envisaged. However, so many other issues have been raised along the way that some readers will doubtless have lost track of where I stand on this vital question. This section therefore seeks to provide a summary of my own conception of the role of the veil of ignorance.

Unlike Harsanyi and Rawls, I am not inspired by Kant. I believe that Kant is wrong about *a priori* moral reasoning for the same reason that he is generally acknowledged to be wrong about *a priori* geometrical reasoning. My own interest in the original position is entirely pragmatic. It derives from the belief that rough-and-ready versions of the device are *already* built into the set of coordinating devices that humans use to get along with each other. In advocating the use of the device of the original position as an instrument for reform, I therefore make no grand metaphysical claims about its merits. All that is suggested is that we try to improve the effectiveness with which citizens in a society cooperate by adapting a coordinating device that is familiar from use on a daily basis in our everyday life to larger-scale coordinating problems for which social evolution has so far failed to generate anything very satisfactory.

When Harsanyi and Rawls discuss the original position, they typically have large-scale applications in mind. Behind the veil of ignorance, utopian societies are created from scratch to serve as standards of comparison against which to measure the gimcrack societies in which we actually live.

For Harsanyi and Rawls, the device of the original position therefore serves as what Rawls [214, p.584] calls an *Archimedean point* from which to judge our current institutions. My own approach to the original position is more complicated, since it forces me to wear different hats at different times. One of these hats is a *prescriptive* or normative hat like that worn by Harsanyi and Rawls. This is the hat I wear when acting the part of a whiggish reformer. But I am not always wearing this prescriptive hat when discussing the original position. Sometimes I am wearing a *descriptive* or positive hat. I wear this hat when attempting to understand how the device of the original position actually works when used for small-scale purposes in current societies.

Why do I need two hats? The reason is to be found in Section 1.2.4, where a distinction was made between the *game of life* and the *game of morals*. The rules of the game of life are made by Nature. They hold whether we believe them or not. If the citizens of a society are motivated by enlightened self-interest like *homo economicus*, they will be led to coordinate on an equilibrium in this game of life. I identify such an equilibrium with a social contract. A social contract is therefore an equilibrium profile of strategies, one for each citizen. When the social contract operates, each citizen will therefore be optimizing when he follows the rules of behavior prescribed by his strategy. But these rules for sustaining an equilibrium do not bind like the rules of the game of life. They are entirely conventional. They survive because we believe in them. If the accidents of social evolution had led society to a different equilibrium, we would believe in a different set of conventional rules.

When wearing the prescriptive hat of a reformer, I advocate shifting from our current social contract to another social contract that we would all prefer. Instead of using the conventional rules that we currently use to sustain an equilibrium in the game of life, I propose that we pretend that we are playing a different game—a game that Section 1.2.4 calls the "game of morals". In the game of morals, each citizen believes that he can invoke the device of the original position whenever he feels unjustly treated. Everybody then disappears behind a veil of ignorance to negotiate a new social contract in ignorance of what their roles in society have been hitherto. Such a game of morals serves as my Archimedean point. In particular, I suggest that a "fair social contract" be defined as an equilibrium in the game of life that calls for the use of strategies which, if used in the game of morals, would leave no player in the game of morals with an incentive to appeal to the device of the original position. Although not bound by the rules of the game of morals, players who behave as though they were so bound will then be coordinating on an equilibrium in the game of life whose rules do really bind. The game of morals therefore serves as an *equilibrium selection mechanism* for the game of life.

My prescriptive hat is needed when proposing the game of morals as an instrument of reform. However, unlike Harsanyi and Rawls, who advance metaphysical arguments in favor of their proposals, I find it necessary to change my headgear when asked why attention should be paid to my game of morals rather than to one of the many other moral systems that have been proposed. In replying to such questions, I find it necessary to wear a *descriptive* hat, since my reason for proposing the game of morals is that our current social contract *already* incorporates simple versions of the device of the original position that we use when coordinating on an equilibrium in one of the many subsidiary games of the game of life that we play every day. In the metaphor of Section 2.3.6, the tide of history has washed this social tool up onto our beach. Why not therefore use it to improve our lives—just as we use whatever tools we find in our toolbox when making repairs around the house? But, before we can adapt the device of the original position to new purposes, we need to describe how it currently works.

How thick is the veil of ignorance when the device of the original position is used in everyday life? For the reasons given in Section 2.3.3, I am very dubious about the usefulness of introspection as a guide in seeking to answer such questions. The psychological mechanisms that we use when operating the original position are so internalized that they impinge very little on our conscious thought, except when they get triggered in situations for which they are ill adapted. The stories that we have invented to explain our behavior to ourselves are therefore not reliable. Nevertheless, some evidence is available about what is going on. In particular, it does seem to be a fact that we are commonly able to articulate empathetic preferences.[93] I find it hard to believe that such a capacity should have evolved unless it serves some social function. My own view is that we reveal such empathetic preferences, *to ourselves* as well as to others, whenever we coordinate on equilibria in situations that we rationalize by talking about "fairness". The device of the original position doubtless fails to capture much of the complexity involved in such interactions, but its intuitive appeal must surely signal that it hits the nail at least partly on the head.

If I am right in thinking that we routinely operate everyday versions of the original position in adjudicating fairness issues, then it follows that we also operate an everyday version of the veil of ignorance. How thick is this everyday veil of ignorance? I believe that it is not thick at all. Indeed, my best guess is that it is as thin as it can possibly be without failing in its function. Why should something complicated evolve when something simple will suffice? Nature doubtless found it hard enough to teach us how to see the world-as-it-is through the eyes of our fellows, without taking on

---

[93]These are not the complete and consistent preferences of *homo economicus*, but some poetic license must be granted if any kind of tractable model is to emerge.

the task of of teaching us to envisage how various worlds-as-they-might-have-been would seem to others.

In expressing this view, I believe that I am in harmony with at least one of the criticisms of Rawls [214] offered by such communitarian authors as Macintyre [160, 162, 161] and Sandel [226, 227]. I am doubtful of the value of articulating such criticism in terms of metaphysical concepts of the self, but I agree very much that a human being capable of cutting himself adrift from his cultural roots in the manner required by the younger Rawls [214] would be an extraordinary prodigy.

A Thin Veil of Ignorance. How does my thin veil of ignorance work? It differs from Rawls' veil of ignorance in that Adam and Eve are not called upon to forget the way society is currently organized. Behind the thin veil of ignorance, they retain their knowledge of the current state of nature. Nor do they forget their empathetic preferences as in Harsanyi's story. This point is particularly important for my theory. I see Adam and Eve's empathetic preferences as being shaped by social evolution in the medium run. Social evolution therefore determines how Adam and Eve make interpersonal comparisons of utility. Since the manner in which different people evaluate the well-being of others seems me the bedrock on which any coherent moral theory must be based, it therefore matters to me very much that I am able to offer the beginnings of an explanation of how and why such evaluations are made. However, no such story would be possible if Adam and Eve were forced to reinvent their empathetic preferences every time they entered the original position.

A formal model that incorporates such a thin veil of ignorance will not be introduced until Chapter 2 of Volume II. At this stage it is therefore only worthwhile to outline the features of a model about which it will be necessary to be more precise in the future. In particular, we shall need to play close attention to modeling the *informational constraints* on those in the original position, the set of *feasible social contracts* available to them, and the mechanics of the *bargaining process* that we are to envisage their using in reaching an agreement.

Informational Constraints. The use of a thin veil of ignorance requires taking a minimalist attitude to the informational constraints that Adam and Eve pretend to observe in the original position. They are to see themselves as one of two abstract entities unimaginatively labeled player I and player II. Player I will always actually be Adam and player II will always actually be Eve, but both act as though this information were unavailable. However, everything else is taken to be an open book.

In particular, the state of nature—the way that society is currently organized—is common knowledge between players I and II.[94] The circumstances that face them in the original position are also common knowledge. Both players know that, after they have negotiated an agreement in the original position, then one player will become Adam and the other Eve. Behind the veil of ignorance, each player therefore has to contemplate lotteries in which the prizes are contingent on two exclusive events, A and E. In the event A, player I turns out to be Adam and player II to be Eve. In the event E, player I turns out to be Eve and player II to be Adam.

Section 4.6 goes on at great length about why Bayesian decision theory applies in such circumstances. It is therefore taken for granted that each player will assign a subjective probability p to the event A and a probability $1 - p$ to the event E. But why should we take $p = \frac{1}{2}$? Indeed why should p be the same for both player I and player II? And how come its value gets to be common knowledge among the players? Rawls [214] evades such questions by denying the applicability of Bayesian decision theory. Harsanyi [109] seeks to answer them by an appeal to the Harsanyi doctrine criticized in Sections 3.4 and 4.3. However, I follow Olson [197] in making no attempt to deduce the circumstances of the original position from metaphysical premises. On the contrary, I think that one goes astray in trying to *prove* things about p. The value of p should be part of the definition of the original position. That is to say, a "fair" social contract should be *defined* to be an agreement that would be negotiated in an original position in which it is *given* not only that $p = \frac{1}{2}$, but that this fact is common knowledge.

If asked to defend the choice of such a definition of the original position, I don my descriptive hat.[95] When "fairness" issues are adjudicated in real life, it is always understood that the principle is that both parties should be placed on as equal a footing as possible.[96] If we want to base our model of the original position on the "fairness" norms that society currently uses, we therefore have little choice but to take $p = \frac{1}{2}$. Of course, it is no accident that the primitive versions of the device of the original position that we use in everyday life ostensibly treat both players equally. Social evolution must be responsible for generating this particular choice of p. A deeper analysis would seek an explanation by studying models in which the evolutionary

---

[94]Of course, certain relevant matters, like next year's rainfall or the foreign policy of a neighboring state, will necessarily be uncertain. However, it is to be understood that players I and II agree on the probabilities to be assigned to such unknowns.

[95]In later chapters, I sometimes work with an unspecified value of p, when this can be done without making the mathematics too messy. But I dislike this expedient for the same reason that I dislike Harsanyi's leaving open the rate at which Adam's utils are to be compared with Eve's.

[96]I do not mean by this to imply that both parties are actually getting treated "equally" because a great deal depends on how interpersonal comparisons of utility are made.

origins of the original position were endogenized. I appreciate that the armchair empiricism that I offer in place of such a formal study is not a satisfactory substitute. However, my armchair empiricism on this aspect of everyday original positions is no less soundly based than my armchair empiricism on their other aspects.

Feasible Social Contracts. Aside from my differences with Harsanyi and Rawls on informational questions in the original position, I differ from both in being unwilling to deny players I and II the opportunity to make their social contract *contingent* on anything that might conceivably be relevant.[97] In particular, I see no reason why players I and II should be confined, as in Section 4.3, to agreements that impose the *same* social contract no matter who turns out to be who. I therefore allow them to agree to *contingent* social contracts in which one set of conventional rules is operationalized if player I turns out to be Adam, and an entirely different set if player I turns out to be Eve.

Suppose that such a contingent social contract leads to the outcome C if the event A occurs and to the outcome D if the event E occurs. Then player i will evaluate the contingent contract as being worth

$$pu_i(C, A) + (1 - p)u_i(D, E),$$

where u_i is player i's empathetic utility function. Thus $u_i(C, A)$ is his Von Neumann and Morgenstern utility for being Adam when C occurs, while $u_i(D, E)$ is his Von Neumann and Morgenstern utility for being Eve when D occurs. These empathetic utility functions are the same as those that Adam and Eve hold in the real world. Thus player I has Adam's empathetic preferences and player II has Eve's.[98] Adam and Eve therefore do not forget their empathetic preferences when passing behind the veil of ignorance as in Harsanyi's theory. Indeed, if my speculations about how everyday "fairness" norms actually operate are anywhere near correct, there would be no point in you or I having empathetic preferences at all if we

---

[97]My differences with Harsanyi on this particular point are very slight, since the issue becomes significant only in out-of-equilibrium situations. However, I think Rawls' neglect of the possibility of contingent contracts in the Dance of the Four Veils described in Section 4.6 leads him badly astray.

[98]Section 1.2.7 explains that, when social evolution has brought the system to an equilibrium, Adam and Eve will have the *same* empathetic preferences. Player I will therefore be unable to deduce that he is Adam by examining his own empathetic preferences and observing that they are Adam's. On the other hand, when considering what is in equilibrium, it is necessary to consider what would happen if there were a deviation from the equilibrium path. In such an out-of-equilibrium situation, Adam would be able to deduce his identity from a study of his empathetic preferences. However, the question of whether he can or cannot deduce that he is Adam from any clues left lying around is really beside the point. After all, Adam actually knows that he is Adam anyway. He only *pretends* to pass behind a veil of ignorance when entering the original position.

forgot them on entering the original position, because it is only when used in this way that they have any impact on how we behave.

The Bargaining Process. Finally, it is necessary to be precise about the mechanics of the bargaining process that players I and II employ in reaching an agreement on a contingent social contract behind their thin veil of ignorance. As always, I take a minimalist view and assume nothing more than one might reasonably assume about rational bargaining in the real world. However, the problem of finding adequate models of how people really bargain when in a rational frame of mind is too large an issue to be pursued here. A new chapter on this topic is required. Unfortunately, this new chapter on the theory of rational bargaining is so long that it will not fit into the current volume. Much water will therefore have passed under the bridge before we return to the problem of bargaining behind the veil of ignorance in Chapter 2 of Volume II.

A Final Word.   The previous sentence was an attempt at a cliff-hanging conclusion to *Playing Fair*—which is only the first volume of *Game Theory and the Social Contract*. But it seems that the irrepressible Hobbes [117] insists on having the final word. He tells us that:

> Of Pleasures, or Delights, some arise from the sense of an object Present ... others arise from the Expectation, that proceeds from foresight of the End.

Nobody could reasonably expect the experience of reading of a book on political philosophy to be an unqualified pleasure or delight. But I feel deeply apologetic to have written so much that I cannot even offer readers of *Playing Fair* the gratification that comes, on reaching the end of a book, from the realization that no more remains to be read. However, I can at least promise that this particular pleasure and delight will not be denied to readers of its sequel *Just Playing*—which will be the second and last volume of *Game Theory and the Social Contract*.

Bibliography

[1] D. Abreu and A. Rubinstein. The structure of Nash equilibrium in repeated games with finite automata. *Econometrica*, 56:1259–1282, 1988.

[2] F. Anscombe and R. Aumann. A definition of subjective probability. *Annals of Mathematical Statistics*, 34:199–205, 1963.

[3] M. Arbib. *Brains, Machines and Mathematics*. Springer-Verlag, Berlin, 1987.

[4] M. Arbib. *In Search of the Person*. University of Massachusetts Press, Amherst, 1985.

[5] Aristotle. *The Philosophy of Aristotle*. Mentor Books, New York, 1963. (Translated by R. Brambrough.).

[6] K. Arrow. Extended sympathy and the problem of social choice. *Philosophia*, 7:233–237, 1978.

[7] K. Arrow. Rawls' principle of just savings. *Swedish Journal of Economics*, 75:323–335, 1973.

[8] K. Arrow. *Social Choice and Individual Values*. Yale University Press, New Haven, 1963.

[9] J. Aubrey. *Brief Lives*. Penguin Books, Harmondsworth, Middlesex, UK, 1962. (Edited by O. Lawson.).

[10] R. Aumann. Agreeing to disagree. *The Annals of Statistics*, 4:1236–1239, 1976.

[11] R. Aumann. Correlated equilibrium as an expression of Bayesian rationality. *Econometrica*, 55:1–18, 1987.

[12] R. Aumann. Interactive epistemology. 1989. Working Paper, Cowles Foundation, Yale University.

[13] R. Aumann. Nash equilibria are not self-enforcing. In J.-F. Richard J.-J. Gabsewicz and L. Wolsley, editors, *Economic Decision-Making: Econometrics and Optimization*, Elsevier Science Publishers, Amsterdam, 1990. (Essays in honor of Jacques Dreze.).

[14] R. Axelrod. *The Evolution of Cooperation*. Basic Books, New York, 1984.

[15] R. Axelrod. The evolution of strategies in the iterated prisoners' dilemma. In L. Davis, editor, *Genetic Algorithms and Simulated Annealing*, Morgan Kaufmann, Los Altos, Calif., 1987.

[16] B. Barry. *Theories of Justice*. University of California Press, Berkeley and Los Angeles, 1989.

[17] J. Bentham. An introduction to the principles of morals and legislation. In *Utilitarianism and Other Essays*, Penguin Books, Harmondsworth, Middlesex, U.K., 1987. (Introduction by A. Ryan, essay first published 1789).

[18] T. Bergstrom. Love and spaghetti, the opportunity cost of virtue. *Journal of Economic Perspectives*, 3:165–173, 1989.

[19] G. Berkeley. *Three Dialogues Between Hylas and Philonus*. Bobbs-Merrill, Indianapolis, 1954. (Edited by C. Turbayne; first published 1713).

[20] D. Bernheim. Rationalizable strategic behavior. *Econometrica*, 52:1007–1028, 1984.

[21] M. Bianchi. How to learn sociality: True and false solutions to Mandeville's problem. 1990. University of Rome Paper.

[22] C. Bicchieri and I. Gilboa. Etude for: Can free choice be known. 1992. Working Paper, Philosophy Department, Carnegie-Mellon University.

[23] K. Binmore. Bargaining and morality: Social contract II. In R. Sugden, editor, *Rationality, Justice and the Social Contract: Themes from 'Morals by Agreement'*, Simon and Schuster, Hemel Hempstead, U.K., 1992.

[24] K. Binmore. Debayesing game theory. In B. Skyrms, editor, *Studies in Logic and the Foundations of Game Theory: Proceedings of the Ninth International Congress of Logic, Methodology and the Philosophy of Science*, Kluwer, Dordrecht, 1992.

[25] K. Binmore. Equilibria in extensive games. *Economic Journal*, 95:51–59, 1984.

[26] K. Binmore. An example in group preference. *Journal of Economic Theory*, 10:377–385, 1975.

[27] K. Binmore. Experimental economics. *European Economic Review*, 31:257–264, 1987.

[28] K. Binmore. Foundations of game theory. In J.-J. Laffont, editor, *Advances in Economic Theory*, Sixth World Congress of the Econometric Society, Cambridge University Press, Cambridge, 1992.

[29] K. Binmore. *Fun and Games*. D. C. Heath, Lexington, Mass., 1991.

[30] K. Binmore. Game theory and the social contract. In R. Selten, editor, *Game Equilibrium Models II: Methods, Morals and Markets*, Springer-Verlag, Berlin, 1991.

[31] K. Binmore. *Game Theory and the Social Contract I*. Technical Report ST/ICERD 84/108, London School of Economics, 1984.

[32] K. Binmore. Modeling rational players I. *Economics and Philosophy*, 3:9–55, 1987.

[33] K. Binmore. Modeling rational players II. *Economics and Philosophy*, 4:179–214, 1987.

[34] K. Binmore. Social contract I: Harsanyi and Rawls. *Economic Journal*, 99:84–102, 1989.

[35] K. Binmore. Social contract III: Evolution and utilitarianism. *Constitutional Political Economy*, 1:1–26, 1990.

[36] K. Binmore. Social contract IV: Convention and evolution. In R. Selten, editor, *Rational Interaction: Essays in Honor of John C. Harsanyi*, Springer-Verlag, Berlin, 1992.

[37] K. Binmore. Social contract IV: Evolution and convention. In R. Selten, editor, *Rational Interaction: Essays in Honor of John Harsanyi*, Springer, Berlin, 1992.

[38] K. Binmore and A. Brandenburger. Common knowledge and game theory. In K. G. Binmore, editor, *Essays on Foundations of Game Theory*, Basil Blackwell, Oxford, 1990.

[39] K. Binmore, P. Morgan, A. Shaked, and J. Sutton. Do people exploit their bargaining power? An experimental study. *Games and Economic Behavior*, 3:295–322, 1991.

[40] K. Binmore and L. Samuelson. Evolutionary stability in repeated games played by finite automata. *Journal of Economic Theory*, 57:278–305, 1992.

[41] K. Binmore, A. Shaked, and J. Sutton. An outside option experiment. *Quarterly Journal of Economics*, 104:753–770, 1989.

[42] K. Binmore, A. Shaked, and J. Sutton. Testing noncooperative game theory: A preliminary study. *American Economic Review*, 75:1178–1180, 1985.

[43] K. Binmore and H. Shin. Algorithmic knowledge and game theory. In C. Bicchieri and M. Chiara, editors, *Knowledge, Belief and Strategic Interaction*, Cambridge University Press, Cambridge, 1992.

[44] K. Binmore, J. Swierzsbinski, S. Hsu, and C. Proulx. Focal points and bargaining. 1992. University of Michigan Discussion Paper.

[45] R. Boyd and P. Richerson. *Culture and the Evolutionary Process*. University of Chicago Press, Chicago, 1985.

[46] R. Braithwaite. *The Theory of Games as a Tool for the Moral Philosopher*. Cambridge University Press, Cambridge, 1955.

[47] S. Brams. *Superior Beings*. Springer-Verlag, New York, 1983.

[48] J. Broome. *Weighing Goods*. Basil Blackwell, Oxford, 1991.

[49] J. Buchanan. A Hobbsian interpretation of the Rawlsian difference principle. *Kyklos*, 29:5–25, 1976.

[50] J. Buchanan. *The Limits of Liberty*. University of Chicago Press, Chicago, 1975.

[51] J. Buchanan. Towards the simple economics of natural liberty. *Kyklos*, 40, 1987.

[52] R. Burton. *The Anatomy of Melancholy*. Tudor, New York, 1927.

[53] G. Calvo. Some notes on time inconsistency and Rawls' maximin principle. *Review of Economic Studies*, 45:97–102, 1978.

[54] H. Carlsson and E. Van Damme. Equilibrium selection in Stag Hunt games. 1991. CenTER discussion paper, Tilburg University.

[55] K. Chatterjee and W. Samuelson. Bargaining under incomplete information. *Operations Research*, 31:835–851, 1983.

[56] R. Coase. The problem of social costs. *Journal of Law and Economics*, 3:1–44, 1960.

[57] V. Crawford. An evolutionary interpretation of Van Huyck, Battalio and Beil's experimental results in coordination games. *Games and Economic Behavior*, 3:25–59, 1991.

[58] P. Dasgupta. Of some alternative criteria for justice between generations. *Journal of Public Economics*, 3:405–423, 1974.

[59] P. Dasgupta. Population and savings: Ethical issues. 1993. Working paper, University of Cambridge.

[60] R. Dawes, A. van der Kragt, and J. Orbell. Not thee or me but we. *Acta Psychologica*, 68:83–97, 1988.

[61] R. Dawkins. *The Blind Watchmaker*. Penguin Books, London, 1986.

[62] R. Dawkins. *The Selfish Gene*. Oxford University Press, Oxford, 1976.

[63] D. Defoe. *The Complete English Tradesman*. Augustus Kelley, New York, 1969. (First published 1727.).

[64] C. Dennett. *Brainstorms: Philosphical Essays on Mind and Psychology*. Harvester Press, Hassocks, Sussex, UK, 1978.

[65] C. Dennett. *Consciousness Explained*. Allen Lane: The Penguin Press, London, 1991.

[66] P. Diamond. Cardinal welfare, individualistic ethics and interpersonal comparison of utility: Comment. *Journal of Political Economy*, 75:765–766, 1967.

[67] W. Dowling. There are no safe virus tests. *American Mathematical Monthly*, 96:835–836, 1989.

[68] F. Edgeworth. *Mathematical Psychics*. Kegan Paul, London, 1881.

[69] D. Ellsberg. *The Theory and Practice of Blackmail: Formal Theories of Negotiation*. University of Illinois Press, Urbana, 1975.

[70] J. Elster. *The Cement of Society: A Study of Social Order*. Cambridge University Press, Cambridge, 1989.

[71] J. Elster. *Making Sense of Marx*. Cambridge University Press, Cambridge, 1985.

[72] J. Elster. Sour grapes–Utilitarianism and the genesis of wants. In A. Sen and B. Williams, editors, *Utilitarianism and Beyond*, Cambridge University Press, Cambridge, 1982.

[73] J. Farrell. Meaning and credibility in cheap-talk games. In M. Dempster, editor, *Mathematical Models in Economics*, Oxford University Press, Oxford, (Forthcoming.).

[74] G. Field. *Moral Theory*. Methuen, London, 1988. (First published 1921.).

[75] R. Frank. *Passions within Reason*. Norton, New York, 1988.

[76] M. Friedman. Lerner on the economics of control. *Journal of Political Economy*, 55:405–416, 1947.

[77] M. Friedman and L. Savage. Utility analysis of choices involving risk. *Journal of Political Economy*, 56:179–304, 1948.

[78] D. Fudenberg. Repeated game explanations of commitment and cooperation. In J.-J. Laffont, editor, *Advances in Economic Theory*, Sixth World Congress of the Econometric Society, Cambridge University Press, Cambridge, 1992.

[79] D. Fudenberg and E. Maskin. Evolution and cooperation in noisy repeated games. *American Economic Review*, 80:274–279, 1990.

[80] Y.-L. Fung. *A History of Chinese Philosophy, Volume 1*. Princeton University Press, Princeton, 1952.

[81] W. Gaertner, P. Pattanaik, and K. Suzumura. Individual rights revisited. *Economica*, 59:161–178, 1992.

[82] D. Gauthier. David Hume: Contractarian. *Philosophical Review*, 88:3–38, 1979.

[83] D. Gauthier. *The Logic of Leviathan*. Oxford University Press, Oxford, 1969.

[84] D. Gauthier. *Morals by Agreement*. Clarendon Press, Oxford, 1986.

[85] D. Gauthier. Uniting separate persons. In D. Gauthier and R. Sugden, editors, *Rationality, Justice and the Social Contract*, Harvester Wheatsheaf, Hemel Hempstead, UK, 1993.

[86] E. Gellner. *Plough, Sword and Book*. Paladin, Grafton Books, London, 1988.

[87] A. Gibbard. A Pareto-consistent libertarian claim. *Journal of Economic Theory*, 7:388–410, 1974.

[88] A. Gibbard. *Wise Choices and Apt Feelings: A Theory of Normative Judgment.* Clarendon Press, Oxford, 1990.

[89] A. Gibbard and W. Harper. Counterfactuals and two kinds of expected utility. *Foundations and Applications of Decision Theory*, 1:125–162, 1978.

[90] R. Goodin. Equal rationality and initial endowments. In D. Gauthier and R. Sugden, editors, *Rationality, Justice and the Social Contract*, Harvester Wheatsheaf, Hemel Hempstead, U. K., 1993.

[91] J. W. Gough. *The Social Contract.* Clarendon Press, Oxford, 1938.

[92] E. Green and K. Osband. A revealed preference theory for expected utility. *Review of Economic Studies*, 58:677–697, 1991.

[93] P. Hammond. Consequentialist foundations for expected utility. *Theory and Decision*, 25:25–78, 1988.

[94] P. Hammond. Harsanyi's utilitarian theorem: A simpler proof and some ethical connotations. In R. Selten, editor, *Rational Interaction: Essays in Honor of John Harsanyi*, Springer-Verlag, Berlin, 1992.

[95] P. Hammond. Why ethical measures of inequality need interpersonal comparisons. *Theory and Decision*, 7:263–274, 1976.

[96] S. Hampshire. Morality and convention. In A. Sen and B. Williams, editors, *Utilitarianism and Beyond*, Cambridge University Press, Cambridge, 1982.

[97] J. Hampton. *Hobbes and the Social Contract Tradition.* Cambridge University Press, Cambridge, 1986.

[98] G. Hardin. The tragedy of the commons. *Science*, 162:1243–1248, 1968.

[99] R. Hardin. *Collective Action.* Johns Hopkins Press, Baltimore, 1982.

[100] R. Hardin. *Morality within the Limits of Reason.* University of Chicago Press, Chicago, 1988.

[101] R. Hare. Ethical theory and utilitarianism. In A. Sen and B. Williams, editors, *Utilitarianism and Beyond*, Cambridge University Press, Cambridge, 1982.

[102] R. Hare. *Moral Thinking: Its Levels, Method and Point*. Clarendon Press, Cambridge, 1981.

[103] R. Hare. The promising game. *Revue Internationale de Philosophie*, 70:398–412, 1964.

[104] R. Hare. Rawls' theory of justice. In B. Daniels, editor, *Reading Rawls*, Basil Blackwell, Oxford, 1975.

[105] J. Harsanyi. Can the maximin principle serve as a basis for morality? A critique of John Rawls' theory. *American Political Science Review*, 69:594–606, 1975.

[106] J. Harsanyi. Cardinal welfare, individualistic ethics, and the interpersonal comparison of utility. *Journal of Political Economy*, 63:309–321, 1955.

[107] J. Harsanyi. Games with incomplete information played by 'Bayesian' players, Parts I - III. *Management Science*, 14:159–182, 1967.

[108] J. Harsanyi. Normative validity and meaning of Von Neumann and Morgenstern utilities. In B. Skyrms, editor, *Studies in Logic and the Foundations of Game Theory: Proceedings of the Ninth International Congress of Logic, Methodology and the Philosophy of Science*, Kluwer, Dordrecht, 1992.

[109] J. Harsanyi. *Rational Behavior and Bargaining Equilibrium in Games and Social Situations*. Cambridge University Press, Cambridge, 1977.

[110] J. Harsanyi. Review of Gauthier's "Morals by Agreement". *Economics and Philosophy*, 3:339–343, 1987.

[111] J. Harsanyi and R. Selten. *A General Theory of Equilibrium Selection in Games*. MIT Press, Cambridge, 1988.

[112] F. Hayek. *The Constitution of Liberty*. University of Chicago Press, Chicago, 1960.

[113] F. Hayek. *The Sensory Order*. University of Chicago Press, Chicago, 1952.

[114] F. Hayek. *Studies in Philosophy, Politics and Economics*. University of Chicago Press, Chicago, 1967.

[115] T. Hobbes. *Behemoth*. University of Chicago Press, Chicago, 1990. (Edited by F. Tönnies, first published 1682.).

[116] T. Hobbes. *Elements of Law.* Frank Cass, London, 1969. (Edited by F. Tönnies).

[117] T. Hobbes. *Leviathan.* Penguin Classics, London, 1986. (Edited by C. B. Macpherson, first published 1651.).

[118] D. Hofstadter. A conversation with Einstein's brain. In D. Hofstadter and D. Dunnett, editors, *The Mind's I*, Basic Books, Harmondsworth, UK, 1981.

[119] D. Hofstadter. Metamagical themes. *Scientific American*, 248(6):14–20, 1983.

[120] K. Hopkins. *Conquerors and Slaves.* Cambridge University Press, Cambridge, 1978.

[121] J. Howard. Cooperation in the Prisoners' Dilemma. *Theory and Decision*, 24:203–213, 1988.

[122] N. Howard. *Paradoxes of Rationality: Theory of Metagames and Political Behavior.* MIT Press, Cambridge, Mass., 1971.

[123] R. Howe and J. Roemer. Rawlsian justice as the core of a game. *American Economic Review*, 71:880–895, 1981.

[124] D. Hume. *Enquiries Concerning Human Understanding and Concerning the Principles of Morals.* 3rd edition. Clarendon Press, Oxford, 1975. (Edited by L. A. Selby-Bigge, revised by P. Nidditch, first published 1777.).

[125] D. Hume. Of suicide. In *Essays Moral, Political and Literary*, Liberty Classics, Indianapolis, 1985.

[126] D. Hume. Of the first principles of government. In *Essays Moral, Political and Literary, Part I*, Liberty Classics, Indianapolis, 1985. (Edited by E. Miller, essay first published 1758.).

[127] D. Hume. Of the original contract. In *Essays Moral, Political and Literary*, Liberty Classics, Indianapolis, 1985. (Edited by E. Miller, essay first published 1748.).

[128] D. Hume. *A Treatise of Human Nature.* 2nd edition. Clarendon Press, Oxford, 1978. (Edited by L. A. Selby-Bigge, revised by P. Nidditch, first published 1739.).

[129] M. Hunt. *The Compassionate Beast.* William Morrow, New York, 1990.

[130] R. Jervis. Cooperation under the security dilemma. *World Politics*, 30:167–214, 1978.

[131] D. Kahneman and A. Tversky. Prospect theory: An analysis of decision under risk. *Econometrica*, 47:263–291, 1979.

[132] E. Kalai and M. Smorodinsky. Other solutions to Nash's bargaining problem. *Econometrica*, 45:1623–1630, 1975.

[133] I. Kant. Critique of judgment. In *The Philosophy of Kant*, Random House, New York, 1949. (Edited by C. Friedrich; first published 1788.).

[134] I. Kant. *Groundwork of the Metaphysic of Morals*. Harper Torchbooks, New York, 1964. (Translated and analyzed by H. Paton. First published 1785.).

[135] I. Kant. Idea of a universal history. In *The Philosophy of Kant*, Random House, New York, 1949. (Edited by C. Friedrich; first published 1788.).

[136] I. Kant. *The Philosophy of Kant*. Random House, New York, 1949. (Edited by C. Friedrich.).

[137] I. Kant. Theory and practice. In *The Philosophy of Kant*, Random House, New York, 1949. (Edited by C. Friedrich. First published 1793.).

[138] G. Kavka. Hobbes' war of all against all. *Ethics*, 93:291–310, 1983.

[139] G. Kavka. *Hobbesian Moral and Political Theory*. Princeton University Press, Princeton, 1986.

[140] J. M. Keynes. *The General Theory of Employment, Interest and Money*. Macmillan, London, 1937.

[141] J. M. Keynes. *A Treatise on Probability*. Macmillan, London, 1921.

[142] R. Kirk. *Edmund Burke: A Genius Reconsidered*. Arlington House, New York, 1967.

[143] A. Kolmogorov. *Foundations of the Theory of Probability*. Chelsea, New York, 1950.

[144] D. Kreps. *Notes on the Theory of Choice*. Westview Press, London and Boulder, Colo., 1988.

[145] C. Kukathas and P. Pettit. *Rawls: A Theory of Justice and its Critics*. Polity Press with Basil Blackwell, Oxford, 1990.

[146] E. Land. Experiments in color vision. *Scientific American*, May:84–90, 1959.

[147] J. Ledyard. Public goods: A survey of experimental research. 1992. Working Paper, California Institute of Technology.

[148] A. Lerner. *The Economics of Control*. Macmillan, New York, 1944.

[149] I. Levi. A note on Newcombmania. *Journal of Philosophy*, 79:337–342, 1982.

[150] C. I. Lewis. *An Analysis of Knowledge and Valuation*. Open Court, La Salle, Ill., 1946.

[151] D. Lewis. Causal decision theory. *Australian Journal of Philosophy*, 51:5–30, 1981.

[152] D. Lewis. *Conventions: A Philosophical Study*. Harvard University Press, Cambridge, Mass., 1969.

[153] D. Lewis. *Counterfactuals*. Basil Blackwell, Oxford, 1976.

[154] D. Lewis. Prisoners' Dilemma as a Newcomb problem. *Philosophy and Public Affairs*, 8:235–240, 1979.

[155] B. Linster. *Essays on Cooperation and Competition*. PhD thesis, University of Michigan, 1990.

[156] J. Locke. *An Essay Concerning Human Understanding*. Clarendon Press, Oxford, 1975. (Edited by P. Nidditch).

[157] J. Locke. *Two Treatises of Government*. Cambridge University Press, Cambridge, 1963. (First published 1690.).

[158] R. Luce and H. Raiffa. *Games and Decisions*. Wiley, New York, 1957.

[159] M. Machina. Choice under uncertainty. *Economic Perspectives*, 1:121–154, 1987.

[160] A. Macintyre. *After Virtue*. Duckworth, London, 1981.

[161] A. Macintyre. *Three Rival Versions of Moral Enquiry*. Duckworth, London, 1990.

[162] A. Macintyre. *Whose Justice? Which Rationality?* Duckworth, London, 1988.

[163] J. Mackie. *Ethics, Inventing Right and Wrong*. Penguin Books, London, 1977.

[164] J. Mackie. *Hume's Moral Theory.* Routledge and Kegan Paul, London, 1980.

[165] J. Mackie. *Problems from Locke.* Clarendon Press, Oxford, 1976.

[166] R. MacMullen. *Corruption and the Decline of Rome.* Yale University Press, New Haven, 1988.

[167] C. Macpherson. The social bearing of Locke's political theory. *Western Political Quarterly*, 7:1–22, 19547.

[168] B. de Mandeville. *The Fable of the Bees—or Private Vices, Publick Benefits.* Liberty Classics, Indianapolis, 1988. (Edited by F. Kaye, first published 1714.).

[169] J. Mansbridge. *Beyond Self-Interest.* University of Chicago Press, Chicago, 1990.

[170] H. Margolis. *Selfishness, Altruism, and Rationality.* Cambridge University Press, Cambridge, 1982.

[171] J. Martinez-Coll and J. Hirshleifer. The limits of reciprocity. *Rationality and Society*, 3:35–64, 1991.

[172] J. Maynard Smith. *Evolution and the Theory of Games.* Cambridge University Press, Cambridge, 1982.

[173] J. Maynard Smith and G. Price. The logic of animal conflict. *Nature*, 246:15–18, 1972.

[174] B. Mayo. *The Philosophy of Right and Wrong.* Routledge and Kegan Paul, London and New York, 1986.

[175] E. McClennen. *Rationality and Dynamic Choice.* Cambridge University Press, Cambridge, 1990.

[176] J. de la Mettrie. *Man a Machine.* Open Court, La Salle, Ill., 1988. (First published 1748.).

[177] P. Milgrom. An axiomatic characterization of common knowledge. *Econometrica*, 49:219–222, 1981.

[178] J. S. Mill. Utilitarianism. In *Utilitarianism and Other Essays*, Penguin Books, Harmondsworth, Middlesex, U.K., 1987. (Introduction by A. Ryan; essay first published 1863.).

[179] J. Milnor. Games against Nature. In *Decision Processes*, Wiley, New York, 1954. (Edited by R. Thrall, C. Coombs, and R. Davies.).

[180] M. de Montaigne. *Essays of Montaigne.* Edwards Brothers, Ann Arbor, 1947.

[181] G. E. Moore. *Principia Ethica.* Prometheus Books, Buffalo, N.Y., 1988. (First published 1902.).

[182] A. de Morgan. *The Encyclopaedia of Eccentrics.* Open Court, La Salle, Ill., 1974.

[183] H. Moulin. Implementing the Kalai-Smorodinsky bargaining solution. *Journal of Economic Theory*, 33:32–45, 1984.

[184] S. Mulhall and A. Swift. *Liberals and Communitarians.* Blackwell, Oxford, 1992.

[185] D. Munro. *The Concept of Man in Early China.* Stanford University Press, Stanford, Calif., 1969.

[186] R. Myerson. *Game Theory: Analysis of Conflict.* Harvard University Press, Cambridge, Mass., 1991.

[187] R. Myerson and M. Satterthwaite. Efficient mechanisms for bilateral trading. *Journal of Economic Theory*, 29:265–281, 1983.

[188] J. Nachbar. The evolution of cooperation revisited. 1989. Working Paper, Rand Cooperation.

[189] T. Nagel. *The Possibility of Altruism.* Clarendon Press, Oxford, 1970.

[190] J. Nash. The bargaining problem. *Econometrica*, 18:155–162, 1950.

[191] F. Nietzsche. *Beyond Good and Evil.* Penguin Books, Harmondsworth, UK, 1973. (Translated by R. Hollingdale, first published 1886.).

[192] F. Nietzsche. Human, all too human. In O. Levy, editor, *The Complete Works of Friedrich Nietzsche*, Russell and Russell, New York, 1964.

[193] F. Nietzsche. *The Will to Power*, Volume II. Foulis, Edinburgh, 1910.

[194] R. Nozick. *Anarchy, State, and Utopia.* Basic Books, New York, 1974.

[195] R. Nozick. Newcomb's problem and two principles of choice. In N. Rescher, editor, *Essays in Honor of Carl G. Hempel*, Reidel, Dordrecht, Netherlands, 1969.

[196] M. Olson. *The Logic of Collective Action.* Harvard University Press, Cambridge, Mass, 1965.

[197] M. Olson. A new approach to the ethics of income distribution. 1986. Manville American Enterprise Lecture, University of Notre Dame.

[198] G. Orwell. *Animal Farm.* New American Library, Signet Classic, New York, 1960. (First published 1946.).

[199] V. Pareto. *Manuale di Economia Politica.* Societa Editrice Libraria, Milan, 1906.

[200] P. Pattanaik and K. Suzumura. Professor Sen on minimal liberty. 1990. Discussion Paper A231, Institute of Economic Research, Hitotsubashi University, Tokyo.

[201] D. Pearce. Rationalizable strategic behavior and the problem of perfection. *Econometrica*, 52:1029–1050, 1984.

[202] R. Penrose. *The Emperor's New Mind.* Oxford University Press, Oxford, 1989.

[203] W. Poundstone. *Labyrinths of Reason.* Doubleday, New York, 1988.

[204] D. Probst. Evolution in the repeated Prisoners' Dilemma. Working Paper (in preparation), University of Bonn.

[205] W. Quine. *The Ways of Paradox and Other Essays.* Harvard University Press, Cambridge, Mass., 1966.

[206] H. Raiffa. Arbitration schemes for generalized two-person games. In H. Kuhn and A. Tucker, editors, *Contributions to the Theory of Games II*, Princeton University Press, Princeton, 1953.

[207] A. Rapoport. *Two-Person Game Theory.* University of Michigan Press, Ann Arbor, Mich., 1966.

[208] J. Rawls. Distributive justice: Some addenda. *Natural Law Forum*, 13, 1968.

[209] J. Rawls. Justice as fairness. *Philosophical Review*, 57:185–187, 1958.

[210] J. Rawls. Kantian constructivism in moral theory. *Journal of Philosophy*, 88:575–582, 1980.

[211] J. Rawls. *Political Liberalism.* Columbia University Press, New York, 1993.

[212] J. Rawls. Social unity and primary goods. In A. Sen and B. Williams, editors, *Utilitarianism and Beyond*, Cambridge University Press, Cambridge, 1982.

[213] J. Rawls. Some reasons for the maximin criterion. *American Economic Review*, 64 (papers and proceedings):141–146, 1974.

[214] J. Rawls. *A Theory of Justice*. Oxford University Press, Oxford, 1972.

[215] P. Redondi. *Galileo: Heretic*. Princeton University Press, Princeton, 1987. (Translated by R. Rosenthal).

[216] W. Riker. *Liberalism against Populism*. Waveland Press, Prospect Heights, Ill., 1982.

[217] L. Robbins. *An Essay on the Nature and Significance of Economic Science*. Macmillan, London, 1935.

[218] L. Robbins. Inter-personal comparisons of utility. *Economic Journal*, 48:635–641, 1938.

[219] A. Robson. Efficiency in evolutionary games: Darwin, Nash, and the secret handshake. *Journal of Theoretical Biology*, 144:379–396, 1990.

[220] A. Rodriguez. Rawls' maximin criterion and time consistency: A generalisation. *Review of Economic Studies*, 48:599–605, 1981.

[221] J.-J. Rousseau. A discourse on political economy. In G. Cole, editor, *Rousseau's Social Contract and Discourses*, pages 249–287, J. M. Dent, London, 1913. (First published 1755.).

[222] J.-J. Rousseau. *Emile*. J. M. Dent, London, 1908. (First published 1762.

[223] J.-J. Rousseau. The inequality of man. In G. Cole, editor, *Rousseau's Social Contract and Discourses*, pages 157–246, J. M. Dent, London, 1913. (First published 1755.).

[224] J.-J. Rousseau. The social contract. In G. Cole, editor, *Rousseau's Social Contract and Discourses*, pages 5–123, J. M. Dent, London, 1913. (First published 1762.).

[225] G. Ryle. *The Concept of Mind*. Hutchinson, London, 1949.

[226] M. Sandel. *Liberalism and the Limits of Justice*. Cambridge University Press, Cambridge, 1982.

[227] M. Sandel. The procedural republic and the unencumbered self. *Political Theory*, 12:81–96, 1984.

[228] L. Savage. *The Foundations of Statistics*. Wiley, New York, 1951.

[229] T. Schelling. *The Strategy of Conflict*. Harvard University Press, Cambridge, Mass., 1960.

[230] A. Schopenhauer. *The World as Will and Representation*. Dover, New York, 1969. (Translated by E. Payne, first published 1819.).

[231] A. Schotter. *The Economic Theory of Social Institutions*. Cambridge University Press, Cambridge, 1981.

[232] A. Schotter. *Free Market Economics*. 2nd edition. Basil Blackwell, Oxford, 1990.

[233] J. Searle. Minds, brains and programs. In D. Hofstadter and D. Dunnett, editors, *The Mind's I*, Basic Books, Harmondsworth, UK, 1981.

[234] J. R. Searle. How to derive "ought" from "is". *Philosophical Review*, 73:43–58, 1964.

[235] R. Selten. Reexamination of the perfectness concept for equilibrium points in extensive-games. *International Journal of Game Theory*, 4:25–55, 1975.

[236] A. Sen. Behaviour and the concept of preference. *Economica*, 40:241–259, 1973.

[237] A. Sen. Choice functions and revealed preference. *Review of Economic Studies*, 38:307–317, 1971.

[238] A. Sen. Choice orderings and morality. In *Practical Reason*, Basil Blackwell, Oxford, 1974. (Edited by S. Korner).

[239] A. Sen. *Collective Choice and Social Welfare*. Holden Day, San Francisco, 1970.

[240] A. Sen. The impossibility of a Paretian liberal. *Journal of Political Economy*, 78:152–157, 1970.

[241] A. Sen. Minimal liberty. *Economica*, 59:139–160, 1992.

[242] A. Sen. *On Ethics and Economics*. Basil Blackwell, Oxford, 1987.

[243] A. Sen. On ignorance and equal distribution. *American Economic Review*, 63:1022–1024, 1973.

[244] A. Sen. Rational fools: A critique of the behavioral foundations of economic theory. *Philosophy and Public Affairs*, 6:317–344, 1977.

[245] A. Sen. Welfare inequalities and Rawlsian axiomatics. *Theory and Decision*, 7:243–262, 1976.

[246] H. Sidgwick. *The Methods of Ethics*. Hackett, Indianapolis, 1981. (Seventh edition of 1907.).

[247] B. Skyrms. *The Dynamics of Rational Deliberation*. Harvard University Press, Cambridge, MA, 1990.

[248] A. Smith. *The Theory of Moral Sentiments*. Clarendon Press, Oxford, 1975. (Edited by D. Raphael and A. Macfie, first published 1759.).

[249] V. Smith. Experimental economics: Induced value theory. *American Economic Review*, 66:274–279, 1976.

[250] R. Solow. Intergenerational equity and exhaustible resources. *Review of Economic Studies*, 41:29–46, 1974.

[251] B. de Spinoza. Ethics. In *Collected Works of Spinoza, Volume I*, Princeton University Press, Princeton, 1985. (Edited by E. Curley, first published 1677.).

[252] B. de Spinoza. Tractatus politicus. In *Chief Works of Benedict de Spinoza*, Volume I, Bell, London, 1909. (Translated by R. Elwes, first published 1674.).

[253] G. J. Stigler. Economics or ethics? In S. McMurrin, editor, *Tanner Lectures on Human Values*, Cambridge University Press, Cambridge, 1981.

[254] R. Sugden. *The Economics of Rights, Cooperation and Welfare*. Basil Blackwell, Oxford, 1986.

[255] R. Sugden. Liberty, preference and choice. *Economics and Philosophy*, 1:213–219, 1985.

[256] R. Sugden. Rational choice: a survey of contributions from economics and philosophy. *Economic Journal*, 101:751–785, 1991.

[257] R. Sugden. Rationality and impartiality: is the contractarian enterprise possible? In R. Sugden, editor, *Rationality, Justice and the Social Contract: Themes from 'Morals by Agreement'*, Simon and Schuster, Hemel Hempstead, U.K., 1992.

[258] W. Sumner. *Essays of William Graham Sumner, Volume II.* Yale University Press, Newhaven, 1934. (edited by A. Keller and M. Davie).

[259] P. Suppes. Some formal models of grading principles. *Synthèse,* 6:284–306, 1966.

[260] C. Taylor. *Sources of the Self.* Cambridge University Press, Cambridge, 1990.

[261] M. Taylor. *The Possibility of Cooperation.* Cambridge University Press, Cambridge, 1987.

[262] E. Ulmann-Margalit. *The Emergence of Norms.* Oxford University Press, New York, 1977.

[263] J. Van Huyck, R. Battalio, and R. Beil. Strategic uncertainty, equilibrium selection principles and coordination failure. *American Economic Review,* 80:234–238, 1991.

[264] V. Vanberg and R. Congleton. Rationality, morality and exit. *American Political Science Review,* 86:418–431, 1992.

[265] H. Varian. *Microeconomic Analysis.* 3rd edition. Norton, New York, 1992.

[266] T. Veblen. The theory of the leisure class. In M. Lerner, editor, *The Portable Veblen,* Viking Press, New York, 1958. (First published 1899.).

[267] W. S. Vickrey. Measuring marginal utility by reactions to risk. *Econometrica,* 13:319–333, 1945.

[268] J. Von Neumann. Zur Theorie der Gesellschaftsspiele. *Mathematische Annalen,* 100:295–320, 1928.

[269] J. Von Neumann and O. Morgenstern. *The Theory of Games and Economic Behavior.* Princeton University Press, Princeton, 1944.

[270] M. Walzer. *Spheres of Justice.* Basic Books, New York, 1983.

[271] J. Weymark. A reconsideration of the Harsanyi-Sen debate on utilitarianism. In J. Elster and J. Roemer, editors, *Interpersonal Comparisons of Well-Being,* Cambridge University Press, Cambridge, 1991.

[272] B. Williams. *Ethics and the Limits of Philosophy.* Fontana Press, London, 1985.

[273] B. Williams. *Morality: An Introduction to Ethics.* Cambridge University Press, Cambridge, 1972.

[274] E. Wilson. *Sociobiology: The New Synthesis.* Harvard University Press, Cambridge, Mass., 1975.

[275] R. Wolff. A refutation of Rawls' theorem on justice. *Journal of Philosophy*, 63:170–190, 1966.

[276] R. Wolff. *Understanding Rawls.* Princeton University Press, Princeton, 1977.

Index